Jesus
Prophet
of Islam

Revised Edition

Muhammad 'Ata'ur-Rahim

and   **Ahmad Thomson**

Ta-Ha Publishers Ltd.
1 Wynne Road
London SW9 0BB
United Kingdom

First Edition published by Diwan Press in 1977.

Reprinted October 2006

Revised Edition published by:

Ta-Ha Publishers Ltd
1 Wynne Road
London SW9 0BB

Revised and typeset by Ahmad Thomson.

The English translations of the *Qur'an* appearing in the
text are based on that of Muhammad Pickthall, *alehi rahma*.

British Library Cataloguing in Publication Data
'Ata'ur-Rahim, Muhammad
Jesus, Prophet of Islam (Revised Edition)
1. Islam   2. Europe – Church history
I. Title II. Thomson, Ahmad

ISBN 1 897940 53 X (paper)
ISBN 1 897940 54 8 (case)

Printed by Deluxe Printers, London.

Contents

Preface to the Revised Edition v

Preface to the First Edition ix

Introduction to the First Edition xi

1   The Unitarian View and Christianity 1

2   An Historical Account of Jesus 9

3   Barnabas and the Early Christians 49

4   Early Unitarians in Christianity 77

5   The Gospel of Barnabas 113

6   The Shepherd of Hermas 141

7   Trinitarian Christianity in Europe 147

8   Later Unitarians in Christianity 157

9   Christianity Today 249

10   Jesus in Hadith and Muslim Traditions 263

11   Jesus in Qur'an 279

Chapter Notes 321

Bibliography 327

Surely the similarity of Jesus with Allah is like
the similarity of Adam. – He created him from
dust, and then said to him: 'Be!' and he is.

This is the truth from your Lord, so do not be
one of those who doubt.

(Qur'an: Surat Ali 'Imran – 3: 59-60)

Preface
to the
Revised Edition

Jesus, Prophet of Islam was originally written between 1975 and 1977. After the death of his wife, Colonel Muhammad 'Ata'ur-Rahim, *alehi rahma*, left everything in Pakistan behind him and came to London to complete his studies on the life of *sayyedina* 'Isa, peace be on him, and to write the book about him which he had always longed to write. Although Colonel Rahim had a good command of the English language and a wonderful sense of humour, his written English was not always grammatically correct. Having been born into a Muslim family and having been brought up as a Muslim, Colonel Rahim had no first-hand experience of what it is like to live and think like a Christian. Since English is my native tongue, and since I had received a Christian education, I was in a position to be of assistance – and had the good fortune to be chosen to help Colonel Rahim with his book.

The days that we spent working together on the growing book – not only structuring the material which Colonel Rahim had already gathered, but also conducting further research, principally in the British Library – were precious days indeed, and we both learned a great deal from each other, not only about the nature and history of Christianity, but also about the nature and history of Islam – and of life itself. Almost every line that came to be written was a source of discussion and argument, and while Colonel Rahim always welcomed my contributions and observations, and often agreed to incorporate them into the text, it was also amicably agreed that he would always have the final say as to what should go and what should stay.

Eventually the book was at last completed, painstakingly typed out by Maryam Toby, may she have peace in her grave, read and re-read for final corrections, finally typeset by Abdal-Hayy Moore and Abu'l-Qasim Spiker, and at last printed, published and distributed. Since that time, the book has rarely been out of print, although the numerous typographical errors and a spurious alternative introduction which were introduced into subsequent editions greatly diminished the quality and content of the first edition.

Although the first edition of the book was, on the whole, well received, one of the few criticisms which was levelled at it from time to time was that it was in places too detailed – and accordingly a little boring – for the general reader. I also recall Colonel Rahim mentioning to me that as far as the chapter entitled *Jesus in the Qur'an* was concerned, there are many more *ayat* in the *Qur'an* that could have been included, especially those which are addressed directly towards the Christians and the 'People of the Book' – a term which refers generally to any group of people whose religion is based to a greater or lesser extent on a divine revelation revealed prior to the *Qur'an*, and which includes especially the Jews and the Christians.

It is with this criticism and with this comment of Colonel Rahim in mind, that I have ventured to revise the first edition – not only by shortening some of the longer passages and by increasing the number of *ayat* which are quoted from the *Qur'an*, but also by including additional material which has come to light during the last eighteen years. This has necessitated a partial re-structuring of the original material, with the addition of an additional chapter entitled *Trinitarian Christianity in Europe*.

In drawing attention to the additional material which appears in this revised edition, I would like to acknowledge with gratitude the excerpts which are quoted from Dr. Maurice Bucaille's book, *The Bible, the Qur'an and Science*, which had not yet been published when the first edition of *Jesus, Prophet of Islam* was originally printed. Dr. Bucaille's scrupulous and impartial consideration regarding the authenticity, accuracy and reliability of the contents of both the *Bible* and the *Qur'an*, together with his rational analysis of whether or not they correspond with the empirical evidence gathered by the practitioners of science, are both informative and illuminating – and anyone who has not read his book should do so!

In presenting this revised edition to the general public, I hope not only that Colonel Rahim would approve of these changes if he were here to see them, but also that whoever reads this book will learn something of value from it and, above all, enjoy it. I certainly enjoyed helping to write the first edition with Colonel Rahim, and it has been a pleasure to revise the original text after so many years, reminding me as it has of what a very human, human being Colonel Rahim was.

Colonel Rahim's warmth and wisdom were extraordinary, and many of the long discussions which we shared and his sharp observations are still with me today. Anyone who ever had the good fortune to meet Colonel Rahim will remember him with deep affection. He was what his name indicated – a gift from a Compassionate Lord – and this revised edition is dedicated to his memory. May we meet again in the next world, in the Garden!

As with any book written by a human being, there are inevitably shortcomings and deficiencies in this book. Thousands of pages have been read in order that tens may be written. Hopefully this book will nevertheless complement the knowledge which the reader already possesses, giving fresh insight into what may have been unknown, or half-forgotten, or too readily assumed.

It should perhaps be emphasised that the title of this book is not intended to be provocative. It has always been understood by the Muslims at least that the way of life which was embodied by all of the Prophets, may the blessings and peace of God be on them and on their families and companions and true followers, was essentially one and the same life-transaction, grounded in the worship of the One Creator of the heavens and the earth and all that exists, both in the Seen and in the Unseen worlds – the way of Islam. Like all the Prophets before him, Jesus, peace be on him, confirmed the Prophets who had come before him – especially Moses, peace be on him – and foretold the coming of the Prophet who would come after him – Muhammad, may God bless him and grant him peace – and as with all of the Prophets, the simple way of life that Jesus followed was the way of total submission to his Lord, the way of Islam. When the way of Islam is viewed from this perspective, then it is clear that not only Jesus, but indeed all the Prophets – and especially Muhammad – were Prophets of Islam. It is, when understood in this sense, impossible to make any distinction between them.

This prophetic way of life, the way of Islam, which has always been characterised by suppleness and by balance between outward form and inward content, has always been susceptible to being corrupted in two main ways: either people have made it too rigid, or they have made it too lax. If it is made too rigid, people end up with a system of rules which they then often try to avoid. If it is made too lax, then there are hardly any rules to avoid – but instead there is a lack of clarity which leads inevitably to confusion. Going to either of these two extremes makes it impossible for a human being to fully understand the nature of existence.

Whenever the balance of the middle way that leads between these two extremes has been lost, human society has tended to endlessly oscillate from one extreme to the other, from rigid orthodoxy to mushy liberalism, and back again – until, that is, Allah has sent another Prophet or Messenger to demonstrate what the middle way is and how its balance can be embodied and maintained.

It is in the light of this pattern of behaviour that the history of what became of Jesus's teaching in Europe can be understood, whether it be Paul's abandoning the Law which Jesus specifically said that he had come to uphold – not only the spirit of it, but also the letter of it – or the tyranny of the Mediaeval and Spanish Inquisitions, or the impetus of what has been labelled 'the Reformation', or the reaction to it – the Counter-Reformation, or the liberal all-embracing approach of the present ecumenical movement, or the ruthless genocide of the current Serbian crusaders, to name but a few of the most significant developments that have occurred within the Paulinian Christian religion during the last nineteen centuries.

It should also be emphasised that the underlying objective in writing *Jesus, Prophet of Islam* was always to increase not only the reader's but also the authors' understanding of Jesus, peace be on him – and not merely to enter that arena of argument and debate, which measures 'success' in terms of numbers of converts conscripted, in order to score points against the opposition. If you, the reader, learn as much as the authors did when this book was being written, or even if you simply learn something, or even one thing, of value – then the purpose of this book has been fulfilled.

Finally, I would like to thank my guide and teacher, *Shaykh Abdal-Qadir al-Murabit*, for it was through him that I came to embrace Islam, and it was thanks to him that I came to work with Colonel Rahim, and if it had not been for him, I could not have completed what I had started. *Al-hamdulillahi wa shukrulillah wa la howla wa la quwwata ila bi'llah* – Praise belongs to God and thanks belongs to God and there is no power and no strength except from God. And, as the Prophet Muhammad said, may God bless him and grant him peace, 'If you do not thank people – then you have not thanked God.'

Ahmad Thomson
London 1416/1995

Preface
to the
First Edition

An eminent scholar of Christian history admits that present-day Christianity is a 'mask' on the face of Jesus, peace be on him, but goes on to say that a mask worn for a long time acquires a life of its own and it has to be accepted as such. The Muslim believes in the Jesus of history and refuses to accept the 'mask'. This, in a nutshell, has been the point of difference between Islam and the Church for the last fourteen hundred years. Even before the advent of Islam, the Arians, the Paulicians, and the Goths, to mention only a few, accepted Jesus, but rejected the 'mask'. The Holy Roman Emperors forced Christians to think alike. To achieve this impossible goal, millions of Christians were killed. Castillo, an admirer of Servetus, said that 'to kill a man is not to prove a doctrine.' Conviction cannot be forced with a dagger.

It is suggested in some quarters that, to achieve integration in England, the Muslims should change their two festivals to synchronise with Christmas and Easter. Those who say this forget that these are pre-Christian pagan festivals. One is the ancient birthday of the sun-god and the other is a sacred festival for the old Anglo-Saxon goddess of fertility. In this situation, one begins to wonder who in reality is 'anti-Christ'.

In this book an attempt is made, perhaps for the first time, to study the sacred life of Jesus, using all available sources, including the *Dead Sea Scrolls*, Christian Scripture, modern research, *Qur'an* and *Hadith*. Christian scholars who attempt to write the history of Jesus never completely free themselves of the idea of his divinity. When they fail to prove his divinity, they sometimes conclude that he did not exist at all, or that he is 'everything to everybody'. An objective study is impossible for anyone with this frame of mind. This book starts with the conviction that Jesus did exist. He was a man and a prophet of God.

This work is the result of thirty years of study. My thanks are due to Amat'ur-Rashid who went to the trouble of searching for out-of-print books sold on the streets of many cities in the USA. These books were unavailable in the libraries of Karachi, so the help she gave me was of vital importance.

His Excellency Mr. Ahmad Jamjoom of Jeddah visited me in Karachi, and his encouragement and support were always available to me whenever I was facing any difficulty.

Thanks are also due to His Eminence Shaykh Mahmoud Subhi of Jamiat Dawa Islamia in Tripoli for making it possible for me to come to London in order to undertake the study of this subject in depth.

In London, I met His Eminence Shaykh 'Abd al-Qadir as-Sufi. At every step, he extended his helping hand to me. This resulted in the collaboration of Mr. Ahmad Thomson with me. He helped me to structure the collected material and without him work would have been painfully slow. Hajj 'Abd al-Haqq Bewley was always ready with useful suggestions and advice.

The affection and heart-warming friendship I received from Dr. Ali Aneizi cannot be described, only deeply felt.

Lastly, in the words of Qur'an,

Nothing from me except with the help of Allah

Muhammad 'Ata'ur-Rahim

London
7 Juma'dah al-'Awal 1397 AH

Introduction
to the
First Edition

To the Muslims, Christianity is a historical reality based on a metaphysical fiction. Because its foundations are mythical and invented, as opposed to existential and revealed, it appears to us as a locked system of negation. Declaring a doctrine of love, it establishes inquisition. Preaching pacifism, it enacts the crusades. Calling to poverty, it constructs the vast edifice of wealth called the Church. Declaring 'mysteries', it involves itself in politics. Reformation, far from resolving the contradictions, revealed them further. Declaring the priesthood of all believers, they established a priesthood, but with a shift of focus by which the inherent insanity in the Christian fiction began to emerge. The qualifications for priesthood in the reformed churches were purely 'academic', while before a man could win a place in the hierarchy through piety and withdrawal from the world. This was the beginning of the concept of the secular – now there was a zone of 'religion' and a zone of politics. Church and state are held to be separate. What we discover is that in fact they have been one, as our author reveals in this fascinating study, from the beginning of the Church's bloody history.

Today Christianity as a body of metaphysics is frankly non-existent. No one is more aware of this than the Vatican. Their desperate attempts to co-opt every and any intellectual movement into the Christian thesis have gone beyond the bounds of satire. The most significant sign of their intellectual fraudulence has been the almost complete defection of the Christian intelligentsia into the Marxist and post-Marxist socialist camp. To unbelievers and to people of other religions, it always appeared baffling how the Christians could accommodate themselves to every power-nexus that appeared, right or left wing. From this work, it is clear that there is no longer any such thing as the Christian religion. Christianity is over. The myth has finally exploded.

Why this work is so welcome is that, first of all, it looks at the roots of the Christian phenomenon from the only point of view from which it can be properly understood – I mean, the Muslim point of view. It is the sole vantage point from which it can be surveyed, because Islam is the inheritor of Jesus. Jesus, peace be upon him, was the Prophet who opened the way to the Seal of the Prophets and the completion of the prophetic cycle. It is sometimes difficult for the Christians to grasp that, while they look on the Jews with amazement at their inability to 'recognise' Jesus as a prophetic manifestation, they themselves are in the same fanatical position of being unable to recognise the sameness of the sublime Prophet and Messenger Muhammad, peace and blessings of Allah be upon him. Moses, Jesus, Muhammad – they are one line, peace be upon all of them – their teaching is Islam. Their teaching is submission to the Divine Creator, worship of the one Lord, and obedience to His Law, or *Shari'a*. Moses, peace be upon him, altered the earlier law to fit the period he lived in, under Divine guidance. Jesus confirmed the Musan Law and may have modified it. The Messenger Muhammad, peace and blessings of Allah be upon him, confirmed the prophets and presented the final version of the Divine Law to fit the last age of man, which would see the tribe of Adam basically living as one people. It was for this reason that Allah in His Mercy simplified and made easier the Musan Law.

Christians have never been permitted to review or discover the prophetic teachings of Islam, because the educational base from which they receive their limited world view does not permit access to the *Deen* of Islam. It is only very recently that the great book of Imam Malik, containing the *Hadith* or teaching-sayings of the Messenger, blessings of Allah and peace be upon him, has been translated into a European language, that is, after thirteen hundred years. The Vatican, while mouthing declarations of friendship with Muslims and talking about 'dialogue', is at the same time deeply involved in an intellectual programme of ruthless censorship, repression and distortion of the message of Islam, of which, regrettably, we have collated powerful evidence.

The second important element in this book is its profound statement of how the 'fiction' of Christianity was invented. It is clearly a pseudo-religion in a way that could not be said about Hindu teaching and Buddhist teaching. Although their doctrines too have been corrupted by lack of an unadulterated text on which to base themselves, through the rubble one can glimpse a superb archeological fragment of unitarian teaching. Embedded in Vedic writings and Buddhist Sutras there is no doubt that one can discover fragments of pure *Tawhid* (Unity). The Christian phenomenon is so solidly established on the trinitarian lie that it, understandably, never produced the pure and lucid gnostic tradition that exists in the radiant sufism of Islam. Christian spirituality is trapped in the mental-phase, and therefore the false-self is given reality. The result is that the spiritual impulse in this pseudo-religion is shot through with sadism, masochism, and incest. According to the pure doctrine of the *Huda*, or ancient guidance that has adhered from the time of our father, Sayyidina Adam, peace be upon him, gnosis lies in the hands of the prophet of the time. When his reign is over it passes to the next prophet. I mean by that, the prophet is the door to knowledge of Allah. This is why for six hundred years there was a living Christian gnostic tradition, and after that there was only an adulterated one full of miracle, stigmata and other neurotic manifestations.

Jesus, Prophet of Islam shows us how the 'true' Christian teaching was diverted, or one might say de-railed, by the powerful Pauline explosion. It is clear from this remarkable work that these unfortunate and persecuted unitarians, who so persistently emerged among the Christians when the human intellect thought the thing out and cut through the fantasy of mystery-constructs to a true understanding of Allah's transaction with men, were denied access to the Islam that would have solved their intellectual dilemma and offered them the homeland of wisdom.

The meaning of this book for Christians can only be that they must examine again with an open mind the fantasy called Christian religion, and look frankly at an organisation fragmented in sects beyond any sane motivation, grasping at every hint of spirituality outside it and trying to annexe it (e.g. Christian Zen and Jung's suggested Christian yoga). They must look at an organisation still trundling on through its commitment to supporting both the status quo and the revolutionary forces that want to destroy the status quo – a religion which at the popular level celebrates its two central rites by tying gifts to a fir tree and rolling eggs down a hill, and at the intellectual level no longer exists at all.

The meaning of the book for Muslims, apart from its fascinating account of the ruthless politics behind the society that tried unsuccessfully to destroy the prophetic teaching of Islam, and which nevertheless successfully brought the khalifate to an end and introduced masonic and atheistic doctrines inside the Muslim community, lies in its clarifying for us exactly why that once so powerful society is now spent, exhausted and bankrupt. In the end of the day, Christianity was, simply, Europe. And Europe is finished. Islam is the world's. And the world is not finished yet. And although we can see signs of its approach, our blessed and generous Prophet, blessings and peace of Allah be upon him, guided us, saying:

> If the Last Day comes upon you when you are planting
> a tree—finish planting it.

And the tree we are planting is Islam.

Shaykh 'Abd al-Qadir as-Sufi al-Murabit

Chapter One

The Unitarian View and Christianity

Historical research has shown that the animism and idol worship of primitive peoples in the world is in all cases a regression from an original unitive belief, and that the One-God of Judaism, Christianity and Islam grew up in opposition to many-gods rather than evolving out of them. Thus in any tradition, the pure teaching is to be found at its beginning and what follows is necessarily a decline, and it is from this perspective that the history of Christianity should be viewed. It began with the belief in One God and was then corrupted, and the doctrine of the Trinity came to be accepted. The result was a confusion which led men more and more away from sanity.

In the first century after the disappearance of Jesus, peace be on him, those who followed him continued to affirm the Divine Unity. This is illustrated by the fact that the *Shepherd of Hermas*, written in about 90 AD was regarded as a book of Revelation by the Church. The first of the twelve commandments which it contains begins:

> First of all, believe that God is One and that He created all things and organised them and out of what did not exist made all things to be, and He contains all things but alone is Himself uncontained ...[1]

According to Theodore Zahn, the article of faith up until about 250 AD was, 'I believe in God, the Almighty.'[2] Between 180 and 210 AD the word 'Father' was added before 'the Almighty'. This was bitterly contested by a number of the leaders of the Church. Bishop Victor and Bishop Zephysius are on record as condemning this movement, since they regarded it an unthinkable sacrilege to add or subtract any word to the Scriptures.

They opposed the tendency to regard Jesus as divine. They laid great stress on the Unity of God as expressed in the original teachings of Jesus and asserted that although he was a prophet, he was essentially a man like other men, even if highly favoured by his Lord. The same faith was held by the Churches which had sprung up in North Africa and West Asia.

It must always be remembered that Jesus, peace be on him, was sent specifically to the Tribe of Israel – that is, to the twelve tribes of the Tribe of Israel, who were the descendants of the twelve sons of Jacob, who was also known as Israel. The teachings of Jesus were intended for those who claimed to be following Moses, but who no longer had access to his original teachings. Thus Jesus was given knowledge of the original *Torah* which had been revealed to Moses, and he always emphasised that he had come to uphold the law of Moses and not to change it even by one jot or tittle.

As soon as the teachings of Jesus spread beyond the Tribe of Israel, they began to be radically altered, especially in Europe and America, where this process of change has continued without interruption up until the present day, so that now the Christian priesthood caters for women priests as well as men – who are equally 'free' to be lesbians or homosexuals, in spite of what the *Bible* has to say about such matters!

Thus as the teaching of Jesus spread out beyond the Holy Land, it came into contact with other cultures and into conflict with those in authority. It began to be assimilated and adapted by these cultures and was also altered to diminish persecution by the rulers. In Greece, especially, it became metamorphosed, both by its being expressed in a new language for the first time, and by its realignment with the ideas and philosophy of that culture. It was the many-gods viewpoint of the Greeks which largely contributed to the formulation of the doctrine of the Trinity, together with the gradual elevation of Jesus by some, notably Paul of Tarsus, from being a Prophet of God to somehow being a separate yet indivisible part of God.

It was only after the Councils of Nicea in 325 AD and of Constantinople in 381 AD that the doctrine of the Trinity was declared to be an essential part of orthodox Christian belief. Even then some of those who signed the creed did not believe in it, as they could find no authority for it in the Scriptures. Athanasius, who is considered to be the father of this creed, was himself not altogether sure of its truth. He admits that, 'Whenever he forced his understanding to meditate on the divinity of Jesus, his toilsome and unavailing efforts recoiled on themselves – that the more he wrote the less capable was he of expressing his thoughts.' At one point he even wrote, 'There are not three but ONE GOD.' His belief in the doctrine of the Trinity was not based so much on conviction as on policy and apparent necessity.

That this historic decision was based just as much on political expediency as on the faulty reasoning of philosophy is shown by the part played by Constantine, the pagan emperor of Rome, who presided over the council of Nicea. The growing communities of Christians were a force whose opposition he had no wish for, who weakened his Empire and whose support would be invaluable in strengthening it. By remodelling Christianity, he hoped to gain the Church's support and at the same time end the confusion which had arisen within it and which was the source of yet more conflict within his Empire.

The process by which he partially achieved this aim may be illustrated by an incident which occurred in the Second World War. Once, as the time for the Muslim festival of the 'Id drew near, propaganda from Tokyo began to concentrate on an 'Id prayer that was going to be held in Singapore, then under Japanese occupation. It would be an historic occasion, it was announced, and its effect would be felt throughout the Muslim world. This sudden emphasis on the prayer abruptly stopped after a few days.

The mystery was solved when a Japanese prisoner was taken in a skirmish and interrogated. He said that Tojo, the head of the Japanese government, was planning to take on the role of the greatest Muslim reformer of modern times. He had a scheme to adjust the teachings of Islam to the requirements of the modern age. It had therefore become necessary, according to him, that the Muslims, instead of facing Makka in prayer, should start facing Tokyo, which would become the future centre of Islam under Tojo. The Muslims refused to accept this reorientation of Islam, and so the whole project was dropped. As a result, there was no 'Id prayer allowed in Singapore that year.

Tojo had realised the importance of Islam and he wanted to use it as a means to further his imperialistic designs, but he was unsuccessful. Constantine succeeded where Tojo failed. Rome replaced Jerusalem as the centre of Pauline Christianity.

This degeneration of the pure One-God teachings of Jesus, which resulted inevitably in the acceptance of a many-god Christianity, never went unchallenged. When, in 325 AD., the doctrine of Trinity was officially proposed as the orthodox Christian doctrine, Arius, one of the leaders of the Christians in North Africa, stood up against the combined might of Constantine and the Catholic Church and reminded them that Jesus had always affirmed the Divine Unity. Constantine tried to crush the troublesome One-God people with all the force and brutality at his command, but he failed. Although, ironically, Constantine himself died a Unitarian, the doctrine of Trinity eventually became officially accepted as the basis of Christianity in Europe.

This doctrine caused much confusion among people, many of whom were told to believe it without trying to understand it. Yet it was not possible to stop people from trying to prove and explain it intellectually. Broadly speaking, three schools of thought developed. The first is associated with St. Augustine, who lived in the early 5th century and was of the view that the doctrine could not be proved but could be illustrated. St. Victor, who lived in the 12th century, is associated with the second school, who believed that the doctrine could both be demonstrated and illustrated. And the 14th century saw the growth of the third school, which believed that the doctrine of Trinity could be neither illustrated nor proved, but should be blindly accepted and believed.

Although the books into which Jesus's teaching had gone were either completely destroyed, suppressed, or changed in order to avoid any blatant contradictions of the doctrine, a good deal of truth remained in the ones which survived, and therefore to sustain belief in the doctrine of Trinity, there was a shift in emphasis from what the Scriptures said to what the leaders of the Church said. The doctrine, it was asserted, was based on the special revelation made to the Church, the 'Bride of Jesus'. Thus, for instance, Fra Fulgentio was reprimanded by the Pope in a letter saying, 'Preaching of the Scriptures is a suspicious thing. He who keeps close to the Scriptures will ruin the Catholic faith.' In his next letter he was more explicit, warning against too much insistence on the Scriptures, '... which is a book if anyone keeps close to, he will quite destroy the Catholic Church.'[3]

The effective abandoning of the teaching of Jesus was largely due to the complete obscuring of his historical reality. The Church

[margin note:] Scriptures over looked emphisis on the sayings of the leaders of the Church.

made their religion not only independent of the Scriptures but also independent of Jesus, so that the man Jesus became confused with a mythological Christ. Belief in Jesus, however, does not necessarily mean belief in a resurrected Christ. Whereas the immediate followers of Jesus had based their lives on his example, Pauline Christianity was based on a belief in Christ after his supposed crucifixion – and the life and teaching of Jesus while he was alive was no longer considered to be so important.

As the established Church distanced itself further and further from the teaching of Jesus, so its leaders became more involved in the affairs of those in authority over the land. As the distinctions between what Jesus had taught and what those in authority desired became blurred and began to merge into each other, the Church, while asserting its separateness from the State, became more and more identified with it, and grew in power. Whereas in the early days the Church was subject to imperial power, once it had compromised itself completely, the position was reversed.

There was always opposition to these deviations from what Jesus had taught. As the Church became more powerful, it became very dangerous to deny the Trinity, and led to almost certain death. Although Luther left the Roman Church, his revolt was only against the authority of the Pope, rather than against the fundamental doctrines of the Roman Catholic Church. The result was that he founded a new Church and became its head. All the basic Christian doctrines, however, were accepted, and remained. This lead to the establishment of a number of Reformed Churches and sects, but pre-Reformation Christianity remained undisturbed. These two main bodies of the Pauline Church have continued to exist up to the present day.

In North Africa and West Asia the teachings of Arius were accepted by the majority of the people who readily embraced Islam when it later came to them. Because they had held to the doctrine of One-God and the pure teaching of Jesus, they recognised Islam as the truth.

In Europe the thread of Unitarianism within Christianity has never been broken, and the movement has in fact grown in strength, surviving the continual and brutal persecution of the established Churches in the past and their indifference today.

More and more people are now aware that the Christianity they know has little to do with the original teaching of Jesus. During the last two centuries the research of the historians has left little room for faith in the Christian 'mysteries', but the proven fact that the Christ of the established Church has almost nothing to do with the Jesus of history does not in itself help Christians towards the Truth.

The present dilemma of the Christians is illustrated by what the Church historians of this present century have written. The fundamental difficulty is, as pointed out by Adolf Harnack, that, 'By the fourth century the living Gospel had been masked in Greek philosophy. It was the historians' mission to pluck off the mask and thus reveal how different had been the original contours of the faith beneath.' But then Harnack points out the difficulty of actually fulfilling this task by saying that if the doctrinal mask is worn long enough then it can reshape the face of religion:

> The mask acquires a life of its own – the Trinity, the two natures of Christ, infallibility, and all propositions seconding these dogmas, were the product of historic decisions and of situations that might have turned out quite differently ... nevertheless ... early or late, product or reshaping force, this dogma remains what it has been from the beginning, a bad habit of intellectualization which the Christian picked up from the Greek when he fled from the Jews.[4]

Harnack enlarges on his theme in another book, where he observes:

> The fourth Gospel does not emanate or profess to emanate from the apostle John, who cannot be taken as an historical authority ... the author of the fourth Gospel acted with sovereign freedom, transposed events and put them in a strange light. He drew up the discussions himself and illustrated great thoughts with imaginary situations.

He further refers to the work of the famous Christian historian, David Strauss, whom he describes as having 'almost destroyed the historic credibility not only of the fourth but also of the first three Gospels as well.'[5]

According to Johannes Lehmann, another historian, the writers of the four accepted Gospels describe a different Jesus from the one who can be identified by historic reality. Lehmann quotes Heinz Zahrnt who points out the consequences of this:

> If historical research could prove that an irreconcilable antithesis exists between the historical Jesus and Christ as preached, and therefore that belief in Jesus has no support in Jesus himself, that would not only be absolutely fatal theologically, as N.A. Dahl says, but would also mean the end of all Christology. Yet I am convinced that even then we theologians would be able to find a way out – was there ever a time when we couldn't? – but we are either lying now or would be lying then.[6]

While these few short quotations illustrate the dilemma Christianity is in today, the words of Zahrnt also demonstrate something far more serious which underlies this: that it is possible to get so involved with the details of what became of Jesus's teaching and the Churches and sects which followed after him, that the original purpose of his teaching is overlooked or forgotten.

Thus Theodore Zahn, for instance, illustrates the bitter conflicts within the established Churches. He points out that the Roman Catholics accuse the Greek Orthodox Church of remodelling the text of the holy Scriptures by additions and subtractions with good and bad intentions, that the Greeks in turn point out that the Catholics themselves in places depart very far from the original text, and that, in spite of their differences, they combine to accuse the nonconformist Christians of deviating from 'the true way' and condemn them as heretics, while the heretics in their turn accuse the Catholics of 'having recoined the Truth like forgers.' He concludes, 'Do not facts support these accusations?'[7]

And in the process, Jesus himself, peace be on him, is completely forgotten. And even those who are aware of the degeneration that has taken place and who wish in all sincerity to return to and live by the original teaching of Jesus are prevented from doing so because the original teaching in its totality has disappeared and is irrecoverable. As Erasmus pointed out:

> The ancients philosophised very little about divine things ... Formerly faith was in life rather than in profession of creeds ... When faith came to be in writings rather than in hearts, then there were almost as many

faiths as men. Articles increased and sincerity decreased. Contentions grew hot and love grew cold. The doctrine of Christ which at first knew no hair-splitting came to depend on the aid of philosophy. This was the first stage in the decline of the Church.

Thus the Church was forced to explain what could not be expressed in words, and recourse was taken by both sides to win the support of the Emperor. Erasmus, commenting on this, continued:

> The injection of the authority of the Emperor into this affair did not greatly aid the sincerity of faith ... When faith is in the mouth rather than in the heart, when the solid knowledge of sacred Scriptures fails us, nevertheless by terrorisation we drive men to believe what they do not believe, to love what they do not love, to know what they do not know. That which is forced cannot be sincere. [8]

Erasmus understood that the first Christians, the immediate followers of Jesus, had a recognition of the Unity which they never had to express, and that when his teaching spread and conflict between the Churches grew up, then the men of understanding were forced to try and explain their knowledge of Reality. They had by then lost the teaching of Jesus in its totality and the language of Unity that went with it. They only had recourse to the vocabulary and terminology of Greek philosophy which looked not to Unity but to a tripartite view of existence. And so simple and pure trust in Reality became inevitably couched in a language foreign to Jesus, and led to the formulation of the doctrine of the Trinity, with the deification of Jesus and the Holy Spirit. Confusion and schism were the inevitable results which followed once people lost sight of the Unity of Existence.

This understanding is essential for anyone who wants to know who Jesus was and what he really taught, as is the realisation that once people no longer have recourse to all the everyday actions of a Prophet, which are no less than the embodiment of his teaching, then they are in loss, whether they believe in the doctrine of the Trinity or vocally affirm the Divine Unity.

○   ○   ○   ○   ○

Chapter Two

An Historical Account of Jesus

The more people have tried to discover who Jesus really was, peace be on him, the more it has been found how little is known about him. There are limited records of his teachings and some of his actions, but very little is known about how he actually lived his life from moment to moment, and how he conducted his everyday transactions with other people.

Certainly, the picture many people have been given of Jesus – of who he was, and what he did – is a distorted one. Although there is some truth in them, it has been established that the four accepted Gospels have not only been altered and censored through the ages, but also are not eyewitness accounts.

The earliest Gospel is that of Mark, written about 60 AD. He was the son of St. Barnabas's sister. Matthew was a tax collector, a minor official who did not travel around with Jesus. Luke's Gospel was written much later, and is, in fact, drawn from the same source as Mark's and Matthew's. Luke was Paul's physician, and, like Paul, never met Jesus.

John's Gospel is from a different source, and was written later still, in Greek, in about 100 AD. The author of this Gospel should not be confused with John, the disciple, who was another man. For two centuries it was hotly debated whether or not this Gospel should be accepted as a reliable account of the life of Jesus, and whether or not it should be included in the Scriptures.

Since none of the Gospels are written by people who personally saw and heard the events and words which they describe, it is hardly surprising that their respective accounts of particular events often differ – and at times even contradict each other – and that even highly significant events in the life of Jesus are not described in all of the Gospels. Thus, as Dr Maurice Bucaille points out in his book, *The Bible, the Qur'an and Science*:

Each of the four Gospels contains a large number of descriptions relating events that may be unique to one single Gospel or common to several if not all of them. When they are unique to one Gospel, they sometimes raise serious problems. Thus in the case of an event of considerable importance, it is surprising to find the event mentioned by only one evangelist; Jesus's Ascension into heaven on the day of Resurrection, for example. Elsewhere, numerous events are differently described – sometimes very differently indeed – by two or more evangelists. Christians are very often astonished at the existence of such contradictions between the Gospels – if they ever discover them. This is because it has been repeatedly said in tones of the greatest assurance that their authors were the eyewitnesses of the events they describe![1]

Fortunately, there are other sources of knowledge concerning Jesus, some of which have survived the repeated attempts of the established Church to either suppress or destroy them:

In the early days of Christianity, many writings on Jesus were in circulation. They were not subsequently retained as being worthy of authenticity and the Church ordered them to be hidden, hence their name '*Apocrypha*'. Some of the texts of these works have been well preserved because they 'benefited from the fact that they were generally valued', to quote the Ecumenical Translation. The same was true for the *Letter of Barnabas*, but unfortunately others were 'more brutally thrust aside' and only fragments of them remain. They were considered to be the messengers of error and were removed from the sight of the faithful. Works such as the Gospels of the Nazarenes, the Gospels of the Hebrews and the Gospels of the Egyptians, known through quotations taken from the Fathers of the Church, were nevertheless fairly closely related to the canonic Gospels. The same holds good for Thomas's Gospel and Barnabas's Gospel.[2]

As regards other sources, the discovery of the famous *Dead Sea Scrolls* has thrown new light on the nature of the society into which

Jesus was born, although some of their contents have been intentionally suppressed, and only selections made available to the general public; the *Gospel of Barnabas* covers Jesus's life more extensively and accurately than the other Gospels; and the *Qur'an* and the *Hadith* further clarify the picture of who Jesus really was.

If these additional sources are consulted, then a picture which is different in many important respects to those fostered by the various Christian churches, emerges:

We find that Jesus, peace be on him, was not the 'son' of God, in the literal sense of the word – but, like Abraham and Moses before him and Muhammad after him, a Messenger of God, blessings and peace be on all of them, who, like all human beings ate food, and had to sleep, and went to the market place.

We find that Jesus inevitably found himself doing battle with those people whose interests were in conflict with what he taught. They either did not accept the guidance he received, or knowing it to be true, nevertheless chose to ignore it in favour of pursuing power, riches and reputation in the eyes of men.

Further, we find that Jesus's life on earth is an integral part of Jewish history, and that to understand his story it is necessary to be aware of theirs. Throughout his life Jesus was an orthodox practising Jew, and the fact that he came to reaffirm and revive the original teachings of Moses, which had been altered through the years, should never be overlooked.

Finally, we find that it was not Jesus who was crucified, but someone who resembled him.

○   ○   ○   ○   ○

Lentulus, a Roman official, described Jesus as follows:

> He has nut brown hair that is smoothed down to the ears, forming soft curls and flowing onto his shoulders in luxuriant locks, with a parting in the centre of his head after the fashion of the Nazarenes. A smooth clear brow and a reddish face without spots and wrinkles. Nose and mouth are flawless. He bears a full luxurious beard which is the same colour as his hair and is parted in the middle. He has blue-grey eyes with an unusually varied capacity for expression. He is of medium height, fifteen and a half fists tall. He is cheerful in seriousness. Sometimes he weeps, but no one has ever seen him laugh.

A Muslim Tradition, however, paints a slightly different picture. According to this source:

> He was a ruddy man inclined to white. He did not have long hair. He never anointed his head. Jesus used to walk barefoot, and he took no house, nor adornment, nor goods, nor clothes, nor provisions, except his day's food. His head was dishevelled and his face was small. He was an ascetic in this world, longing for the next world and eager for the worship of God. (*Ath-Tha'labi*).

The exact date of Jesus's birth is not known. According to Luke, it is associated with a census which was held in 6 AD. It is also stated that he was born in the reign of Herod, who died in 4 BC. Vincent Taylor, however, concludes that his date of birth could be as early as 8 BC [3], since Herod's decree – which was set in motion by the news of Jesus's actual or imminent birth – that all newly born infants in Bethlehem should be killed, obviously must have preceded Herod's death. Even if we follow Luke, the discrepancy between the two verses in the same Gospel is of ten years. Most of the commentators believe the second verse, which infers that he was born in 4 BC – i.e. four years 'Before Christ' – that is, four years before he was subsequently and officially said to have been born.

The miraculous conception and birth of Jesus have been the subject of much discussion. Some people believe that he was no more than the flesh and blood son of Joseph. While others, believing in the immaculate conception, therefore conclude that he was the 'son of God,' but remain divided as to whether this term should be taken literally or figuratively. Luke, who somehow traces Jesus's ancestry back through Joseph and simultaneously confirms the fact that Jesus had no human father, says:

> The angel Gabriel was sent from God to a virgin ... the virgin's name was Mary. And the angel came in unto her and said: 'Hail, thou art a highly favoured woman.' And when she saw him, she was troubled at his saying and cast in her mind what manner of salutation this should be. And the angel said unto her: 'Fear not, Mary, for thou hast found favour with God. And behold, thou shalt conceive in thy womb and bring forth a son and shalt call his name Jesus ...' Then said Mary unto the

angel: 'How shall this be, seeing I know not a man?' ...
And the angel answered ...'With God, nothing shall be
impossible.' And Mary said: 'Behold the handmaid of
the Lord, be it unto me according to thy word.' And the
angel departed from her. (*Luke 1: 26-38*).

The same incident is described in the Qur'an as follows:

And (remember) when the angels said, 'O Mary, surely
Allah has chosen you, and He has made you pure, and
He has preferred you above all women in all the worlds.
O Mary, be obedient to your Lord, and prostrate and
bow down in worship (before Him) with those who bow
down in worship ... O Mary, surely Allah gives you good
news of a word from Him, whose name is the Messiah,
Jesus son of Mary, who will be honoured in this world
and in the next world, and who will be one of those
who are near (to Allah) – and he will speak to people
from his cradle and when he is a man, and he will be
one of those who are righteous.' She replied, 'My Lord,
how can I have a child, when no man has touched me?'
He replied, 'Just like that – Allah creates whatever He
wants. When He decrees something, then all He says to
it is, "Be!" and it is.' (*Qur'an 3. 42-47*).

Out of the four Gospels, Mark and John are silent about Jesus's
birth, and Matthew only casually mentions it. Both Luke and Matthew contradict themselves by giving a human genealogy on the
father's side to Jesus, while Mark and John do not mention it. As
between Matthew and Luke, the former gives twenty-six persons
between David and Jesus, while Luke has forty-two names in his
list. Thus, there is a discrepancy between the two of sixteen people. If we accept only forty years as the average age of a person,
then there is a gap of six hundred and forty years between the two
records of Jesus's supposed lineal descent! As Dr. Maurice Bucaille
points out, however:

One must straight away note that the male genealogies
have absolutely no relevance to Jesus. Were one to give
a genealogy to Mary's only son, who was without a bio-
logical father, it would have to be the genealogy of his
mother Mary. [4]

There are no such contradictions in the Qur'anic doctrine of the immaculate conception and the miraculous birth of Jesus. Yet the *Qur'an* – which confirms that the father of Mary, who was descended from Solomon the son of David, was called 'Imran – firmly rejects the divinity of Jesus, as is shown in this description of what happened shortly after Jesus's birth:

> Then she brought him to her people, carrying him. They said, 'O Mary, you have indeed come with something deceitful! O sister of Aaron, your father was not a wicked man, and your mother was never immoral!' Then she pointed to him. They said, 'How can we talk to a baby in his cradle?' He said, 'Surely I am the slave of God – He has given me the Book, and He has made me a Prophet, and He has made me blessed wherever I may be, and He has made the prayer and *zakat* obligatory for me as long as I live, and He has made me obedient towards the one who bore me, and He has not made me tyrannical or ungrateful – and peace be on me the day I was born, and the day I die, and the day I shall be brought back to life!'
>
> Such was Jesus son of Mary – (this is) a statement of the truth about which they are in doubt. It is not how it is for God to choose any son – glory be to Him! When He decrees something, then all He says to it is 'Be!' and it is.
>
> 'And surely God is my Lord and your Lord, so worship Him. This is the straight path.' (*Qur'an* 19.27-36).

The birth of Adam was the greatest miracle, as he was born without a father or mother. The birth of Eve too was a greater miracle than the birth of Jesus, inasmuch as she was born without a mother. The *Qur'an* says:

> Surely the similarity of Jesus with God is like the similarity of Adam. – He created him from dust, and then said to him: 'Be!' and he is. (*Qur'an* 3. 59).

o   o   o   o   o

It is very important to examine Jesus's life in the context of what was happening politically and socially in the society into which he was born. It was a time of great unrest in the Jewish world.

The Jews in their history had been trampled under the feet of invaders one after another in a series of invasions, which will be examined in greater detail further on in this account. Because of the defeats which resulted in their helplessness, the fire of hatred always remained burning in their hearts. But even in the days of their blackest despair, a large proportion of the Jews retained their mental balance, and continued in the expectation of a new Moses, whose coming was described in the *Torah*, and who, it was hoped, with his staff would succeed in driving away the invader, so that the rule of Jehovah would be ushered in. He would be the Messiah, the Anointed One.

As well as this group, there was always a section of the Jewish nation who worshipped every rising sun, trimming their sails to whatever wind prevailed at the time, in order to make the best of a bad bargain. They acquired wealth and position, both temporal and religious, but were hated by the rest of the Jews as traitors.

Apart from these two groups, there was a third group of Jews who differed widely from them. They took refuge in the wilderness where they could practise the teachings of the *Torah* more easily, and prepare themselves to fight the invaders whenever the opportunity arose. During this period, the Romans made many unsuccessful attempts to discover their hideouts, but the numbers of these patriots continued to grow. They are described by Josephus the historian, who categorises these three parties of the Jews as the Pharisees, the Sadducees, and the Essenes, respectively.

The existence of the Essenes was known of but not in any great detail. This group of people is not once mentioned in the Gospels. Then, with dramatic suddenness, the documents known as the *Dead Sea Scrolls* came to light in the mountains of Jordan near the Dead Sea. This discovery took the whole intellectual and ecclesiastical world by storm. The story of how these documents came to be found is this:

In 1947, an Arab boy, tending his flock near Qumran, found one of his sheep was missing, so he decided to climb the nearby mountain in search of the missing animal. During his search, he came upon the mouth of a cave into which he thought the sheep had gone. He threw a stone into it, expecting to hear the sound of stone hitting stone. Instead the stone made a clinking noise as if it had hit an earthen pot. His imagination was fired. He thought that perhaps he had stumbled upon a treasure trove. Next morning, he returned to the cave and, with a friend to help him, entered it.

Inside they found several clay jars amongst the fragments of broken pottery. They took one of them to the camp where they were living and were bitterly disappointed when all that they found was a foul smelling leather scroll. They unrolled it until it reached from one side of the tent to the other. It was one of the scrolls which were later sold for a quarter of a million dollars. They sold it to a Syrian Christian named Kando for a few shillings. Kando was a cobbler, and he was only interested in the leather as it might come in handy for resoling old shoes. Kando, however, noticed that the leather sheet was over-written in letters unknown to him. After a closer look, he decided to show it to the Syrian Metropolitan of St. Mark's Monastery in Jerusalem. These two shadowy figures carted the scrolls from one country to another, hoping to make money.

In the American Oriental Institute of Jordan, the scrolls were found to be the oldest known copy of the Book of Isaiah in the Old Testament. Seven years later, the scrolls were placed in the Shrine of the Book in Jerusalem by the government of Israel.

At a rough guess, there are about six hundred caves dotted around the hillside above the bank of the river Jordan. In these caves lived the Essenes, a community of people who had renounced both the world and Roman rule, because by their understanding a true Jew could only live under the sovereignty of Jehovah and was not permitted to obey any authority except His. So, according to their beliefs, any Jew living under and recognising the Roman Emperor as overlord was committing a sin.

Tired of the pomp and show of the world and overwhelmed by its uncontrollable forces which lead inevitably to conflict and self-destruction, they sought refuge in the silence of the cliffs rising above the shores of the Dead Sea. They withdrew into the solitude of the mountain caves so that they could concentrate on living a life of purity and so gain salvation. Unlike many of the Jews of the Temple, they did not use the *Old Testament* to make money, but tried to live according to its teachings. By leading this life, they hoped to achieve perfection and holiness. Their aim was to set an example to the rest of the Jews of how they could escape from the road leading to destruction, which they knew was fast approaching, unless the Jews followed the Word of God.

The Essenes wrote gnostic songs that must have stirred the hearts of the people who sang and heard them too deeply for words to express. A gnostic's life is like a ship in a storm, says one song. In another, a gnostic is described as a traveller in a forest full of lions, each having a tongue like a sword. At the beginning of the path, a gnostic experiences distress like a woman in labour giving birth to her first child. If he succeeds in enduring this distress, he becomes illuminated by God's perfect Light. Then he realises that man is a vain and empty creature moulded of clay and kneaded with water. Since he has passed through the crucible of suffering and endured the limits of doubt and despair, he attains peace in turmoil, joy in sorrow, and a new life of happiness in pain. Then he finds himself enveloped in God's love. At this stage, with humble thanks, he realises how he has been snatched from the pit, and placed on a high plain. Walking there in the Light of God, he stands erect, unbending before the brute force of the world.

Before the discovery of the *Dead Sea Scrolls*, only a little was known about the Essenes. Pliny and Josephus mention them, but they were virtually ignored by later historians. Pliny describes them as a race apart, more remarkable than any other in the world:

> They have no women, they abjure sexual love, they have no money ... Their membership is steadily increasing through the large number of people who are attracted to their way of life ... in this way, their race has lasted for thousands of years though no one is born within it.

Josephus, who started life as an Essene, writes that the Essenes 'believe that the soul (*ruach*) is immortal. It is a gift from God. God purifies some for Himself, removing all blemishes of the flesh. The person so perfected attains a holiness free of all impurities.'

These cave-dwellers continued to lead their life unaffected by the waves of conquerors who had already destroyed the Temple of Solomon once in 586 BC – and who were destined to do so again, in 73 AD – and who had conquered the Jews so many times. Their life in the wilderness was not an escape from the responsibility of every Jew to struggle for the purity of his religion, and to free Judea from foreign aggression. Side by side with the daily prayers and study of the Scriptures, some of them were formed into an efficient force which not only preached the guidance of Moses, but was also ready to fight for the freedom to live in the way that their teaching indicated. Thus their fighting could only be in the service of God and not to gain power or for any personal consideration.

The members of this fighting force were called 'Zealots' by the enemy. They were organised under one flag, and each tribe had its own banner. The Zealots were divided into four divisions, and at the head of each stood a chief. Each division was composed of people from three of the tribes of Israel. In this way, all the twelve Jewish tribes were organised under one flag. The chief had to be a Levite. He was not only a military commander, but also a teacher of the Law. Each division had its own *Midrash* (school), and the Levite, apart from performing the duties of a military commander, had to give regular *darsh* (lessons) in the school.

Thus, living in the wilderness in these caves, the Essenes shunned pleasure-seeking, scorned wedlock and were contemptuous of wealth. They formed a secret society and their secrets were never divulged to a non-member. The Romans knew about their existence, but could not penetrate the mask of secrecy surrounding them. The dream of every adventurous Jew was to become a member of this society, for this was the only practical method available to him of fighting the foreign invaders.

The Essenes, as we already know from Pliny's record, disdained marriage, but instead adopted other men's children, while they were still pliable and docile, accepting them as their kin and moulding them according to their way of life. Thus, for centuries, incredible though it may seem, the Essene society had perpetuated itself, although no one was ever born into it.

And when Elizabeth, the wife of Zachariah – the High Priest in the Temple of Solomon who had looked after Mary, the mother of Jesus, when she was a child – had a son in her old age, Zachariah sent him to the Essenes in the wilderness, where the child was brought up. He is known to history as John the Baptist.

Now that we know that the Essene community did exist in the wilderness, Zachariah's action is understandable. He was not sending his cherished son alone into the desert, but was entrusting him to the most reliable of communities, a community which sought to live in a manner pleasing to Jehovah.

Mary, who was either the cousin or the niece of Zachariah's wife, Elizabeth, was brought up by Zachariah because she had been handed over to the Temple in accordance with a vow taken by her mother, who was called Hannah.

It was in this environment and in this political and social climate that the birth of Jesus took place.

O   O   O   O   O

As we have already seen, there was among the Jews an expectation of the Messiah, a new leader who would be baptised and anointed their king. The rumour circulating among the Jews of his imminent birth led to Herod's decision to kill all the babies born in Bethlehem where, according to tradition, the Messiah was to appear. The powerful secret society of the Essenes was set in motion by Zachariah, and Mary succeeded in escaping the clutches of the Roman soldiers. She went with Jesus to Egypt where the Essenes had another colony.

The sudden disappearance of Jesus and Mary and their safe escape from the Roman authorities had, until the discovery of the *Dead Sea Scrolls*, been a mystery and source of speculation. None of the Gospels describe this episode in any detail. The existence of the Essene community shows how it was possible for them to evade their pursuers with such success despite the publicity which must have surrounded the birth. Under other circumstances, a child who spoke coherently and with authority from the cradle, and who was visited by shepherds and Magi might not have been able to disappear so easily.

In 4 BC – using the official dating – when Jesus was three or four years old, Herod died. And so the immediate danger to the life of Jesus was removed and he could move freely. It appears that he was educated under the hard discipline of the Essene teachers and, being an intelligent pupil, he learned the *Torah* very quickly. When Jesus was twelve years old, he was sent to the Temple of Solomon where it was found that instead of merely repeating his lessons, he was speaking with a certain confidence and authority.

There are several Muslim traditions which tell of the singular gifts which Jesus was given so early on in his life. The following accounts are taken from Ath-Tha'labi's *Stories of the Prophets*:

> As-Sadi said: When Jesus, peace be upon him, was in the school, he used to tell the boys what their fathers were doing, and he would say to a boy, 'Go home, for your people have been eating such and such and have prepared such and such for you and they are eating such

and such.' So the boy would go home to his people and would cry until they gave him that thing. Then they would say to him, 'Who told you about this?' and he would say, 'Jesus.' So they gathered them in a house and Jesus came looking for them. Then they said, 'They are not here.' He said to them, 'Then what is in this house?' They replied, 'Swine.' He said, 'Let them be swine.' So when they opened the door for them, lo! they were swine. The Children of Israel were troubled about Jesus, so when his mother was afraid concerning him, she put him on an ass of hers and went in flight to Egypt.

Wahb said: The first sign which the people saw from Jesus was that his mother was living in the house of a village headman in the land of Egypt, to which Joseph, the carpenter, had brought her when he went with her to Egypt; and the poor used to repair to that headman's house. Some money belonging to that headman was stolen from his treasury, but he did not suspect the poor. Mary was grieved over the affliction of that headman. When Jesus saw his mother's grief over her host's affliction, he said to her, 'Mother, do you want me to guide him to his money?' She replied, 'Yes, my son.' He said, 'Tell him to gather the poor for me in his house.' So Mary said that to the headman and he gathered the poor for him. When they had collected, he went to two of them, one of whom was blind and the other lame, and lifted the lame man onto the blind man's shoulders, and said to him, 'Rise up with him.' The blind man replied, 'I am too weak for that.' Jesus said to him, 'How were you strong enough for it yesterday?' When they heard him saying that, they beat the blind man till he arose, and when he stood up, the lame man reached to the window of the treasury. Then Jesus said to the headman, 'Thus they schemed against your property yesterday, because the blind man sought the help of his strength and the lame man of his eyes.' Then the blind man and the lame man said, 'He has spoken the truth, by God!' and restored all his money to the headman. He took it and put it in his treasury and said, 'O Mary, take half of it.' She replied, 'I was not created for that.' The headman said, 'Then give it to your son.' She replied, 'He is greater in rank than I.' ... And at that time he was twelve years old.

Ata' said: When Mary had taken Jesus from the school, she handed him over to various trades, and the last to which she entrusted him was to the dyers; so she handed him over to their chief that he might learn from him. Now the man had various clothes with him, and he had to go on a journey, so he said to Jesus, 'You have learned this trade, and I am going on a journey from which I shall not return for ten days. These clothes are of different colours, and I have marked every one of them with the colour with which it is to be dyed, so I want you to be finished with them when I return.' Then he went out. Jesus, peace be upon him, prepared one container with one colour and put all the clothes in it and said to them, 'Be, by God's permission, according to what is expected of you.' Then the dyer came, and all the clothes were in one container, so he said, 'O Jesus, what have you done?' He replied, 'I have finished them.' He said, 'Where are they?' He replied, 'In the container.' He said, 'All of them?' He replied, 'Yes.' He said, 'How are they all in one container? You have spoiled those clothes.' He replied, 'Rise and look.' So he arose, and Jesus took out a yellow garment and a green garment and a red garment until he had taken them out according to the colours which he desired. Then the dyer began to wonder, and he knew that this was from God, Great and Glorious is He. Then the dyer said to the people, 'Come and look at what Jesus peace be upon him, has done.' So he and his companions and they were the disciples, believed in him; and God Great and Glorious is He, knows best.

During the early manhood of Jesus, John left the Essene society and began to live alone in the wilderness. 'He dressed himself in a simple garment of camel's hair with a leather girdle round his waist. He ate only locusts and wild honey.' (*Matthew 3: 4*). He began to preach to people directly and did not insist on the long period of apprenticeship which was usually necessary for a person who desired full membership in the Essene brotherhood. His was thus a public movement. He called on everyone to turn to Jehovah, and assured them that the Kingdom of God would soon be established, since their promised Messiah would soon be making himself known to them.

In connection with this, it is of interest to read in the history written by Josephus of another hermit whose disciple this historian was: Josephus spent three years in the desert as an ascetic. During this time he was under the guidance of a hermit called Bannus who clothed himself with what grew on trees, ate only such food as grew wild and disciplined himself to chastity by constant cold baths. Thus it is apparent that John was following the tradition common to hermits.

The wilderness had been the place of refuge for David and other Prophets before him. It was a place where the Jews could be free from the domination of their foreign rulers and from the influence of false gods. In the wilderness, there were no aspirations towards the favours of the pagan rulers. In this atmosphere, there could only be dependence on the Creator and worship of Him alone. It was the cradle of monotheism. The desert wilderness removed any false sense of security, and a man learned to rely on Reality alone:

> In the barrenness of the wilderness, all other support falls and one is laid bare to the One God, the Power, the Constant Source of all life, and the Root of all security.[5]

Thus the struggle in the wilderness had two aspects. Primarily, it took place within the hearts of men who had to do battle with themselves if they were to live in a manner pleasing to their Lord. And, as we have already seen, the choice of this course of action inevitably resulted in conflict with those who wished to live otherwise. The first struggle was a question of faith in Jehovah, and of spiritual gain, irrespective of whether the second battle was won or lost.

The clarion call of John began to attract large crowds. He had ceased to observe one important stipulation in the Essene code of conduct – namely, 'to disclose none of the secrets of the sect to others even though tortured to death.'[6] His failure to follow this rule made it all the more easier for the Romans to infiltrate the movement with spies. John, with his prophetic vision, saw through their guise, and called them 'vipers'. (*Matthew 3: 7*). Jesus, his younger cousin, was part of this movement and was probably one of the first to be baptised. It is likely that Barnabas, who was his constant companion, was baptised with Jesus, and also his other companion, Mathias.

John knew that the 'vipers' were going to succeed before he could start the fight and, therefore, the baptism of Jesus gave him great satisfaction inasmuch as he was sure that his movement would not end with his life. As was foreseen by John, Herod the tetrarch had him beheaded and his mantle fell upon the shoulders of Jesus.

Jesus was now thirty years old. His mission lasted for not more than three years. He realised that his period of preparation was over. The most significant part of his life had begun.

In order to appreciate the full significance of this time, we will have to view the life of Jesus against the background of history, and in particular, the history of the Jews. This will further clarify the picture which has already begun to emerge – that the existence of the Essene community, the activities of John, and finally, the conflict between Jesus and the Romans, were all a part of one pattern which repeats itself again and again throughout the history of the Jews: In every case, what finally moved the Jews to revolt against their foreign invaders was the attempt of these rulers to make them associate partners with their Lord. Their recognition of the Divine Unity, and the conviction that there is no object of worship other then God, was categoric.

O   O   O   O   O

As rulers, the Jews often displayed an utter lack of statesmanship, although they flourished in political slavery. After the twelve tribes of the Tribe of Israel had escaped with Moses and his brother Aaron from Egypt, in approximately the 13th century BC, and after they had eventually settled in their promised land, a succession of Prophets was sent to guide them and to keep the teachings of Moses which had been revealed to him on Mount Sinai – the *Torah* – pure and alive. Amongst these Prophets were David, to whom the Psalms – the *Zabur* – were revealed, and his son Solomon, who was given great wisdom and an extraordinary mastery over the creation by God. It has been estimated that David ruled from approximately 1,000 to 960 BC, and that Solomon ruled from approximately 960 to 922 BC. Under their combined rule, therefore, peace be on them, the twelve tribes of the Tribe of Israel were united in one kingdom under rightly-guided prophetic rule for almost a century.

After the death of Solomon, however, the kingdom of the Tribe of Israel divided and split in two. The people of the southern kingdom, which was based in Judah, became known as the Judahites. The people of the northern kingdom became known as the Israelites.

The Judahites, who eventually became known simply as 'the Jews' – which was an abbreviation of either the word 'Judahites' or of the word 'Judeans' – comprised the tribes of Judah and Levi, together with some of the tribe of Benjamin. They considered themselves the true inheritors and guardians of the teachings of Moses – although in fact Prophets, including Elijah and Elisha, were still sent by God to the remaining nine and a half tribes in the northern kingdom of Israel.

In 722 BC, the northern kingdom of the Israelites was over-run by the Assyrians. According to Judahite historians, the nine and a half tribes of the Tribe of Israel who comprised the Israelites were almost totally annihilated, with the exception of some 27,000 captives who were taken off as slaves to Nineveh – which no longer exists today, but which was situated on the banks of the river Tigris, opposite the site of today's modern city of Mosul in northern Iraq. The Israelites are then said to have subsequently 'disappeared from history' – although even the *Bible* confirms that the Prophet Jonah was sent specifically to Nineveh to guide the captive Israelites there aright, and according to the *Qur'an*, '100,000 people or more' (*Qur'an: 37.147*), eventually accepted and followed him.

In 598 BC, King Nebuchadnezzar of Babylon invaded the southern kingdom of the Judahites and took Jerusalem. The Temple of Solomon was left intact, but the treasure, both from the Temple and from the royal palace, was appropriated by the new ruler – and so the Jews lost no time in rebelling against their Babylonian overlord. This prompted another attack by Nebuchadnezzar, in 586 BC, in which the Temple and the city were destroyed. In the aftermath of both of these invasions, a large number of Judahites were taken back to Babylon as slaves, but unlike the Israelites of the northern kingdom, they were not written out of history.

The wheel of fortune took another turn, and the Persians, under Cyrus, conquered Babylon – partly as a result of the captive Jews intriguing for the benefit of the invaders. Cyrus immediately realised the danger of having such a large population of aliens in Babylon, and asked them to leave and go back to Jerusalem, where they would be permitted to rebuild the Temple.

The cavalcade moving towards Jerusalem was composed of 42,360 Jews. In addition, they carried with them 7,337 servants and women, including 200 singing men and singing girls. This caravan was mounted on 736 horses, 245 mules, 435 camels, and 6,720 asses. (*Ezra 2: 64-69*). This was in addition to the animals which carried the treasure which they had amassed.

On reaching Jerusalem, the Jews began to plan the reconstruction of the Temple, and for this purpose, they collected 61,000 drams of gold and 5,000 pounds of silver. This was in addition to the treasure which they had brought with them from Babylon which was comprised of thirty horses laden with gold, and one thousand carrying silver. In addition, there were 5,400 gold and silver vessels to be placed in the Temple once it had been rebuilt. (*Ezra 1: 9-11*). The captives who returned to Jerusalem had grown both in number and in wealth.

Not all of the Jews who had been exiled in Babylon returned to Jerusalem immediately. Although the rebuilding of the Temple was completed by about 515 BC, some of the 'Babylonian' Jews did not return until about 458 BC. They were led by Ezra, who was later joined by Nehemiah, a Jew appointed by the Persians as their new governor of Judah.

It is said that one of the reasons for Ezra's delay in returning to Jerusalem was that he was busy writing down the *Torah* – which had been destroyed by the forces of Nebuchadnezzar – from memory, although it is clear from even a brief look at the five books of the *Pentateuch* – which is usually alleged to be the same as the *Torah* which was revealed to Moses – that they contain historical accounts of what is alleged to have happened both during and after the life of Moses, peace be on him, and which therefore cannot possibly be part of the original revelation of the Torah which was actually revealed to Moses by God.

As rulers of Jerusalem, the Jews did not enjoy peace for very long, and the next conquest of Jerusalem was that of Alexander the Great who, before he died in 323 BC, had reached India. His generals divided up his empire between them after his death. Ptolemy ruled Egypt, with his capital in Alexandria. The kingdom of Seleucus was divided into two parts – Antioch became the capital of the Northern kingdom and Babylon was the centre of the remainder of Alexander's former empire.

The Ptolemaic and Seleucian rulers were soon locked in a constant feud and, in one of their early encounters, Jerusalem fell into the hands of the Egyptian Greeks. The new rulers were not happy with the large concentration of Jews in the area, so a large number of them were forcibly transported to Egypt. This resulted in what was to become the largest Jewish colony outside Judah. The Jews in Alexandria came into close contact with Greek civilization, and as a result the Hebrew scriptures were translated into Greek, between approximately 275 and 150 BC.

To the Ptolemaic rulers based in Alexandria, Judah was a far-off colony and the Jews, after they had paid the annual tribute, were very much left to themselves. Then in 198 BC, the Seleucian rulers took over Jerusalem from the Ptolemaic rulers. For them, Jerusalem was very much nearer at hand and they took a much greater interest in the affairs of the people of Jerusalem than had the earlier rulers. The process of Hellenisation, which had occurred gradually and at a natural pace under Ptolemaic rule, was accelerated by the new rulers in a deliberate attempt to assimilate the Jews into their way of life. This forced cultural conformity reached its extreme expression during the reign of Antiochus Epeplianus. He made the mistake of installing a statue of Zeus in the Temple of Solomon. This outraged the Jews and they revolted under Judah Maccabees. The hammer and sickle were their emblem of revolt. Although Antiochus Epeplianus sacked both Jerusalem and the Temple, in 161 BC, the Jews refused to give in, and eventually the Greeks were pushed out of Jerusalem.

The victorious Jews found the Temple in ruins, the sanctuary desolate, the altar profaned and the Temple gate burnt. They repaired the Temple in accordance with its description in the *Torah*. The new rulers were so popular that they became both the high priests of the Temple and the new kings of Israel. With the concentration of power in the same hands, the rulers became very strict in the observation of the Law, and the people began to pine for the benevolent administration of foreign rulers. Finding dissatisfaction against their rule, the Maccabees became all the more haughty and arrogant. The Jews once again began to intrigue against their rulers, and this played no small part in ushering in Roman rule over Jerusalem, which was under their effective control by about 63 BC.

At about the time that Jesus was born, in approximately 4 BC, the Romans repeated the same mistake as that of the earlier rulers. They erected a large golden eagle over the main gate of the Temple. This infuriated the Jews and resulted in a series of revolts against the Romans. Two descendants of the Maccabees were the

first to unfurl the banner of revolt. Their aim was to destroy the
eagle. To the Romans, this was not only an act of sedition, but also
an insult to their religion. So, after much bloodshed, the revolt was
crushed. The two leaders were caught and burnt alive. Shortly afterwards, the Romans had to face another rebellion. The fight went
against the Jews and two thousand rebels were crucified. Thus the
resentment of the defeated Jews was still running very high when
in 6 AD the Emperor Augustus ordered a census of the Jews in
order to facilitate the levying of the taxes.

To pay taxes to the deified emperor was against the teaching of
the *Torah*. The Jews recognised only one king: Jehovah. A distur-
bance followed. The more moderate elements realised that if the
situation escalated, the conflict would result in a complete massacre of the Jews and so they counselled compromise and agreed to
pay the taxes, in order to save the people from committing sense-
less suicide. The leaders who purchased peace at this price were
not popular, and were regarded as traitors to the Jewish nation.

It is against this historical backdrop and into this tense situation that the birth of Jesus took place.

o   o   o   o   o

It is, within this historical context, easy to understand the opposition of the Roman rulers to Jesus – but in order to understand why
it was that some of the leaders of the Jews were also equally opposed to Jesus, it is necessary to briefly examine what had happened to the *Torah* during the 13 centuries that had elapsed since it
was first revealed.

As we have already seen, the original *Torah* was probably destroyed during the invasions of Nebuchadnezzar in the 6th century BC. Ezra attempted to write down the *Torah* from memory
during the exile of some of the Jews in Babylon – but it is generally
accepted that this compilation was in turn destroyed during the
sack of Jerusalem by Antiochus Epeplianus in 161 BC. Thus
Maulana M. Rahmatullahi Kairanvi, in his book *Izhar-ul-Haq*, quotes
the nineteenth century Catholic scholar, John Mill, as stating:

> All the scholars unanimously agree that the original
> *Torah* (*Pentateuch*) and other original books of the *Old
> Testament* were destroyed by the forces of Nebuchad-
> nezzar. When the books were recompiled through Ezra,
> these too were later on destroyed during the invasion
> of Antiochus.

During the four centuries between 450 and 50 BC, and especially after the destruction of Ezra's compilations by Antiochus in his invasion of Jerusalem in 161 BC, the book which was called the *Torah* – together with the additional books which purported to record the history of the Tribe of Israel after the time of Moses, and which were often written and compiled from remnants of various sources centuries after the events which they purported to describe had taken place – continued to be revised and rewritten, and what was to become the religion of Judaism began to take definite shape, headed by a strong Levitical priesthood who regarded themselves as the rightful guardians of this ancient knowledge. Thus by the time the *Torah* was first translated into Greek by seventy-two scholars from Alexandria between approximately 275 and 150 BC, the Hebrew version had already been re-written 'from memory' twice – and in the process, significant changes were introduced.

The *Talmud*, which is alleged to record the oral traditions of Moses, did not actually appear in written form until some seventeen centuries after the death of Moses, and at least nine centuries after the *Torah* itself had ceased to exist in its original form: The *Mishnah*, the written form of the alleged oral traditions of Moses was not collated in its present form until the beginning of the third century AD. The two commentaries on the *Mishnah*, the *Jerusalem Gemara* and the *Babylonian Gemara*, were not completed until the fifth and seventh centuries AD respectively, while the commentaries written on these commentaries, the very extensive *Midrash* literature, were written between 400 and 1200 AD.

As Dr Maurice Bucaille points out in his book, *The Bible, the Qur'an and Science*, by the time the Hebrew Scriptures came to be translated into Greek, they no longer truly represented the original teachings of Moses – nor had they done so for some considerable time:

> The *Old Testament* is a collection of works of greatly differing length and many different genres. They were written in several languages over a period of more than nine hundred years, based on oral traditions. Many of these works were corrected and completed in accordance with events or special requirements, often at periods that were very distant from one another. [7]

As we have already seen, only the first five books of this collection, which are usually referred to as the *Pentateuch*, are linked directly with Moses, although it is clear that they neither constitute the original *Torah* which was revealed to him, nor were they written 'by' him. Even as regards these first five books, Dr Maurice Bucaille points out that prior to the versions which were written during and after the exile in Babylon – the first of which (said to be compiled by Ezra) is commonly known as the *Sacerdotal* version – there were already at least three sources: the *Yahvist* version (in which God is named Yaweh), the *Elohist* version (in which God is named Elohim) and *Deuteronomy* – all of which were used to produce the *Sacerdotal* version, which was preached in the Temple after its reconstruction in about 515 BC, and all of which have been dated and located in time and place:

1. The *Yahvist* version was situated in the Ninth century BC (written in Judah).
2. The *Elohist* version was probably a little more recent (written in Israel).
3. *Deuteronomy* was from the Eighth century BC for some (E. Jacob), and from the time of Josiah [the Seventh century BC] for others (Father de Vaux).
4. The *Sacerdotal* version came from the period of exile or after the exile: Sixth century BC. [8]

Dr Bucaille continues:

> It may be seen that the arrangement of the text of the *Pentateuch* spans at least three centuries.
> The problem is, however, even more complex. In 1941, A. Lods singled out three sources in the *Yahvist* version, four in the *Elohist* version, six in *Deuteronomy*, nine in the *Sacerdotal* version, 'not including the additions spread out among eight different authors,' writes Father de Vaux. More recently, it has been thought that, 'many of the constitutions or laws contained in the *Pentateuch* had parallels outside the Bible going back much further than the dates ascribed to the documents themselves,' and that, 'many of the stories of the *Pentateuch* presupposed a background that was different from – and older than – the one from which these documents were

supposed to have come.' This leads on to 'an interest in the formation of traditions'. The problem then appears so complicated that nobody knows where they are anymore.

The multiplicity of sources brings with it numerous disagreements and repetitions. Father de Vaux gives examples of this overlapping of traditions in the case of the Flood, the kidnapping of Joseph, his adventures in Egypt, disagreement of names relating to the same character, and differing descriptions of important events.

Thus the *Pentateuch* is shown to be formed from various traditions brought together more or less skilfully by its authors. The latter sometimes juxtaposed their compilations and sometimes adapted the stories for the sake of synthesis. They allowed improbabilities and disagreements to appear in the texts, however, which has led modern man to the objective study of the sources.

As far as textual criticism is concerned, the *Pentateuch* provides what is probably the most obvious example of adaptations made by the hand of man. These were made at different times in the history of the Jewish people, taken from oral traditions and texts handed down from preceding generations. It was begun in the Tenth or Ninth century BC with the *Yahvist* tradition which took the story from its very beginnings. The latter sketches Israel's own particular destiny to 'fit it back into God's Grand Design for humanity' (Father de Vaux). It was concluded in the Sixth century BC with the *Sacerdotal* tradition that is meticulous in its precise mention of dates and genealogies. [9]

Thus, continues Dr Bucaille:

> For *Genesis* alone, the division of the Book into three sources has been firmly established: Father de Vaux in the commentary to his translation lists for each source the passages in the present text of *Genesis* that rely on them. On the evidence of these data it is possible to pinpoint the contribution made by the various sources to any one of the chapters. For example, in the case of the

Creation, the Flood and the period that goes from the Flood to Abraham, occupying as it does the first eleven chapters of *Genesis*, we can see alternating in the Biblical text a section of the *Yahvist* and a section of the *Sacerdotal* texts. The *Elohist* text is not present in the first eleven chapters. The overlapping of *Yahvist* and *Sacerdotal* contributions is here quite clear. For the Creation and up to Noah (first five chapters), the arrangement is simple: a *Yahvist* passage alternates with a *Sacerdotal* passage from beginning to end of the narration. For the Flood and especially chapters 7 and 8 moreover, the cutting of the text according to its source is narrowed down to very short passages and even to a single sentence. In the space of little more than a hundred lines of English text, the text changes seventeen times. It is from this that the improbabilities and contradictions arise when we read the present-day text. [10]

Thus it is clear that the version of the *Torah* which existed at the time that Jesus came into this world was not the original *Torah* which had been revealed to Moses by God on Mount Sinai. It was, to use Dr. Bucaille's words, 'a collection of works with highly disparate contents written over at least seven centuries, using extremely varied sources before being amalgamated inside a single work.'

We know from the *Qur'an*, however, that God not only gave Jesus his own revelation – the *Ingil* – but also knowledge of the original *Torah* which He had revealed to Moses – and the former confirmed the latter in every respect. Thus Jesus was in a unique and divinely-guided position to be able to see exactly how and where the original teachings of Moses had been changed and thereby distorted. As we are about to see in more detail further on, this made things very difficult for the priesthood of the Jews who prior to the arrival of Jesus had been able to claim, virtually unchallenged, that they were the true guardians of the original teachings of Moses, and who had made this claim the basis of their leadership and their livelihood. Jesus showed up their hypocrisy and endangered the source of their authority and wealth – and this was why they opposed him so vehemently.

As Mrs. Iftekhar Bano Hussain points out in *Volume Two* of her book *Prophets in the Qur'an – The Later Prophets*:

There is no known copy of the original revelation which was given to *sayyedina* 'Isa, peace be on him – the *Ingil* – in existence today, which perhaps partly explains why his teachings have been rewritten and redefined so often during the last two millennia. According to the *Gospel of Barnabas*, the *Ingil* was never actually contained in a written form – being more like a well of wisdom in *sayyedina* 'Isa's heart from which he drew when it was needed – but it is clear that as well as speaking Aramaic, *sayyedina* 'Isa also knew Hebrew, since his purpose was to re-establish the original teachings of Musa among the Tribe of Israel, in accordance with the *Taurah*, which was written in ancient Hebrew, and which had already been so significantly changed and corrupted by the time of his miraculous birth, that he was in fact rejected by the very Jewish priesthood who claimed to be the rightful custodians of *sayyedina* Musa's teachings!

Indeed, perhaps one of the main reasons why the Jewish priesthood opposed *sayyedina* 'Isa and wished to have him killed was because he knew exactly which parts of the *Taurah* which had originally been revealed to *sayyedina* Musa had been subsequently changed by the Jews, having been given direct knowledge of the original *Taurah* by Allah.

Sayyedina 'Isa was also most probably equally aware of the distortions and amendments contained in the additional books which had been written *after* the death of *sayyedina* Musa, and which purported to faithfully record the history of the Tribe of Israel thereafter.

In other words, with the coming of *sayyedina* 'Isa, all the misrepresentations and changes to the original teachings of *sayyedina* Musa which had gradually been introduced by the Jewish priesthood during the nine centuries that had elapsed after the reign of *sayyedina* Sulayman had come to an end were suddenly in grave danger of being exposed, and their hierarchy of being destroyed. This is why they rejected *sayyedina* 'Isa, peace be on him, and this is why they plotted with the Romans to have him killed. [11]

○   ○   ○   ○   ○

Returning now to the historical account of the life of Jesus, it will be remembered that the political and social situation at the time of Jesus's birth, along with the events leading up to the death of John the Baptist have already been mentioned. The point had now been reached where the entire resistance movement was concentrated around the divinely inspired figure of Jesus:

Before doing anything else, Jesus had to undergo forty days living and praying in the wilderness. He was now thirty years old. Under Jewish law, this was the age when a man was freed from the domination of his father. Unlike John, he did not openly teach, when he preached to the multitudes, that they should take a stand against the Roman rulers. Discreet preparations needed to be made. Previous attempts had ended in disaster and the recent death of John was fresh in the mind of Jesus. With foresight and prudence, he began to prepare and organise the Jews. He baptised no one. This would have unnecessarily attracted too much attention from the Romans, and would have been a dangerous practice, as he could not have prevented the 'vipers' from infiltrating the resistance movement.

Jesus appointed twelve disciples, a traditional number representing the twelve tribes of Israel. They further enlisted seventy-two patriots to serve under their command. The Pharisees had always kept the *Am Al-Arez*, the able-bodied Jews who lived in the villages, at arm's length. Jesus took them under his wing. These peasants, many of whom were of the Essene community, became the zealous followers of Jesus, and were ready to lay down their lives for his cause. They were known as Zealots. According to the Bible, at least six of the twelve disciples are known to have been Zealots.

Jesus, who had come to reaffirm and not to reject the teaching of Moses, issued the *Old Testament* appeal: 'Whosoever is zealous for the Law and maintains the Covenant, let him come forth after me.' (*Maccabees* 2: 27-31). A large number began to enlist, but they were kept underground, and their training was carried out in the wilderness. They were also called *Bar Yonim*, which means 'sons of the wilderness'. From among these, those who had learned to use the dagger were known as *Sicarii* (dagger-men). A further hand-picked group of men formed a kind of bodyguard, and they were known as *Bar Jesus*, or 'sons of Jesus'. A number of persons known as *Bar Jesus* are mentioned in historical sources, but a curtain of mystery surrounds these men, and not much is known about them. This is understandable. They belonged to the closest circle of Jesus's followers, and their identities had to be hidden from the eyes of the Roman spies.

Jesus gave the command to his followers: 'But now he that hath a purse, let him take it and likewise his scrip; and he that hath no sword, let him sell his garments and buy one.' (*Luke 22: 36*). And the number of his followers, inspired also by his teaching and miracles, grew. The net result of all these preparations was that Pilate's successor, Sossianus Hierocles, (quoted by the Church father, Lactanius), says offhandedly that Jesus was the leader of a band of highway robbers numbering nine hundred men. A mediaeval Hebrew copy of a lost version of a work by Josephus also reports that Jesus had between 2,000 to 4,000 armed followers with him. [12]

Jesus took great care not to deviate from the teaching of the Essenes, which is known by the fact that 'the rites and precepts of the Gospels and the Epistles are to be found on every page of the literature of the sect.' [13] During his mission, however, Jesus did not disclose the totality of his teaching to most of his followers. The whole truth was known to very few:

> I have yet many things to say unto you, but you cannot bear them now. Howbeit, when he, the Spirit of truth, is come, he will guide you into all truth, but he shall not speak of himself, but whatsoever he shall hear, that shall he speak. (*John 16: 12-14*).

It is interesting to note in passing that this passage is said to be one of the few passages referring to the coming of the Prophet Muhammad, blessings and peace be on him, which has not been removed from the four official Gospels. The 'Spirit of truth' to which the above verses refer is identified by John with 'the Paraclete'. The Greek word for Paraclete is '*Parakletos*' or '*Parakleitos*', meaning 'the Comforter' or 'the Praised One'. Its equivalent in Arabic is '*Ahmad*', meaning 'the Most Praiseworthy', 'the One who Distinguishes between Truth and Falsehood', and 'the Comforter' – and Ahmad is one of the names of the Prophet Muhammad. Dr Bucaille, after considering the four references to the Paraclete in the New Testament (who is only mentioned by John, but not by anyone else), and after considering the textual variations in the various versions, as well as the natural meaning of the vocabulary used, concludes:

According to the rules of logic therefore, one is brought to see in John's Paraclete a human being like Jesus, possessing the faculties of hearing and speech formally implied in John's Greek text. Jesus therefore predicts that God will later send a human being to Earth to take up the role defined by John, i.e. to be a Prophet who hears God's word and repeats his message to man. This is the logical interpretation of John's texts arrived at if one attributes to the words their proper meaning. [14]

○   ○   ○   ○   ○

It is clear from virtually all the sources available to us today that Jesus's popularity amongst the common people was largely due to his extraordinary purity and compassion which were expressed not only by the wisdom in his words and the simplicity of his behaviour, but also by his many miracles – which were only made possible, as he always said, by the grace of God.

Jesus was not seeking worldly power, either as ruler of the country, or within the closed hierarchy of the Scribes and Pharisees. However, his popularity with the common people and the large number of his following caused the Romans and those priests who supported them to fear that this was his intention. It was this apparent threat to their position of power which, as has already been stated, prompted them to try to dispose of him.

Jesus's mission was solely to establish worship of the Creator in the manner in which the Creator had ordained. He and his followers were prepared to fight anyone who tried to prevent them from living as their Lord wished them to.

The first fighting took place with the Jews loyal to the Romans. It was led by Bar Jesus Barabbas, and it completely demoralised this group of Jews, as their leader was killed in the encounter. Bar Jesus Barabbas was arrested.

The next objective was the Temple itself. The Romans had a strong force near at hand, since it was the time of the annual festival and the feast of the Passover was approaching. The Romans who at that time of year were always ready for minor disturbances, were even more alert than usual. In addition, there were the Temple police who guarded the sacred place. The entrance made by Jesus was so well planned that the Roman soldiers were taken completely by surprise, and Jesus took over the control of the Temple.

This encounter is known as the 'cleansing of the Temple'. John's Gospel describes the event in these words:

> In the Temple (Jesus) found those who were selling oxen and sheep and pigeons, and the money-changers at their business. And making a whip of cord, he drove them all, with the sheep and oxen, out of the Temple, and he poured out the coins of the money-changers and over-turned their tables. (*John 2: 14-15*).

Commenting on the words, 'whip of cord', Carmichael says:

> They unmistakably imply violence and equally unmis-takably represent a sort of minimal toning down of what actually must have been a massive undertaking. If we simply imagine the size of the Temple, the tens and thou-sands of pilgrims thronging into and through it, the numerous attendants, the police force, the Roman sol-diers, as well as the normal reaction of the ox-drivers themselves, to say nothing of the money-changers, we see that it must have taken much more than mere sur-prise to have accomplished it at all. The scene behind this fragmentary recollection in the fourth Gospel must have been vastly different. The chronicler has softened it by 'spiritualising' it out of all reality. [15]

One of the lessons of every freedom fighter has been that the local police tend to have their sympathies with the patriots and not with the army of occupation. This could have been a contributing factor in the complete collapse of the defence of the Temple.

The Romans had suffered a local setback, but their power was not crushed. They called for reinforcements, and fresh troops be-gan to move towards Jerusalem. The defence of the gate of Jerusa-lem lasted for a few days, but ultimately the Roman army proved too strong for the patriots, and all the followers of Jesus melted away. Even the disciples ran away, leaving Jesus with very few men around him. Jesus went underground, and the Romans began an intensive search to find him.

The 'arrest', the 'trial', and the 'crucifixion' are hedged about with so many contradictions and mis-statements, that it is extremely difficult to untangle and penetrate through them in order to arrive at what actually happened. It is clear, however, that the Roman government succeeded in utilising the services of the small minority of Jews who had a vested interest in the continuation of Roman rule over Jerusalem.

Judas Iscariot, a disciple of Jesus, was won over on the promise of receiving thirty pieces of silver, if, through his help, Jesus was arrested. In order to avoid any further trouble, it was decided to make the attempt at night. On reaching the place where Jesus had gone with a few of his followers, Judas was told to kiss Jesus, so that the foreign Roman soldiers could identify him. The plan miscarried. When the soldiers materialised from the darkness, a tumult ensued. The two Jews were mixed up in the dark, and the soldiers mistakenly arrested Judas instead of Jesus. Thus, the latter made good his escape. The *Qur'an* says:

> And they did not kill him and they did not crucify him, but it appeared so to them. And surely those who disagree about it are certainly in doubt about it – they have no knowledge about it except that they follow speculation. And they did not kill him for certain – but God took him up to Himself. And God was ever Mighty, Wise. (*Qur'an* 4. 157-158).

It is not altogether clear who, if anyone, was aware of the 'mistake' that had been made at the time. Certainly none of the official Gospels in their present form mention it. If the Romans did become aware of the true identity of their prisoner when he was brought before Pilate, the Roman Magistrate, then it is possible that the dramatic turn of events may still have satisfied everyone. The Romans would have made an example of someone – whoever that someone was – which was sure to act as a deterrent. The majority of the Jews would have been happy for, due to a miracle, the traitor was standing in the dock instead of Jesus. Even the pro-Roman Jews would be happy, for, with the death of Judas, the proof of their guilt would be destroyed. And furthermore, with Jesus officially dead, he would be far less likely to come out into the open to give them trouble.

This possible explanation, however, appears to be unlikely, given the descriptions of what is said to have happened in the four official Gospels. It is far more likely that everyone really believed that it was Jesus who had been arrested, even though they were wrong.

The part played by Pontius Pilate, the Roman Magistrate, is hard to determine. His indecisiveness, as described in the *Bible*, his partiality towards the Jewish leaders, together with his good will towards Jesus, make a story hard to believe. It has been suggested that this could be the result of an attempt by the writers of the Gospels to twist the facts in order to shift the responsibility of the 'crucifixion' entirely onto the whole Jewish nation and so to exonerate the Romans completely from their part in Jesus's supposed death.[16] The only way an official account of Jesus's life could survive would be by describing it in a manner which was not offensive to the foreign rulers, and by either omitting, disguising, or even changing those details which would be displeasing to those in authority.

Another possible explanation is provided by a strong tradition that Pilate was 'got at' with a sizeable bribe amounting to the equivalent of £30,000. If what is described in the Gospels is true, then it is obvious that Pilate did have a vested interest in the drama enacted that day in Jerusalem.

There is one other significant fact which it is interesting to note in passing: In the calendars of the Saints of the Coptic Church, both in Egypt and in Ethiopia, Pilate and his wife appear as 'saints'. This can only make sense if we accept that Pilate, knowing full well that his soldiers had made a wrong arrest, knowingly condemned Judas in place of Jesus, and allowed the latter to escape.

In the account given by Barnabas, we are told that at the time of the arrest, which took place after the Last Supper – and which according to him took place 'in the house of Nicodemus beyond the brook Cedron', outside Jerusalem – Judas was transformed by the Creator so that not only his enemies but even his mother and his closest followers believed him to be Jesus:

> Having gone forth from the house, Jesus retired into the garden to pray, according as his custom was to pray, bowing his knees an hundred times and prostrating himself upon his face. Judas, accordingly, knowing the place where Jesus was with his disciples, went to the high priest, and said: 'If you will give me what was promised, this night will I give into your hand Jesus whom you seek; for he is alone with eleven companions.'
>
> The high priest answered: 'How much do you seek?'

Said Judas: 'Thirty pieces of gold.'

Then straightway the high priest counted unto him the money, and sent a Pharisee to the governor to fetch soldiers, and to Herod, and they gave a legion of them, because they feared the people; wherefore they took their arms, and with torches and lanterns upon staves went out of Jerusalem.

When the soldiers with Judas drew near to the place where Jesus was, Jesus heard the approach of many people, wherefore in fear he withdrew into the house. And the eleven were sleeping.

Then God, seeing the danger of his servant, commanded (the angels) Gabriel, Michael, Rafael and Uriel, His ministers, to take Jesus out of the world.

The holy angels came and took Jesus out by the window that looks toward the South. They bare him and placed him in the third heaven in the company of angels blessing God for evermore.

Judas entered impetuously before all into the chamber from where Jesus had been taken up. And the disciples were sleeping. Whereupon the wonderful God acted wonderfully, insomuch that Judas was so changed in speech and in face to be like Jesus that we believed him to be Jesus. And he, having awakened us, was seeking where the Master was. Whereupon we marvelled, and answered: 'You, lord, are our master; have you now forgotten us?'

And he, smiling, said: 'Now are you foolish, that know not me to be Judas Iscariot!'

And as he was saying this the soldiery entered, and laid their hands upon Judas, because he was in every way like to Jesus.

We having heard Judas' saying, and seeing the multitude of soldiers, fled as beside ourselves.

And John, who was wrapped in a linen cloth, awoke and fled, and when a soldier seized him by the linen cloth he left the linen cloth and fled naked. For God heard the prayer of Jesus, and saved the eleven from evil.

The soldiers took Judas and bound him, not without derision. For he truthfully denied that he was Jesus; and the soldiers, mocking him, said: 'Sir, fear not, for we are come to make you king of Israel, and we have bound you because we know that you are refusing the kingdom.'

Judas answered: 'Now have you lost your senses! You are come to take Jesus of Nazareth, with arms and lanterns as (against) a robber; and you have bound me that has guided you, to make me king!'

Then the soldiers lost their patience, and with blows and kicks they began to flout Judas, and they led him with fury into Jerusalem.

John and Peter followed the soldiers afar off; and they affirmed to him who writes that they saw all the examination that was made of Judas by the high priest, and by the council of the Pharisees, who were assembled to put Jesus to death. Whereupon Judas spake many words of madness, insomuch that every one was filled with laughter, believing that he was really Jesus, and that for fear of death he was feigning madness. Whereupon the scribes bound his eyes with a bandage, and mocking him said: 'Jesus, prophet of the Nazarenes,' for so they called them who believed in Jesus, 'tell us, who was it that smote thee?' And they buffeted him and spat in his face.

When it was morning there assembled the great council of scribes and elders of the people; and the high priest with the Pharisees sought false witness against Judas, believing him to be Jesus: and they found not that which they sought. And why say I that the chief priests believed Judas to be Jesus? Nay, all the disciples, with him who writes, believed it; and more, the poor virgin mother of Jesus, with his kinsfolk and friends, believed it, insomuch that the sorrow of every one was incredible. As God lives, he who writes forgot all that Jesus had said: how that he should be taken up from the world, and that he should suffer in a third person, and that he should not die until near the end of the world. Wherefore he went with the mother of Jesus and with John to the cross.

The high priest caused Judas to be brought before him bound, and asked him of his disciples and his doctrine.

Whereupon Judas, as though beside himself, answered nothing to the point. The high priest then adjured him by the living God of Israel that he would tell him the truth.

Judas answered: 'I have told you that I am Judas Iscariot, who promised to give into your hands Jesus the Nazarene; and you, by what art I know not, are beside yourselves, for you will have it by every means that I am Jesus.

The high priest answered: 'O perverse seducer, you have deceived all Israel, beginning from Galilee even unto Jerusalem here, with your doctrine and false miracles; and now do you think to flee the merited punishment that befits you by feigning to be mad? As God lives, you will not escape it!' And having said this he commanded his servants to smite him with buffetings and kicks, so that his understanding might come back into his head. The derision which he then suffered at the hands of the high priest's servants is past belief. For they zealously devised new inventions to give pleasure to the council. So they attired him as a juggler, and so treated him with hands and feet that it would have moved the very Canaanites to compassion if they had beheld that sight.

But the chief priests and Pharisees and elders of the people had their hearts so exasperated against Jesus that, believing Judas to be really Jesus, they took delight in seeing him so treated.

Afterwards they led him bound to the governor, who secretly loved Jesus. Whereupon he, thinking that Judas was Jesus, made him enter into his chamber, and spake to him, asking him for what cause the chief priests and the people had given him into his hands.

Judas answered: 'If I tell you the truth, you will not believe me; for perchance you are deceived as the (chief) priests and the Pharisees are deceived.'

The governor answered (thinking that he wished to speak concerning the Law): 'Now do you not know that I am not a Jew? but the (chief) priests and the elders of your people have given you into my hand; wherefore tell us the truth, that I may do what is just. For I have power to set you free and to put you to death.'

Judas answered: 'Sir, believe me, if you put me to death, you will do a great wrong, for you will slay an innocent person; seeing that I am Judas Iscariot, and not Jesus, who is a magician, and by his art has so transformed me.'

When he heard this the governor marvelled greatly, so that he sought to set him at liberty. The governor therefore went out, and smiling said: 'In the one case, at least, this man is not worthy of death, but rather of compassion.' 'This man says,' said the governor, 'that he is not Jesus, but a certain Judas who guided the soldiery to take Jesus, and he says that Jesus the Galilean has by his art magic so transformed him. Wherefore, if this be true, it were a great wrong to kill him, seeing that he were innocent. But if he is Jesus and denies that he is, assuredly he has lost his understanding, and it were impious to slay a madman.'

Then the chief priests and elders of the people, with the scribes and Pharisees, cried out with shouts, saying: 'He is Jesus of Nazareth, for we know him; for if he were not the malefactor we would not have given him into your hands. Nor is he mad; but rather malignant, for with this device he seeks to escape from our hands, and the sedition that he would stir up if he should escape would be worse than the former.'

Pilate (for such was the governor's name), in order to rid himself of such a case, said: 'He is a Galilean, and Herod is king of Galilee; wherefore it does not pertain to me to judge such a case, so you take him to Herod.'

Accordingly they led Judas to Herod, who for a long time had desired that Jesus should go to his house. But Jesus had never been willing to go to his house, because Herod was a Gentile, and adored the false and lying gods, living after the manner of the unclean Gentiles. Now when Judas had been led there, Herod asked him of many things, to which Judas gave answers not to the purpose, denying that he was Jesus.

Then Herod mocked him, with all his court, and caused him to be clad in white as the fools are clad, and sent him back to Pilate, saying to him, 'Do not fail in justice to the people of Israel!'

And this Herod wrote, because the chief priests and scribes and the Pharisees had given him a good quantity of money. The governor having heard that this was so from a servant of Herod, in order that he also might gain some money, feigned that he desired to set Judas at liberty. Whereupon he caused him to be scourged by his slaves, who were paid by the scribes to slay him under the scourges. But God, Who had decreed the issue, reserved Judas for the cross, in order that he might suffer that horrible death to which he had sold another. He did not suffer Judas to die under the scourges, notwithstanding that the soldiers scourged him so grievously that his body rained blood. Thereupon, in mockery they clad him in an old purple garment, saying: 'It is fitting to our new king to clothe him and crown him.' So they gathered thorns and made a crown, like those of gold and precious stones which kings wear on their heads. And this crown of thorns they placed upon Judas' head, putting in his hand a reed for sceptre, and they made him sit in a high place. And the soldiers came before him, bowing down in mockery, saluting him as King of the Jews. And they held out their hands to receive gifts, such as new kings are accustomed to give; and receiving nothing they smote Judas, saying: 'Now, how are you crowned, foolish king, if you will not pay your soldiers and servants?'

The chief priests with the scribes and Pharisees, seeing that Judas died not by the scourges, and fearing lest Pilate should set him at liberty, made a gift of money to the governor, who having received it gave Judas to the scribes and Pharisees as guilty unto death. Whereupon they condemned two robbers with him to the death of the cross.

So they led him to Mount Calvary, where they used to hang malefactors, and there they crucified him naked, for the greater ignominy.

Judas truly did nothing else but cry out: 'God, why have you forsaken me, seeing the malefactor has escaped and I die unjustly?'

Verily I say that the voice, the face, and the person of Judas were so like to Jesus, that his disciples and believers entirely believed that he was Jesus; wherefore some departed from the doctrine of Jesus, believing that Jesus had been a false prophet, and that by art magic he had done the miracles which he did: for Jesus had said that he should not die till near the end of the world; for that at that time he should be taken away from the world.

But they that stood firm in the doctrine of Jesus were so encompassed with sorrow, seeing him die who was entirely like to Jesus, that they remembered now what Jesus had said. And so in company with the mother of Jesus they went to Mount Calvary, and were not only present at the death of Judas, weeping continually, but by means of Nicodemus and Joseph of Arimathea they obtained from the governor the body of Judas to bury it. Whereupon, they took him down from the cross with such weeping as assuredly no one would believe, and buried him in the new sepulchre of Joseph; having wrapped him up in an hundred pounds of precious ointments.

Then returned each man to his house. He who writes, with John and James his brother, went with the mother of Jesus to Nazareth.

Those disciples who did not fear God went by night and stole the body of Judas and hid it, spreading a report that Jesus was risen again; whence great confusion arose. The high priest then commanded, under pain of Anathema, that no one should talk of Jesus of Nazareth. And so there arose a great persecution, and many were stoned and many beaten, and many banished from the land, because they could not hold their peace on such a matter. (*The Gospel of Barnabas: 214-218*).

According to Barnabas, it was not until Jesus subsequently appeared to Mary and some of the disciples, after his supposed death, that they were informed of what had really happened:

Jesus came, surrounded with splendour, to the room where abode Mary the Virgin with her two sisters, and Martha and Mary Magdalen, and Lazarus, and him who writes, and John and James and Peter. Whereupon, through fear they fell as dead. And Jesus lifted up his mothers and the others from the ground, saying: 'Fear not, for I am Jesus; and weep not, for I am alive and not dead.' They remained every one for a long time beside himself at the presence of Jesus, for they altogether believed that Jesus was dead. Then the Virgin, weeping, said: 'Tell me, my son, wherefore God, having given you power to raise the dead, suffered you to die, to the shame of your kinsfolk and friends, and to the shame of your doctrine? For every one that loves you has been as dead.'

Jesus replied, embracing his mother: 'Believe me, mother, for verily I say to you that I have not been dead at all; for God has reserved me till near the end of the world.' And having said this he prayed the four angels that they would manifest themselves, and give testimony how the matter had passed.

Thereupon the angels manifested themselves like four shining suns, insomuch that through fear every one again fell down as dead.

Then Jesus gave four linen cloths to the angels that they might cover themselves, in order that they might be seen and heard to speak by his mother and her companions. And having lifted up each one, he comforted them, saying: 'These are the ministers of God: Gabriel, who announces God's secrets; Michael, who fights against God's enemies; Rafael, who receives the souls of them that die; and Uriel, who will call every one to the judgement of God at the Last Day.'

Then the four angels narrated to the Virgin how God had sent for Jesus, and had transformed Judas, that he might suffer the punishment to which he had sold another. (*The Gospel of Barnabas: 219-220*).

According to Barnabas, Jesus remained with his mother and close disciples for three days, thereby giving them and some of his other closest followers the opportunity to be with him for just a little while longer:

And then Jesus commanded us to call his faithful disciples that they might see him. Then did James and John call together the seven disciples with Nicodemus and Joseph, and many others of the seventy-two, and they ate with Jesus.

The third day Jesus said: 'Go to the Mount of Olives with my mother, for there will I ascend unto heaven, and you will see who shall bear me up.'

So there went all, saving twenty-five of the seventy-two disciples, who for fear had fled to Damascus. And as they all stood in prayer, at mid-day came Jesus with a great multitude of angels who were praising God: and the splendour of his face made them sore afraid, and they fell with their faces to the ground. But Jesus lifted them up, comforting them, and saying: 'Be not afraid, I am your master.'

And he reproved many who believed him to have died and risen again, saying: 'Do you then hold me and God for liars? For God has granted to me to live almost unto the end of the world, even as I said unto you. Verily I say unto you, I died not, but Judas the traitor. Beware, for Satan will make every effort to deceive you, but you be my witnesses in all Israel, and throughout the world, of all things that you have heard and seen.'

And having thus spoken, he prayed God for the salvation of the faithful, and the conversion of sinners. And, his prayer ended, he embraced his mother, saying: 'Peace be unto you, my mother, rest you in God Who created you and me.' And having thus spoken, he turned to his disciples, saying: 'May God's grace and mercy be with you.'

Then before their eyes the four angels carried him up into heaven.

After Jesus had departed, the disciples scattered through the different parts of Israel and of the world, and the truth, hated of Satan, was persecuted, as it always is, by falsehood. For certain evil men, pretending to be disciples, preached that Jesus died and rose not again. Others preached that he really died, but rose again. Others preached, and yet preach, that Jesus is the Son of God,

among whom Paul is deceived. But we, as much as I
have written, that preach we to those who fear God, that
they may be saved in the Last Day of God's Judgement.
Amen. (*The Gospel of Barnabas: 221-222*).

Although – as is the case with all of the Gospels – it is impossible to
verify the contents of the *Gospel of Barnabas* with complete certainty,
in the absence of an early, original, authentic manuscript, his account of what happened does make sense, and it does explain why
there is such confusion surrounding the events which took place
at the time of the arrest and the crucifixion, and it does explain
why some accounts, written by people who were not present at
those events, support the mistaken belief that it was Jesus who
was crucified. Perhaps most significantly, it does not contradict the
account given in the *Qur'an*, which is the only totally reliable statement concerning this matter in existence today.

There are also several historical sources other than the *Bible* and
the *Qur'an* which confirm that many of the early Christians did
not believe that Jesus died on the cross, although not everyone is
in complete agreement as to whether it was Jesus's would-be be-
trayer who was the one crucified. The Cerinthians and later the
Basilidians, for example, who were among the first of the early
Christian communities, denied that Jesus was crucified, but believed that it was Simon of Cyrene who was crucified instead.
Cerinthus, a contemporary of Peter, Paul and John, also denied the
resurrection of Jesus. The Carpocratians, another early Christian
sect, believed that it was not Jesus who was crucified, but one of
his followers who very closely resembled him. Plotinus, who lived
in the fourth century, tells us that he had read a book called *The
Journeys of the Apostles* which related the acts of Peter, John, Andrew,
Thomas and Paul. Among other things, it stated that Jesus was not
crucified, but another in his place, and therefore, he laughed at
those who believed that they had crucified him.[17] Thus, although
it is clear that Jesus was not crucified, sources either differ or are
not specific as to who was crucified in his place – while others,
some two thousand centuries later, find it hard to believe anything:

> When one reflects that the catalogue of outrage ascribed
> to the Roman soldiery, repeats almost *verbatim* certain
> passages of the *Old Testament* ... one begins to suspect
> that the entire episode is a sheer invention.[18]

There is no other known historical record of what happened to Jesus after the 'crucifixion' other than in the *Gospel of Barnabas* and the *Qur'an*, which as we have already seen, both describe the event which is generally known as the 'Ascension' – in which Jesus was taken away from this world – and which is described in the Gospel of Luke and in the Acts of the Apostles, but which, as Dr. Maurice Bucaille points out, is not even mentioned by the other three officially accepted Gospels:

> Neither Matthew nor John speaks of Jesus's Ascension. Luke in his Gospel situates it on the day of the Resurrection, and forty days later in the Acts of the Apostles of which he is said to be the author. Mark mentions it (without giving a date) in a conclusion thought today not to be authentic. The Ascension therefore has no solid scriptural basis. Commentators nevertheless approach this important question with incredible lightness. [19]

Finally, since Jesus has not yet returned to this world, as promised by him and as foretold by the Prophet Muhammad, may the blessings and peace of God be on both of them, it is clear that the life of Jesus on this earth has not yet been concluded, and accordingly this historical account of his life must remain incomplete – although as we shall see in Chapter Ten, there are already some reliable records in existence of some of the main events in the life of Jesus which will take place after his return.

o   o   o   o   o

Chapter Three

Barnabas
and the
Early Christians

Barnabas, or *Bar Nabe*, which means 'son of consolation' or 'son of exhortation', was a Jew and was born in Cyprus. He was known as Joses, or Joseph, but was given this new name by the disciples of Jesus, peace be on him and them. Although little mention is made of him in the four accepted Gospels, it is evident from some of the other books in the New Testament that he became one of the leaders of the disciples after Jesus had disappeared. It was he above all who endeavoured to hold to the pure teaching of Jesus and opposed any innovators, notably Paul of Tarsus. Luke, who also wrote the Acts of the Apostles, was Paul's personal physician and therefore gave Paul's point of view. This explains why Barnabas is only mentioned by him when it serves to illustrate Paul's story.

Unfortunately, books like *The Travels and Teachings of the Apostles* were destroyed by the Pauline Church, once it had adopted the doctrine of Trinity, in its attempts to eliminate any record which contradicted this dogma. Therefore, much that was known about Barnabas and the early Christians has been lost. It is this policy of the Trinitarians which probably indicates why any reference to Barnabas during Jesus's mission is strangely missing from the four accepted Gospels; and why Barnabas, who, according to Luke, acquires an importance second to none soon after the disappearance of Jesus, himself disappears from the pages of history as soon as he and Paul have a disagreement and part company.

Barnabas was with Jesus from the very start of his mission. His Gospel clearly demonstrates his great loyalty to Jesus and the love he had for him. Barnabas was not only his constant companion, but also absorbed and retained his teaching, so that very soon he must have acquired the reputation, which is attested to so clearly in the Acts, as a man who had the ability to transmit what he had learned from his master.

The name which the other disciples gave to Barnabas indicates his power and eloquence as a speaker who was a source of solace and encouragement. He was sincere, as well as generous. After meeting Jesus, he sold all that he possessed and gave the money for the use of the followers of Jesus. The affection Jesus and the disciples had for him is shown in the number of different names by which he was known.

When the apostles decided to elect an apostle in the place of Judas from among those who had constantly been with Jesus 'beginning from the baptism of John,' they selected two people to choose from: 'Joseph, called Barsabas, who was surnamed Justus, and Mathias.' (*Acts 1: 22-23*) There is no other Joseph who accompanied Jesus during his life referred to in the *New Testament* except the one who was popularly known as Barnabas. Thus, although Clement of Alexandria always refers to Barnabas as an apostle in his writings, there is nevertheless a possibility that Barsabas – who, Goodspeed tells us, once drank a deadly poison but experienced no ill-effects – was none other than Barnabas.

If this is so, then it also confirms that even if Barnabas was not one of the first twelve apostles, he was certainly one of the first seventy-two disciples – and if this is the case, then the fact that he was regarded highly enough to be proposed as someone suitable to make up the number of the first apostles to the original twelve is supported by the tradition that as Mary, the mother of Jesus, lay on her deathbed, she called for the apostles, and Barnabas was one of those who came.

It is more likely, however, that Barnabas was indeed one of the original twelve apostles – which is what he himself states in his Gospel, when he describes what Jesus first did after his fast of forty days in the wilderness had been completed:

> Jesus, having returned to the region of Jerusalem, was found again of the people with exceeding great joy, and they prayed him that he would abide with them; for his words were not as those of the scribes, but were with power, for they touched the heart.
>
> Jesus, seeing that great was the multitude of them that returned to their heart for to walk in the law of God, went up into the mountain, and abode all night in prayer, and when day was come he descended from the moun-

tain, and chose twelve, whom he called apostles, among whom is Judas, who was slain upon the cross. Their names are: Andrew and Peter his brother, fishermen; Barnabas, who wrote this, with Matthew the publican, who sat at the receipt of custom; John and James, sons of Zebedee; Thaddaeus and Judas; Bartholomew and Philip; James, and Judas Iscariot the traitor. To these he always revealed the divine secrets; but the Iscariot Judas he made his dispenser of that which was given in alms, but he stole the tenth part of everything. (*The Gospel of Barnabas: 14*).

It is interesting to note in passing that although the names of the apostles which Barnabas gives do not all correspond to those listed in the Gospels of Matthew, Mark and Luke, the same observation can equally be made as regards the three groups of names given in *Matthew 10.2-4, Mark 3.14-19* and *Luke 6:13-16* respectively: Luke does not mention Thaddaeus, whereas Barnabas, Matthew and Mark do. Both Matthew and Mark do not mention the other Judas, the son of James, whereas Barnabas and Luke do. Matthew, Mark and Luke mention Thomas and Simon the Zealot, whereas Barnabas does not. Neither Matthew, Mark nor Luke refer to Barnabas, whereas Barnabas does. The Gospel of John in its present form does not provide a complete list of the twelve apostles. As always, when faced with gaps or contradictions, it is up to the reader to decide which of these Gospels in their present form is the most divinely inspired and the least altered, and accordingly the most accurate and reliable!

As we have already seen, it is likely that Jesus was brought up by the Essene community, and there is a tradition that Barnabas was a student of Gamaliel, the greatest teacher of orthodox Judaism at that time. Thus the meeting of Jesus and Barnabas meant the fusing together of all that was best in the gnostic teaching of the Essenes and the orthodox Judaism of the Temple. Doubtless this contributed to the harmonious understanding between them. Since Barnabas was a Levite, he could well have been the commander of a division of the Zealots.

Although so little is known about Barnabas, the latest historical research is slowly uncovering the importance that was undoubtedly his while Jesus was on earth. It is now generally agreed by historians that the Last Supper was held in the house of Barnabas's sister – although it must be remembered that, as we have already seen, Barnabas states that it took place 'in the house of Nicodemus beyond the brook Cedron', which was on the outskirts of Jerusalem. Albert Schweitzer, however, who may not have had access to the Gospel of Barnabas, in his book *The Kingdom of God and Primitive Christian Belief* writes:

> It may be inferred from the Acts that the disciples and the believers from Galilee met in the house of the mother of John Mark, who later accompanied Barnabas and Paul on the First Missionary Journey (*Acts 12: 25*) ...The meeting place of the believers was the 'upper room', which means the room situated immediately under the flat roof (*Acts 1: 12-14*). It must have been a large one to hold the entire company. It was in this room that the believers were 'all together in one place' on the day of Pentecost (*Acts 2: 1*). How did it come to be identified with the one in which Jesus celebrated the Last Supper with the disciples?
>
> When Jesus sent two disciples from Bethany to the city with instructions to prepare the Passover meal for him, he told them that they were to follow a man who would meet them with a pitcher of water. He would lead them to a house with a large upper room furnished with rugs, where they were to prepare the meal. We owe this valuable piece of information to the Gospel of Mark (*Mark 14: 13-15*), which rests on a tradition going back to John Mark. Matthew only relates that Jesus sent the two disciples with directions to inform someone in the city, 'The Master saith, "My time is at hand; I keep the Passover at thy house with my disciples."' (*Matthew 26: 8*). Theodore Zahn was one of the first to put forward the view that the house of the last meal of Jesus with his disciples was identical with that of John Mark's mother, in which the disciples met together with the believers from Galilee. [1]

Although Schweitzer says the house was that of John Mark's mother, he does not remind us that Mark's mother was the sister of

Barnabas. Since Barnabas had by then sold all that he possessed, it is likely that he stayed with his sister when in Jerusalem, especially if she had a house with a room big enough for all the disciples to meet in. Perhaps the reason why none of this is clearly stated in the *New Testament* is because the disciples wished to keep their meeting place a secret at a time when they were being persecuted for their beliefs.

If Albert Schweitzer's hypothesis is correct, it might be asked why no mention of Barnabas is made in the descriptions of the Last Supper in the four accepted Gospels, since clearly he would have been the host to any gathering of men in his sister's house. Either mention of him was made, but has been removed, or else he simply was not present. It is possible that he was unable to be there because he was in prison. It is recorded that a man named Barabbas, with a company of men, attacked a group of pro-Roman Jews in the fighting which took place shortly before the feast of the Passover. Although the leader of these Jews was killed, Barabbas was captured and put in jail. Heinrich Holtzman, who examined the records of this fighting in detail, says that among those arrested was 'the famous Barabbas who was certainly a patriot and a political 'prophet' and was tried at almost the same time as Jesus.' [2]

Since Barnabas was a Levite and one of Jesus's foremost disciples, he could well have been a chief of one of the divisions of the Zealots. These four divisions, as we know from the *Dead Sea Scrolls*, were an integral part of the Essene community and were committed to freeing the land of its foreign aggressors and their supporters. Only a band of Zealots could have been capable of an organised attack on the pro-Roman Jews at that time, and thus it may well be that Barabbas and Barnabas were one and the same person. It is quite possible that, along with its other amendments, the Pauline Church either eradicated, or at least altered, Barnabas's name when he was mentioned in connection with an event which was not a part of Paul's story. They could not adopt this procedure every time Barnabas was mentioned in the books of the *New Testament*, however, since, as the Acts of the Apostles indicates, without the support which Barnabas gave Paul in the early days of the Church, Paul may well have had no place in the history of Christianity at all.

o   o   o   o   o

There is scant record of what happened to the close followers of Jesus after he had disappeared. It appears that many of them scattered after his supposed crucifixion. After some time they began to re-group in Jerusalem. Exactly how many of the twelve disciples and seventy-two closest followers came back is not known. It is certain, however, that those who did were men of faith, sincerity, and courage, and possessed a very deep love for Jesus.

Barnabas's eminence as a man who had been close to Jesus made him a prominent member of this small group of disciples. They continued to live as Jews and practice what Jesus had taught them, observing the Law of the Prophets, which Jesus had come 'not to destroy, but to fulfil.' (*Matthew 5: 17*). That the teaching of Jesus could ever be regarded as a new religion did not occur to any of them. They were sincere practising Jews and were distinguished from their neighbours only by their faith in the message of Jesus. In these early days, they did not organise themselves as a separate sect and did not have a synagogue of their own. There was nothing in the message of Jesus, as understood by them, to necessitate a break with what was clearly the continuance and revivifying affirmation of the guidance which Moses had brought.

The conflict between some of the Jews and the true followers of Jesus, which had already arisen during the time that Jesus had been delivering his message, peace be on him, had been started by those Jews who had changed and adapted Moses's message to suit their own ends, and who feared, quite correctly, that to support Jesus and his followers would inevitably lead to their losing the wealth, the power and the position which they enjoyed. The pact which the upper echelon of Jews had made with the Romans, to safeguard their vested interests and the privileges which they had enjoyed for centuries, had necessitated their departing even further from the guidance they had been given.

This group of Jews continued to actively support the Romans after the disappearance of Jesus in the persecution of those whose actions and words threatened to expose what they had done. Thus it was that a follower of Jesus accepted Jesus while a Jew rejected him. It could not have been an easy time for the early followers of Jesus. On the one hand, they were hounded by the Romans who regarded them as a threat to their political power, and on the other hand they were pursued by the Jews who feared that their own 'religious authority' would be undermined by them.

In the years that followed, the gulf between the Jews who re-fused to acknowledge Jesus and those who followed him began to widen. During the siege of Jerusalem in 70 AD – after which the Temple of Solomon was utterly destroyed by the Romans – the followers of Jesus left the city; and, by the time of the *Bar Koch'eba* rebellion in 132 AD, they refused to fight with the Jews. These two major confrontations which occurred between the Romans and the Jews demonstrate the main difference between the Jews and the true followers of Jesus. The former sought political power, the lat-ter to live in a manner pleasing to their Lord. Although there were certainly Jews who fought because they wished to be able to fol-low their religion, free from foreign invaders, there were also fol-lowers of Jesus who disassociated themselves from the Jews in or-der to avoid the persecution which was being directed specifically at the Jews.

The questions of the origin of Jesus, his nature and his relation to God, which were later to become a source of much contention, were not raised among the first followers of Jesus. That Jesus was a man who was a Prophet and one who had been given many gifts by God, was accepted without question. Nothing in the words of Jesus or in the events in his life on earth had led them to modify this certainty. According to Aristides, one of the earliest apologists, the worship of the early Christians was more purely monotheistic than even that of the Jews.

It was into this circle of sincere followers that Paul of Tarsus walked. He had never met Jesus, nor had he been well acquainted with any of Jesus's closest disciples. He had the reputation of be-ing one of the greatest enemies of Jesus. He had watched over the stoning of Stephen, who had been 'full of faith and the Holy Ghost,' (*Acts 6: 5*), and who was one of the growing number of people who had joined the followers of Jesus after his disappearance. When Paul's own teacher, the famous Gamaliel, had tried to protect Stephen, he too had been stoned to death, without Paul attempt-ing to intercede.

And it is recorded that Paul, who was then called Saul, was responsible for 'a great persecution against the Church' at that time, and that he 'made a havoc of the Church, entering into every house and haling men and women and committed them to prison.' (*Acts 8: 1-3*). Paul himself admitted that:

> You have heard ... how that beyond measure I perse-
> cuted the Church of God and wasted it – and profited
> in the Jews' religion above many of my equals in mine
> own nation, being more exceedingly zealous of the tra-
> ditions of my fathers. (*Galatians 1: 13-15*).

And, as it is related in *Acts 9: 41*:

> Saul yet breathing out threatenings and slaughter
> against the disciples of the Lord, went unto the high
> priest, and desired of him letters to Damascus to the
> synagogues, that if he found any of this way, whether
> they were men or women, he might bring them bound
> unto Jerusalem.

It was on this journey to Damascus that Paul is said to have met
Jesus in a vision and become one of his followers as a result.

Not long before all these events took place, it is recorded that
Paul had desired to marry a woman called Popea, who was the
attractive but ambitious daughter of the high priest of the Jews.
She possessed haunting beauty and an intriguing mind. She liked
Paul, but she rejected his offers of marriage and went to Rome as
an actress. Starting on the stage, she climbed step by step until she
reached Nero's bed. Ultimately she married him and so became
the Empress of the Roman Empire. Paul therefore had good reason
to resent both the Jews and the Romans. Paul's conversion coin-
cided with his being rejected by Popea. He must have been under
considerable emotional and mental strain at the time. It is possible
that this crisis in his life had some bearing on this sudden change
from his being one of the greatest supporters of the Jewish Law to
one of its greatest enemies.

After his conversion, Paul stayed with the followers of Jesus
who were in Damascus and 'straight away, he preached Christ in
the synagogues, that he is the son of God.' (*Acts 9: 20*). As a result,
he began to taste the persecution in which he himself had so recently been involved. If he actually used the term 'son of God' to
describe Jesus, then it was probably this which helped to anger the
Jews. The idea of God having a child ascribed to Him was abhor-
rent to them, since they firmly believed in the Unity of God.

Paul then left Damascus and, instead of seeking out the company of the other followers of Jesus, he went into the Arabian desert

where he remained hidden for three years. It may well have been here that he began to formulate his own version of what Jesus had taught. This involved a rejection of the Law of Moses, which in turn meant his turning away from the fact that throughout his life Jesus had remained a true practising follower of the Law of Moses, and had always sought to uphold the teachings which Moses had brought before him.

It was after this long period of withdrawal in the desert that Paul came to the apostles in Jerusalem. The sudden arrival of Paul caused more suspicion than surprise. The stories of his persecution of the followers of Jesus must still have been fresh in their minds. Could a leopard change its spots? It seems that the disciples had no reason to accept him into their circle. Not only had he been their persecutor, but also he now claimed to know what Jesus had taught, although he had never even seen him and had spent little time, if any, with those who had been with him. Instead of trying to learn from those who had been so closely and strongly connected with Jesus while he was on earth, Paul wanted to teach them. Paul later justified this approach in his epistle to the Galatians where he states:

> I certify you brethren that the Gospel which was preached of me is not after man. For I neither received it of man, neither was I taught it, but by the revelation of Jesus Christ. (*Galatians 1: 11-12*).

Thus, Paul claimed to have an access to Jesus which had been denied to even the closest followers of Jesus while he had been on earth. The teaching which Paul claimed he had been given did not tally with what the apostles had heard from the very lips of Jesus. It is understandable that they were therefore suspicious of his conversion and considered his 'revelations' unreliable. Many probably suspected that he was no more than a spy, posing as a follower of Jesus. [3] The dispute as to whether Paul should be accepted was therefore a bitter one and its outcome must have seemed a foregone conclusion.

Barnabas, however, who according to tradition had been Paul's class fellow under Gamaliel, intervened and spoke in favour of Paul. Against their unanimous opposition, he succeeded in having Paul accepted by the followers of Jesus. This indicates the degree of influence which Barnabas had over the apostles, and therefore

also points to the degree of intimacy which he must have enjoyed
with Jesus when he was on earth.

Paul must have realised that he had been accepted by virtue of
Barnabas's authority and not because of his own efforts. He probably felt dissatisfied as a result. This may well have been one of the
main reasons why he decided to return to Tarsus, his home town,
shortly afterwards, although it is also recorded that he left because
his life was in danger.

⊙   ⊙   ⊙   ⊙   ⊙

The persecution of the followers of Jesus, not only by the Romans
but also by the Jews, forced many of them to disperse throughout
the Holy Land. After the martyrdom of Stephen, some of the apostles made their way to Antioch where they hoped to escape any
further persecution by Paul and his followers. Originally founded
by Seleucus Necator, Antioch had grown in size until by then it
was the third largest city of the Roman Empire after Rome and
Alexandria. It had once been the capital of the Greek kingdom and
had grown into a centre of trade and commerce. With the accumu-
lation of wealth, its people had begun to lead a life of luxury and
decadence and so Antioch had acquired the reputation of being a
city of loose living.

It was here that this small group of strangers, dressed in rags,
began to lead a God-fearing life with simplicity and honesty. Those
who had grown tired of an immoral life began to gather around
them, but the majority of those who met them regarded them with
contempt and ridicule and nick-named them 'Christians'. For a very
few people, this might have been a term of respect, but to a large
number of people it was used as a term of hatred and abuse.

Up until this point, the followers of Jesus had always been
known as Nazarenes. The root of this word in Hebrew means 'to
keep' or 'to guard.' Thus the adjective indicated their role as keepers and guardians of the guidance which Jesus had brought.
Libanius records that the Jews in Antioch used to pray three times
a day: 'Send the curse of God upon the Nazarenes.' Prophery, another historian, who always opposed the Nazarenes, described their
way of life as a 'barbarous, new and strange religion.' Celsus records
that, according to Jerome, the Christians were called 'Greek im-
posters and deceivers' because they wore the same Greek cloaks
which the priests of the Greek temple wore.

In spite of the opposition which they faced, people continued to visit these strange newcomers and their number increased. Encouraged by this interest, the disciples in Antioch sent word to Jerusalem asking the apostles there to send a man to help spread the truth and teaching of Jesus among the pagans who surrounded them. The disciples selected Barnabas as the most suitable person for this task, and thus Barnabas became the first missionary in Christian history. Barnabas came to Antioch and met with unexpected success. Due to his efforts, 'much people was added unto the Lord,' (*Acts 11: 24*), for 'he was a good man, and full of the Holy Ghost and faith.'

After a year had passed, Barnabas decided that the time had come to extend his activity beyond Antioch. He was sure that Paul would make a good helper and with this in view he went to Tarsus and brought Paul back with him. ¹ Thus, again, Paul came face to face with some of the people who had suffered persecution at his hands, and again he met with hostility and opposition.

Once more, the importance of and respect for Barnabas can be assessed by the fact that he had his way, and Paul was received into the community. Perhaps Barnabas was looking to the best in his former class-mate and felt that if Paul's zeal and enthusiasm, which had made him such a thorough persecutor, could only be re-channelled, he would make an outstanding and invaluable follower of Jesus.

Not all the apostles shared this view, and Peter came out in open opposition to Paul. As well as the hostility kindled by Paul's past actions, there was a difference of opinion over two other issues. They could not agree to whom the teaching of Jesus should be taken and what should be taught. Peter held that Jesus had come to revivify the guidance given to the Jews and that, therefore, what he had taught could only be preached among the Jews. On the other hand, there was Paul who not only believed in spreading the truth to everyone, Jew or otherwise, but also asserted that he had been given additional instruction from Jesus after his disappearance. He felt that any necessary adjustments should be made to adapt the teaching according to the apparent demands of time and situation.

Barnabas held the middle position between the two. He held that they should only teach what they had been taught by Jesus, but felt that they should bring this guidance to anyone who would benefit from it and was receptive to it, Jew or non-Jew.

Both Barnabas and Peter regarded the guidance they had been given as a continuation and an extension of Judaism. They could not accept Paul's teaching where it differed from what they themselves had heard from Jesus. They believed that Paul's new doctrine was in the main a purely personal creation of his own. Albert Schweitzer, in his book *Paul and His Interpreters*, says that, 'Paul never appealed to the sayings and commands of the Master.' [5]

It is likely that Barnabas hoped that the two extremes would mellow, and that Paul, especially, by keeping company with the followers of Jesus, would forsake his own ideas in favour of their own knowledge of what must still have been a fairly complete understanding and embodiment of what Jesus had taught. It is clear how important Barnabas's support was to Paul at this stage, since Barnabas shielded and protected him against the unanimous opposition of the Apostles. It is probably for this reason that this part of Barnabas's life is recorded with such detail in the Acts of the Apostles. The relationship between Barnabas and Paul is indicated in *Acts 13: 1-2*:

> There was in the church that was at Antioch certain prophets and teachers as Barnabas, and Simeon that was called Niger and Lucius of Cyrene and Manaen, which had been brought up with Herod the Tetrarch, and Saul. As they ministered to the Lord, and fasted, the Holy Ghost said: 'Separate me Barnabas and Saul for the work whereunto I have called them.'

In this list of these followers, Luke mentions Barnabas first and Paul last. Having been selected to work together, they set out, accompanied by John Mark, who was Barnabas's nephew, to spread the teaching of Jesus in Greece. James, who was related to Jesus on his mother's side, was left at the head of the followers of Jesus. Peter also stayed behind.

It is recorded in the Acts of the Apostles that, in spite of being stoned in some places, these three missionaries were on the whole successful. Their reputation as men of Truth spread far and wide. When they reached Lucaonia and healed a cripple in Lystra, it was rumoured that:

> ... the gods are come down to us in the likeness of men. And they called Barnabas, Jupiter and Paul, Mercurius.

Then the priests of Jupiter ... brought oxen and garlands
unto the gates, and would have done sacrifice with the
people. Which when the apostles, Barnabas and Paul,
heard of, they rent their clothes and ran in among the
people crying out. And saying: 'Sirs, why do ye these
things? We also are men of like passions with you, and
preach unto you the living God, which made heaven
and earth and the sea and all things that are thereon.'
(*Acts 14: 11-15*).

If this reaction by the inhabitants of Greece was typical, it is an
indication of some of the practical difficulties which must have
faced Barnabas and Paul. A true Jew would have immediately recognised the teaching of Jesus as a reaffirmation of what Moses had
taught. But to many a pagan, it must have seemed new and strange
and perhaps a little complicated.

Most of the pagans in Europe still believed in a multitude of
gods who, it was thought, mixed freely with human beings, mated
with them, and took part in every sphere of human life. To the
common people of Greece, any description of Jesus must have
seemed like a description of one of their gods, and they were probably quite ready to accept Jesus in this capacity. There was always
room for one more god. However, the actual teaching of Jesus negated all their gods, since it affirmed the Divine Unity. This could
not have been received with favour by many of these idol worshippers.

Furthermore, the code of behaviour which was an integral part
of Jesus's guidance, would have necessitated an immediate and
far-reaching change in the way of life of anyone who decided to
follow it unless, of course, that person was already a practising
Jew, which these pagans were clearly not. The Jews, who were regarded as a nation of money-lenders, were not at all liked by those
who were not Jews. Toland, in his book *The Nazarenes*, says that:

> ... amongst the Gentiles, so inveterate was the hatred of
> the Jews that their observing of anything, however rea-
> sonable or necessary, was sufficient motive for a Gen-
> tile convert to reject it. [6]

To anyone not as sincere and steadfast as Barnabas, the task of establishing Jesus's way of life in Greece without making any com-

promises must have seemed overwhelming. To Paul, who had already displayed his tendency to change what little teaching he did know, it must have now seemed absolutely necessary to make what adjustments were needed to make Jesus's teaching palatable to the common people. Greece was now part of the Roman Empire. The Roman gods bore a marked resemblance to the Greek ones and belief in them only served to support the same misconceptions which a belief in the Greek gods entailed. Paul had previously spent some time in Rome and was a Roman citizen. It is possible that his own reasoning had been influenced by his contact with the Roman way of life. He was well aware of the strong hold which the Graeco-Roman religions had on the common people within the Roman Empire. It is clear that he seems to have felt that it would not be possible to change their ways without making changes too. Barnabas, on the other hand, as is recorded of Jesus in *Matthew 5 : 17-18*, knew that his Creator did not wish His Law to be diminished or changed 'one jot or one tittle.' He therefore held firm to the guidance he had been given.

At this stage in the spread of Christianity, the main source of contention was not of a metaphysical nature. The subtle arguments and fine distinctions of the intellectuals were a development which was to come later. The issues over which Barnabas and Paul disagreed were principally those which affected a human's everyday existence and way of life. Paul wished to avoid making any abrupt changes in those customs which the Greeks had probably taken for granted before his and Barnabas's arrival in Greece. He therefore wished to abandon the commandments transmitted through Moses as to what meat it was lawful to eat and how the animal was to be sacrificed. He also wished to relinquish, where it seemed expedient, the commandment established by Abraham regarding the necessity of circumcision for males. Faced with the practical difficulty of establishing and implementing these aspects of Jesus's teaching, the difference between Paul and Barnabas must have been emphasised rather than diminished.

However, at this stage, these differences were probably not that marked. Both Paul and Barnabas were faced with the practical challenge of establishing Jesus's way of life. The teaching of the affirmation of the Divine Unity was essential to this, but initially it was necessary to establish a pattern of behaviour which was probably different in many ways to the one to which the pagans had been accustomed. Clearly, this new way of doing things could only be learned and assimilated into the texture of everyday life gradually. No pagan community could have adopted overnight the whole way of life which Jesus embodied.

From what records there are, it seems that Barnabas and Paul never stayed for very long in any one place. It would have been impossible in any case to have transmitted the whole of Jesus's teaching in such a short space of time. They must, therefore, have taught what seemed to be the most important parts first, with the intention of returning later and supplementing what they had shown the people with further instruction. Whereas Barnabas intended to transmit the whole teaching of Jesus, Paul was prepared to dispense with many of its aspects altogether, since, according to the new doctrine he was developing, they were no longer necessary. Thus, on their return to Jerusalem, they must have defended their actions each for a different reason. Despite their descriptions of the miracles they had performed together, this underlying difference remained, and finally there was a parting of the ways.

It is said that they fell out with each other because Paul refused to take John Mark with them on any future mission, while Barnabas insisted that John Mark should continue to accompany them. It is recorded in *Acts 15: 39-40* that, 'the contention was so sharp between them, that they departed asunder one from the other – and so Barnabas took Mark and sailed unto Cyprus,' which was Barnabas's birth-place.

The fact that John Mark accompanied Barnabas clearly indicates that his beliefs were in harmony with his uncle's. This was probably one of the reasons why Paul had no desire to keep his company. Hardly any mention of Barnabas is made in the *New Testament* after this point.

It is interesting to note that Barnabas, who, it is recorded in the Acts, was chosen by the Holy Ghost, was rejected by Paul. Perhaps Paul felt that he no longer needed Barnabas. In his early days as a Christian, no one would have relied on him once they knew that he had not been with Jesus. Now that he had become a leader and an established figure with his own community, this was no longer the case. Paul's reputation was now such that perhaps he felt that he could go out and preach his doctrine without fear of being rejected, and without the restraining hand of Barnabas to check him, whenever he deviated from what Jesus had taught.

Furthermore, Paul was a Roman citizen. He must have learned the language of Rome. He certainly spoke Greek, which was the official language of the area in which he was born. The epistles he later wrote to the Christian communities in Greece must have been written in their native tongue. This meant that Paul could travel in Greece and probably in Italy without any difficulties over language.

Barnabas, on the other hand, spoke neither of these two languages. John Mark, who spoke Greek, had accompanied him on the first missionary journey into Greece to act as his interpreter. If Barnabas were to go there by himself, he would not be able to make himself understood. Thus Paul's refusal to travel with John Mark may have been a round about way of ensuring that Barnabas would refuse to travel with him. Commenting on their parting in his *History of Christianity in the Apostolic Age*, MacGiffert says:

> That Barnabas ... whose right to work among the Gentiles had been recognised in Jerusalem ... should have drawn back and separated himself from them is very strange. Barnabas was not in full sympathy with Paul's doctrine of the Christian's complete liberty from all laws of whatever kind ... The separation of Paul and Barnabas is stated by the author of the Acts to be the result of a disagreement concerning Mark, but the real reason lay deeper than that ... The man who stood closest to Paul and was most intimately associated with him during the early years of his Christian career was Barnabas, who was a member of the Church in Jerusalem in its primitive days ... His friendship meant much to Paul and doubtless contributed in no small degree to his credit and influence with the Christians. Barnabas stood sponsor for Paul in the early days when the memory of his persecuting career was fresh in the mind of the Church.[7]

The change in Barnabas's attitude towards Paul could only have come about as a result of his experiences while travelling with Paul. Any hopes that Paul would change his views and become a true follower of Jesus must have been dispelled by what happened on that first missionary journey. Perhaps too Barnabas realised the futility of trying to spread a guidance, which had only been intended for the Jews, among the Gentiles, and, seeing the folly of this course of action, left it.

Before it had been attempted, perhaps spreading Jesus's message among the Gentiles had seemed a viable proposition. But, having actually tried it, experience had proved that it was not possible. Perhaps the reason why his experience in Antioch had seemed to be so successful was because there the Gentiles had been coming to the followers of Jesus and asking to be accepted as Christians – whereas, when he, Mark and Paul went to Greece, it was they who had been asking the Gentiles to come to them and become Christians.

There is no record of what happened to Barnabas after he returned to Cyprus, but it is known that, like so many who held to a new prophet's teaching, he died as a martyr. In spite of the fact that Barnabas has been blocked out from many of the pages of the *Bible*, it is evident that he acquired an integral position in the history of Christianity and cannot be forgotten. He was willing to openly affirm and teach what he had learned from Jesus in the early days of the Church, at a time when even some of those who were nearest to Jesus were afraid to acknowledge their association with him. Barnabas's loyalty to Jesus is accepted as a fact by friends and foes alike. As we have already seen, it is possible that it was his sister's house where Jesus had his last Passover meal, and it must have remained a meeting place for the followers of Jesus after he had disappeared. Furthermore, the influence of Barnabas over the Apostles and other followers of Jesus has been established from the *Bible* itself. In it he is called a prophet, a teacher, and also an apostle by Luke, whose unquestioned loyalty was to Paul. Above all, Barnabas is remembered as a man who was not prepared to compromise or change Jesus's message in the least.

○　　　○　　　○　　　○　　　○

After Barnabas had left for Cyprus, Paul continued with what he had begun. Although he had now been with many of the early Christians long enough to be accepted as one of them, he was still conscious of the weakness of his position. He might now be called an Apostle of Jesus, yet this did not alter the fact that he had never met Jesus in his life. Although he claimed to have had access to Jesus by revelation, he still needed someone who had lived with Jesus to accompany him on his journeys among the Gentiles. The company of an eye-witness would provide him with invaluable support and serve to back up his arguments with additional authority. He therefore persuaded Peter to join him.

That these two, who had opposed each other so vehemently in the past, should now come together is perhaps surprising. However, the situation had changed. Paul was now accepted by many as a Christian and was no longer regarded as a possible spy or persecutor. Celsus, a Greek philosopher and a bitter critic of the Christians, said that the root of the disagreement between the two in Antioch had been Paul's jealousy of Peter's popularity. Obviously, Paul's jealousy would by now have dwindled with his own increase in reputation, especially among the Gentiles.

The persecution of the first Christians had also probably played its part in drawing them together. The persecution by the Romans and those Jews who supported them was quite severe by now. Peter had already demonstrated his weakness when, under pressure or faced by immediate danger, he denied his being a companion of Jesus at the time of Jesus's supposed trial and crucifixion. He was probably now more willing to fall in line with Paul's approach to Jesus's message, since changes here and there might mean less confrontation with established customs, and accordingly perhaps less persecution.

Thus the situation in these early days was such that it seemed expedient to some to change and adapt the message of Jesus not only so that people who were not Jewish would accept it, but also so that it would not offend or apparently threaten those in authority in the land. This policy of obeying rulers indiscriminately, whether their laws were in accord with those of the Creator of the Universe or not, is evident in Peter's first Epistle:

> Submit yourselves to every ordinance of man for the Lord's sake: whether it be to the king, as supreme; or unto governors, as unto them that are sent by him for the punishment of evildoers, and for the praise of them that do well. For so is the will of God, that with well-doing ye may put to silence the ignorance of foolish men: as free, and not using your liberty for a cloak of maliciousness, but as the servants of God. Honour all men. Love the brotherhood. Fear God. Honour the king. Servants, be subject to your master with all fear; not only to the good and gentle, but also to the froward. (*1 Peter 2: 13-18*).

Paul travelled West with Peter. Without the sincerity and restraining influence of Barnabas, he must have met with little opposition to his new doctrines and adapted ways of conduct and behaviour. In *Romans 15: 20-21*, he says, referring to *Isaiah 52:15*:

> Yea, so have I strived to preach the Gospel, not where Christ was named, lest I should build upon another man's foundation: but as it is written: 'To whom he was not spoken of, they shall see: And they that have not heard shall understand.'

If Paul had been spreading the original teaching of Jesus, then 'another man's foundation' would have been the same as his. They would both have been involved in building the same structure. The people who were hearing about Jesus, or rather Christ, for the first time from Paul's lips, had no means of comparing his account with that of the Apostles who still held to Jesus's teaching. Paul's version was the only one to which they had access.

Paul was helped a great deal in spreading his message by a learned Jew from Alexandria called Appolos. He was very successful in spreading the ideas of Paul among people. Paul, it was said, planted and Appolos watered. Ultimately, even Appolos could not accept all the innovations of Paul, and, like Barnabas, parted company with him.

Paul deviated further and further from the original teaching which Jesus had embodied, and laid more and more emphasis on the figure of Christ whom he claimed had appeared to him in his visions. His defence against those who accused him of changing the guidance which Jesus had brought was that what he was preaching had its origin in a direct revelation which he had received from Christ. This, in effect, gave Paul Divine Authority. It was by virtue of this 'authority' he claimed, that the blessings of the Gospel were not limited to the Jews, but to all who believed. Furthermore, he asserted that the requirements of the Law of Moses were not only unnecessary, but also contrary to what had been directly revealed to him from God. In fact, he said, they were a curse.

As a result, Paul incurred not only the wrath of the followers of Jesus, but also that of the Jews, since he was now contradicting both of their Prophets. It is clear why he chose to spread his teaching among people who hated the Jews and who had not heard the truth about Jesus.

Paul justified his new doctrine with the use of this analogy:

> Know ye not, brethren, (for I speak to them that know
> the law) how that the law hath dominion over a man as
> long as he liveth? For the woman which hath an hus-
> band is bound by the law to her husband so long as he
> liveth; but if the husband be dead, she is loosed from
> the law of her husband. So then, if, while her husband
> liveth, she be married to another man, she shall be called
> an adulteress: but, if her husband be dead, she is free
> from that law, so that she is no adulteress, though she
> be married to another man. Wherefore, my brethren, ye
> also are become dead to the law by the body of Christ;
> that ye should be married to another, even to him who
> is raised from the dead, that we should bring forth fruit
> unto God. (*Romans 7: 1-4*).

The use of this analogy clearly indicates that Paul made a distinction between Jesus and 'Christ'. According to his reasoning, the
law which had bound Jesus and his followers was no longer necessary, since Jesus had died. Now they were no longer 'married' to
Jesus, but to Christ, who had brought another law. It was, therefore, necessary to follow Christ and not Jesus. Thus, anyone who
still persisted in holding to Jesus's original teaching had gone astray.

It was with the use of spurious reasoning such as this that Paul
assembled his doctrine of redemption and atonement, a theory
which Jesus had certainly never taught. It was a great success, since,
in so many words, it preached that a man could do what he wanted
and not face the inevitable consequences of his actions, provided
that, at the end of the day, he said: 'I believe in Christ.'

The basic premise on which Paul's reasoning was based, however, is false, since Jesus was neither crucified nor resurrected. Thus
Paul's doctrines of redemption and atonement are clearly fallacious
and mis-leading.

Paul's reasoning had two major consequences. It not only resulted in further changes being made to what Jesus had taught,
but also prepared the way for completely changing people's ideas
of who Jesus was. He was being transformed from a man to a conception in people's minds. As has already been noted, divinity had
been attributed to Jesus even when he was on earth by some of
those who marvelled at his words and miracles, and who, mistakenly, considered him to be more than a Prophet.

Some of his enemies had also spread the rumour that Jesus was the 'son' of God, hoping to arouse the orthodox Jew's anger against him for associating himself with God. Thus, even before Jesus disappeared, there had been a tendency to obscure his true nature and attributes, and to ascribe Godhood to Jesus. This imaginary figure of Christ, who apparently had the power to annul what Jesus had previously taught, was clearly no ordinary mortal, and, inevitably, became simultaneously confused by many both with Jesus and with God. It did not take very long before this imaginary super-human figure became an object of worship, and was associated with God.

This shift of emphasis from Jesus as a man to the new image of Christ, who was divine, enabled the intellectuals in Greece and Rome to assimilate into their own philosophy what Paul and those who followed him were preaching. Their view of existence was a tripartite one, and, with the Pauline Church's talk of 'God the Father' and the 'Son of God', it only needed the inclusion of the 'Holy Ghost' to have a Trinity which matched theirs. With the passage of time, these two pictures merged into one, and the doctrine of Trinity was born.

Not only the philosophical ideas prevalent in Greece at that time coloured Paul's teaching, but also the very language of Greece itself influenced the expression of that teaching, trapping and limiting its meaning. Greek could contain the philosophy of the Greeks, but was neither vast nor supple enough to carry the entire meaning of what Jesus had taught. Thus, even a true follower of Jesus who spoke fluent Greek could not have expressed the totality of Jesus's teaching in this language. It had to be re-worded – and in the process changes were inevitably made. When the time came to translate the Hebrew Gospels into Greek, these limitations were made permanent, and finally sealed, when nearly all the Gospels in Hebrew were subsequently destroyed.

Although Paul never actually preached the divinity of Jesus, nor the doctrine of Trinity, his manner of expression and the changes he made opened the door to both these misconceptions, and prepared the way for their becoming established doctrines in Europe. It was these doctrines which eventually lead to Mary being put in the impossible position of being regarded as the 'mother' of God – even though most Christians in every age who have been heard repeating, 'Hail Mary, mother of God!' in one breath have also been equally willing to emphasise that God has no beginning and no ending – and no mother – in another breath.

It appears that Paul rationalised his actions by holding that there was no link between the period in which Jesus had lived and the period in which he himself now lived. Times had changed and the conditions which now prevailed were such that the teaching of Jesus was out of date and could no longer be applied. It had therefore become necessary to find a new basis for human ethics and behaviour. Paul took stock of the conditions which existed at the time and taught what they seemed to require him to believe:

> All things are lawful unto me, but I will not be brought under the power of any. (*I Corinthians 6: 12*).

Thus Paul not only rejected the divine law which both Moses and Jesus had followed in all humility, peace be on them, but also he asserted that he was a law to himself. The followers of Moses and Jesus, obviously, could not accept this. Paul responded by claiming that God does not measure a person's righteousness by looking at how much he or she follows and obeys the commandments of God by following His Prophets and Messengers – but by whether or not a person puts their faith in Jesus Christ:

> We who are Jews by birth and not 'Gentile sinners' know that a man is not justified by observing the law, but by faith in Jesus Christ. So we, too, have put our faith in Christ Jesus that we may be justified by faith in Christ and not by observing the law, because by observing the law no-one will be justified. (*Galatians 2: 15-16*).

Thus, argued Paul:

> Now that faith has come, we are no longer under the supervision of the law. (*Galatians 3: 25*).

From this anarchistic statement, it appears that the basis of Paul's arguments was the implied – and never expressly stated – claim that out of all of the Jews and Christians in the Holy Land at the time, Paul alone knew what was most pleasing to God:

> For we maintain that a man is justified by faith apart from observing the law. (*Romans 3: 28*).

Assuming that this assumption was correct, and assuming that the means justifies the end, Paul then apparently assumed that this viewpoint must therefore be pleasing to God, Whose commands and Prophets he had just rather clumsily but nevertheless almost completely negated:

> Therefore, since we have been justified through faith, we have peace with God through our Lord Jesus Christ, through whom we have gained access by faith into this grace in which we now stand. And we rejoice in the hope of the glory of God. (*Romans 5: 1-2*).

Paul's attitude towards the Law of Moses is, to some extent, understandable, perhaps at times even laudable, because as we have already seen, by the time that Jesus began his mission, the Jews had already re-written and re-defined the Law of Moses on more than one occasion, transforming it into their own religion. Thus Jesus had upbraided them in no uncertain terms, when referring to *Isaiah 29: 13*, for passing off their own man-made laws and interpretations as being the 'Law of God':

> You hypocrites! Isaiah was right when he prophesied about you: (The Lord says:) 'These people honour Me with their lips, but their hearts are far from Me. They worship Me in vain; their teachings are but rules taught by men.' (*Matthew 15: 7-9*).

This, as we have already seen, is one of the main reasons why the Pharisees and the Sadducees plotted to kill Jesus – because he was fully aware of just how much they had changed the original teaching of Moses. Jesus had, however, while he was on earth, succeeded in restoring the original teaching of Moses, breathing back into it the mercy and justice which had all but been squeezed out of it.

It is highly significant that whereas Jesus rejected the rewritten law of the Jews but reaffirmed the original Law of Moses, Paul rejected both the rewritten law of the Jews *and* the original Law of Moses. To use that well-known phrase, Paul threw the baby out with the bath water – claiming that this was exactly what its mother wanted – and his followers, perhaps mistakenly thinking that they were following Jesus when they were really following Paul, have been paying for it ever since!

o   o   o   o   o

Thus Paul produced a religion which encompassed different contradictory elements. He took the Unitarianism of the Jews and
added to it the philosophy of the pagans. This admixture was combined with some of what Jesus had taught and some of what Paul
claimed Christ had revealed to him. Paul's theology was based on
his personal experience interpreted in the light of contemporary
Greek thought. Jesus was deified and the words of Plato were put
in his sacred mouth.

The theory of redemption was Paul's brainchild, a belief entirely unknown to Jesus and his disciples. It was based on the mistaken belief in 'original sin', the 'crucifixion', and the 'resurrection', none of which have any validity. In this way a synthetic religion was produced: Christianity – mathematically absurd, histori-
cally false, yet psychologically impressive, guaranteeing simultaneously, as it apparently did, both absolute guilt and complete freedom from retribution.

In the magnificent temple of the religion which Paul helped so
zealously to erect, he built doors on all sides. The result was that
people who came across his brand of Christianity for the first time,
when they entered its temple, were given the impression that they
were paying homage to the same deity that they had worshipped
all along, whether they were Jew or Gentile. As the basic misconceptions introduced by Paul evolved and became established, many
a man who thought that he was following Jesus followed Paul without knowing it.

There is, therefore, some justification for Heinz Zahrnt calling
Paul a 'corrupter of the Gospel of Jesus,'[8] and for Werde describing him as 'the second founder of Christianity'. Werde says that,
due to Paul:

> ... the discontinuity between the historical Jesus and the
> Christ of the Church became so great that any unity be-
> tween them is scarcely recognisable.[9]

And Schonfield concluded that:

> The Pauline heresy became the foundation of Christian
> orthodoxy and the legitimate Church was disowned as
> heretical.[10]

And so Barnabas who had been regarded by the disciples of Jesus as one of the most reliable of his close followers subsequently came to be considered an arch-heretic, and, as we shall see in greater detail further on, every attempt was made by the followers of Paul to destroy his writings and diminish his influence.

◯   ◯   ◯   ◯   ◯

Thus it was that very soon after the disappearance of Jesus, there was a sharp disagreement, followed by a parting of the ways, between the true followers of Jesus and the enthusiastic followers of Paul, which in time was to develop into all-out war between what became the Unitarian church on the one hand, and the Trinitarian church on the other.

To the followers of Jesus, the path of Truth, like a geometrical straight line, had length but no breadth. They were not prepared to change the teaching of Jesus merely because it seemed expedient. To them what Jesus had taught was the Truth and the whole Truth. Barnabas and his followers continued to preach and practise the Christianity they had learned from Jesus himself. They were always and still are to be reckoned with as a force. From among them came many saints and scholars respected by every sect of Christianity.

The true followers of Jesus and Barnabas never developed a central organisation, yet, due to the devotion of their leaders for the Truth, their number increased rapidly. These leaders were wise and learned men who loved and feared God. They went into the deserts and mountains. Small communities formed around each saint. They were independent of each other, largely due to the rough terrain which surrounded them. Their lack of a structured organisation was a source of strength because it was not so easy for their persecutors to pick them out or up.

While Paul's version of Christianity spread northwards up through Greece and Italy, and then Europe, these men of God – the 'real' Christians – spread with their knowledge to the east and to the south and, eventually, right across North Africa. The communities they formed retained the life-style of Jesus. Although the time came when what these people knew by heart began to be recorded in writing, those who still embodied Jesus's teaching transmitted much of their knowledge directly from person to person. Behaviour was imitated and the doctrine of Jesus passed on orally. They continued to affirm the Divine Unity.

Thus there are records of various sects who lived in the early centuries after Jesus's disappearance, such as, for example, the Ebionites, the Cerinthians, the Basilidians, the Carpocratians, and the Hypisistarians, who refused to worship God as a father. They revered Him as the Almighty Ruler of the Universe, the Highest of all with no one equal to Him.

In time, many different written accounts of Jesus's life and teachings – some clearly more reliable than others – appeared and were used. Jesus had spoken in Aramaic, a dialect of Arabic, which was not commonly written. The first Gospels were therefore usually recorded in Hebrew. In these early days, none were formally accepted or rejected. It was up to the leader of each Christian community to decide what books he would use. Depending on whom they had been taught by, each community or sect went to a different source. Those who followed Barnabas's example, for instance, went to one source – and those who followed Paul went to another.

Thus, quite soon after Jesus's disappearance from earth, there was a definite and widening divergence between the followers of Jesus and the members of the Pauline Church, which was later to become known as the Roman Catholic Church. Differences between the two were not only evident in life-style and belief, but were also clearly delineated geographically.

As the Pauline Church became more established, it became increasingly hostile to the followers of Jesus. It aligned itself more and more with the rulers of the Roman Empire, and the persecution which to begin with had been directed at all who called themselves Christians, now began to fall mainly on those who affirmed the Divine Unity. Attempts began to be made to change their beliefs and forcefully to remove those who refused to do so, together with the books they used. Most of the early martyrs were Unitarians. The more the doctrines of Paul became accepted, the more its adherents opposed those who affirmed the Divine Unity. By the time the Emperor Julian came to power, this infighting had reached such a stage that he said: 'No wild beasts are so hostile to man as Christian sects in general are to one another.'

Naturally, those who deviated from the teaching of Jesus were prepared to change the Scriptures too, and even to introduce false writings in order to support their opinions. Toland, in his book *The Nazarenes*, records these words of Iranaeus, who was one of the early Unitarian martyrs:

In order to amaze the simple and such as are ignorant of the Scriptures of Truth, they obtrude upon them an inexpressible multitude of apocryphal and spurious scriptures of their own devising.

Toland continues:

We know already to what degree imposture and credulity went hand in hand in the primitive times of the Christian Church, the last being as ready to receive as the first was to forge books ... This evil grew afterwards not only greater when the Monks were the sole transcribers and the sole keepers of all books good or bad, but in process of time it became almost absolutely impossible to distinguish history from fable, or truth from error as to the beginning and original monuments of Christianity ...

How immediate successors of the Apostles could so grossly confound the genuine teaching of their masters with such as were falsely attributed to them? Or since they were in the dark about these matters so early how came such as followed them by a better light? And observing that such Apocryphal books were often put upon the same footing with the canonical books by the Fathers, and the first cited as Divine Scriptures no less than the last, or sometimes, when such as we reckon divine were disallowed by them. I propose these two other questions: Why all the books cited as genuine by Clement of Alexander, Origen, Tertullian and the rest of such writers should not be accounted equally authentic? And what stress should be laid on the testimony of those Fathers who not only contradict one another but are also often inconsistent with themselves in their relations of the very same facts?

Toland goes on to say that when these questions are asked of the 'wooden priests and divinilings,' instead of meeting the arguments, they react by calling those who raise the questions 'hereticks or concealed atheists.' He continues:

This conduct will make them suspect all to be a cheat
and imposture, because men will naturally cry out when
they are touched in a tender part ... No man will be
angry at a question who is able to answer it ...

Finally Toland asks:

Since the Nazarenes or Ebionites are by all the Church
historians unanimously acknowledged to have been the
first Christians, or those who believed in Christ among
the Jews with which, his own people, he lived and died,
they having been the witness of his actions, and of whom
were all the Apostles, considering this, I say how was it
possible for them to be the first of all others (for they
were made to be the first heretics), who should form
wrong conceptions of the doctrines and designs of Jesus? And how came the Gentiles who believed on him
after his death by the preaching of persons that never
knew him to have truer notions of these things, or
whence could they have their information but from the
believing Jews? [11]

How, or whence, indeed!

o   o   o   o   o

Chapter Four

Early Unitarians
in
Christianity

The Apostolic Christians, as the true followers of the followers of Jesus came to be known, peace be on him and them, produced a number of scholars and saints whose piety and learning is respected and admired even today. Apostolic, or, as it is generally known, Antiochene, exegesis of the Scriptures was historical, and, unlike what is now the orthodox approach, looked not for a hidden allegorical meaning in the text, but accepted the plain meaning of the words spoken by the inspired Prophet. They were also critical of holding some parts of the Bible to be of more value than the others. They insisted on the One-ness of God and abhorred any dogma which to the slightest degree savoured of tri-theism. They emphasised the historical Jesus and avoided the use of the term 'son' when talking of him. They endeavoured to live as Jesus had lived and to behave as he had behaved. As well as living in the Holy Land, many of them lived in North Africa. Some of the most important of these followers of the followers of Jesus were:

Iranaeus (130-200 AD)

By the time Iranaeus was born, Antiochene Christianity had spread right across North Africa and up into Spain and the South of France. Mention is first made of him carrying a petition on behalf of Pothinus, the Bishop of Lyons, to Pope Elutherus in Rome. In this petition, a request was made to the Pope to stop the persecution of Christians who did not agree with the doctrine of the Pauline Church. Iranaeus was still in Rome when he heard that all the dissenting Christians, including Bishop Pothinus, had been killed. On his return, Iranaeus succeeded Pothinus as Bishop of Lyons.

In 190 AD Iranaeus himself wrote to Pope Victor urging him to stop the massacre of Unitarian Christians who were being killed solely for their differences in belief. The story was again repeated – and like Bishop Pothinus, he himself was murdered in 200 AD for espousing the cause of Christians who did not follow the Pope.

Iranaeus believed in One God and supported the doctrine of the manhood of Jesus. He strongly criticised Paul for being responsible for injecting doctrines borrowed from the European pagan religions and Platonic philosophy into Christianity. Iranaeus quoted extensively from the *Gospel of Barnabas*. It was after reading the writings of Iranaeus that Fra Marino became interested in this Gospel, which in turn led to his discovery, in the Papal library, of the Italian manuscript of the *Gospel of Barnabas* – which as we shall see further on, is the earliest version known to be in existence today.

Tertullian (160-220 AD)

Tertullian belonged to the African Church. He was a native of Carthage. He believed in the Unity of God and identified Jesus with the Jewish Messiah. He opposed Pope Callistus for teaching that capital sin was forgiven after doing canonical penance. He stressed the unity of the heart with existence.

He wrote: 'Common people think of Christ as a man.'

Ironically it was Tertullian who introduced the term 'trinitas' into Latin ecclesiastical writings when analysing and refuting this strange new doctrine. The term 'trinity' is not once used in the inspired Scriptures – which strongly confirms that it was a concept with which Jesus was entirely unfamiliar.

Origen (185-254 AD)

Origen was an Egyptian by birth. Perhaps he was born in Alexandria. His father, Leonidas, founded a centre of learning and appointed the famous theologian Clement as its head. Origen received his education here. The Pauline Church did not approve of the beliefs held by Leonidas, who followed Apostolic Christianity and refused to accept the interpretations and innovations of Paul. He was murdered in 208 AD. Origen was so affected by this event that he too wished to offer himself as a martyr, but was prevented from doing so by his mother.

Origen's teacher, Clement, finding his life to be in danger, fled from Alexandria. With his father dead, and his teacher gone, Origen felt obliged to step into the breach. As the new head of the school, he soon acquired a reputation for learning and courage. Owing to his piety and excessive zeal, he mutilated himself, following the words of *Matthew 19: 12*:

> There are some eunuchs, which were so born from their mother's womb: and there are some eunuchs, which were made eunuchs of men: and there be eunuchs, which have made themselves eunuchs for the kingdom of heaven's sake. He that is able to receive it, let him receive it.

In 230 AD Origen was ordained a priest in Palestine, but Bishop Demerius deposed and exiled him. He found refuge in Caesarea in 231 AD. Following the example of his father, he started a centre of learning in Caesarea and this school also became highly renowned.

Jerome – *not* the Jerome who was the author of the famous *Vulgate Bible*, the first Latin translation of the Greek Bible – supported Origen to begin with, but then later began to believe in the doctrine of Trinity and became his enemy. Jerome tried to have Origen condemned by the Church, but because of Origen's popularity, Bishop John did not dare do so. In fact, Jerome himself was exiled. However, Jerome finally succeeded in 250 AD, when Origen was condemned by the Council of Alexandria. He was put in prison and subjected to prolonged torture, which eventually resulted in his death in 254 AD.

The reason given for the imprisonment of Origen was that he rejected the doctrine of Trinity and preached the Unity of God. He believed that God was supreme and that Jesus was not equal to Him, but was His slave.

Origen wrote about six hundred tracts and treatises. He has been described as 'one of the most appealing characters in Church History'. From the early days of his youth right up until his last hour, he showed an uncommon fearlessness. He was conscientious and patient. He had all the qualities of a true teacher and those whom he taught loved him. His power of discrimination, creative energy and catholicity of knowledge were almost unparalleled among the Christians.

Diodorus

Diodorus was a Bishop of Tarsus. He is regarded as one of the most important leaders of the Antiochene branch of Christianity. He held that the world is subject to change, but that change itself is a condition which implies a beginning and an end and requires the onlooker to conclude that there is constancy behind it. Thus both the infinite variety of forms in existence and the wisdom displayed in the very process of change itself, to which all forms are subject, points to their underlying unity of origin and indicates the existence and presence of their Creator and Sustainer – and there could only be one such Creator.

Diodorus emphasised the complete manhood of Jesus whom, he emphasised, had a human soul and human flesh.

Lucian (Died in 312 AD)

Lucian's reputation for his fear of God was no less than his fame as a man of learning. He knew both Hebrew and Greek. He remained outside the communion of the Church from 220 to 290 AD. His purity and profound knowledge attracted a large number of people and soon his school became the seedbed of what later became branded as Arian doctrine. Arius was one of his pupils.

Lucian believed in the grammatical and literal exegesis of the Scriptures. He opposed the tendency to look for symbolic and allegorical meanings within them and believed in an empirical and critical approach towards them. The very fact that this controversy existed at all demonstrates that by the end of the 3rd century AD, people were beginning to rely more and more on the written record and less and less on the oral transmission of what Jesus had taught. This in itself is an indication of how quickly the teaching of Jesus in its totality was lost.

Lucian was a great scholar. He revised the *Septuagent*, the first Greek translation of the *Old Testament*, and also eliminated many of the changes which had been made to some of the Gospels when they were translated from Aramaic or Hebrew into Greek. He also selected the four Gospels which, according to him, were the most reliable of the true Gospels. These Gospels were not the same as the four Gospels commonly accepted by the Pauline Church today.

Lucian believed that Jesus was not equal to God and that he was subordinate to Him. It was for this that he incurred the enmity of the Pauline Church, and after many tortures he was put to death in 312 AD.

Arius (250-336 AD) and Donatus (died 355 AD)

The lives of Arius and Donatus are so intertwined both with each other and with the life of the Emperor Constantine that it is not possible to understand one without knowing the others. The story of how Constantine first became involved with the Christian Church begins in Rome:

Constantine became jealous of his eldest son and heir, Crispus. The young prince had become very popular because of his good looks, his charming manner and his bravery on the field of battle. To make sure of his own position as Emperor, Constantine had him murdered. The death of Crispus cast a gloom over the whole realm. It was known that the step-mother of Crispus had wanted her own son to succeed Constantine. She therefore had a motive for killing Crispus. Constantine accordingly put the blame for his crime on her, and killed her by immersing her in a bath full of boiling water. He hoped to mitigate one crime by the other. The result, however, was just the opposite of what he had planned – the supporters of the dead queen joined forces with the followers of his dead son, and both sought revenge. In desperation he turned to the priests of the Roman temple of Jupiter for help, but they told him there was no sacrifice or prayer which could absolve him from the two murders. It became so uncomfortable to be in Rome that Constantine decided to go to Byzantium.

On his arrival there, Constantine modestly re-named the city after himself, and called it Constantinople. Here he met with unexpected salvation from the Pauline Church, whose leaders said that if he did penance in their Church his sins would be forgiven. Constantine made full use of this facility. His hands were not only stained with the blood from the two murders in Rome, but also full of the problems associated with governing his Empire. Having salved his conscience with his confession, the life to come ceased to worry him as much as it had, and he turned his attention to the affairs of the Empire. Constantine recognised the possibilities of using the Christian Church to his own ends provided that he could win its loyalty, and so he gave the Church his full support.

With this unexpected backing, the Christian Church became a much stronger force almost overnight, and Constantine made full use of her. By now the countryside bordering the Mediterranean was dotted about with Christian churches, and the Emperor utilised them to great advantage in the wars he was fighting. Many of the priests carried out very useful intelligence work for him, and their help was an important factor in his efforts to unite Europe and the Middle East under him. Partly as a token of his gratitude and partly in order to diminish the power of the Roman priests in the temple of Jupiter who had refused to support him, Constantine encouraged the Christians of Constantinople to open a church in Rome. However, he did not become a Christian himself, for many of his subjects still believed in Jupiter and the other gods in the Pantheon of Rome. In order to allay any suspicions they might have, he made a number of decisions which seemed to prove that he too worshipped the Roman gods. Everything appeared to be going very well when the old controversy between the Pauline and Apostolic Churches again flared up and intensified.

The leader of the Apostolic Church, which continued to affirm belief in One Reality, was at this time a presbyter known to history as Arius. He was a Libyan by birth. He gave new strength to the Apostolic Church. He followed the teaching of Jesus implicitly, and refused to accept the innovations introduced by Paul. 'Follow Jesus as he preached,' was the motto of Arius. His importance can be gauged by the fact that his name became and has remained a synonym for Unitarianism even up until today.

The Pauline Church received a violent jolt from Arius. He was no mere 'bustling schemer' as his enemies would have people believe, and even they were forced to admit that he was a sincere and blameless presbyter. At a time when the oral tradition which had kept the teaching of Jesus alive was beginning to weaken, and when the understanding of what had been written down was starting to diminish, Arius revived both and renewed them with his vigour and wisdom. He remained aloof from the alliance which the organised Church had made with the Emperor Constantine.

Arius was the disciple of the greatest critic of the Pauline Church at that time, the venerated martyr, Lucian of Antioch, who was known for his great learning and who, like his predecessors, was killed for holding views not approved of by the Pauline Church. Thus Arius was fully aware of the dangers involved in entertaining beliefs which differed from those acceptable to this Church.

Although his early life is hidden in mystery, it is recorded that in 318 AD, Arius was in charge of the Church of Baucalis in Alexandria. It was the oldest and one of the most important of the city's churches. From the scanty record which is available, it is known that Arius was tall and thin. He would have been handsome but for his general emaciation, the deadly pallor of his face and a downcast look which was imparted by the weakness of his eyesight. His dress and demeanour were those of a dedicated ascetic. He wore a long coat with short sleeves. His hair hung in a tangled mass from his head. He was usually silent, but, if occasion arose, he would break into fierce and exciting words. There was a sweetness to his voice and he had an earnest but winning manner about him which fascinated those who came into contact with him. He was regarded as one of the most remarkable presbyters in Alexandria, and was held in high esteem by anyone who met him:

> His fame soon spread, even outside Alexandria, as an earnest worker who led a strict and ascetic life, a powerful preacher who dealt boldly and frankly with the great principle of faith. He was gifted with great conversational powers and charm of manner. He was also capable of injecting others with the enthusiasm which he himself felt. Like all the great religious leaders of the world, he was fanatically sincere and the doctrine he preached was vital and fecund. [1]

It is also known that he had the following of not less than seven hundred of the Christian ladies of Alexandria. [2]

○ ○ ○ ○ ○

Up until this time, a Christian's faith had not really been a matter of compulsion. There were differences between sects, sometimes deep and bitter, but whatever belief an individual held was based on his own personal conviction and sincerity. In this period after Jesus's disappearance from earth, saints and martyrs had gladly given up their lives rather than compromise their belief. The swords wielded by those in authority over the land had only ever been used in an attempt to destroy such beliefs and certainly not to enforce them. When, however, Constantine made his first alliance with the Church, there was a dramatic change in the situation.

Although he remained Pontifex Maximus, and continued in his capacity as head of the pagan state religion, Constantine began to openly support the Christian Church, probably making little distinction between the Pauline and the Apostolic branches at this early stage. This sign of favour put Christianity in a new light and it became virtually the only official cult of the Roman Emperor. For many people, Christianity had suddenly become a matter of policy and expediency. Some of those who held back soon joined with the aid of a little governmental pressure. Thus many of the conversions to Christianity ceased to come from the heart, but were the result of an entirely different kind of conviction. Christianity had become a mass movement. [3] However, it was a movement which re-emphasised the split between the Pauline Church and the Apostolic Church. Those who became Christians out of expediency naturally chose the less rigorous approach of the Pauline Church. The Apostolic Church welcomed only those who sincerely wished to follow the way of Jesus.

Constantine, who at this stage neither understood nor believed in Christianity, saw the political advantage of having a united Church which would obey him, and whose centre would be based in Rome, and not in Jerusalem. When the members of the Apostolic Church refused to comply with these wishes, he tried to compel them by means of force. This pressure from without, however, did not produce the desired result. A number of the Apostolic Christian communities still refused to accept the overlordship of the Bishop of Rome. They recognised this move as a political ploy by a foreign ruler, and as something entirely apart from the teaching of Jesus.

The first revolt came from among the Berber communities of North Africa. It was led not by Arius but by a man named Donatus. On the whole the Berbers have always retained certain basic beliefs, the strongest of which was their belief in the Divine Unity. They could believe in Jesus as a Prophet, but never as God. Since Jesus had never said anything about Rome being the centre of his teaching, they could not entertain such an idea, let alone attribute it to him retrospectively. In 313 AD Donatus was chosen from among these people as their bishop. For forty years he remained the leader of their Church which continued to flourish in opposition to the Bishop of Rome. According to Jerome, 'Donatism' became the religion of nearly all North Africa within a generation, and neither force nor argument could change it.

The Bishop of Rome tried to install one of his own bishops in Carthage to replace Donatus. His name was Cacealian. The prestige of Constantine was such that, in the conflict which ensued, both parties appealed to him. It appears that they thought that whoever won his support would have no further battles to fight. This attempt to win the patronage of Constantine brought with it a very important change in the history of Christianity. For the first time it had become possible for schism and unorthodoxy to become an offence punishable by secular law. This secular coat of armour stood at the disposal of whoever could prove himself to be 'orthodox', and could then be used against those who differed from this new standard of orthodoxy. Constantine decided in favour of Cacealian.

When the news of Constantine's decision reached Carthage, the general populace there gathered around the office of the Roman proconsul and denounced Cacealian. Constantine was annoyed by their action, but nevertheless appointed a tribunal under the Bishop of Rome to hear the case of the two parties once again. Donatus was not present and no one was there to argue his case. The decision went against him *in absentia*, but the Apostolic church in North Africa refused to accept the *ex parte* verdict of the Roman Bishop.

Constantine was scandalised that the 'ministers of God were wrangling amongst themselves like ordinary litigants.'[4] In spite of his disappointment, he set up a new tribunal at Arles. The two parties were told to travel there by different routes, in order to prevent any clashes before the hearing took place. The Donatists lost again. The decision was that 'the bishops found themselves dealing with dangerous men who had no respect for authority or tradition. They were fit only for condemnation.'[5]

This decision was no more acceptable to the North African Christians than the previous rulings. As it was, they had little respect for the Roman proconsul and the other imperial officials. For generations now the Christians had suffered persecution at their hands, and regarded them as emissaries of Satan. Formerly, they had been persecuted because they were Christians. Now they were to be persecuted because they were not the right kind of Christians. The North African Christians could not accept that the officials of the Roman Empire had become servants of God overnight, merely because they sought to enforce a ruling of the Pauline Bishop of Rome. Up until this point, Donatus had been their bishop. He now became their popular leader.

Very little is known about this remarkable man. The books which Donatus wrote and his precious library of manuscripts were all burned by the Roman soldiers. They performed these deeds in the name of the Roman Christian Church, which, with the support of a pagan Emperor, was now beginning to grow in importance and strength. Thus, little is known about his background, his personal appearance, his friends and the events in his life.

It is known that Donatus was a fine orator and a great leader of men. He was met with such enthusiasm wherever he went that these times were remembered long after he had died. His followers used to swear by his 'white hairs'. He seems to have personified the popular loathing for the worldly ecclesiastics who were sure they would do well both in this life and the next if they performed the correct manoeuvres. His integrity and honesty were recognised by friend and foe alike. He was known as the religious reformer 'who purified the Church of Carthage from error.' [6] He was regarded by the people as a worker of miracles and a saint wiser than Daniel. He stood as firm as a rock against all attempts to erode and alter the original teaching of Jesus.

Constantine wrote a letter to the two Churches urging them to forget their differences and to unite under the Church favoured by him. This letter is significant in that Constantine regarded himself as being superior to the Church, whatever its form, and any reference to Jesus was conspicuous by its absence. The letter had no effect on anyone, and no progress was made in enforcing the decision of the tribunal which had met at Arles.

In July 315 AD the Emperor returned to Rome. It was necessary to go to Milan to suppress the Frankish incursions which had begun in the north of Italy. When he again had some time at his disposal, he appointed a commission to travel to Africa, examine the situation and settle the dispute. When the commission arrived, it was boycotted, and such a violent riot took place that its members were forced to return to Italy without having achieved anything. This disquieting news reached Constantine in 316 AD. He decided to go to North Africa in person and himself give a clear ruling as to exactly how the Supreme Deity should be worshipped.

It is interesting that Constantine considered it within his competence to pass such a judgement. In the letter which he wrote to the two Churches in Africa, he concluded:

> What more can be done by me, in accord with my con-
> stant practice and with the very office of a prince, than
> after expelling error and destroying rash opinion, to
> cause all men to argue together to follow true religion
> and simplicity of life, and to render to Almighty God
> the worship which is His due. [7]

It is clear that once the example of Jesus was forgotten or ignored,
then 'true religion' became a matter of opinion – and there was no
opinion that Constantine favoured more than his own. It was only
by approaching Christianity in this manner that Constantine could
take such a keen interest in the internal affairs of a religion which
he did not yet follow. Constantine regarded himself as a man who
spoke with greater authority than the leaders of the Churches, and
seems to have regarded himself more as God's own vicar than as
an ordinary mortal. The Pauline bishops who had sat on the tribunal at Arles appear to have been of the same opinion as Constantine. They claimed that their 'devising' was recorded 'in the presence of the Holy Ghost and His angels.' [8] Yet when their ruling was
ignored, it was to the Emperor that they turned for help.

 As it happened, Constantine did not make the journey to Africa
that he had planned. The Donatists had become so strong, he was
told, that it was inadvisable to take part personally in the dispute
between Donatus and Cacealian. For should his personal intervention meet with failure, it would be a great blow to his prestige.
Instead, he issued a decree condemning Donatus and drawing his
attention to 'the advantage of worshipping the Supreme Deity in
the proper manner.' [9] When this was ignored, 'a most severe law'
was dispatched to Africa: the churches held by the Donatists were
to be confiscated, and their leaders were to be sent into exile.
Cacealian at first tried to bribe the leaders of the Donatist Church,
but without success. They defied the imperial command, ignored
his bribes and made his offers of money publicly known. Cacealian
then resorted to force, and was soon branded as 'a man more cruel
than a butcher and more brutal than a tyrant.' [10]

 The Church of Rome, which had by now adopted the epithet
'Catholic' to indicate the universality of its approach in the worship of God, appealed to the Donatists to unite. The appeal had no
effect, and Donatus refused to hand over his churches to Cacealian.
Finally, the Roman army came into action:

There was a mass slaughter of people. Dead bodies were thrown into wells, and bishops were murdered in their churches. However, the surviving Donatists remained firm, and if anything, their movement became stronger than before. They named their Church the 'Church of Martyrs'. These events widened the rift between the Donatists and the Catholic Church even further. Since the Catholic Church was working in alliance with the pagan magistrates and their soldiers, the Catholics were called schismatics and their churches were identified as places of 'hated idolatry'.

Constantine, who was a good administrator, realised the futility of trying to restore religious harmony and unity by force. Deciding that discretion was the better part of valour, he left the people in North Africa to themselves. However, it was these events and their consequences which played a large part in his later making the decision to call the famous Council of Nicea.

○   ○   ○   ○   ○

Before returning to the story of Arius, who at this point was just beginning to make his voice heard, it would be of interest to give a very brief summary of the history of the Donatists up until the coming of Islam: once Constantine had turned his attention away from North Africa to other parts of his Empire, the persecution of the Donatists lessened considerably, and their numbers again began to increase rapidly. They became so powerful that when the Emperor had a church built for the Catholics of North Africa in 330 AD, the Donatists took possession of it. The Emperor was enraged, but could do nothing about it except promise the Catholics sufficient money to build another church for themselves. The Donatist movement spread even to Rome. They too had a Bishop of Rome, but he was regarded as being a rank below the Bishop of Carthage and Nicomedia. [¹

Donatus acquired sovereign authority at Carthage. He was regarded by the masses as a being superior to other mortals. He was never called a bishop, but was known as 'Donatus of Carthage'. Augustine once complained that the Donatists reacted more sharply to an insult against Donatus than to a blasphemy against Jesus, a fact which is easily explained by the strong and unkind language which many of the Catholics used when talking about Donatus.

When the reign of Constantine ended, the Donatists continued to work for the independence of their Church and to oppose any interference from the Emperor or his officials in matters of religion. They were not, however, narrow-minded sectarians. Augustine himself observes that the Donatists did not oppress the Catholics even when they outnumbered them.

The Catholics, who were always ready to claim toleration for themselves, were not prepared to grant it to the Donatists when once more the imperial forces were sent to subdue these fearless people. However, despite this continued persecution, the Donatists refused to allow the Emperor to alter the way they worshipped God. In their opinion, 'the Catholics were evil priests working with the kings of the world. Relying on royal favours, they had renounced Christ.' [12]

After the death of Donatus, the people of North Africa continued to follow his example, and for three hundred years his teaching of what Jesus had brought was followed by them. When Islam came to them, they embraced it, so well-prepared were they for what was, after all, an extension and reaffirmation of the guidance they had been following.

○   ○   ○   ○   ○

There was another movement similar to that of Donatus which took place simultaneously, yet quite independently of it, in the south of Egypt. Constantine was just about to make another attempt at unravelling the tangled skein of North African Christianity in 324 AD, when his attention was drawn to Egypt, a country which was seething with discontent and revolt.

When the persecution of the Christians by Diocletian had been at its height, many of them had compromised their beliefs in order to avoid it. A priest called Meletius was now saying that those priests who had publicly renounced Christianity during the persecution of Diocletian should be prevented from re-assuming their clerical functions. He felt that they should also be stopped from attending all the assemblies of pure worship unless they demonstrated sufficient proof of their penitence. Peter, who was patriarch of Alexandria at that time, advised a more lenient course. The majority of the people, however, supported Meletius. When Alexander came on the episcopal throne, he banished Meletius to the mines. When Meletius returned, however, many followers gathered around him once more. He ordained bishops, priests and deacons and was responsible for building many churches. They refused to submit to their persecutors. Like the Donatists, Meletius called his Church the 'Church of Martyrs' – as opposed to the followers of Alexander who called themselves Catholic and followed the Pauline version of Christianity.

After the death of Meletius, Alexander forbade his followers to hold their assemblies of worship. In opposition to this order, they sent a deputation to Constantine. It was only with the help of Eusebius of Nicomedia that they were allowed to see the Emperor. Their presence in his court was yet another factor which led to his calling the Council of Nicea. Eusebius was a friend of Arius, and it was through this meeting that contact was made between the Arian and Meletian movements.

⊙   ⊙   ⊙   ⊙   ⊙

The movement led by Arius took place against the background of these two separate yet similar Churches of Martyrs. Anything written in favour of Arius or any independent assessment of his movement has virtually been destroyed. Nearly all the books referring to Arius which still exist have been written by his enemies. It is, therefore, impossible to give a full account of his life. Connecting the pieces of information which still exist, the following picture emerges:

Peter, the Bishop of Alexandria, ordained Arius as a deacon but then later excommunicated him. Achillas, Peter's successor, again ordained him a priest. Arius became so popular that when Achillas died, he had every chance of taking his place. However, Arius had no desire to be involved in any kind of election, and so it was Alexander who was chosen to sit on the episcopal throne. A complaint was made against Arius because of what he preached. His rival became his judge, and eventually Arius was again excommunicated.

Up to this point, there had been a great latitude in the beliefs of the Christians. The beliefs which are inherent in the doctrine of Trinity were now accepted by many of those who called themselves Christians, even though no one was very sure about what they actually meant. Some blindly affirmed them; others, like Meletius and Donatus, strongly rejected them, and those who fell between these two poles were at liberty to explain the new doctrines in whatever way they thought best. After more than two centuries of discussion, no one had been able to summarise these beliefs in terms which were free from equivocation. Arius stood up and challenged anyone to clearly define them.

Alexander was completely taken aback. The more he tried to explain them, the more confused he became. Arius, by the use of reason, and relying on the authority of the Scriptures, proved the new doctrines to be false.

Arius began his refutation of Alexander's explanations with reference to Jesus: if Jesus was in reality the 'son of God', he argued, then it followed that the father must have existed before the son. Therefore, there must have been a time when the son did not exist. Therefore, it followed that the son was a creature composed of an essence or being which had not always existed. Since God is in essence Eternal and Ever-Existent, Jesus could not be of the same essence as God.

Arius always appealed to reason and logic, and since Alexander could not furnish any reasonable counter-arguments, he always ended up by losing his temper. 'Given the premises', Arius would say, 'where is the fault of my deduction and where does my syllogism break down?' By the year 321 AD, Arius was a popular rebellious priest, profoundly confident and certain of what he believed.

After receiving this personal setback, Alexander called a provincial synod to pronounce judgement on the doctrine of Arius. About one hundred Egyptian and Libyan bishops attended. Arius boldly maintained the stand he had taken, and with great ability stated his case: there was a time when Jesus did not exist, whereas God existed even then. Since Jesus was created by God, his being was finite and so he could not possess the attribute of Eternity. Only God is Eternal. Since Jesus was a creature, he was subject to change like all other rational creatures. Only God is unchanging. Thus, he asserted, it was clear that Jesus was not God. As well as his appeal to logic, Arius backed up his arguments with numerous verses from the *Bible* which nowhere teaches that Jesus is God.

If Jesus said, 'My father is greater than I,' [13] then to believe that God and Jesus were equal or somehow identical, argued Arius, was to deny the truth of the Scriptures.

The arguments of Arius were irrefutable, but Alexander, by virtue of his position in the Church hierarchy, excommunicated him. However Arius had such a large following that he could not be ignored by the Pauline church, especially since many of the Eastern Bishops did not accept Alexander's decree. The controversy which had been simmering for nearly three hundred years came to a boil. Alexander was troubled and annoyed that so many of the Eastern bishops supported Arius, whose greatest ally was Eusebius of Nicomedia.

Eusebius of Nicomedia and Arius were old friends, since both had been students of Lucian, a man who, as we have already seen, had been universally respected for his purity and learning. It is possible that Lucian's martyrdom in 312 AD helped to strengthen the friendship and the resolve which these two shared.

There is a letter which Arius wrote to Eusebius in Constantinople after his excommunication by Alexander, and which still exists. Arius complains of his persecution by Alexander, who was trying to expel him from Alexandria as an impious atheist because he and his friends did not subscribe to the outrageous doctrines which the bishop professed:

'We are persecuted,' wrote Arius, 'because we say that Jesus had a beginning, while God had no beginning.' [14]

As a result, Arius received increased support from Eusebius who had much influence, not only among the common people, but also in the imperial palace itself. In spite of this backing, Arius appears always to have inclined towards reconciliation rather than opposition, so far as discipline within the Church was concerned.

Unfortunately, the records of this dispute which still exist are very scanty, but there are a few letters in existence which show that Arius's intention was solely to keep the teachings of Jesus pure and free from alteration, and not to cause disruption among the Christians. On the other hand, the letters written by Alexander show that the Bishop was always using intemperate language against Arius and his supporters. In one letter he writes: 'They are possessed of the Devil who dwells in them and goads them to fury; they are jugglers and tricksters, clever conjurors with seductive words; they are brigands who have lairs for themselves wherein day and night they curse Christ … they make proselytes through the agency of loose young women of the town.' [15] The use of such violent and outrageous language by the Patriarch raises the suspicion that he too must have been aware of the weakness of his case.

Eusebius hotly resented the tone of the Patriarch of Alexandria. He summoned the synod of Eastern bishops and laid the whole matter before them. The result of this gathering was a letter, which was sent to all the bishops of both the East and the West, begging them to induce Alexander to accept Arius back into the Church. Alexander, however, wanted Arius's total surrender. Arius returned to Palestine and continued to hold services for his followers. Alexander issued a long letter addressed to 'all his fellow workers of the Catholic Church,' in which he again attacked Arius. He also made a pointed reference to Eusebius, mentioning him by name and accusing him of believing 'that the welfare of the Church depended on his nod.' [16] He added that Eusebius supported Arius, not because he sincerely believed in Arian doctrine, but in order to further his own ambitious interests. Thus the ecclesiastical controversy degenerated into a personal conflict between the Eastern and Western bishops.

The questions in issue spread from the circle of the bishops out among the common people. Gregory of Nyssea writes:

> Every corner of Constantinople was full of their discussions: the streets, the market place, the shops of the money-changers, the victuallers. Ask a tradesman how many obols he wants for some article in his shop, and he replies with the disquisition on generated and ungenerated being. Ask the price of bread today and the baker tells you: 'The son is subordinate to the father.' Ask your servant if the bath is ready and he makes an answer: 'The son arose out of nothing.' 'Great is the only Begotten,' declared the Catholics, and the Arians rejoined: 'But greater is He that begot.' [17]

The arguments ranged from the sublime to the ridiculous, until people would even ask women whether a son could exist before he was born. The debate in the higher ecclesiastic circle was equally hot and bitter. It is recorded that 'in every city, bishops were engaged in obstinate conflict with bishops. People were against people ... and came into violent collision with each other.' [18]

As far as Constantine was concerned, things were going from bad to worse. He was obliged to intervene and addressed a letter to both Alexander and Arius. He said that his consuming passion was for unity of religious opinion, since it was the best guarantee of peace in the realm. Deeply disappointed by the events in North Africa, he had hoped for better things from the 'bosom of the East' whence had arisen the 'dawn of Divine Light'. He then continues:

> But Ah! Glorious and Divine Providence, what a wound was inflicted not alone on my ears but on my heart, when I heard that divisions existed among yourselves even more grievous than those in Africa; so that you, whose agency I hoped to bring healing to others, need a rem-

edy worse than they. And yet, after making a careful enquiry into the origin of these discussions, I find that the cause is quite insignificant and entirely disproportionate to such a quarrel ... I gather that the present controversy originated as follows: for when you, Alexander, asked each of the presbyters what he thought about a certain passage in the Scriptures or, rather, what he thought about a certain aspect of a foolish question; and you, Arius, without due consideration, laid down propositions which never ought to have been conceived at all, or if conceived ought to have been buried in silence, dissensions arose between you – communion was forbidden, and the most people, torn in twain, no longer preserved the unity of a common body.

The Emperor then exhorts them to let both the unguarded question and the inconsiderate answer be forgotten and forgiven:

The subject never ought to have been broached, but there is always mischief found for idle hands to do and idle brains to think. The difference between you has not arisen on any cardinal doctrine laid down in the Scriptures, nor has any new doctrine been introduced. You both hold one and the same view. Reunion, therefore, is easily possible.

The Emperor then went on to quote the example of pagan philosophers who agree to disagree on details while holding the same general principles. How then, he asked, can it be right for brethren to behave towards one another like enemies, because of mere trifling and verbal differences. Such conduct in his opinion was:

... vulgar, childish, and petulant, ill-fitting priests of God and men of sense ... It is the wile and temptation of the Devil. Let us have done with it. If we cannot all think alike on all topics, we can at least all be united on great essentials. As regards the Divine Providence, let there be one faith and one understanding, one united opinion in reference to God.

Constantine's letter concludes:

Restore me then my quiet days and untroubled nights
that I may retain my joy, the gladness of peaceful life.
Else I must groan and be defused wholly in tears, and
no comfort of mind till I die. For while the people of
God, my fellow servants, are thus torn asunder in un-
lawful and pernicious controversy, how can I be tran-
quil of mind? [19]

This letter demonstrates the profound ignorance of the Emperor,
not only of Christianity, but also of any religion, since it assumes
that it is the same whether a man either worships God as he pleases
or in the manner which God has indicated is pleasing to Him. To
say that the controversy between Alexander and Arius was merely
a verbal quarrel over an insignificant and non-essential point is
absurd. To regard the difference between the two as 'trifling' clearly
shows that Constantine did not understand what he was talking
about. A certainty in the Divine Unity, on the one hand, and the
belief in a concept which would inevitably lead towards a Trinity
of God, on the other hand, could hardly have been more fundamentally opposed. The contents of the letter indicate that Constantine was not concerned with the nature of Reality, but with his own
peace of mind and the stability of his Empire. It is not surprising
that his letter achieved nothing. It was carried to Alexandria by
Hosius of Cordoba. After a short stay, he returned empty-handed
to report the failure of his mission to the Emperor.

   While all this was going on, Constantine had clashed with his
brother-in-law, Licinus, on the battlefield, and Licinus had been
killed. Licinus had been a supporter of Arius, and his death further weakened the position of Arius in the Emperor's court. However, Constantine did realise that it is possible to win a war and yet
lose the peace. Since the failure of Hosius's mission, the situation
in the East had become very unsettled. The songs and arguments
of Arius had resulted in blood being shed in Alexandria, and unrest had spread throughout the eastern parts of the Empire. There
was already turmoil in North Africa. Constantine realised that his
friends in the Pauline Church were not powerful enough to dispel
any of this trouble. His experience in dealing with the North Afri-
cans, which had partly resulted in his coming east after almost
burning his boats in Rome, seemed to have taught him a lesson:
that he should not take sides openly.

Constantine accordingly decided to call a meeting of Christian bishops in order to settle the matter once and for all. His position as a pagan, he said, was a great advantage since by virtue of his not belonging to any sect or either party, he would make an impartial judge. This would resolve the problem which had faced the bishops up until then, for they had not been able to agree on any one Christian to preside over such a meeting as their arbitrator. This gathering of the bishops under Constantine is known today as the Council of Nicea (which is now in Turkey):

The Council of Nicea: 325 AD

Invitations were despatched, and all expenses paid for by Constantine from the imperial state treasury. Apart from the leaders of the two contending parties, the majority of those who were invited were not on the whole very knowledgeable. It is significant that no one from the Church of Donatus was asked to attend – although Cacealian, Donatus's chief opponent, was invited. Among the more important bishops who participated in the council were:

Eusebius of Caesaria

Eusebius of Caesaria is the father of ecclesiastical history. His book is the chief repository of the traditions which link the 1st century AD with the 4th century AD of the Christian era. Apart from his extensive knowledge, the degree of his influence rested on the fact that he alone of the Eastern prelates could often tell what was going on in the mind of the Emperor. This was partly because he was the interpreter and nominal chaplain and confessor of the Emperor. He was at heart an Arian, and enjoyed the support of most of the bishops in Palestine.

Eusebius of Nicomedia

Eusebius of Nicomedia came from an aristocratic family, and was a follower of Lucian at the same time as Arius. His spiritual eminence was universally recognised. Thus, there were two important men of God in this age who bore the same name, a fact which has caused much confusion in some of the minds of the historians of this period.

Eusebius of Nicomedia was the most resolute supporter of Arius, whose other followers called Eusebius 'the great'. Miracles were attributed to him. Originally the bishop of Beyruth, he was later transferred to Nicomedia, the capital of the Eastern Empire. He had been a good friend of the Emperor's brother-in-law and rival, Licinus, and thus exercised an influence on Constantina, the sister of Constantine. Licinus had recently fought the Emperor and lost his life. After the death of her husband, Constantina went to stay in the Imperial Palace. Thus, through her and through his own distant relationship with the Imperial family, Eusebius kept a hold on the court which he never lost. It was to be through his influence that the Emperor eventually accepted Christianity in the Church of Arius, and finally died a believer in the Divine Unity.

Athanasius

Athanasius was a young and fiery supporter of the beliefs and concepts which eventually led to the formation what became known as the Trinitarian school of theology. Alexander, who was growing old, and who had been routed so many times before by Arius, decided to send Athanasius to Nicea as his representative, instead of going there himself.

Hosius

Hosius was the Chief Councillor of the Emperor. His importance lay in the fact that he represented the Pauline Church in the West where the Emperor's influence was weakest. Hosius was recognised as a profound scholar of theology in his own right. In history he is known as the venerable old man who was called 'holy' by Athanasius. His high character was known to everyone. His importance had increased due to his intimacy with the Emperor.

○   ○   ○   ○   ○

Apart from these few learned men, the Council was composed of men with a reputation of piety, but not of learning, men whose hearts were pure, but whose tongues were not always articulate:

○   ○   ○   ○   ○

Spiridem

Spiridem was one of the rough and simple, almost illiterate bishops who formed the majority of the bishops in the Christian Church at that time. A closer study of him will help illustrate the kind of men they were. He was a shepherd who had suffered persecution and yet remained firm in his faith. His knowledge of the politics of religion was superficial. He had been appointed bishop because many miracles had been attributed to him. After becoming a bishop, he did not change his rough and ready rural attire. He always walked on foot. The other 'princes' of the Pauline Church did not like him, and were anxious that he should not reach Nicea in time for the Council.

When Spiridem received his invitation from the Emperor, he realised that he would have to travel by mule if he was to arrive in time. He set out with one attendant, unlike other bishops who went with a whole retinue. They travelled on two mules, one white, the other piebald. It is said that one night they were staying in an inn when there also arrived those bishops who were not sure whether Spiridem was the right kind of person to take part in the deliberations of the Council. Early the next morning, while Spiridem was still asleep, they chopped off the heads of his two mules and departed. When he awoke, he asked his attendant to feed and saddle the mules. The attendant discovered the dead animals and reported the loss to Spiridem. Spiridem told the attendant to put the head of each mule near the dead body it had been a part of. In the darkness, the attendant put each head next to the wrong body. As soon as he had done this, the mules got up alive, and they continued on their journey. After a while, they overtook the bishops, who thought they had left Spiridem well behind and were sure that he would not reach Nicea in time. Their surprise was even greater when they found that the white mule had a piebald head, and the piebald, a white head! [20]

Patammon

Patammon was a hermit.

Oesius

Oesius was known only for his puritanical zeal.

Myser of Nicholas

The name of Myser of Nicholas is preserved, especially by Church historians, by virtue of the fact that when Arius was speaking, he boxed his ears.

○   ○   ○   ○   ○

Thus, the Council was composed largely of bishops who held their faith earnestly and sincerely, but without much intellectual knowledge of the grounds on which they maintained it. These men were suddenly brought face to face with the most agile and most learned exponents of Greek philosophy of the age. Their manner of expression was such that these bishops could not grasp the significance of what was being said. Incapable of giving rational explanations of their knowledge or entering into arguments with their opponents, they were to either stick to their beliefs in silence or to agree to whatever the Emperor decided.

○   ○   ○   ○   ○

All the delegates reached Nicea a few days before the Council was due to start. They collected together in small groups where the questions in issue were publicly debated with earnestness and with feeling. In these gatherings, which took place either in the gymnasium or in some open space, the Greek philosophers placed their darts of argument and ridicule with great effectiveness. This caused no small confusion among the delegates.

At last the day arrived, and everyone gathered for the inauguration of the Council which was to be conducted by the Emperor himself. The chamber prepared for the meeting was a long, oblong hall in the palace. In the centre of the room were placed copies of all the known Gospels, which at that time numbered about three hundred. Every eye lay upon the Imperial throne, which was carved in wood and richly covered in gilt. It was placed at the upper end of the hall between two rows of seats which faced each other.

The deep silence was disturbed by the faint sounds of a distant procession. It was approaching the palace. Then the officers of the court came in one by one. At last a signal from without announced that the Emperor was close at hand. The whole assembly stood up, and for what was the first time for many of them, they set their wondering gaze on the Roman Emperor, Constantine, the Conqueror, the August, the Great.

His towering stature, his well-built frame, his broad shoulders, and his handsome features were all in keeping with his grand position. His expression was such that many thought him to be the manifestation of Apollo, the Roman sun-god. Many of the bishops were struck by the dazzling, albeit barbaric, magnificence of his dress. His long hair was crowned with an imperial diadem of pearls. His scarlet robe blazed with precious stones and gold embroidery. He was shod in scarlet shoes, then worn only by the Emperor – and now worn by the Pope!

Hosius and Eusebius sat on either side of the Emperor. Eusebius started the proceedings with an address to the Emperor. The Emperor replied with a short speech translated from Latin into Greek which very few understood, including the Emperor, whose knowledge of Greek was sparse. With the meeting under way, the floodgates of the controversy were opened wide. Constantine with his broken Greek concentrated all his energy on one point, which was to achieve a unanimity of decision. He informed everyone that he had burned all the petitions which he had received from different parties a few days earlier. He assured them that since he had not read any of them, he had an open mind and was not inclined one way or the other.

The representative of the Pauline Church wanted to put three 'parts' of God on the Divine Throne, but could produce arguments from their Scriptures in favour of only two. In spite of this, the third 'part' of God, namely 'the Holy Ghost', was declared to be the third person of the Trinity, although no reasons were given in support of this innovation. The disciples of Lucian, on the other hand, were sure of their ground, and forced the Trinitarians to shift from one impossible position to the next.

The Trinitarians found it difficult to define a Christian in such a way as to exclude Arius and the other Unitarian Christians from their definition, especially since belief in the doctrine of the Trinity, which they asserted was the distinguishing factor between the two parties, was never actually mentioned in the Gospels. They said that the 'Son' was 'of God'. The Arians replied that they themselves were 'of God' since it is written in the Scriptures, 'All things are of God.'[21] Therefore, if this argument was used, they argued, then it also proved the Divine nature of all things.

The Pauline bishops then argued that Jesus was not only 'of God', but also 'of the Essence of God'. This distinction roused opposition from all the orthodox Christians since, they pointed out, these words were not to be found in the Scriptures. Thus, this attempt to prove that Jesus was God, instead of uniting the Christians, further divided them. In desperation, the Trinitarians argued that the Scriptures say that, 'Jesus is the eternal image of the Father and True God.' [22] The Arians replied that the Scriptures also say, 'We men are the image and glory of God.' [23] Therefore, if this argument was used, they argued, then not only Jesus but all men could claim to be Divine.

The discussion continued, not only in the meeting hall but also within the Imperial Palace: Helena, the queen mother, supported the Pauline Church. She was a political animal, and administrative expediency ran in her blood. On the other hand, Constantina, the sister of the Emperor, was a believer in the Divine Unity and supported Arius. In her opinion, Arius was following the original teachings of Jesus. She hated politics and loved and feared God. The debate spread throughout the court. What had started as a Council, had also developed into a palace intrigue, in which the imperial eunuch and the palace cook also played a significant role. The Emperor, a master of strategy, remained aloof from the two factions, and kept everyone guessing. Being a pagan, he did not belong to any of the sects. This, he believed, was the strongest point in his favour.

As the debate continued, it became evident to both parties that no clear-cut decision would be reached on the floor of the Council. However, they still both desired the support of the Emperor since, for the Pauline Church, it would mean an increase in power, and for the North African Church an end to persecution. In order to keep the favour of Constantine, all the bishops present agreed to make some changes in their religion. Princess Constantina had advised Eusebius of Nicomedia that the Emperor strongly desired a united Church, since a divided one endangered his Empire. However, if no agreement was reached within the Church, he might lose patience and withdraw his support for Christianity altogether. Should he take this course of action, the situation of the Christians would be even worse than before, and the teaching itself would be endangered even further. Counselled in turn by Eusebius, Arius and his followers adopted a passive role, but disassociated themselves from the following changes to which the Council agreed:

Since worship of the Roman sun-god was very popular throughout the Empire at this time, and since the Emperor was considered to be the embodiment of the sun-god on earth, the Pauline Church therefore:

- Declared the Roman 'sun' day to be the Christian Sabbath – which is why it is called Sunday, and not because Jesus gave it that name;

- Adopted the traditional birthday of the sun-god, the twenty-fifth of December, as the birthday of Jesus, for by then no one could remember which day his real birth day had been;

- Borrowed the emblem of the sun-god, the cross of light, to be the emblem of Christianity; and

- Although the statue of Jesus replaced the idol of the sun-god, decided to incorporate many of the ceremonies which were performed at the sun-god's birthday celebrations into their own ceremonies.

It must have been very comforting for Constantine to see the gulf which existed between Christianity and the religion of the Empire narrowed so considerably. The Pauline Church especially must have gone up in his estimation, and the likelihood of his continued support for that Church, once apparently weak, was now much firmer.

Finally, the new beliefs and concepts which underpinned the dogma of Trinity were accepted as fundamental doctrines of what could now be termed 'official Christianity'.

It is possible that even at this relatively late stage some of the advocates of the Paulinian beliefs and concepts still had a degree of direct experience of the Divine Unity, and that they still affirmed it, in spite of the language they were now using. For them, the new doctrines, which were to eventually become enshrined in the official doctrine of Trinity, were in fact no more or less than the means by which they were attempting to describe what they witnessed.

Since the language of Unity which Jesus had once used was by now largely lost, they had resorted to using the terminology of neo-Platonic philosophy which, although it was not really adequate for the purpose, was all that they had left at their disposal to indicate what they knew. Such a perspective, however, was only open to very few people. 'I pass over in silence,' wrote Apuleius, 'those sublime and Platonic doctrines understood by very few of the pious, and absolutely unknown to every one of the profane.' [24]

Similarly, Plato observed that, 'To discover the Creator was difficult, but to explain it to the vulgar is impossible.' [25] Pythagoras said, 'To tell of God among men of prejudicial opinion is not safe. To tell the truth or falsehood is equally dangerous.' [26]

Although the use of Greek terminology was justified by some of those who were attempting to express the nature of the Divine Unity, in fact the attempt was doomed to failure. There was no way in which the Greek concept of '*theos* ', which was not based on any revealed message, could successfully encompass the superior teaching which had been revealed to Jesus. It was only the innovations made by Paul and his followers that had made this 'marriage' of concepts even seem possible in the first place.

And for those who were unable to grasp the ideas of the Greek philosophers, there was only added confusion. This was the case with the majority of people who came into contact with the new beliefs and concepts which eventually syncretised into and gave birth to the 'official' doctrine of Trinity. The confusion into which they fell led to endless speculation – as the course which the Council of Nicea itself had taken so clearly demonstrated. Thus even though the doctrine of Trinity itself remains unintelligible to anyone who is intellectually honest and sincere, it is at least possible to understand how the doctrine came into being and why it was accepted, informally to begin with, and then officially at the Council of Nicea. It is also clear, on account of the confusion which the doctrine caused, why Arius insisted on returning to the source of Christianity for guidance, rather than resorting to the thinking of the Greek philosophers, which clearly did not stem from any of the revelation which was granted to the Prophet Jesus.

Once these changes had been secured at the Council of Nicea, the next step away from Jesus's teaching was made possible, and what is today known as the Nicene Creed was drawn up and attested to in writing by those present with the full support of the Emperor Constantine. It enshrined the view of the Paulinian Christians and had the following anathema appended to it as a direct rejection of Arius's teaching:

> But as for those who say, 'There was when he was not, and, before being born he was not, and that he came into existence out of nothing,' or who assert that the Son of God is of a different hypostasis or substance, or is created, or is subject to alteration or change – these the Catholic Church anathematises.

Of those who signed the Nicene Creed, some believed in it, some pretended to believe in it, even though they did not really know what they were putting their names to, and some, the majority of the delegates at the Council, did not agree with the doctrine of Trinity at all, but nevertheless signed the Creed with silent mental reservation, in order to please the Emperor. One of them is recorded as having said: 'The soul is nothing worse for a little ink.' [27] Referring to this statement, Professor Gwatkin moans that this was not a pleasant scene for a historian. Perhaps this is because Professor Gwatkin was not writing as a historian, but as an advocate who accepts a brief to plead a weak case!

These were the people who decided, under a pagan Emperor, what should be the test for an orthodox Christian. The result was as much a surprise to the Paulinian Christians as it was to the Unitarian Arian party. It is probable that no one except Constantine had expected the turn which events had taken. The idea of a having universal test of what it is to be a Christian was a revolutionary change. It was not liked by anyone.

The insertion of a direct condemnation of Arianism was a still more serious step. Even those who had consented to attesting the Creed, did so with misgiving – and when it came to endorsing an anathema which contained a form of terminology which was not to be found in any of the Scriptures, and which had apparently never been utilised by either Jesus or his close companions, they told themselves that they had signed it under duress.

The Council which had begun with such a fanfare had in reality completely failed to achieve anything.

The one person who knew exactly what he was doing was the Emperor Constantine. He realised that a Creed which was based not on conviction but on votes could not be taken seriously. One could believe in God, but could not elect Him by the democratic method. Constantine knew how and why the bishops had signed the Creed, but he was determined not to let the impression remain that he had somehow managed to force the bishops to sign against their convictions. So it was decided to resort to a miracle of God in order to affirm and confirm the decision of the Council:

All the various Gospels – the written record both of Jesus's teaching and, in some cases, of what had become of that teaching after it had been changed – still lay in a pile in the middle of the hall where they had been placed at the beginning of the Council. Which of these Scriptures were the most accurate and reliable?

According to one source, there were at least 270 versions of the Gospel at this time, while another states there were as many as 4,000 different Gospels. Even if one accepts the most conservative record, the number must have been quite overwhelming for a literate Christian of that time. The drawing up of a creed which contained ideas not to be found in the Gospels and, in some cases, in direct contradiction of what was in the Gospels, must have made matters even more confusing for those who relied on them, while the continued existence of such Gospels must have been very inconvenient for others.

It was decided that all the different Gospels should be placed under a table in the Council Hall. Everyone then left the room and the door was locked. The bishops were asked to pray for the whole night that the correct or most accurate and reliable versions of the Gospel of Jesus might find their way onto the top of the table. There is no record of who kept the key to the Council Hall that night.

In the morning, the Gospels most acceptable to Athanasius, the representative of Alexander – Matthew, Mark, Luke and John – were found neatly placed on top of the table. It was then decided, in order to simplify matters, that all the other Gospels which still remained under the table should be burned.

It subsequently became a capital offence to possess an unauthorised Gospel. As a result, over a million Unitarian Christians were killed in the years following the Council's decisions. This was how Athanasius tried to achieve unity among the Christians.

On their return from the Nicea, the bishops soon picked up the threads of the dispute which they had left on being summoned by the Emperor. The battle resumed and the old conflict continued. They soon forgot about the fact that the Nicene Creed which they had signed was meant to be an agreed profession of belief. The supporters of Arius especially did nothing to hide the fact that they did not consider the Creed to be an affirmation of true Christianity. Only Athanasius was perhaps loyal to it, but even his supporters had their doubts.

In the West, the Nicene Creed remained almost unknown. Saint Hillary was still a stranger to it thirty years after the Council of Nicea had taken place. Of it he eventually wrote:

> We anathematise those we defended. We condemn either the doctrine of others in ourselves or our own in others, and, reciprocally tearing one another to pieces,

we have become the cause of each other's ruin. The translation (of the Creed) from Greek into Latin was imperfect, for the Greek terms of Platonic philosophy, which had been consecrated by the Church, failed to express the mysteries of the Christian faith. Verbal defects in Scriptures might introduce into Latin theology a long train of errors or perplexity. [28]

Sabinas, one of the early bishops of Thrace, describes all those who assembled in Nicea as being ignorant simpletons. He brands the faith they declared there as having been set forth by ignorant persons who had no intelligence in the matter. Socritus, the historian, compares the two combatants to armies engaged in battle at night, neither knowing the meaning of the words used by the other. Dr. Stanley writes that if Athanasius, when young, had adopted the moderation which he showed in his old age, then the Catholic Church would not have been divided, and much bloodshed would have been avoided.

o o o o o

Thus the Council of Nicea, instead of bridging the gulf between the Christian sects, succeeded in widening it, and the bitterness between them was not diminished, but increased. Such was the temper of the Church, that, withstanding reason and persuasion, it learned the efficacy of force, and the first major bloodbath of the Arians began. At a later stage, the Goths and the Lombards were 'converted' by the same means. The fearful loss of life which was the inevitable result of the Crusades followed. During the Thirty Years War in Europe, it was established that even belief in the Trinity was not enough: the ruling elite of the Pauline Church had to be obeyed. By the time of the Reformation, the situation was such that even Luther's actions were not really directed towards any serious attempt to return to the true teaching of Jesus, but rather demonstrated a mere struggle for power.

o o o o o

Returning to the events which took place immediately after 325 AD, we find that Bishop Alexander died in 328 AD. A stormy election for the bishopric of Alexandria followed. The Arians and Meletians put up a strong fight, but Athanasius was declared, elected, and consecrated as a bishop. His election was disputed. Those who opposed his election complained of persecution, political intrigue and even magic.

Meanwhile, at Constantine's court, Constantina, his sister who feared and loved God, continued to voice her opposition to the killing of the Christians. She never tried to hide the fact that she thought Arius represented true Christianity. She also opposed the treatment of Eusebius of Nicomedia who had been banished by the Emperor for his beliefs. At long last, she had her way, and Eusebius was allowed back. His return was a great blow to the Athanasian faction. The Emperor gradually began to lean towards the side of Arius. When he received news that the election of Athanasius was being disputed, he summoned the new Bishop to the capital. Athanasius, however, made excuses and did not go to Constantinople.

In 335 AD, a Council was held in Tyre to celebrate the thirtieth year of Constantine's reign. This time Athanasius was obliged to attend. He was accused of episcopal tyranny, and the atmosphere was so charged with feeling against him that he left the Council without waiting to hear what decisions would be made. He was condemned. The bishops then gathered in Jerusalem where the condemnation of Athanasius was confirmed. Arius was taken back into the Church and allowed to receive communion.

The Emperor then invited Arius and his friend Euzous to Constantinople. The peace between Arius and the Emperor was now virtually complete, and to further this, the bishops again officially condemned Athanasius. In desperation, Athanasius decided to try and face the lion in his own den. He came in person to Constantinople, and audience was granted to him by the Emperor. Eusebius of Nicomedia was also present on this occasion. He well knew that the decision made at the Council of Nicea had gone against Arius for political reasons. So, instead of starting an ecclesiastical debate which the Emperor would not have understood anyway, he accused Athanasius of hindering the supply of corn to the capital. This tactic caught Athanasius completely by surprise. He discovered that someone else could also play the game at which he was so expert. The charge was easily proved and Athanasius was sent away to Trier in Gaul.

Arius was then appointed the Bishop of Constantinople. He died soon after, however, from poisoning, in 336 AD. The Paulinian Church called it a miracle, but the Emperor suspected murder. He appointed a commission to investigate the death which had taken place in such a mysterious manner. Athanasius was found to be responsible, and was condemned for the murder of Arius.

The Emperor, greatly moved by the death of Arius, and doubtlessly influenced by his sister, became a Christian soon after. He was baptised by Eusebius of Nicomedia. He died only a year later, in 337 AD. Thus Constantine, who had spent so much of his reign persecuting those who affirmed the Divine Unity and supporting their opponents, died in the faith of those he had killed.

○   ○   ○   ○   ○

Arius played an important part in the history of Christianity. He was not only largely the means by which Constantine finally accepted Christianity, but also represented those people who have attempted to follow the teaching of Jesus implicitly. At a time when this guidance was beginning to be seriously eroded, and when the memory of Jesus as a man who embodied his message was beginning to fade, Arius stands out as a man who was not prepared to accept this course of events with complacency.

Arius believed that God is absolutely One, and that therefore this belief is absolutely simple. He believed that God is alone ingenerate, alone eternal, alone without beginning, alone good, alone almighty, alone unchangeable and unalterable, and that His Being is hidden in eternal mystery from the outward eye of every creature. Arius opposed any idea of the manhood of God.

Arius earnestly pressed in favour of following Jesus implicitly. He was willing to recognise in him every attribute which was compatible with his being a human being, and which, in turn, did not contradict the unique attributes and Unity of God, and accordingly he refused to compromise or come to terms with any idea which led to a concept of or a belief in multiple Divinity. Thus he automatically felt bound to reject any dogma which promoted or accepted the alleged divinity of Jesus. In his view, since ingenerateness is the very essence of Divinity, there could be no 'son' of God in any strict or primary sense.

If the act of generation is attributed to God, he said, this concept constitutes an attack on the unique singularity of God. It also, even if only indirectly, ascribes to God corporeality and passion which are attributes of man and imply that the Almighty is subject to necessity – which He clearly is not. Thus, on every ground, he argued, it is impossible to ascribe the act of generation to God.

Arius also stated that since Jesus was finite, he was other than God – Who is Eternal. It is also possible, he argued, to visualise a time when Jesus did not exist – which again demonstrates that he is other than God. Jesus is not of the Essence of God, but a creature of God, essentially like other creatures, albeit definitely unique among men on account of his having no human father and because of his being singled out as a Prophet. Instead of somehow sharing in the Divine Essence, Arius argued, Jesus did not even fully comprehend his own essence. He had to depend, like every other creature, on the help of God's grace – while God is dependant on nothing. Like all mankind, continued Arius, he had free will and a human nature which was capable of leading him to acts which were either pleasing or displeasing to God. However, Arius added, although Jesus was potentially capable of acting in a manner displeasing to God, the purity and virtue which God had granted to him, kept him from doing so.

These basic tenets of Arius's belief have survived right up to the present day, and are still the foundation of the belief of many Unitarian Christians.

        ◎   ◎   ◎   ◎   ◎

After Constantine's death in 337 AD, the next Emperor, Constantius, also accepted the faith of Arius, and belief in the Divine Unity continued to be officially accepted as 'orthodox' Christianity. A conference held in Antioch in 341 AD accepted monotheism as the true basis of Christianity. This ruling was confirmed by another Council that was held in Sirmium in 351 AD, again with the concurrence of the Emperor then in power. Thus at this stage the teaching to which Arius had held with such certainty was accepted by an overwhelming majority of Christians both in the Eastern Roman Empire as well as in North Africa. Saint Jerome wrote in 359 AD that, 'the whole world groaned and marvelled to find itself Arian.' [29]

In the years that followed, the Trinitarian Christians grew in number, but even as late as 381 AD, the official religion of the Emperor in Constantinople was still declared to be that of Arius. It was at the Council of Constantinople in 381 AD, however, that the Holy Ghost was officially granted divine status, and once this had been 'achieved' it then became even easier than before to argue that the doctrine of Trinity was not only plausible but also correct. From that point on, therefore, the doctrine of Trinity gradually came to be the accepted basis of Christianity in Western Europe.

This phenomenon of 'councils' meeting and passing 'official' resolutions demonstrates just how far even 'orthodox' Christianity in Eastern Europe had departed from what Jesus had taught, peace be on him. He himself had never resorted to this kind of procedure, which was usually to be found solely within the courts of rulers – for wisdom and debate are mutually incompatible!

In 387 AD, Jerome completed his famous *Vulgate Bible*. This was the first Latin translation of some of the Scriptures which had been translated into Greek from the Hebrew texts. It included what is known today as the *Old Testament*. It was this *Bible* which became the basis of all other Bibles translated into other languages, and which was adopted by the Roman Catholic – and at a later stage by the Protestant – Churches as their official canonical book. Once this version had become established, all other Gospels and Scriptures not included in Jerome's selection were almost completely destroyed by these two Trinitarian Churches at one stage or another. Thus all contact with the real Jesus continued to be gradually lost, as the 'official' version became more deeply and widely established.

Today, for example, relatively few Christians are aware of just how many Gospels there used to be, or why they were destroyed. Of those who are aware of this historical fact, most will explain it away by stating that either these missing Gospels were written by 'heretics', or that they must have merely duplicated what is already in the officially accepted Gospels, or that they must have been unreliable for some other reason.

Furthermore, most Christians today are totally unaware of the research which has been conducted, especially during the present century, into the authenticity, accuracy and reliability of the contents of the *Bible*. Not having been informed of the inescapable findings and conclusions of that research, they will probably assert, in direct contradiction of what the leaders of all the established Churches must surely know by now, that the contents of the *Bible* are 'the Word of God' – reliably translated into their own language from authentic texts which accurately record the accounts written by actual eyewitnesses. This, as Dr Maurice Bucaille points out in his book, *The Bible, the Qur'an and Science*, is often because they have been deliberately misled:

> In editions of the Bible produced for widespread publication, introductory notes more often than not set out a

collection of ideas that would tend to persuade the reader that the Gospels hardly raise any problems concerning the personalities of the authors of the various books, the authenticity of the texts and the truth of the descriptions. In spite of the fact that there are so many unknowns concerning authors of whose identity we are not at all sure, we find a wealth of precise information in this kind of introductory note. Often they present as a certainty what is pure hypothesis, or they state that such-and-such an evangelist was an eye-witness of the events, while specialist works claim the opposite. The time that elapsed between the end of Jesus's ministry and the appearance of the texts is exaggeratedly reduced. They would have one believe that these were written by one man from an oral tradition, when in fact specialists have pointed out adaptations to the texts. Of course, certain difficulties of interpretation are mentioned here and there, but they ride rough shod over glaring contradictions that must strike anyone who thinks about them. In the little glossaries one finds among the appendices complementing a reassuring preface, one observes how improbabilities, contradictions or blatant errors have been hidden or stifled under clever arguments of an apologetic nature. This state of affairs, which shows up the misleading nature of such commentaries is very disturbing. [30]

Dr. Bucaille continues:

The majority of Christians believe that the Gospels were written by direct witnesses of the life of Jesus and therefore constitute unquestionable evidence concerning the events highlighting his life and preachings. One wonders, in the presence of such guarantees of authenticity, how it is possible to discuss the teachings derived from them and how one can cast doubt upon the validity of the Church as an institution by applying the general instructions Jesus himself gave. Today's popular editions of the Gospels contain commentaries aimed at propagating these ideas among the general public.

The value the authors of the Gospels have as eyewitnesses is always presented to the faithful as axiomatic. In the middle of the Second century, Saint Justin did, after all, call the Gospels the *'Memoirs of the Apostles'*. There are moreover so many details proclaimed concerning the authors that it is a wonder that one could ever doubt their accuracy; it is even said that they spoke Aramaic and Greek. Matthew was a well-known character, 'a customs officer employed at the toll-gate or customs house at Capharnaum'; Mark is also easily identifiable as Peter's colleague; there is no doubt that he too was an eyewitness. Luke is the 'dear physician' of whom Paul talks: information on him is very precise. John is the Apostle who was always near to Jesus, son of Zebedee, fisherman on the Sea of Galilee.

Modern studies on the beginnings of Christianity show that this way of presenting things hardly corresponds to reality. We shall see who the authors of the Gospels really were. As far as the decades following Jesus's mission are concerned, it must be understood that events did not at all happen in the way they have been said to have taken place and that Peter's arrival in Rome in no way laid the foundations for the Church. On the contrary, from the time Jesus left earth to the second half of the Second Century, there was a struggle between two factions. One was what one might call Pauline Christianity and the other Judeo-Christianity. It was only very slowly that the first supplanted the second, and Pauline Christianity triumphed over Judeo-Christianity. [31]

Since, as a result of this 'triumph', the nature of the struggle itself has been covered up by the Trinitarian Church – to the extent that most Christians are taught that Trinitarian Christians are 'true' Christians, and that Unitarian Christians are misguided 'heretics', whose beliefs should not even be considered under any circumstances – it would be helpful at this point to briefly consider the origins, authenticity, accuracy and reliability of not only the *New Testament*, but also of two of the early Scriptures which were condemned by the Trinitarian Church, but which survived its attempts to destroy them: *The Gospel of Barnabas* and *The Shepherd of Hermas*.

○   ○   ○   ○   ○

Chapter Five

The Gospel
of
Barnabas

Although none of today's officially accepted Gospels – or, for that matter, the *Gospel of Barnabas*, whose authenticity continues to be attacked by the established Church because its contents contradict official dogma on several fundamental issues – are capable of being objectively authenticated (instead it is sweepingly claimed that they are 'divinely inspired'), the *Gospel of Barnabas* does nevertheless remain interesting reading, especially since it appears to be, on the face of it, the only known surviving Gospel written by a close disciple of Jesus, that is, by a man who spent most of his time in the actual company of Jesus, peace be on him, during the three years in which he was delivering his message.

Barnabas therefore had a direct experience and knowledge of Jesus's teaching, unlike all the authors of the four officially accepted Gospels. It is not known when he wrote down what he remembered of Jesus and his guidance, whether events and discourses were recorded as they happened, or whether he wrote it soon after Jesus had left the earth, fearing that otherwise some of his teaching might be changed or lost. It is possible that he did not write down anything until he had returned to Cyprus with John Mark. As we have already seen, the two made this journey some time after Jesus had left the earth, after parting company with Paul of Tarsus, who had refused to make any further journeys with Barnabas on which Mark was also present. But no matter when it was written, and although it, too, like the four accepted Gospels, has inevitably suffered from being translated and filtered through several languages, it is, at least on the face of it, an eyewitness account of Jesus's life.

Both those who have a vested interest in attempting to 'prove' that the *Gospel of Barnabas* is a 'forgery' and those who simply want to be able to establish the truth of the matter, whatever it may be, are quick to point out that although the early church fathers often referred to the *Gospel of Barnabas* in their writings, this does not necessarily mean that what appears to be a sixteenth century Italian translation of the Gospel in the Imperial Library in Vienna is a faithful translation of the early first century original. Any number of changes could have been introduced during the intervening centuries.

This observation, it should also be pointed out, applies almost equally to the four officially accepted Gospels, (of which the earliest surviving manuscripts on which today's text is based are written in Greek – not Hebrew or Aramaic – and date from the 4th century AD, some three centuries after the late first century originals were probably written), although this possibility has never been too carefully considered by the established Church, since its authority would have been – and still could be – inevitably and seriously undermined as a result.

On the other hand, it can also be argued that if, on the balance of probabilities, the four accepted Gospels are more or less accurate, then this must also be more or less equally true of the *Gospel of Barnabas*, since much of its contents have very much in common with the four accepted Gospels and are often in complete agreement – although of course there are two very significant major differences between the *Gospel of Barnabas* and the four official Gospels, namely the account of just who it was who was crucified, and also the several specific references to the coming of the Prophet Muhammad, blessings and peace be on him, which appear in the *Gospel of Barnabas*, but not in the other Gospels.

Ultimately any reader's assessment of the contents of any of the Gospels must be highly subjective. Either the words in any given verse ring true, or they do not – and the reaction of any particular reader will probably be different to that of any other reader.

As regards the various references to the *Gospel of Barnabas* which are known to have been made during the course of the last eighteen centuries or so – and which accordingly confirm that such a Gospel was written and did exist, even if it no longer entirely exists in its original form today – it has been well established that the *Gospel of Barnabas* was accepted as a Canonical Gospel in the churches of Alexandria up until 325 AD.

It is also known that it was being circulated in the first and second centuries after the birth of Jesus from the writings of Iraneus (130-200 AD) who wrote in support of the Divine Unity. Iraneus opposed Paul and his followers whom he accused of being responsible for the assimilation of the pagan Roman religion and Platonic philosophy into the original teaching of Jesus. He quoted extensively from the *Gospel of Barnabas* in support of his views.

It is also clear from relatively recent research – which has been conducted more in the spirit of genuinely trying to find out what actually happened, rather than with the intention of merely attempting to present further 'evidence' either for or against established dogmas and theories which are clearly untenable in the light of undisputed historical facts and blatant contradictions – that the conflict between the Unitarian followers of Jesus who belonged to the Tribe of Israel on the one hand, and the European followers of Paul who did not belong to the Tribe of Israel and whose lives were rooted in an entirely different culture and philosophical heritage, on the other hand, occurred at a very early stage in the history of the Christian Church – and even before the early Christians began to rely more on the written word than on what had been transmitted by word of mouth.

In his book, *The Bible, the Qur'an and Science*, Dr Maurice Bucaille refers to these two groups as the Judeo-Christians and the Pauline Christians. His overview of the origins of and the interaction between these two groups – an overview at which he clearly arrived only after extensive research and careful consideration and analysis – confirms that this conflict was, at least to begin with, not so much an ideological conflict as a behavioural one, as his summary of an article published by Cardinal Daniélou in 1967, including many quotations from it, indicates:

> After Jesus's departure, the 'little group of Apostles' formed a 'Jewish sect that remained faithful to the form of worship practised in the Temple'. However, when the observances of converts from paganism were added to them, a 'special system' was offered to them as it were: the Council of Jerusalem in 49 AD exempted them from circumcision and Jewish observances; 'many Judeo-Christians rejected this concession'. This group is quite separate from Paul. What is more, Paul and the Judeo-Christians were in conflict over the question of pagans

who had turned to Christianity, (the incident of Antioch, 49 AD). 'For Paul, the circumcision, Sabbath, and
form of worship practised in the Temple were hence-
forth old fashioned, even for the Jews. Christianity was
to free itself from its political-cum-religious adherence
to Judaism and open itself to the Gentiles.'

For those Judeo-Christians who remained 'loyal Jews',
Paul was a traitor: Judeo-Christian documents call him
an 'enemy', and accuse him of 'tactical double-dealing'
... 'Until 70 AD, Judeo-Christianity represents the majority of the Church' and 'Paul remains an isolated case'.
The head of the community at that time was James, a
relation of Jesus. With him were Peter (at the beginning)
and John. 'James may be considered to represent the
Judeo-Christian camp, which deliberately clung to Judaism as opposed to Pauline Christianity.' Jesus's family
has a very important place in the Judeo-Christian
Church of Jerusalem, 'James's successor was Simeon,
son of Cleopas, a cousin of the lord'.

Cardinal Daniélou here quotes Judeo-Christian writings which express the views on Jesus of this community which initially formed around the apostles: the
Gospel of the Hebrews (coming from a Judeo-Christian
community in Egypt), the writings of Clement: *Homilies
and Recognitions*, '*Hypotyposeis*', the *Second Apocalypse* of
James, the *Gospel of Thomas*. (One could note here that
all these writings were later to be classed as *Apocrypha*,
i.e. they had to be concealed by the victorious Church
which was to be born of Paul's success. It was to make
obvious excisions in the Gospel literature and retain only
the four Canonic Gospels.) 'It is to the Judeo-Christians
that one must ascribe the oldest writings of Christian
literature.' Cardinal Daniélou mentions them in detail.

'It was not just in Jerusalem and Palestine that Judeo-
Christianity predominated during the first hundred
years of the Church. The Judeo-Christian mission seems
everywhere to have developed before the Pauline mission. This is certainly the explanation of the fact that the
letters of Paul allude to a conflict.' They were the same
adversaries he was to meet everywhere: in Galatia, Corinth, Colossae, Rome and Antioch.

The Syro-Palestinian coast from Gaza to Antioch was Judeo-Christian 'as witnessed by the Acts of the Apostles and Clementine writings'. In Asia Minor, the existence of Judeo-Christians is indicated in Paul's letters to the Galatians and Colossians. Papias's writings give us information about Judeo-Christianity in Phrygia. In Greece, Paul's first letter to the Corinthians mentions Judeo-Christians especially at Apollos. According to Clement's letter and the *Shepherd of Hermas*, Rome was an 'important centre'. For Suetonius and Tacitus, the Christians represented a Jewish sect. Cardinal Daniélou thinks that the first evangelisation in Africa was Judeo-Christian. The *Gospel of the Hebrews* and the writings of Clement of Alexandria link up with this.

It is essential to know these facts to understand the struggle between communities that formed the background against which the Gospels were written. The texts that we have today, after many adaptations from the sources, began to appear around 70 AD, the time when the two rival communities were engaged in a fierce struggle, with the Judeo-Christians still retaining the upper hand. With the Jewish war and the fall of Jerusalem in 70 AD, the situation was to be reversed. This is how Cardinal Daniélou explains the decline:

'After the Jews had been discredited in the Empire, the Christians tended to detach themselves from them. The Hellenistic peoples of Christian persuasion then gained the upper hand: Paul won a posthumous victory; Christianity separated itself politically and sociologically from Judaism: it became the third people. All the same, until the Jewish revolt in 140 AD, Judeo-Christianity continued to predominate culturally.'

From 70 AD to a period situated sometime before 110 AD the Gospels of Mark, Matthew, Luke and John were produced. They do not constitute the first written Christian documents: the letters of Paul date from well before them. According to O. Culmann, Paul probably wrote his letter to the Thessalonians in 50 AD. He had probably disappeared several years prior to the completion of Mark's Gospel.

Paul is the most controversial figure in Christianity. He was considered to be a traitor to Jesus's thought by the latter's family and by the apostles who had stayed in Jerusalem in the circle around James. Paul created Christianity at the expense of those whom Jesus had gathered around him to spread his teachings. He had not known Jesus during his lifetime and he proved the legitimacy of his mission by declaring that Jesus, raised from the dead, had appeared to him on the road to Damascus. It is quite reasonable to ask what Christianity might have been without Paul and one could no doubt construct all sorts of hypotheses on this subject. As far as the Gospels are concerned however, it is almost certain that if this atmosphere of struggle between communities had not existed, we would not have had the writings we possess today. They appeared at a time of fierce struggle between the two communities. These 'combat writings', as Father Kannengiesser calls them, emerged from the multitude of writings on Jesus. These occurred at the time when Paul's style of Christianity won through definitively, and created its own collection of official texts. These texts constituted the *'Canon'* which condemned and excluded as unorthodox any other documents that were not suited to the line adopted by the Church.

The Judeo-Christians have now disappeared as a community with any influence, but one still hears people talking about them under the general term of 'Judaistic'. This is how Cardinal Daniélou describes their disappearance:

'When they were cut off from the Great Church, that gradually freed itself from its Jewish attachments, they petered out very quickly in the West. In the East however it is possible to find traces of them in the Third and Fourth centuries AD, especially in Palestine, Arabia, Transjordania, Syria and Mesopotamia. Others joined in the orthodoxy of the Great Church, at the same time preserving traces of Semitic culture; some of these still persist in the Churches of Ethiopia and Chaldea.' [1]

The 'official' confirmation of the 'victory' over the true followers of Jesus by Paulinian Christianity was enshrined, as we have already seen, in the outcome of the famous Council of Nicea which was held in 325 AD – when the Roman Emperor Constantine, who at the time claimed to be 'neutral' on the grounds that he was not a Christian, decided that the Paulinian version of Christianity represented the true teachings of Jesus, and that the gospels of Matthew, Mark, Luke and John should become the officially accepted gospels, and that all other gospels, including the *Gospel of Barnabas*, were to be destroyed – along with whoever was found to have them in their possession – a decision which resulted in many of the early gospels being lost for good, and millions of Unitarian Christians being martyred in the years that followed.

It was also at the Council of Nicea, after over two centuries of debate, that Jesus was officially granted divine status, and, with the official instatement at the Council of Constantinople in 381 AD of 'the Holy Ghost' as the 'third person', the doctrine of Trinity which had begun to emerge during the intervening period finally came of age, some three and a half centuries after the disappearance of Jesus.

Shortly after the Council of Constantinople, the Roman Emperor Theodosius made it a capital offence to reject the doctrine of Trinity, thereby laying the foundations for the Mediaeval and Spanish Inquisitions which were to flourish centuries later – by which time the doctrines of the New Covenant, and of Original Sin, and of the Atonement and Forgiveness of Sins, and of the Trinity, had become so deeply embedded in the Christian psyche that no amount of reformations, ancient or modern, and however well-intentioned, could dislodge them.

Thus it is a matter of historical fact that it took several centuries for the doctrine of Trinity to be developed – as part of a long drawn out cultural and philosophical process, characterised by fierce conflict and at times often confused debate – which explains why the doctrine is never actually described in detail within any of the texts of even the official Paulinian version of the *New Testament* as being central to Jesus's teaching. This can only be because the contents of the early Christian writings – both of the Judeo-Christians and of the Paulinian Christians – had already been finalised prior to the formulation of the doctrine, and were already too well-known to be tampered with too extensively, by the time that the doctrine had reached the stage where it was formally expressed in writing.

The most that the Paulinian Church could hope to achieve was the systematic and complete suppression of all the Judeo-Christian writings which clearly and unequivocally affirmed the Oneness of God as well as confirming the continuity of both teaching and behaviour which existed between Moses and Jesus, peace be on them.

Thus once the doctrine of Trinity had been formally adopted and declared to be the official doctrine of the Pauline Church, one of the inevitable consequences of this decision was that out of the three hundred or so Gospels extant at that time, only the four which were selected as the official Gospels of the Pauline Church were permitted to survive. The remaining Gospels, including the *Gospel of Barnabas*, were ordered to be destroyed completely. It was also decided that all Gospels written in Hebrew should be destroyed. Edicts were issued stating that anyone found in possession of an unauthorised Gospel would be put to death. This was the first well-organised attempt to remove all the records of Jesus's original teaching, whether in human beings or books, which contradicted the doctrine of Trinity. In the case of the *Gospel of Barnabas*, these orders were not entirely successful, and mention of its continued existence has been made up to the present day:

Pope Damasus (304-384 AD), who became Pope in 366 AD, is recorded as having issued a decree that the *Gospel of Barnabas* should not be read. This decree was supported by Gelasus, Bishop of Caesaria, who died in 395 AD. The Gospel was included in his list of Apocryphal books. '*Apocrypha*' simply means 'hidden from the people'. Thus, at this stage, the Gospel was no longer available to everyone, but was still being referred to by the leaders of the Church. In fact, it is known that the Pope secured a copy of the *Gospel of Barnabas* in 383 AD, and kept it in his private library.

There were a number of other decrees which referred to the Gospel. It was forbidden by the Decree of the Western Churches in 382 AD, and by Pope Innocent in 465 AD. In the Gelasian Decree of 496 AD, the *Evangelium Barnabe* is included in the list of forbidden books. This decree was reaffirmed by Hormisdas, who was Pope from 514 to 523 AD. All these decrees are mentioned in the Catalogue of Greek Manuscripts in the Library of Chancellor Seguier (1558-1672), prepared by B. de Montfaucon (1655-1741).

The writings of Barnabas – which include his Epistle as well as his Gospel – are also mentioned in the *Stichometry* of Nicephorus as follows:

Serial No. 3 : Epistle of Barnabas ... Lines 1,300

and again in the list of *Sixty Books* as follows:

Serial No. 17 : Travels and teaching of the Apostles.
Serial No. 18 : Epistle of Barnabas.
Serial No. 24 : Gospel According to Barnabas.

This famous list was also known as the *Index*, and Christians were not supposed to read any of the books listed in it on pain of eternal punishment.

It is interesting to note in passing that a Greek version of the *Epistle of Barnabas* (which is mentioned by two of the most well-known early church fathers, Origen (185-254 AD) and Eusebius (265-340 AD) in their writings) is in fact to be found in the *Codex Sinaiticus* – perhaps the earliest Greek version of the New Testament known to be in existence today and dating from the 4th or 5th century AD – although it has been excluded from all modern versions of the Bible.

Although Christian polemicists have repeatedly attempted to allege not only that the Italian translation of the *Gospel of Barnabas* is a mediaeval forgery, but also by implication that the Gospel itself is a forgery – written by a Muslim convert in the fifteenth or sixteenth century AD – this clearly cannot be correct, given the number of recorded references to the *Gospel of Barnabas* which were often made long before the coming of the Prophet Muhammad, blessings and peace be on him.

As regards other later references to the *Gospel of Barnabas*, the Gospel is also, recorded in the 206th manuscript of the Baroccian Collection in the Bodleian Library in Oxford which dates from the 6th or 7th century AD. [2] Cotelerius, who catalogued the manuscripts in the Library of the French king, listed the *Gospel of Barnabas* in the *Index of Scriptures* which he prepared in 1789. There is also a solitary fragment of a Greek version of the *Gospel of Barnabas* to be found in a museum in Athens, which is all that remains of a copy which was burnt:

Βαρνάβας ὁ ἀπόστολος ἔφη· ἐν ἁμίλλαις πονηραῖς ἀθλιώτερος ὁ νικήσας, διότι ἀπέρχεται πλέον ἔχων τῆς ἁμαρτίας [3]

It is interesting to note that consistent with the observation by Grabe in *Spicilegium Patrum, i, 302,* Toland found that the 39th Baroccian manuscript contains a fragment that is an Italian equivalent to the Greek text. Thus Toland's conclusion was that the extant Italian translation of the *Gospel of Barnabas* was identical to the ancient *Gospel of Barnabas.* In the same year, Reland in *De religione Mahommedica* (1718) discovered that the Gospel also existed in Arabic and Spanish.

Mr. Johnson's conclusions regarding all the various references to the various versions of the *Gospel of Barnabas* are significant:

> Grabe's knowledge of a Greek version of the Gospel and its equivalence to the later Italian manuscript makes it highly plausible that today's *Gospel of Barnabas* is in fact the *Evangelium Barnabae* listed by the Sixth century Gelasian Decretal and the Sixth or Seventh century Cod. Barocc. 206's list of 60 books. I say, 'highly plausible' because no early Greek manuscript is known to be in existence today. However, it is equally certain that Christian claims that the *Gospel of Barnabas* is a forgery of some fifteenth or sixteenth century renegade Muslim, are simply vain attempts to dismiss a Gospel that strikes at the heart of contemporary Christian christology. Paul in his letter to the Corinthians admitted the centrality of this doctrine to the entire body of Christian faith:
>
> 'Tell me, if Christ is preached as raised from the dead, how is it that some of you say there is no resurrection of the dead? If there is no resurrection of the dead, Christ himself has not been raised. And if Christ has not been raised, our preaching is void of content and your faith is empty too. Indeed, we should then be exposed as false witnesses of God, for we have borne witness before Him that He raised up Christ ...' (*I Corinthians 15: 12-15*). [4]

Clearly, if there is an early Greek or Hebrew copy of the *Gospel of Barnabas* in existence somewhere, then a comparison between it and the Italian translation would end the dispute as to the authenticity and reliability of the Italian version once and for all.

In the fourth year of the Emperor Zeno's rule in 478 AD, the remains of Barnabas were discovered, and a copy of the *Gospel of Barnabas*, written in his own hand, was found on his breast. This is recorded in the *Acta Sanctorum*, Boland Junii, Tome II, pages 422-450, published in Antwerp in 1698. It has been claimed by the Roman Catholic Church that the Gospel found in the grave of Barnabas was that of Matthew, but no steps have been taken to display this copy. The exact contents of the twenty-five mile long library of the Vatican continue to remain in the dark.

The manuscript from which the current English translation of the *Gospel of Barnabas* was made, was originally in the possession of Pope Sixtus V (1589-1590). He had a friend, a monk called Fra Marino, who became very interested in the *Gospel of Barnabas* after reading the writings of Iraneus, who quoted from it extensively. One day he went to see the Pope. They lunched together and, after the meal, the Pope fell asleep. Father Marino began to browse through the books in the Pope's private library and discovered an Italian manuscript of the *Gospel of Barnabas*. Concealing it in the sleeve of his robe, he left and came out of the Vatican with it. This manuscript then passed through different hands until it reached 'a person of great name and authority' in Amsterdam, 'who, during his lifetime, was often heard to put a high value to this piece.' After his death, it came into the possession of J.E. Cramer, a Councillor of the King of Prussia. In 1713, Cramer presented this manuscript to the famous connoisseur of books, Prince Eugene of Savoy. In 1738, along with the library of the Prince, it found its way into the Hofbibliothek in Vienna, where it now rests.

Toland, a notable historian of the early Church, had access to this manuscript, and he refers to it in his *Miscellaneous Works*, which was published posthumously in 1747. He says of the Gospel: 'This is in scripture style to a hair,' and continues:

> The story of Jesus is very differently told in many things from the received Gospels, but much more fully ... and particularly this Gospel ... being near as long again as many of ours. Someone would make a prejudice in favour of it; because, as all things are best known just after they happen, so everything diminishes the further it proceeds from its original. [5]

The following extract from the *Gospel of Barnabas*, for example, (which is taken from the translation of Lonsdale and Laura Ragg) describes what is alleged to have taken place immediately before the miraculous feeding of the five thousand – an account which, as well as furnishing an explanation as to why such a large crowd had gathered in the first place, cannot be found in the four officially accepted Gospels, and for obvious reasons, since it describes how Jesus publicly demonstrated that he could not possibly be identified with God, simply by comparing his human attributes with God's divine attributes:

> Accordingly the governor and the priest and the king prayed Jesus that in order to quiet the people he should mount up into a lofty place and speak to the people. Then went up Jesus on to one of the twelve stones which Joshua made the twelve tribes take up from the midst of Jordan, when all Israel passed over there dry shod; and he said with a loud voice: 'Let our priest go up into a high place whence he may confirm my words.'
>
> Thereupon the priest went up thither; to whom Jesus said distinctly, so that everyone might hear: 'It is written in the testament and covenant of the living God that our God has no beginning; neither shall He ever have an end.'
>
> The priest answered: 'Even so it is written therein.'
>
> Jesus said: 'It is written there that our God by His word alone has created all things.'
>
> 'Even so it is,' said the priest.
>
> Jesus said: 'It is written there that God is invisible and hidden from the mind of man, seeing He is incorporeal and uncomposed, without variableness.'
>
> 'So it is truly,' said the priest.
>
> Jesus said: 'It is written there how that the heaven of heavens cannot contain Him, seeing that our God is infinite.'
>
> 'So said Solomon the Prophet,' said the priest, 'O Jesus.'
>
> Said Jesus: 'It is written there that God has no need forasmuch as He eats not, sleeps not, and suffers not from any deficiency.'
>
> 'So is it,' said the priest.

Said Jesus: 'It is written there that our God is every-where, and that there is not any other god but He, Who strikes down and makes whole, and does all that pleases Him.'

'So it is written,' replied the priest.

Then Jesus, having lifted up his hands, said: 'Lord our God, this is my faith wherewith I shall come to Your judgement: in testimony against every one that shall believe the contrary.'

And turning himself towards the people, he said, 'Repent, for from all that of which the priest has said that it is written in the book of Moses, the covenant of God for ever, you may perceive your sin; for that I am a visible man and a morsel of clay that walks upon the earth, mortal as are other men. And I have had a beginning, and shall have an end, and am such that I cannot create a fly over again.' (*The Gospel of Barnabas: 95*).

The publicity which Toland gave to the Vienna manuscript made it impossible for it to share the same fate as another manuscript of the Gospel in Spanish which also once existed. This manuscript was presented to a college library in England at about the same time that the Italian manuscript was given to the Hofbibliothek. It had not been in England long before it mysteriously disappeared.

The Italian manuscript was translated into English by Canon Lonsdale and Laura Ragg, and was printed and published by the Oxford University Press in 1907. Nearly the whole edition of this English translation abruptly and mysteriously disappeared from the market. Only two copies of this translation are known to exist, one in the British Museum, and the other in the Library of Congress in Washington. A microfilm copy of the book in the Library of Congress was obtained, and a fresh edition of the English translation was printed in Pakistan. A copy of this edition was used for the purposes of reprinting a revised version of the *Gospel of Barnabas* thereafter.

The new English edition, understandably, has caused the present Christian Church a certain degree of irritation – for if the contents of the *Gospel of Barnabas* are true, then it clearly follows that most of the versions of Christianity which exist today – and accordingly the various Churches which promote them – do not have very firm foundations.

This is because the *Gospel of Barnabas* confirms that Jesus was not God, nor the 'son' of God, and that he was neither crucified in the first place, nor subsequently 'raised from the dead' thereafter. As we have already seen, it was Paul himself who pointed out that if Jesus was neither crucified nor raised from the dead, then the bottom falls out of the Paulinian thesis:

> And if Christ has not been raised, our preaching is use-less and so is your faith. More than that, we are then found to be false witnesses about God, for we have tes-tified about God that he raised Christ from the dead ... (*I Corinthians 15: 14-15*).

Accordingly virtually all the established churches, however near or far they are to each other, have united in their various efforts to discredit the English version of the *Gospel of Barnabas* by discrediting the Italian edition from which it was translated.

In a manner reminiscent of the way in which the Russian edition of *The Protocols of the Elders of Zion* has been constantly branded as 'a forgery' in order to discredit any translation of it into another language, so with the Spanish and English translations of the *Gospel of Barnabas*, it has been claimed that the Italian version is a forgery – and, by implication, that even the much earlier Hebrew and Greek versions which, as we have just seen, are known to have existed at a very early stage in the history of Christianity, must also have been 'forgeries'!

Perhaps the most sustained and scholarly attempt aimed at discrediting the English edition of the *Gospel of Barnabas* has been the book written by David Sox entitled, somewhat misleadingly, '*The Gospel of Barnabas*'. Only a few lines of the English translation are actually quoted by him, and the underlying purpose of his book is clearly to put off as many people as possible from actually reading the *Gospel of Barnabas* itself and making their own minds up about its authenticity!

Given that David Sox's brief was to 'prove' that the Italian version of the *Gospel of Barnabas* is a forgery, his methodology is transparently clear: Having ascertained that the *binding* of the manuscript in Vienna dates from approximately the 16th or 17th century – although not necessarily the manuscript itself, which may date from an earlier period and which could have been bound and rebound several times before ending up in its present binding for all we know, but certainly not an earlier manuscript from which it may have been copied, let alone an even earlier manuscript in Greek or Hebrew from which it may have been translated – David Sox then had to find a likely forger:

It had to be someone who was clearly familiar with both the *Old* and the *New Testaments* as represented in the *Vulgate Bible* – so that repeated references could be made to *Old Testament* events and prophecies whenever this was appropriate; it had to be someone who had converted to Islam, but who nevertheless would be 'clever' enough not to make the 'forgery' correspond too closely or entirely with what the *Qur'an* says about Jesus (for example, describing the Prophet Muhammad as 'the Messiah' who would come after Jesus, whereas the *Qur'an* confirms that Jesus *was* the Messiah whose coming had been foretold by Moses; or, for example, confirming the traditional nativity story given in the officially accepted Gospels, rather than giving an account of the birth of Jesus which corresponded with the account which is given in the *Qur'an*; or, for example, not mentioning various miracles of Jesus which, as we shall see in Chapter Eleven, are described in the *Qur'an*, but not in the officially accepted Gospels); and it had to be someone who had the ability to ensure not only that the 'forgery' did not correspond exactly with what is in the Qur'an, but also that at least a third of the contents of the 'forgery' confirmed exactly what is in the other officially accepted Gospels, that at least another third expanded on what is in the other officially accepted Gospels without contradicting them, and that the remaining third – even if it contradicted what is in the other officially accepted Gospels – nevertheless appeared to be 'in scripture style to a hair', to use the phrase coined by Toland. It could not have been a particularly easy brief!

There was, however, one obvious possible candidate: According to the Preface to the Spanish translation of the *Gospel of Barnabas*, Fra Marino – the monk who is said to have stolen the Pope's copy of the Italian version – had subsequently embraced Islam. 'If we can only prove that he did not really steal the Pope's copy at all,' we can see David Sox thinking, 'but that in fact he actually wrote it himself – then we will have succeeded!' Naturally this hypothesis would depend heavily on establishing beyond any doubt that not only the binding, but also the Italian manuscript itself was written between approximately 1580 and 1600 – any proof of which is very conspicuous by its absence.

Of course, short of having access to an authentic and voluntary confession by Fra Marino, it would be impossible to 'prove' such a thesis, some four centuries after the alleged event, even 'on the balance of probabilities', and let alone 'beyond any reasonable doubt', – as David Sox in a roundabout way himself accepts, when he admits that 'the reader is faced with a great amount of specula-tion' in his book. However he nevertheless attempts the impossi-ble, perhaps in the hope that, by at least raising this possibility and making it seem plausible, any version of the *Gospel of Barnabas* might as a result be sufficiently discredited not to be taken too seriously by anyone who happened to come across it.

We are accordingly presented with the fruits of David Sox's la-borious searches through the official records for the period within which the Italian manuscript was probably bound to see if there is any mention of a Fra Marino who not only had the requisite tal-ents to be able to produce such an interesting 'forgery', but who also would have had the necessary motive needed to sustain what would have been such a demanding and, if he were to be found out by the Inquisition, such a dangerous, task.

David Sox was only able to come up with one possible candi-date: a former Inquisitor of Venice – who probably would have been more likely to have burnt the *Gospel of Barnabas* than written it! – who according to the records was officially reprimanded on two occasions for being too lenient with heretics, and who was subsequently demoted from his position and replaced. From these scant details, David Sox concludes that Fra Marino was not only somehow driven to embrace Islam, but also must have decided to forge the Italian version of the *Gospel of Barnabas* as an act of re-venge against his successor – although how such an act could have actually adversely affected his successor (who probably would have been delighted to burn the offending 'forgery' had he ever come across it) is never clarified.

This scenario is extremely tenuous, to say the least, especially when in fact the Italian manuscript receives hardly any publicity whatsoever for the next four hundred years – and not until the English version of it begins to be widely circulated some seventy years after the Italian version has been translated into English by Canon Lonsdale and Laura Ragg!

Unfortunately for David Sox there are no contemporary records which depict the successor of an ex-Inquisitor (who happens to be called Fra Marino) tearing his hair out in desperation as hundreds of gullible Italians inexplicably embrace Islam after reading the infamous *Gospel of Barnabas*. Indeed there is no real 'proof' that the Fra Marino to whom the Preface to the Spanish version refers is none other than our ex-Inquisitor from Venice. In all probability there were literally tens, if not hundreds, of Fra Marinos in Italy during the time of Pope Sixtus V, not all of whom would have been recorded in what few records have survived up until today, and any one of whom might have been the Fra Marino who stole the Pope's copy of the *Gospel of Barnabas*.

Furthermore, as regards the Fra Marino selected by David Sox, although it is recorded that he was an Inquisitor, and that he was reprimanded, and that he was demoted (but not dismissed), there is no record that he either subsequently embraced Islam, or that he was burnt at the stake for embracing Islam, or that he fled the country in order to avoid the clutches of the Inquisition after accepting Islam. If, as David Sox has attempted to argue, Fra Marino himself wrote the *Gospel of Barnabas* 'in revenge against his successor', surely the Gospel would have been publicised at the time, and surely there would have been a public outcry as a result. It appears that David Sox could find no such record.

Thus in spite of all his long hours of research, his carefully arranged footnotes and cross-references, and his lucid style, David Sox's hypothesis remains unlikely, implausible and unconvincing. It is highly unlikely that any impartial court of law today could possibly conclude, on the 'evidence' presented by David Sox, that the link needed to substantiate his allegation of forgery which he seeks to establish in his book has been proved. Indeed one cannot help concluding that perhaps the main reason why he has gone to such great lengths in his attempts to prove the highly improbable, may well be that it is because the contents of the *Gospel of Barnabas* are in fact true.

It is however to his credit that in spite of all the far-fetched speculation – of which, as we have already seen, he admits there is 'a great amount' – David Sox does have the intellectual honesty to admit that, 'The Jesus of the *Gospel of Barnabas* is on many occasions similar to that of the canonical Gospels,' [6] – although he then adds, ' because, of course, the former book depends on material contained in the latter.' It is possible, however, that it is in fact the converse of that statement which is nearer the truth:

It is possible that the reason why there is in fact such a marked similarity between the contents of *The Gospel of Barnabas* and that of the other Gospels is that the Italian translation is not a 'forgery', but rather a faithful translation of a much earlier Greek or Hebrew or even Aramaic version, which was in existence long before the *Qur'an* was revealed, and on which the writers of the four officially accepted Gospels perhaps depended – for it is now generally accepted that the three earliest accepted Gospels, known as the Synoptic Gospels, were in part derived from an earlier unknown Gospel which today's researchers often refer to as the 'Q' Gospel, for want of a better name.

It is possible that this earlier unknown Gospel could be the original *Gospel of Barnabas*, although it is clear from the following analysis contained in Dr. Maurice Bucaille's book, *The Bible, the Qur'an and Science*, that the 'Q' Gospel may well have been a collection of different narrations, rather than one complete document:

> The problem of sources was approached in a very simplistic fashion at the time of the Fathers of the Church. In the early centuries of Christianity, the only source available was the Gospel that the complete manuscripts provided first, i.e. Matthew's Gospel. The problem of sources only concerned Mark and Luke because John constituted a quite separate case. Saint Augustine held that Mark, who appears second in the traditional order of presentation, had been inspired by Matthew and had summarised his work. He further considered that Luke, who comes third in the manuscripts, had used data from both; his prologue suggests this, and has already been discussed.
>
> The experts in exegesis at this period were as able as we are to estimate the degree of corroboration between the texts and find a large number of verses common to two or three synoptics. Today, the commentators of the *Ecumenical Translation of the Bible* provide the following figures:
>
> verses common to all three synoptics 330
> verses common to Mark and Matthew 178
> verses common to Mark and Luke 100
> verses common to Matthew and Luke 230

The verses unique to each of the first three Gospels are as follows: Matthew 330, Mark 53, and Luke 500.

From the Fathers of the Church until the end of the Eighteenth century AD, one and a half millennia passed without any new problems being raised on the sources of the evangelists: people continued to follow tradition. It was not until modern times that it was realised, on the basis of these data, how each evangelist had taken material found in the others and compiled his own specific narration guided by his own personal views. Great weight was attached to actual collection of material for the narration. It came from the oral traditions of the communities from which it originated on the one hand, and from a common written Aramaic source that has not been rediscovered on the other. This written source could have formed a compact mass or have been composed of many fragments of different narrations used by each evangelist to construct his own original work. [7]

Thus the question inevitably arises as to whether the Apocryphal *Gospel of Barnabas* is, in fact, either this missing Gospel or at least a part of the possible collection of different narrations. It must be remembered that John Mark, whose Gospel is the earliest of the four accepted Gospels, was the son of the sister of Barnabas. He never met Jesus. Thus, what he related of Jesus's life and teaching in his Gospel must have been related to him by others. It is known from the books of the *New Testament* that he accompanied Paul and Barnabas on many of their missionary journeys up to the point when there was a sharp conflict between them, resulting in Barnabas and Mark going to Cyprus together. It is unlikely that Mark relied on Paul as a source of information since Paul had never met Jesus either.

The only reasonable conclusion appears to be that he must have repeated what his uncle Barnabas told him about Jesus. It is said by some that he acted as Peter's interpreter and wrote down what he had learned from Peter. This may be correct, for Mark must have had some contact with the other apostles when he was not journeying with Barnabas or Paul. However, Goodspeed shows us from his research that anything he did learn from Peter was by no means comprehensive:

He had been an interpreter of Peter and wrote down accurately, though not in order, everything that he remembered that had been said or done by the lord. For he neither heard the lord, nor followed him, but afterwards, as I said, attended Peter who adapted his instructions to the needs of the hearers, but had no design of giving a connected account of the lord's oracles. [8]

Luke, who also wrote the Acts of the Apostles, never met Jesus. He was Paul's personal physician. Matthew, who also never encountered Jesus, was a tax collector.

It has been argued that Mark's Gospel might be the 'Q' Gospel and that Matthew and Luke used his Gospel when writing theirs. However, they record details which Mark does not, which implies that Mark's Gospel could not have been their only source. Some have said that this is not important, since it is known that Mark's Gospel was written in Hebrew, then translated into Greek, and the Greek translation then translated once again into Latin. All the Hebrew and early Greek versions of Mark's Gospel have been destroyed, and people can only speculate as to how much of the Gospel was changed or altered during these transitions from one language to another, although it has now been generally accepted that the final section (*Mark 16: 9-20*) was tacked on to the end of the basic work at a later stage in order to round it off, which is why it is not to be found in the two oldest complete manuscripts of the Gospels, the *Codex Vaticanus* and the *Codex Sinaiticus* which are said to date from the late 4th or 5th century AD.

It is interesting to note in passing that there have even been attempts to return to the source by synthesising the Gospels, since the contradictions that arise between them have, at times, proved a little awkward for the established Church. Titian attempted to synthesise the four accepted Gospels, which had already been earmarked by the Pauline Church as their official Scriptures during the second century AD. In this Gospel, Titian used 96% of John's Gospel, 75% of Matthew's Gospel, 66% of Luke's Gospel, and 50% of Mark's Gospel. The rest he rejected. It is significant that he placed little trust in the earliest Gospel and relied most heavily on the last Gospel to be written. His synthesised Gospel was not a success.

Thus it is debatable whether Mark's Gospel can be regarded as the common source of the three Synoptic Gospels, whereas most of the events recorded in these three Gospels are contained within the *Gospel of Barnabas* – although, as has already been remarked, there are some notable and deeply significant differences – which is why, according to the Introduction to the *Gospel of Barnabas*, Barnabas wrote his Gospel in the first place:

> Dearly beloved, the great and wonderful God has during these past days visited us by his Prophet Jesus Christ in great mercy of teaching and miracles, by reason whereof many, being deceived of Satan, under pretence of piety, are preaching most impious doctrine, calling Jesus son of God, repudiating the circumcision ordained of God for ever, and permitting every unclean meat: among whom also Paul has been deceived, whereof I speak not without grief; for which cause I am writing that truth which I have seen and heard, in the intercourse that I have had with Jesus, in order that you may be saved, and not deceived of Satan and perish in the judgement of God. Therefore beware of every one that preaches unto you new doctrine contrary to that which I write, that you may be saved eternally.
>
> The great God be with you and guard you from Satan and from every evil. Amen. (*The Gospel of Barnabas*).

If the Italian version of the *Gospel of Barnabas* is a faithful translation of an earlier manuscript which actually did contain what Barnabas originally wrote – and there is no way of conclusively 'proving' this, just as there is no way of conclusively 'proving' that the contents of the four officially accepted Gospels which exist today actually contain what their original authors in fact wrote – then it does follow that the *Gospel of Barnabas* could well be the 'Q' Gospel, the common source of the synoptic Gospels, although as yet no one has ventured to make a verse by verse comparison between the contents of the *Gospel of Barnabas* and the contents of the four official Gospels in order to establish exactly which verses are shared and which verses are unique.

If the *Gospel of Barnabas* is the 'Q' Gospel, and given the manner in which Paulinian Christianity developed, it then makes it easier to understand why not only the manuscripts of all the other Gospels – which are known to have existed in the early years of Christianity and which were rejected at the Council of Nicea – were destroyed, but also all the early manuscripts of even the four official Gospels, probably after the original texts had been radically altered.

It should be emphasised that as regards the four officially accepted Gospels, there are no versions in the original Hebrew or Aramaic, and that, as Dr Maurice Bucaille confirms, the earliest Greek versions date from *after* the Council of Nicea:

> Documents prior to this, i.e. papyri from the Third century AD and one possibly dating from the Second, only transmit fragments to us. The two oldest parchment manuscripts are Greek, Fourth century AD. They are the *Codex Vaticanus*, preserved in the Vatican Library and whose place of discovery is unknown, and the *Codex Sinaiticus*, which was discovered on Mount Sinai and is now preserved in the British Museum, London. The second contains two apocryphal works.
>
> According to the *Ecumenical Translation*, two hundred and fifty other known parchments exist throughout the world, the last of these being from the Eleventh century AD. 'Not all the copies of the New Testament that have come down to us are identical' however. 'On the contrary, it is possible to distinguish differences of varying degrees of importance between them, but however important they may be, there is always a large number of them. Some of these only concern differences of grammatical detail, vocabulary or word order. Elsewhere however, differences between manuscripts can be seen which affect the meaning of whole passages.' If one wishes to see the extent of textual differences, one only has to glance through the *Novum Testamentum Graece* (Nestlé-Aland, Pub., United Bible Societies, London, 1971). This work contains a so-called 'middle-of-the-road' Greek text. It is a text of synthesis with notes containing all the variations found in the different versions.[9]

Thus not only is it possible – indeed it is highly likely – that significant changes were made to the original texts which pre-dated the Council of Nicea and which have all been destroyed, but also even the texts which date from *after* the Council of Nicea do not fully agree with each other, cannot therefore be entirely accurate, and in fact have themselves been altered:

The authenticity of a text, and of even the most venerable manuscript, is always open to debate. The *Codex
Vaticanus* is a good example of this. The facsimile reproduction edited by the Vatican City, 1965, contains an
accompanying note from its editors informing us that,
'several centuries after it was copied (believed to have
been in circa the Tenth or Eleventh century), a scribe
inked over all the letters except those he thought were a
mistake.' There are passages in the text where the original letters in light brown still show through, contrast-
ing visibly with the rest of the text which is in dark
brown. There is no indication that it was a faithful restoration. The note states moreover that, 'the different
hands that corrected and annotated the manuscript over
the centuries have not yet been definitively discerned;
a certain number of corrections were undoubtedly made
when the text was inked over.' In all the religious manu-
als the text is presented as a Fourth century copy. One
has to go to sources at the Vatican to discover that various hands may have altered the text centuries later.

One might reply that other texts may be used for comparison, but how does one choose between variations
that change the meaning? It is a well known fact that a
very old scribe's correction can lead to the definitive
reproduction of the corrected text. We shall see further
on how a single word in a passage from John concerning the Paraclete radically alters its meaning and completely changes its sense when viewed from a theological point of view.

O. Culmann, in his book, *The New Testament*, writes
the following on the subject of variations:

'Sometimes the latter are the result of inadvertent flaws:
the copier misses a word out, or conversely writes it
twice, or a whole section of a sentence is carelessly omitted because in the manuscript to be copied it appeared
between two identical words. Sometimes it is a matter
of deliberate corrections, either the copier has taken the
liberty of correcting the text according to his own ideas
or he has tried to bring it into line with a parallel text in
a more or less skilful attempt to reduce the number of

discrepancies. As, little by little, the New Testament writings broke away from the rest of early Christian literature, and came to be regarded as Holy Scripture, so the copiers became more and more hesitant about taking the same liberties as their predecessors: they thought they were copying the authentic text, but in fact wrote down the variations. Finally, a copier sometimes wrote annotations in the margin to explain an obscure passage. The following copier, thinking that the sentence he found in the margin had been left out of the passage by his predecessor, thought it necessary to include the margin notes in the text. This process often made the new text even more obscure.'

The scribes of some manuscripts sometimes took exceedingly great liberties with the texts. This is the case of one of the most venerable manuscripts after the two referred to above, the Sixth century *Codex Bezae Cantabrigiensis*. The scribe probably noticed the difference between Luke's and Matthew's genealogy of Jesus, so he put Matthew's genealogy into his copy of Luke, but as the second contained fewer names than the first, he padded it out with extra names (without however balancing them up).

    Is it possible to say that the Latin translations, such as Saint Jerome's Sixth century Vulgate, or older translations (Vetus Itala), or Syriac and Coptic translations are any more faithful than the basic Greek manuscripts? They might have been made from manuscripts older than the ones referred to above and subsequently lost to the present day. We just do not know. [10]

The truth of the matter is that there are no complete *pre*-Council of Nicea manuscripts of any of the writings contained in the *New Testament* extant today – nor of the *Gospel of Barnabas* for that matter – or if there are, then whoever has them has been keeping very quiet about them for a good many centuries, and probably for not the right reasons.

    It must be emphasised therefore that the contents of the earliest Greek manuscripts of the four officially accepted Gospels are in fact just as capable of having been 'forged', albeit during an earlier period, as are the contents of the Italian manuscript of the *Gospel of Barnabas*. We just do not know.

The converse possibility, however, is equally true, and although, to quote the Introduction to the *Ecumenical Translation*, 'there can be no hope of going back to the original text itself,' there is still the possibility that on the whole all the Gospels – including *The Gospel of Barnabas* – in their present form do contain a certain degree of accuracy and truth. It is possible to read all of these Gospels and find elements of what must be true in all of them – but it is impossible to claim that any of them are entirely accurate or to rely completely and unreservedly on any one of them.

Furthermore, the one Gospel which we do not have is the Gospel *of* Jesus, the original revelation that he received, in the original language in which it was revealed – so that the accuracy and authenticity of any translation of that original text could always be ascertained and assessed simply by referring back to that original text whenever the occasion might arise.

It is interesting to note, as has already been stated, in this context that according to the *Gospel of Barnabas*, the revelation which was given to Jesus – the *Ingil* – was never preserved as a written text at any stage, but was more in the nature of a well of wisdom which was placed in the heart of Jesus by the angel Gabriel, and from which he could draw as he needed:

> Jesus having come to the age of thirty years, as he himself said unto me, went up to the Mount of Olives with his mother to gather olives. Then at midday as he was praying, when he came to these words: 'Lord, with mercy ....,' he was surrounded by an exceeding bright light and by an infinite multitude of angels, who were saying: 'Blessed be God.' The angel Gabriel presented to him as it were a shining mirror, a book, which descended into the heart of Jesus, in which he had knowledge of what God has done and what has said, and what God wills insomuch that everything was laid bare and open to him; as he said unto me: 'Believe, Barnabas, that I know every prophet with every prophecy, insomuch that whatever I say the whole has come forth from that book.' (*The Gospel of Barnabas: 10*).

This account of the nature of the revelation which Jesus received is not contradicted by any historical record which states otherwise. There is no record of Jesus being presented with inscribed tablets as happened with Moses, for example, or of his receiving a series of revelations like Muhammad, blessings and peace be on all of them, with certain disciples being appointed to record these revelations as they occurred – but not any of Jesus's own words – in order to ensure that the revelation was preserved exactly as it was revealed.

There can be no doubt, however, that Jesus was an illuminated being whose words contained a clarity and directness which reflected all the qualities of light – and which must have entered people's hearts and remained in them just as light does when it enters a room.

And when these words came to be recorded in writing, then surely at least some of these words – together with the accounts of the situations in which they were uttered – must have survived intact, even if the darkness in other people tried to cloud some of them up or shut them out by changing or removing them.

In spite of all the imperfections which exist in the present contents not only of the *Old* and the *New Testaments*, but also of *The Gospel of Barnabas* and other similar works, there can be no doubt that at least some of their contents must accurately record at least some of the words and actions of Jesus, peace be on him – although it will never be possible to actually differentiate between what is reliable and what is not with complete accuracy or certainty.

It does remain a great pity, therefore, that there is no complete original authentic text of the Gospel *of* Jesus, which has been verified beyond any reasonable doubt, in existence today.

It therefore follows that what David Sox says of the four officially accepted Gospels applies equally to the *Gospel of Barnabas*:

> The differences, even the contradictions, between the Gospel accounts do not detract from the spiritual truths that they contain; if anything, they give us a better understanding of the world in which they were written. [11]

Nevertheless, there is still the necessity – wherever fundamental contradictions between the various accounts do exist – of having to decide which account is the most accurate and the nearest to the truth of the matter:

Was Jesus a Prophet of God or a 'son' of God? Was it Jesus or Judas, or someone else, who was crucified? Did Jesus tell his disciples that there would be a Prophet who would come after him who would be called Muhammad, may the blessings and peace of God be on all the Prophets, and are the references to the Paraclete in John's Gospel in fact references to him?

And the answers to these questions can only be sensed if the reader does indeed understand the world in which they were written – and accordingly the nature of the disagreement that clearly existed between the two groups of Christians whom Cardinal Daniélou termed the Judeo-Christians and the Pauline Christians, between those who sincerely followed the example of Jesus and those who followed Paul, putting words into the mouth of Jesus that he, peace be on him, never himself uttered, and granting him a divine status which he neither claimed nor possessed.

Even though none of the contents of either the *New Testament* or the *Gospel of Barnabas* are capable of being fully authenticated; and even though it is impossible to establish exactly what has been altered, or added, or removed, or allowed to remain intact; and whether or not the authors of the officially accepted Gospels, each with such a differing background, derived their knowledge from the same source or not; and if they did, then whether or not that source was in fact *The Gospel of Barnabas*, about Barnabas the commandment is:

If he comes unto you, receive him.
(*Epistle to the Colossians 4: 10*).

o   o   o   o   o

Chapter Six

The Shepherd
of
Hermas

It has been established that *The Shepherd* was a book written by
Hermas between 88 and 97 AD at Patmos, near Ephesus. Like the
Gospel of Barnabas, it affirmed the Divine Unity, and it was for this
reason that concerted efforts were made to destroy it, once the doctrine of Trinity had become firmly rooted in the established Pauline
Church. It was one of the books which was banned as a result of
the decisions made by the Council of Nicea in 325 AD.

It appears that Hermas wrote *The Shepherd* at about the same
time that John was writing his Gospel, although some people think
that *The Shepherd* was written before this. However, there is no difference of opinion as regards the fact that Hermas had not read or
seen any of the four Gospels included in the *New Testament*. Some
believe that *The Shepherd* was inspired by the *Gospel according to the
Hebrews*, an earlier Gospel which no longer exists, but this is not
supported by the account given by Hermas himself of how the book
came to be written.

Up until the Council of Nicea, the book was accepted and widely
used by the early followers of Jesus, peace be on him and them,
who regarded Hermas as a prophet. Towards the end of the second century AD, *The Shepherd* was accepted as part of the *New Testament* by Clement of Alexandria. Origen (185-254 AD) also accepted
it as a revealed book, and it was placed, along with the *Epistle of
Barnabas*, at the end of the *Codex Sinaiticus* which, as we have already seen, dates from about the late 4th or 5th century AD.
Tertullian (160-220 AD) at first accepted it, but later repudiated it
when he became a Montanist. Iranaeus (130-200 AD) accepted it as
a Scripture. Eusebius of Caesaria rejected it, but Athanasius accepted it, in 367 AD, as being suitable for the private reading of
new converts. Manichaeus, a Christian from Persia, took it far into
the East. Dante was also definitely influenced by the book.

Thus, *The Shepherd* was a book which obviously could not be ignored and which was accepted as a revealed book by the majority of early Christian thinkers and lovers of God. It was written when the movement to 'Hellenise' the teachings of Jesus was in its infancy, and at a time when many of those who followed Jesus were still aware that Jesus had come to restore and expand the teaching which Moses had brought to the Jews. Like Jesus, they were practising Jews whose understanding of what they were doing was illuminated by the knowledge Jesus had brought. They still believed in and followed the writings of the *Old Testament*, and since *The Shepherd* affirmed what they already knew, they accepted Hermas's book into their body of Scriptures.

As we have already seen, with the teaching by some, notably Paul, that the laws of the Jews need not be followed by Christians, contradictions began to arise between the body of newly written Scriptures, which later became known as the 'New' Testament, and what accordingly came to be re-defined as the 'Old' Testament. However, the *Old Testament* was retained by the established Church in spite of these contradictions, since an outright rejection of the *Old Testament* would have been regarded by many of the people as a rejection of Jesus himself. Confusion was the inevitable result. In the attempt to accept and reject the *Old Testament* simultaneously, contradictions arose within the *New Testament* itself, since it had to be 'new' without openly rejecting the 'old'. But, in the early days of the Church, there was no real attempt to formally arrange the books and ensure that all the accounts and doctrines tallied with each other. The leaders of the first Christian communities were free to use their discretion and to refer to those Scriptures which they thought best contained the teachings of Jesus.

With the development, formulation and official acceptance in 325 AD of the doctrine of Trinity, such latitude was no longer acceptable to the established Pauline Church. As we have already seen, the four accepted Gospels were selected and all the other Scriptures written after Jesus's birth were banned. However, the leaders of the Pauline Church, who were not entirely satisfied with their doctrine of 'mysteries', which was now beginning to develop, and who recognised the validity of some of the banned books, wished to retain some of these books even though they directly contradicted the new doctrines of their Church. Accordingly books such as these were gathered together and their availability limited to the people in power in the Church. They became known as *The Apocrypha*, which means 'hidden from the people'.

When the contents of the *Bible* became more accessible to people, the books in the *Apocrypha* were then removed from the *Bible*, at a time when only very few people had copies of these books which were publicly being destroyed, along with those who were found in possession of them. This, as with the *Gospel of Barnabas*, was the fate of *The Shepherd* of Hermas. It was removed from the *New Testament*, and, since the first 'command' in it created confusion in the minds of those who were being asked to believe in the doctrine of the Trinity, attempts were made to destroy it completely.

These attempts proved unsuccessful. There are records of references being made to it, but no one in the West had had the opportunity of reading it for a long time. Then, suddenly, in 1922, a third century papyrus manuscript of the text came to light.

It was found that the Greek used by Hermas was a simple vernacular. The language could be understood by the common people and it is clear that the book was written for everyone and not just for an intellectual elite. His style was frank and informal and he possessed an originality of expression which made the book easy to read.

Hermas begins by telling of four visions he experienced, the last of which he calls a revelation since on this occasion an angel visited him dressed as a shepherd. The angel informed Hermas that he had been sent by the 'most reverend angel' (that is, the angel Gabriel), to live with Hermas for the rest of the days of his life.

The angel then ordered Hermas to write down all 'the Commands and the Parables.' Since these were dictated to him by the angel, who only related what he was told to say by the 'most reverend angel', *The Shepherd* was accepted as a revealed book by the earlier Christians.

The commands he was told to write down were these:

> 1.   First of all believe that God is One and that He created all things and organised them, and out of what did not exist made all things to be, and He contains all things but Alone is Himself uncontained. Trust Him therefore and fear Him, and, fearing Him, be self-controlled. Keep this command and you will cast away from yourself all wickedness, put on every virtue of uprightness, and you will live to God if you keep this commandment.

2.   Be sincere and simple minded. Speak evil of nobody and do not enjoy hearing anyone do so. Do right, and give generously.

3.   Love truth.

4.   Observe purity. Be pure not only in action but in thinking.

5.   Be patient and understanding. The Lord dwells in patience, but the devil in ill temper.

6.   Trust what is right, and do not trust what is wrong. Uprightness has a straight and level way, but wrong doing a crooked one. There are two of angels with men, one of uprightness and one of wickedness.

7.   Fear the Lord and keep God's commands.

8.   Be self-controlled about what is wrong and do no wrong. But do not be self-controlled about what is right, but do what is right. Restrain yourself from all evil and follow the right path.

9.   Cast off doubt from yourself. Ask the Lord without doubting, and you will receive everything. God is not like men who hold grudges, but He is forgiving and feels pity for what He has made. So cleanse your heart of all the vanities of this world.

10.   Put sadness away from you, for it is the sister of doubt and bad temper.

11.   A man who consults a false prophet is an idolater and void of the truth.

(Hermas asked the angel how to distinguish a true prophet from a false one. The angel replied that in the first place the man who has the spirit that is from above is gentle, quiet, and humble. He abstains from all wickedness and the futile desires of the world ... (He) does not speak by himself ... but speaks when God wishes him to speak ... but all power belongs to the Lord. Whereas a false prophet exalts himself and wants to have a front seat. He is bold, shameless, and talkative, lives in great luxury and accepts pay for his prophesying. Can a divine spirit accept pay for prophesying? The false prophet avoids upright men and attaches himself to those who are doubtful and vain; and he says everything to them falsely in line with their desires. An empty vessel put among empty ones does not break, but they harmonise with one another. Take a stone and throw it up to heaven; see if you can reach it. Earthly things are impotent and weak. On the other hand, take the power that comes from above. Hail is a very small grain, yet when it falls on a man's head what pain it causes! Or again, take a drop of water which falls on the ground from the roof and makes a hole in the stone. So the Divine Power that comes from above is Mighty.)

12. Cast off from yourself every evil desire and clothe yourself in good and holy desires. God created the world for man's sake and made his whole creation subject to man, and gave him complete authority to have dominion over all things under heaven. A man who has the Lord in his heart is able to master all things. Behave as a slave of God. The devil cannot get control of the slaves of God. The devil can wrestle with them, but he cannot throw them. [1]

As we have already seen, once Paulinian Christianity had separated itself from Unitarian Christianity and from its Judaic roots, it developed into its own peculiar religion, Trinitarian Christianity, which then continued to evolve along the lines which had, perhaps unwittingly, been laid for it by Paul. As time passed, the various forms of Trinitarian Christianity which developed in Europe turned out to be very different to the Unitarian Christianity which was being practised in the Holy Land and North Africa.

o   o   o   o   o

Chapter Seven

Trinitarian Christianity
in
Europe

After the decisions which were reached at the Councils of Nicea in 325 AD and of Constantinople in 381 AD had paved the way for the 'final' formulation and ratification of the doctrine of Trinity – a doctrine which even Paul himself had not expounded back in the 1st century AD – the doctrinal evolution and transition from Pauline to Trinitarian Christianity proceeded in leaps and bounds, especially in the Western Roman Empire.

One of the main intellectual stumbling blocks for the new doctrine's main exponents, however, was what had always been the impossible task of explaining and reconciling in one person both the human and the divine aspects which were logically required as soon as Jesus came to be regarded not only as a man but also as a 'son' of God. This reconciliation of opposites could only ever be achieved by flatly stating that there was no contradiction and by then accepting the doctrine as an act of unconditional and uncritical blind faith. This was not always intellectually satisfying, and was sometimes interpreted as in fact being an act of surrender and an acknowledgement of defeat. Whenever anyone tried to rationally explain why or how there was no contradiction, however, they were often eventually driven to conclude that Jesus must be one or the other but that he could not be both – which was always the point at which the Unitarians would gleefully point out that if he was not one, then he must be the other, and that if he had indeed possessed all the attributes of a mortal human being, then Jesus could not possibly have been God as well.

One of the important figures in the history of early Christianity in the context of this debate is that of Pope Honorius. A contemporary of the Prophet Muhammad, may the peace and blessings of

God be on him, Pope Honorius was aware of the rising tide of Islam, whose tenets very much resembled those of Arius. The mutual killing of Christians by each other was still fresh in his memory, and perhaps he thought that what he had heard about Islam might be applied in healing the differences between the various Christian sects. In his letters he began to support the doctrine of 'one mind' within the doctrine of Trinity. He argued that if God had three independent minds, the result would be chaos. This logical and reasonable conclusion pointed to the belief in the existence of One God.

The Council of Chalcedon in 451 AD had already ruled – in attempting to reconcile the impossible contradiction that if Jesus had been a man as well as being God, then this meant that he must have had two natures, one human, the other Divine – that Christ's natures were indivisible. This decision may well have influenced Honorius in concluding that there was a single will in Christ. He therefore argued that Christ took to himself a human nature free from the curse of original sin. According to this view, Christ therefore had human will. Thus, even at this stage, belief in One God was being indirectly affirmed within Pauline Christianity.

That this kind of controversy had arisen at all – for it is certainly never mentioned in any of the Gospels – is an indication of the degree to which Paul's innovations and arguments had taken over and confused people's minds.

Pope Honorius died in October 638 AD. In the same year, the Emperor Heraclius – who had already refused the Prophet Muhammad's invitation to embrace Islam – officially accepted the doctrine of Honorius and issued an order that, 'All the Emperor's subjects are to confess the one will of Jesus.' [1] The Synod of Constantinople which also took place in 638 AD supported the doctrine as 'truly agreeing with Apostolic preaching.' [2]

The doctrine of Honorius was not officially challenged for about half a century. In 680 AD, however, forty-two years after his death, yet another Council was held in Constantinople and Pope Honorius was officially anathematised, since he 'did not extinguish the flame of heretical teaching in its first beginning but fostered it by negligence,' and therefore, 'allowed the immaculate faith to be stained.' [3]

This decision, whereby a Pope was denounced by his successor with the support of the Church, is unique in the history of the Papacy, especially as regards the doctrine of papal infallibility, since it seems to indicate that, at least at this stage, some Popes were less infallible than others!

In fact this decision illustrates how the boundaries of what constituted papal infallibility were only gradually defined over a period of time until they had been sufficiently formulated to be officially accepted as being immutable and certain because, like 'Gospel Truth', they had reached a stage where it could be plausibly argued that they had been determined not by man, but by God.

The Pauline Church, or rather, the Roman Catholic Church, as it came to be known, gradually grew in size and power. This was largely due to its associations with the Roman Emperors. The more it compromised itself with those in authority, the more identified it became with them. During the eight centuries which followed the first Council of Nicea, the Roman Catholic Church became firmly established, with her headquarters not in Jerusalem, but in Rome – where she acquired vast amounts of land and property both in and around this city. These were known as the 'Gift of Constantine'.

It soon became very dangerous for anyone to differ from the Roman Catholic Church, which came to have the support of the imperial army, as well as its own power. After 325 AD, millions of Christians were killed for not subscribing to the doctrines of the Catholic Church. These were indeed dark ages for those who wished or professed to follow Jesus, and few people in Europe dared to openly affirm the Unity of God.

While the Catholic Church in Europe was busy eliminating any dissenters, who were branded as 'heretics', the Muslims began to make themselves known on the periphery of the Christian world. Nearly all of the Unitarian followers of Jesus in the Holy Land and in North Africa recognised Islam as a further message from their Lord, which directly followed, confirmed and superseded the guidance by which they had been living. They naturally became Muslims – which is why there are so very few Unitarian Christians in the Middle East and North Africa today. Thus from about the middle of the 8th century AD onwards, only the Paulinian version of 'Christianity', which was practised mainly in Europe, remained.

The leaders at the Vatican must have seen the marked similarity between the teachings of Islam and the Unitarianism preached by Arius. Both believed in One God. Both accepted Jesus as a Prophet who, nevertheless, was still a man. Both believed in the Virgin Mary and in the immaculate conception of Jesus. Both accepted the Holy Spirit. Both rejected the divinity which had been attributed to Jesus. It is hardly surprising that the hatred which the Roman Catholic Church had directed at the Unitarian Arians for centuries was now turned against the Muslims as well.

When viewed from this perspective, the mediaeval Crusades – as indeed is also the case with the more modern Crusades being waged in the Balkans today – cease to be an isolated phenomenon of Church history, and become an extension of the massacre of the Arians and the Donatists by the early Pauline Church.

It is interesting to note in passing that it was as Islam was spreading up from Arabia, up through the Holy Land and into Syria and Turkey – at about the time when a tribe living in the Caucasus who were descended from Gog and Magog, the tribe of the Khazars, embraced Judaism for reasons of political expediency – that the first major division within the Trinitarian church occurred, between the Roman Catholic Church and what became known as the Greek Orthodox Church. This split concerned the issue of image worship:

During the early years of the history of Christianity, when the religion was still not very far removed from its origin and source – Jesus, peace be on him – the use of images for whatever reason had been avoided by all Christians, by both the true followers of Jesus and by the followers of Paul, in compliance with the second commandment of the *Old Testament* which clearly forbids making a representation of any living thing:

> Thou shalt not make unto thee any graven image, or any likeness of any thing that is in heaven above, or that is in the earth below, or that is in the water under the earth; thou shalt not bow down thyself to them, nor serve them: for I the Lord thy God am a jealous God, visiting the iniquity of the fathers upon the children unto the third and fourth generation of them that hate Me; and showing mercy unto thousands of them that love Me, and keep My commandments. (*Exodus 20: 4-6*).

Once the teachings of Paul had taken hold in Europe, however, the veneration and subsequently the adoration of images and relics increasingly crept into the practices and rites of the Trinitarian Church, until by the 7th century AD this practice was firmly established, especially in the Western Roman Empire.

There was, however, yet another revival of Unitarianism in the Eastern Byzantine Empire, centred in and around Constantinople, and culminating in the campaign of Leo the Iconoclast who literally set about breaking up images and idols in earnest in 726 AD. Pope Gregory II, fearing that Leo's puritanical zeal might spread to Italy, warned him of dire consequences if he did not stop smashing idols. Leo ignored his threats and subsequently invaded Italy, determined to purify the Western as well as the Eastern Church. Leo and his army were, however, heavily defeated by the Roman Catholic troops near Ravenna.

After this confrontation, the two Churches never re-united – in spite of the fact that they both subscribed to basically the same Paulinian and Trinitarian doctrines – especially after Leo's son, Constantine the Adoptionist, called the seventh Synod of Constantinople, in 774 AD, which duly declared that image worship was a corruption of Christianity and a renewal of paganism and that accordingly all images should be destroyed.

There was, predictably, a backlash against this attempt to eradicate and eliminate the use of images which had been so easily and so comfortably accommodated into European Christianity, and it comes as no surprise to learn that in 787 AD the second Council of Nicea re-endorsed the permissibility of using images. This ruling finally resulted, after many years, in the widespread use again of images not only by the Greek Orthodox Church, but also by what became known as the Russian Orthodox Church. By the time that both the Eastern and Western Trinitarian Churches were united once more in this practice of permitting and using images, however, they had drifted so far apart in other respects – especially as regards their respective ruling hierarchies – that it would have been impossible for them ever to re-unite again under a single head of 'the Christian Church'.

It is in the light of this split between the Eastern and the Western Churches that the sack of Constantinople during the fourth Crusade, in 1203 AD, by a Roman Catholic army – which had ostensibly set out to 'liberate' Jerusalem from the Muslims – can be understood. Although the majority of the inhabitants of Constantinople at the time were Trinitarian Christians, and accordingly subscribed to the same basic religious doctrines as the majority of the members of the army which was attacking them, the two 'sides' were nevertheless far enough apart ideologically for one to be able to regard the other as 'the enemy'.

Indeed it was at this stage in the evolution of European Christianity – when the supremacy of the Roman Catholic Church was being threatened not only by the Byzantine Church to the East, but also by the rapidly expanding Muslim Empire to the South; and now that its doctrines and practices were obviously more deeply rooted in the culture and philosophies of Europe than in the way of life and teachings of Jesus and his followers from among the twelve tribes of the Tribe of Israel; and when almost inexplicably Unitarian Christians kept on surfacing and appearing throughout Europe and especially in France – that the Roman Catholic Church established the Mediaeval Inquisition, in the early 13th century AD, in order to put its house in order by tirelessly eliminating corruption from among its priesthood, and by relentlessly rooting out 'heretics' from among its congregations, in a demonstration of such heartless 'compassion' and ruthless 'mercy' that has probably never been equalled since.

It is perhaps not surprising that the Mediaeval Inquisition concentrated more on the congregations than on the priesthood in its efforts to investigate and eliminate any traces of 'deviation' from the now firmly, albeit erroneously, established doctrines of the Trinitarian Church. The exact record of how many people were murdered in the name of Jesus by this notorious institution of mediaeval gangsters is not known, but certainly a great number suffered and perished at their hands, especially after the Mediaeval Inquisition had developed both its techniques of torture and its tortuous polemics in its extended role as the Spanish Inquisition – which was used as part of the elaborate and brutal mechanism whereby all Jews, Unitarian Christians and Muslims living in the Iberian peninsula were systematically hunted down and either killed or forced to flee for their lives during the period between the 13th and 16th centuries AD.

Having been tested and perfected in Europe, the Trinitarian Inquisition was then exported to the 'New World', where hundreds of thousands of the indigenous inhabitants of the Americas and the West Indies were either wiped out or enslaved for the greater glory of God, and lots of gold.

This extreme expression of tyranny and greed, which so obviously contradicted the example of compassion and generosity which had been demonstrated by Jesus, was feared but not accepted by many of Europe's Trinitarian Christians, especially once most of the Jews, Unitarian Christians and Muslims in Europe had been eliminated for the time being – for this inevitably meant that the Inquisitors were obliged to turn on their fellow Christians, even if it meant having to accuse them of practising witchcraft and magic, in order to sustain and finance the lifestyle to which they had all become accustomed.

The inevitable result of all this was a growing feeling of resentment and protest which resulted in several movements – including those of Luther and Calvin – during the 15th and 16th centuries AD, in what is generally known as 'the Reformation'.

Although the Inquisition eventually fell into decline and was finally disbanded, on the 15th of July 1834, the overall result of the Reformation movement – and of the inevitable counter-Reformation movement which was triggered off within the Roman Catholic Church – was merely the institution of yet more Trinitarian Church hierarchies, accompanied by a deeper entrenchment of all the fundamental Trinitarian doctrines.

Thus with the event of the Reformation, and the subsequent establishment of various Protestant Churches, which like the Roman Catholic Church also eventually became very powerful, the doctrine of Trinity became even more firmly established, even though the Protestants and the Roman Catholics remained bitterly opposed to each other over other issues such as who should be the head of the Trinitarian Church, and what about the validity of the document which authorised the 'Gift of Constantine' – whereby, it will be remembered, the Roman Catholic Church had acquired so much property in and around Rome. (Some scholars took a closer look at the deed and discovered that it was a forgery. Since then, the Vatican has ceased to boast of it.)

The famous Thirty Years War which took place in the 17th century AD (1618-1648) between the Protestants and the Catholics was yet another indication that these Churches' battles were not really fought with the intention of establishing the true guidance of Jesus in the land. Like the Pauline Church's aggression towards the followers of Arius and Donatus, and later the Muslims, this war clearly demonstrated that what the various Church hierarchies wanted was power. Indeed ever since its inception, the Pauline Trinitarian Church had only fought in order to establish and consolidate its own existence as an institution, and not in order to spread what Jesus had taught.

Although it was always claimed by the various Reformist movements, from the 15 century AD onwards, that their desire was to return to the original teachings of Jesus, these original teachings had in fact by then already long been lost. All Christians, whatever their denomination and however sincere, were by then stuck with Scriptures which were neither complete, nor accurate, nor reliable, and accordingly they were stuck with the doctrines which stemmed from them and came with them.

Thus although all the new Reformist movements challenged the authority of the Pope and the behaviour of the established priesthood, they never even dreamed of challenging the validity of the doctrines of the 'New' Covenant, and of the Trinity, and of Original Sin, and of the Atonement and Redemption of Sins – none of which had been preached by Jesus, and all of which depended for their efficacy on an alleged crucifixion and resurrection that had never actually taken place.

When one considers the amount of effort and sacrifice and misplaced inspiration that has gone into the 'sacred' art and music that have been utilised to perpetuate these myths, it is difficult to know whether to laugh or weep!

Perhaps the most honest of the various re-formers was King Henry VIII of England who, after being given the title of 'Defender of the Faith' by the Pope in 1521 – presumably the Roman Catholic faith – because he had opposed the ideas of the mainstream Reformers, then promptly separated from the Church of Rome and made himself the head of the new 'Church of England'. This was so that he could divorce Catherine of Aragon, remarry and divorce thereafter as he pleased, and help himself to the wealth of the Church whenever he wanted.

King Henry VIII never claimed to be following the original teachings of Jesus, peace be on him, and neither did he try to disguise his reasons or motives which were always clear. He even went so far as to legalise usury, a parasitical practice which had always been forbidden by all of the Prophets including Moses, Jesus and Muhammad, may the blessings and peace of God be on all of them.

It is therefore more than a little ironic that ever since that time, the monarchs of England have continued to retain the title of 'Defender of the Faith' – which was originally conferred on King Henry VIII by the Roman Catholic Pope – while remaining legally obliged by English statute not to be or to marry a Roman Catholic!

It is also perhaps only right that the monarchs of England have now finally agreed to pay income tax – much of which is now needed to service the national debt which was first instituted by King William of Orange, and which as a result of the compound interest legalised by King Henry VIII has continued to spiral upwards in ever increasing circles ever since!

It is also interesting to note that it was during the period of the Reformation that the European Christians – both Trinitarian and Unitarian, and both Roman Catholic and Protestant – began to expand out of Europe and re-form on foreign soil and in the midst of different cultures. They could not go very far overland, for their way both to the East and to the South was blocked by the Muslims, and so they went by sea, converting as many people as they could as and wherever they went.

As Islam continued to expand, with many of the Unitarian Christians who encountered it becoming Muslims, a grand strategy – which was to be implemented principally by the Trinitarian Christians and financed primarily by the European Jews (many of whom were descended from the Khazar Jews and accordingly, like the European Christians, no longer descended from the twelve tribes of the Tribe of Israel) – was formulated to attack the Muslims both from the East and the West in a global pincer movement.

It was hoped that it would be possible to join forces with a legendary Indian Christian king and, with his aid, to conquer the whole world. In his efforts to reach India the long way round, Columbus 'discovered' America, approximately two centuries after Muslims from West Africa had already settled there, while Vasco da Gama 'discovered' a new sea route to India via the Cape of Good Hope. Both of these discoveries turned out to be very profitable ventures financially. The European Christians did not discover their legendary king, nor did they eliminate Islam, but along with the European Jews they colonised much of the world – including eventually Palestine, which the European Khazar Jews successfully claimed as their long lost 'homeland' even though they were 'turkic' and not 'semitic' and in fact originated from the Caucasus – and as a result their respective leaders and merchants and bankers became very wealthy.

Thus the conflict between the Roman Catholics and the Protestants – and, from time to time, whenever a fresh Unitarian Christian movement emerged, the conflict between the Trinitarians and the Unitarians – continued to be played out, only now on a world stage, with each 'side' united in their opposition to and dependence on the financial services of the European Jews, and with each 'side' united in their attempts to subvert the Muslims, and with each 'side' still involved in an ideological war for both political as well as doctrinal supremacy.

By the beginning of the 19th century AD, any meaningful connection between the Christians (whether Trinitarian or Unitarian) and the original followers of Jesus – who were all members of the twelve tribes of the Tribe of Israel – had long been lost; the doctrinal controversies and debates which had characterised the early Christian Councils and Synods had all been simplified and decided one way or the other; and any serious opposition to Trinitarian Christianity in Europe had been overcome.

Despite the tremendous power which came to be wielded by the Trinitarian Roman Catholic and Protestant Churches in Europe, however, they could not quite stamp out belief in the Divine Unity amongst those who professed to be Christians – and whether it became known as Arianism or Socianism or Unitarianism, belief in the Divine Unity – in One God – has survived within the Christian movement right up to the present day, as the following short biographies of some of its most outspoken adherents demonstrate.

O   O   O   O   O

Chapter Eight

Later Unitarians in Christianity

Whereas the early Unitarians in the history of Christianity tended to come from the Holy Land and North Africa and were Unitarians because they had access to the original teachings of Jesus, peace be on him, the later Unitarians tended to come from Europe – and then later from America and the rest of the colonised world as well – and became Unitarians largely as a result of the exercise of common sense and rational thought.

In other words, whereas the early Unitarians were in a position to benefit from direct transmission of both behaviour and knowledge, the later Unitarians no longer had access to this kind of wisdom, but were nevertheless still in a position to work things out for themselves – sometimes because of and sometimes in spite of what limited written records there still were in existence, and often in spite of the misconception shared with the Trinitarians that Jesus was crucified and then rose from the dead.

The later Unitarians no longer had access to the original teachings of Jesus in their entirety, nor to his way of life, both of which had long been lost to posterity and in any case superseded by the advent of Islam, but when they looked at what had become of the Trinitarian Church and its doctrines, then they realised that something was seriously amiss and, after using their intellects to critically appraise the main doctrines and practices of the Trinitarians – neither of which derived from Jesus – they at least arrived at an intellectual recognition of the Divine Unity, especially once they had the good fortune and the courage to realise and appreciate that much of the dogma and religious practices which had been evolved by the European Trinitarian Christians, during the course of many centuries, not only had not come from Jesus in the first place, but also simply did not make any sense anyway.

158 Jesus, Prophet of Islam

This intellectual recognition of the Divine Unity which Christian Unitarians experienced from time to time – of the underlying unity of everything in existence and therefore of the One Who has brought everything that exists into existence – could never have the same depth and quality as the understanding of the Divine Unity which is granted by God to those who follow the Prophetic way of life and pattern of worship which has been constantly embodied and taught by all of the Prophets from Adam to Muhammad – and including Abraham, Moses and Jesus – may the blessings and peace of God be on all of them, but nevertheless this recognition was clearly a gift to them from their Creator.

Knowledge of God appears in many ways, and everyone knows something that nobody else knows, and only God knows everything!

As far as the original followers of Jesus are concerned, access to the Prophetic way of life through Jesus had been lost by the end of the 7th century AD, for with the coming of the Prophet Muhammad, may God bless him and grant him peace – who died in 632 AD after delivering his message and establishing the way of Islam as a living social reality – the last of the relatively few Christians who still had access to the original teachings of Jesus, peace be on him, recognised the Prophet whose coming Jesus had foretold and embraced Islam.

From this point onwards – when Pope Honorius was still struggling to reconcile the impossible, poor man – the only way that anyone could actually follow the Prophetic way of life, and accordingly really understand the nature of the Divine Unity, was by accepting Islam and following the way of Muhammad – an option which, as we shall see, many Unitarian Christians in fact exercised as soon as they realised that this option did exist and was available, and in spite of all the concerted attempts by the Trinitarian Christians to misrepresent Islam and prevent this from happening.

The short biographies which follow are simply a small selection of some of the more well-known later Unitarians who have surfaced from time to time in the history of Christianity, both from Europe and America. They do not purport to represent either a detailed or a comprehensive account of the Unitarian movement within European Christianity. The excerpts which are quoted from their writings may at times appear to be somewhat mind-bound, but given the philosophical elements which were gradually and continually introduced into Christianity during those long centuries in which this mutant religion was subjected to 'European thought', this tendency was as inevitable as the more emotional forms of Christianity which have appeared as a reaction to this tradition during the present century: 'Forget all the arguments – Jesus loves you!'

It must nevertheless be remembered, as we travel back in time once more, that although born-again Christians in the twentieth century can twang their guitars and clap their hands as they sing 'Jesus loves you,' (while Trinitarian Serb Christians further east carve crosses into the bodies of the Muslim prisoners whom they are about to slaughter because they refuse to be forcibly baptised) – the other side of the coin is never very far away, and everything lies in its opposite – in the sixteenth century any Christian in Europe who simply wrote or publicly announced, 'I believe God is One,' faced impoverishment, torture and death:

Michael Servetus (1511-1553)

Michael Servetus was born in Villanueva in Spain in 1511. He was the son of a local judge. He lived at a time when there was unrest in the established Church, and in a period when everyone was questioning the nature of Christianity. In 1517, when Servetus was six years old, Martin Luther started his revolt against the Roman Catholic Church. This resulted in his being excommunicated, and he became a leader of the new reformed 'protestant' religion. This movement, known today as the Reformation, spread like wild fire, and even those who did not agree with Luther were forced to take notice of him. As well as this conflict, there was another closer to home: although the Muslims and the Christians in Spain had enjoyed better relations in the past, the results of the Crusades in the East caused the Christians to direct their anger against the Muslims in Spain. The organisation known as the Spanish Inquisition set about converting all people who were not Christians to Roman Catholicism. Any laxity in observing the outward rites of the Church resulted in severe punishment, if not death.

As he grew older and more informed, the young Servetus was appalled by the shedding of so much blood. There was a large number of Muslims and some Jews in the country – although by now most of the Jews had either been killed or driven out of both

Spain and Portugal – and they were spared the sword only if they publicly confessed their faith to be that of the Roman Catholics, publicly affirmed the formula of the Trinity, submitted to forced baptism, and lived thereafter as Paulinian Trinitarian Christians.

On examining the *Bible* more closely, Servetus found that the doctrine of Trinity was nowhere a part of its teaching. He further discovered that the *Bible* did not always support what was being taught or practised by the representatives of the established Church. Servetus was only twenty years old when he decided to tell the world the truth as he had found it, for it followed from his discoveries that if the Christians accepted that there is only One God, then all cause for strife between the Christians and the Muslims would be ended, and both communities could live together in peace.

This sensitive but inexperienced youth, his imagination fired with enthusiasm, felt that this end would most easily be achieved with the help of the leaders of the Reformation, who had, after all, already broken away from the Roman Catholic Church. The new Protestant Churches would become Unitarian, he thought, and with their help the Christians, the Muslims and the Jews would be able to live together in peace. A world of toleration would then become possible, based on One God, the 'Father' of the family of mankind.

Servetus was too young to realise that the minds of the leaders of the Reformation were still trapped in the same false metaphysics as those of the Roman Catholics. He was to find that both Luther and Calvin would have nothing to do with his belief in the Unity of God. They feared that the Reformation would go too far. A number of the ceremonies practised by the Catholic Church had been abolished, and they had rejected the authority of the Pope, but they were afraid to rediscover the original teaching of Jesus, since this would have added to their difficulties and entailed a diminishing of their own power and reputation. Perhaps they were unaware of just how far the practices of the Roman Catholics had deviated from the life which Jesus lived. Certainly, they took great pains to contain the reformed religion within the framework of Catholic orthodoxy. Their quarrel was not so much with the theology of Rome as with its organisation, and particularly over the question as to who should rule the Church.

The beliefs of Servetus posed a threat to both organisations, the old and the new, because their authority depended on the same Paulinian sources – and so, ironically, the appeal of Servetus to the Reformists only caused them to join forces with the Roman Catholics in order to protect their common interest, although this was probably not how they perceived their respective reactions to the conclusions of Servetus at the time. None of this was fully grasped by the young Servetus.

Servetus had every hope in the leaders of the Reformation, for he was convinced that Roman Catholicism was not the religion of Jesus. His studies had shattered his belief in the doctrine of Trinity and resulted in his believing that there was only One God and that Jesus was one of His Prophets. His convictions were strengthened after he witnessed the coronation of Charles V of Spain by the Pope.

In 1527 AD, Charles V had invaded and sacked Rome. At first, he had imprisoned the Pope, but then realised the expediency of having the Pope as an ally. A captive Pope would hardly influence the people in the way he wanted, so he restored some measure of freedom to him. To demonstrate the good terms they were now on, Charles V decided to have a coronation at the hands of the Pope. Strictly speaking, this was not necessary. It was like having a church wedding after a civil ceremony. The king's predecessors – who did not wish to be subject to the authority of the Church in any way – had discontinued this practice, but Charles V felt that he was now powerful enough, and the Pope weak enough, for him to revive it.

The coronation ceremony was not held in Rome, but in Bologna, since, according to one of the doctrines of the Church, 'where the Pope is, there is Rome.' Servetus witnessed the gorgeous spectacle and it filled him with revulsion for the Catholic Church. When describing the event, he wrote:

> With these very eyes I saw him (the Pope) borne with pomp on the shoulders of princes, making with his hand the sign of the cross, and adored in the open streets by all the people kneeling to such a point that those who were able to kiss his feet or slippers counted themselves more fortunate than the rest and declared that they had obtained many indulgences, and that on this account the infernal pains would be remitted for many years. Oh vilest of all beasts, most brazen of harlots! [1]

Thus Servetus's hopes were directed towards the leaders of the Reformation. He felt sure that if he could bring the error of the doctrine of Trinity to their notice, then they would abandon their belief in this dogma. This misconception was to cost him his life.

Servetus left Spain and resided in Toulouse where he studied medicine and eventually took his doctor's degree in 1534. In the years that followed, he soon became a working physician, but, during all this time, his interest was primarily directed towards re-establishing pure Christianity. He did not stay long at any one place, but travelled far and wide in search of people who were open-minded enough to listen to what he was sure was the true Christianity as taught by Jesus.

Servetus eventually went to Basle to meet the then famous Oeclompadius, who was one of the leaders of the Reformation. He had several meetings with him and the talk mainly centred on the two natures of Christ. Servetus denied the belief that Jesus had existed before the creation of the world. He pointed out that the Jewish Prophets had always referred to the 'Messiah' in the future tense. However, he found that his views were not acceptable to the Protestants in Switzerland, and so he left Basle in 1530.

This rejection was a great shock to Servetus, since he had hoped that, unlike Catholic France, the Protestants would give a patient ear to what he had to say about Jesus and his teaching. He went to Strasbourg only to find that he could not earn a living there. Due to his ignorance of German, he was unable to practice medicine, and so he was forced to go to Lyons.

Servetus also conducted a lengthy correspondence with Calvin throughout this period after his departure from Spain, but without any favourable response from Calvin, who was not altogether interested in trying to embody the teaching of Jesus, but who did want to remain leader of his movement.

Since all his attempts to influence people by personal contact had failed, Servetus printed his views in a book which he called *The Errors of Trinity*. It was published in 1531. In the same year, he published another book called *Two Dialogues on Trinity*. The two books took the whole of Europe by storm. No one had ever written such a daring book within living memory. The result was that the Church hounded Servetus from one place to another. Servetus was forced to change his name, but not his views. From 1532 onwards, up until his death, he lived under an assumed name.

Servetus still appeared to have a childlike faith in Calvin, who, after reading the two books, developed a deep dislike for this presumptuous young man who dared teach him theology. Servetus continued to write to Calvin and the leader's anger only increased when he found that Servetus still refused to accept his views. The leaders of the Protestant movement feared that it might suffer a set-back if the views of this young enthusiast became known to the people. The reformers also feared that persecution by the Catholic Church might increase if Protestant doctrine deviated too far from the Roman Catholic norm.

Thus, Servetus, instead of converting the Protestants to his views, forced them to embrace the dogma of Trinity even more zealously. Luther, for instance, publicly condemned him in 1539.

Throughout this time, Servetus continued to practice as a doctor, and he became a very popular physician. In spite of the fact that a doctor's profession is very time-consuming, Servetus still found time to supervise the printing of a *Bible*. It was published in 1540. Servetus wrote a preface to it in which he questioned whether a text of Scripture could have more than one meaning. Calvin wrote and replied in the affirmative, but Servetus disagreed with him. Servetus stated that he was following the views held by the early apostles who belonged to the Antiochene school of Christianity. Today the Calvinist Church accepts the very principle of interpretation which Calvin alleged was one of the greatest offences against orthodoxy committed by Servetus.

It is refreshing to discover that at the height of this bitter controversy, Servetus found refuge and peace in the house of his old friend, Peter Palmier, who at that time was the Roman Catholic Archbishop of Vienna. He lived there for thirteen years, enjoying the freedom to practice medicine, and became quite renowned as a physician. He was one of the first people in Europe to write about the principle of the circulation of the blood. He also wrote a book on geography.

In spite of his literary attainments, the issues facing Christianity always held the centre of his attention. Servetus continued to write to Calvin, still hoping to win him over to his views, but Calvin firmly rejected the beliefs expressed in his letters. Servetus refused to accept the *obiter dicta* of Calvin. Calvin, who was at that time recognised as the foremost thinker of the Protestant religion, felt he was justified in expressing annoyance with Servetus for daring to challenge his rulings in matters of religion, but Servetus refused to accept Calvin as an indisputable authority. Calvin wrote back in anger and Servetus replied in turn with sarcasm. Servetus then wrote another book called *The Restoration of Christianity*, and sent an advance copy of the manuscript to Calvin. When the book was published, it was found to have seven chapters, the first and last of which were devoted entirely to the doctrines of Christianity. The fifth chapter contained copies of thirty letters which had passed between Servetus and Calvin. It exposed the fact that, whatever merits Calvin might have possessed, he lacked what is known as Christian meekness. The book resulted in Servetus being condemned yet again, both by the Catholic and Protestant Churches. They united in their efforts to have the book completely destroyed, and were so thorough that not more than two copies are known to exist today. A facsimile of the book was published in 1791, but copies of this book were also destroyed.

In a letter written in 1546, Calvin threatened Servetus, saying that if he ever came to Geneva he would not allow him to escape with his life. It appears that Servetus did not seem to believe him, but Calvin was as good as his word. When Servetus later came to Geneva and went to see him, still convinced that a meeting of minds was possible, Calvin had him arrested by the Roman Catholics and thrown into prison on a charge of heresy.

Servetus had become so popular as a physician that he succeeded in escaping from the prison with the help of some of his former patients. He decided to go to Naples. His route lay through the city of Geneva. He thought he had disguised himself sufficiently to escape detection, but he was wrong. While passing through the city, he was recognised and arrested once more. This time he did not escape. At his trial, he was found guilty of heresy. Some of the judgement ran as follows:

Servetus confesses that in his book he called believers in the Trinity, Trinitarians and Atheists. He called this Trinity a diabolical monster with three heads ... He called infant baptism an invention of the devil and sorcery ... This entails the murder and ruin of many souls. Moreover, he wrote a letter to one of the ministers in which, along with other and numerous blasphemies, he declared our evangelical religion to be without faith and without God, and that in place of God we have a three-headed Cerberus. Addressing Servetus, the Court says that you had neither shame nor horror of setting yourself against the Divine Majesty of the Holy Trinity, and so you have obstinately tried to infect the world with your stinking heretical poison ... For these and other reasons desiring to purge the Church of God of such infection and cut off the rotten member ... we now, in writing, give final sentence and condemn you, Michael Servetus, to be bound and taken to the Chapel and there attached to a stake and burned with your book to ashes. And so you shall finish your days and give example to others who would commit the like. [2]

On the 26th of October, 1553, Servetus was fastened to the trunk of a tree fixed in the earth, his feet just touching the ground. A crown of straw and leaves sprinkled over with brimstone was placed on his head. Bundles of wood intermingled with green oaken faggots still in leaf were piled around his legs. His body was then bound to the stake with an iron chain and a course twisted rope thrown around his neck. The wood was then lit. The fire tormented him, but did not burn him severely. Seeing this, a few onlookers felt compassion for him and added more fuel in order to end his misery. According to one eye-witness, Servetus was writhing for about two hours before he died. A copy of *The Errors of Trinity* had been tied to his waist before the wood was lit. It is said that the book was rescued by someone, and that the half-burnt book still exists.

Celsus relates that the constancy of Servetus in the midst of the fire induced many to go over to his beliefs. Calvin made it an express subject of complaint that there were so many people who cherished and revered his memory. As Castillo, a follower of Servetus, said: 'To burn a man is not to prove a doctrine.' [3] In later years, the people of Geneva were to remember him by erecting a statue, not to Calvin, but to the man he was responsible for burning alive. Cowper was moved to write these lines:

> They lived unknown
> Till persecution dragged them into fame
> And chased them up to heaven. Their ashes flew
> No marble tells us whither. With their names
> No bard embalms and sanctifies his song.
> And history so warm on meaner themes
> Is cold on this. [4]

Servetus's death was by no means an isolated incident. This kind of thing was happening throughout Europe at this time, as the following passage from Motley's *Rise of the Dutch Republic* indicates:

Upon the 15th of February 1568, a sentence of the Holy Office condemned all the inhabitants of the Netherlands to death as heretics. From this universal doom only a few persons, especially named, were excepted. A proclamation of King Philip II of Spain, dated ten days later, confirmed this decree of the Inquisition, and ordered it to be carried into instant execution ... Three millions of people, men, women and children, were sentenced to the scaffold in three lines. Under the new decree, the executions certainly did not slacken. Men in the highest and the humblest positions were daily and hourly dragged to the stake. Alva, in a single letter to Philip 11, cooly estimates the number of executions which were to take place immediately after the expiration of Holy Week at 'eight hundred heads.' [5]

A few excerpts from *The Errors of Trinity*, which cost Servetus his life, follow. Servetus writes:

The philosophers have invented a third separate being truly and really distinct from the other two, which they call the third Person, or the Holy Spirit, and thus they have contrived an imaginary Trinity, three beings in one nature. But in reality three Gods, or one threefold God, are foisted upon us under the pretence, and in the name of Unity ... For with them it is very easy, taking the words in their strict sense, for three beings to exist, which they say and yet strictly, simply, and really, so different or distinct yet one is born of another, and one is breathed out of the others, and yet all these three are shut up in one jar. Since I am unwilling to misuse the word Persons, I shall call them the first being, the second being, and the third being, for in the Scripture I find no other name for them ... Admitting therefore these three, which after their fashion they call Persons, they freely admit a plurality of beings, a plurality of entities, a plurality of Essences, a plurality of substances, and taking the word God strictly, they will have a plurality of Gods.

He continues:

If this is so, then why the Tritorites are blamed, who say that there are three Gods, for they also contrive three Gods or one threefold one. These threefold Gods of theirs form one composite substance. And although some will not use the word implying that the three have been put together, yet they do use a word that they are constituted together, and that God is constituted out of three beings. It is clear therefore that they are Tritorites and we have a threefold God. We have become Atheists, men without any God. For as soon as we try to think about God, we are turned aside to three phantoms, so that no kind of Unity remains in our conception. What else is being without God but being unable to think about God, when there is always present to our understanding a haunting kind of confusion of three beings, by which we are forever deluded into supposing that we are thinking about God ... They seem to be living in another world while they dream of such things for the kingdom of heaven knows none of this nonsense and it is in another way unknown to them, that Scripture speaks of the Holy Spirit.

He adds:

How much this tradition of the Trinity has alas, alas! been the laughing stock of Muhammedans only God knows. The Jews also shrink from giving adherence to this fancy of ours, and laugh at our foolishness about the Trinity, and on account of its blasphemies, they do not believe that this is the Messiah promised in their Law. And not only the Muhammedans and the Hebrews, but the very beasts of the field, would make fun of us, did they grasp our fantastic notion, for all the workers of the Lord bless the One God ... This most burning plague, therefore, was added and superimposed, as it were, on the new gods which have recently come, which our fathers did not worship. And this plague of philosophy was brought upon us by the Greeks, for they above all men are most given to philosophy; and we, hanging upon their lips, have become philosophers, and they never understood the passages of the Scriptures which they adduced with regard to this matter.

Servetus also stressed what he believed to be the true nature of Jesus:

> Some are scandalised at my calling Christ the Prophet, because they happen not themselves to apply to him the epithet, they fancy that all who do so are chargeable with Judaism and Mohametism, regardless of the fact that the Scriptures and ancient writers call him the Prophet. [6]

Michael Servetus was one of the most outspoken critics of the established Church of his time. It earned him the singular distinction of being burnt to death by the Catholics with the aid of the Protestants. He combined within himself all that was best in the Renaissance and the Reformation, and came near to fulfilling the ideal of his age which was to produce a 'universal man' with 'pansophic' knowledge. He was proficient in medicine, geography, Biblical scholarship and theology. The diversity of his learning gave Servetus a breadth of vision which was denied to men who were less educated than he. Perhaps the most significant part of his life was his clash with Calvin. It was certainly a personal conflict, but it was more than that: It was also a rejection of the Reformation which was only prepared to alter the form, but not the content of a decadent Church. This cost Servetus his life, but although he is dead, his belief in the Divine Unity still lives. He is still regarded by many as 'the founder of modern Unitarianism'.

O   O   O   O   O

Not everyone who shared the beliefs of Servetus also shared his fate, as is shown by the following letter written by Adam Neuser, who was his contemporary. It was addressed to the leader of the Muslims in Constantinople, Emperor Selim II. It is included in the *'Antiquities Palatinae'* which is now in the Archives at Heidelberg.

> 1, Adam Neuser, a Christian born in Germany and advanced to the dignity of Preacher to the people in Heidelberg, a city where the most learned men at this day in Germany are to be found, do fly for refuge to your Majesty with a profound submission conjuring you for the love of God and your Prophet, on whom be the peace of God, to receive me into the number of your

subjects and those of your people that believe in God. For by the grace of the Omnipotent God, I see, I know, and I believe with my whole heart that your Doctrine and your Religion are pure, clear, and acceptable to God. I am firmly persuaded that my Retreat from among the idolatrous Christians will engage many persons of Consideration to embrace your Belief and your Religion, especially since many of the most learned and most considerable amongst them are herein of the same sentiments with me as I shall inform your Majesty by word of mouth. As to what concerns myself I am certainly one of those of whom it is said in the thirteenth chapter of the Al Coran: The Christians show us more good will than the Jews; and when their Priests and Bishops, provided they are not imprudent and opinionated, understand the commandments which the Prophet of God gave, and thereby acknowledge the truth, they say with tears in their eyes, O God! We hope from our Hearts that since we believe the same things that the good people do, Thou wilt also make us enter into the communion: For why should not we believe in God and in Him who is manifested to us by the Truth?

Certainly, O Emperor! I am one of those that read the Al Coran with joy. I am one of those that desire to be of our People and I give testimony before God that the Doctrine of your Prophet, upon whom be the peace of God, is of undoubted Truth. For this reason I most humbly supplicate your Majesty for the love of God and of your Prophet to be graciously pleased to hear me and know after what manner the God of Mercy hath revealed this Truth to me.

But first of all your Majesty ought to be entirely persuaded that I have not recourse to your protection as some Christians are accustomed, who because of their crimes, thefts, murders, or adulteries, cannot live with safety among the people of their own Religion. For I had resolved above a year ago to fly for Refuge to you, and was advanced in my way as far as Presburg but not understanding the Hungarian language I could go no further and against my will was constrained to return to my country which I should not have ventured to do if I had fled for any crime. Besides nothing constrains me to embrace your Religion, for who could force me to it being unknown to our people, and at so great a distance from them?

So your Majesty ought not to place me in the number of those Christians who being conquered and made prisoners by your subjects embrace your Religion but not with good will and who so soon as they find occasion run away and renounce the true faith. Wherefore I again supplicate your Majesty to lend attention to what I am going to say and to be informed of the true course of my retreat to your Dominion.

Being promoted to the dignity of Preacher in the famous University of Heidelberg by the Elector Palatine who next to the Emperor is the most powerful prince in Germany, I began to weigh maturely within myself the divers dissensions and divisions of our Christian religion: for so many persons as there are amongst us there are so many opinions and sentiments. I began with abstracting from all the Doctors and Interpreters of the Scriptures who have wrote and taught since the days of the Prophet Jesus Christ. I tied myself only to the commandments of Moses and to the Gospel. Then I called upon God inwardly with a most religious application and prayed Him to show me the right way that I may not be in the danger to mislead myself and my hearers. Then it pleased God to reveal to me the 'Articles of the Invocation of the One Only God', upon which Article I composed a book in which I prove that the Doctrine of Jesus Christ did not consist in asserting that he was himself a God as the Christians falsely allege: but that there is only One God who has no son consubstantial with Him. I dedicated this book to your Majesty and I am very sure that the most able men amongst the Christians are not capable of refuting it. And wherefore indeed should I associate to God another god like unto Him? Moses had forbid it and Jesus Christ never taught it. Afterwards fortifying myself from day to day by the grace of God, and understanding that the Christians abuse all the benefits of Jesus Christ as formerly the Jews abused the brazen serpent ... I concluded that nothing pure is to be found amongst the Christians and that all they have is falsified. For they have perverted by their false interpretations almost all the writing of Moses and the Gospel which I have shown in a book wrote with my own hand and which I shall present to your Majesty. When I say that the Christians have falsified and corrupted the commandments of Moses and the Gospel I mean only the words and the sense. For the doctrine of Moses, of Jesus and of Mahomet agree in everything and are not contrary to anything ... the Al Coran gives a very advantageous testimony to Moses and Jesus Christ. But it insists principally upon the Christians corrupting the commandments of Moses and the Gospel of Jesus Christ by their false interpretations. Indeed if the Word of God was faithfully interpreted there would be no difference amongst the Jews, Christians and Turks. Thus what the Al Coran so often repeats is true. The doctrine of Mahomet destroys all the false interpretations of the Scriptures and teaches the true sense of the Word of God ...

After that by the grace of God I understood there was but One only God, that I had observed that the doctrine of Jesus Christ was not taught as it ought to have been, that all the ceremonies of the Christians were very much different from their first institutions. I began to think I was the only man of my opinion in the World. I had not seen Al Coran and among us Christians there was care taken to spread in all parts such infamous and scandalous reports against everything that concerns the doctrines of Mahomet that the poor people who are made to believe things as so many truths are seized with horror and run out of themselves at the very name of Al Coran. Nevertheless by the effect of Divine Providence that book fell into my hands for which I give thanks to God. To God I say Who knows that in my prayers I invoke Him for your Majesty and for all those that belong to you. I sought all effects of ways to impart the knowledge of these truths to my Auditors and in case they would not receive this doctrine I resolved to ask leave of the Electors to abandon my charge and retire to you. I began to attack by way of dispute in all the churches

and in the schools some points of our doctrine and obtained what I wished: For I brought the matter to such a
point that it was known to all the States of the Empire
and I drew several learned men to my side. The Elector
(fearing an invasion from the Emperor Maximillian) ...
deposed me ... [7]

This letter fell into the hands of Emperor Maximillian. Neuser was
arrested along with his friends who included two men called Sylvan and Mathias Vehe. They were thrown into prison. On the 15th
of July 1570 Neuser escaped only to be retaken. He escaped a second time but was again arrested. Their trial continued for two years,
after which it was decided to behead Sylvan. At this point, Neuser
again escaped. This time he reached Constantinople and embraced
Islam.

Francis David (1510-1579)

Francis David was born in Kolozsar, Transylvania, in 1510. He was
a brilliant student, winning a scholarship to Wittenberg where he
trained for the Catholic priesthood for four years. On his return to
Kolozsar, he was appointed as rector of a Catholic school. He then
accepted Protestantism, left the Catholic school and in 1555 became
the rector of a Lutheran school. When the split in the Reform movement between Luther and Calvin took place, David joined the Calvinist party. The Reformation was still in its early days and in this
atmosphere the spirit of enquiry was not yet completely inhibited.
Discussion was allowed on every aspect of Christianity. The Reformed Church had not yet adopted a fixed doctrine and there was
room to think freely. In such an intellectual climate, it was possible
to advocate a freedom of belief in which each individual was only
accountable to God.

The two dogmas which caused most confusion in the minds of
the general public at this time, and which defied rational explanation, were those concerning the divinity of Jesus and the Trinity.
David's mind was troubled by these inexplicable articles of faith.
He could not see why anyone who believed in these 'mysteries'
without trying to understand them was considered a better Christian than those who did. He was not prepared to follow any faith
blindly. Gradually he arrived at the conclusion that Jesus was not
divine, and affirmed belief in the existence of One God.

This belief already had strong adherents in Poland. The leaders of this group were two: Blandrata, the court physician, and a man called Socianus. While David was still formulating his concept of faith, King John of Transylvania fell ill and Blandrata was called to treat him. David met Blandrata during his stay there and his conclusion that belief in One God is the true basis of Christianity was confirmed.

In 1566, David produced a confession of faith which showed the status of the dogma of Trinity in the light of what the Bible actually said. In it he disowned the scholastic concept of Father, Son and Holy Ghost. Blandrata, for his part, published a paper in which he formulated seven propositions refuting these doctrines both positively and negatively. In the same year, and on the recommendation of Blandrata, King John appointed David as his court preacher. As such, David became spokesman for the Unitarian party in the national debates called by the king to clarify the religious issues of that time. He was an incomparable public speaker, one who, as a contemporary said of him, 'seemed to have the Old and New Testaments at his tongue's end.' [8]

The major debates held during King John's reign were at Gyualafehervat in 1566 and 1568, and at Nagyvarad in 1569. The first debate was inconclusive. The king, however, was impressed by the arguments of Blandrata and David. So, in 1567, a Decree of Toleration was passed. It declared that:

> In every place the preachers shall preach and explain the Gospel according to their understanding of it, and if the congregation likes, so far so good; if not, no one shall compel them, and they shall keep the preacher whose doctrine they approve. None shall annoy or abuse the preacher, or allow anyone to be imprisoned or punished … on account of his teaching, for faith is the gift of God. [9]

The second synod, held in 1568, was called in order to establish conclusively whether or not the doctrines of the Trinity and the eternal deity of Jesus were taught in the Scriptures. David, who was a very powerful and convincing speaker, could not be disproved. When his opponents realised that they were losing the debate, they resorted to abuse, which only served to help convince the king that David's arguments were genuine. The debate lasted for ten days. It established Unitarianism as a popular faith and David as its champion.

During this period the writings of Michael Servetus, which had been almost completely destroyed by the Trinitarian Church authorities, were smuggled into Transylvania and translated into the local language. They were widely read and served to strengthen the Unitarian movement in Eastern Europe.

The third synod, held in Hungary in 1569, was, in the judgement of one Hungarian historian, 'the decisive debate' which produced the 'final triumph of Unitarianism.' [10] The king himself presided over it, and it was attended by all the highest ranking civil and military officials of the kingdom. David's arguments were these:

- The view of Trinity held by the Pope in Rome is really a belief in four or five gods: one substance, God, three separate persons, each of whom are said to be God, and one man, Christ, who is also regarded as being God. God, however, is only One, the Father from Whom and by Whom everything exists – Who created everything and Who is above everything and besides Whom there is no other god, neither three, nor four, neither in substance, nor in persons – for the Scripture does not teach anything anywhere about a triple God.

- The Church's God/Son who is alleged to have been born of the same substance as God from the beginning of eternity is not mentioned anywhere in the Scriptures – and neither is the God/Son who is alleged to be the second person of the Trinity descended from heaven and become flesh. This is only human invention and superstition and as such should be discarded.

- Jesus did not create himself – it was God Who gave him his eminence. God had him begotten by the Holy Spirit. God sanctified him and sent him into the world.

- The relationship of Christ to God was determined by God alone, with God in his absolute Divine Sovereignty remaining distinct from and above everything in His creation – including Jesus.

- There is no passage of time for God – for Him everything is in the present tense. Jesus was born into time,
  and was taken out of time – and the Scriptures do not
  teach anywhere that Jesus was born from the beginning of eternity.

The debate lasted for five days. It was again conclusive. In his final
address, the king ordered that the Unitarians be given full liberty
of conscience. Melius, the leader of the Lutheran party, was warned
not to play the Pope, nor to burn books, nor to use force to convert
people. David later summed up the debate in these words:

> I followed the line of Scripture, but my opponents hid it
> in a bag; they turned light into darkness when they made
> three of the Father God, and two of Christ. Their reli-
> gion is self-contradictory to the extent that even they
> cannot present it as a whole. Nevertheless, they will see
> that even against their will God will prove His Truth. [11]

The result of this debate was that nearly the whole city of Kolozsar
became believers in One God. This belief spread out into the countryside and became the faith of a large majority of the people there.
Unitarianism became one of the four officially 'received religions',
that is, one protected by law, and by 1571, there were almost five
hundred Unitarian congregations in Transylvania.

It was in this year that King John died. Although the popularity
of Unitarianism continued to grow, the new king, King Stephen,
did not share King John's tolerance, and he reversed the policy of
the freedom of conscience initiated by his predecessor. Life was
made difficult for those who affirmed the Divine Unity, and, to
make matters worse, David fell out with both Blandrata and
Socianus. David was an uncompromising Unitarian and could not
bear anything to be associated with God, even indirectly. Socianus
made a distinction between adoration and invocation directed towards Jesus. One could not invoke him, but one could adore him.
David could not accept or tolerate this.

Even the Polish Unitarians found the distinction too subtle, since
little difference could be perceived between the two. In common
thought and daily practice, this distinction tended to become
blurred, and, during the course of worship, it could not be hon-
estly said whether a person was adoring or invoking.

The Roman Catholics enjoyed the support of the new king, and the division between the leaders of the Unitarian movement gave them additional strength. In a Diet at Torda in 1571, a general complaint was made that some pastors were guilty of innovations. This was repeated in Diets of 1573, 1576, and 1578, and the complaints which were made became more and more specific until they were pointedly made against Francis David. Blandrata had in the meanwhile become increasingly friendly with the king, appreciating the reputation and wealth which this association brought, and in 1578 he openly opposed David, and advised him not to pursue his beliefs any more. David, however, was not prepared to abandon his convictions merely to save his own skin. Blandrata, after a lifelong struggle to establish belief in the Divine Unity, had become infirm and old and wanted a rest. He did not want to invite fresh trouble on himself or his friends. They knew that what David was doing was very dangerous, and felt that matters would be made much easier for them all if he followed their example.

David remained unmoved. He not only continued to preach, but also began to write and distribute leaflets containing his beliefs, despite opposition. Blandrata invited Socianus to Transylvania in order to persuade David to change his views and accept the distinction which he made between the adoration and the invocation of Jesus. Socianus came and stayed as David's guest. His persuasion was to no avail, but it was agreed that David should summarise his beliefs in writing, and that they should then be presented to a synod of the Polish Unitarian Church. David did this, making the following four points:

- The strict command of God is that no one should be invoked save God the Father, the Creator of heaven and earth.

- Christ, the teacher of Truth, taught that no one is to be invoked besides the heavenly Father.

- True invocation is defined as that which is directed to the Father in spirit and in truth.

- All forms of simple prayer are directed not to Christ, but to the Father.

Socianus wrote against these views, and David responded again in writing in support of his views. The discussion became heated and then gradually grew bitter and personal. The result was that Blandrata and David were now open enemies. This gave the Catholic king the support that he needed and the order was given to place David under house arrest and to allow no one to see him. David found out about the order before it had been executed. He immediately began to preach in as many places as was possible, both in churches and in the public square, and openly told the people the reason for his impending arrest. He declared: 'Whatever the world might try to do, it will nevertheless become clear to the whole world that God is One.' [12]

After his arrest, David was taken before a Diet. Blandrata acted both as chief prosecutor and as chief witness for the prosecution. The strain on David was so great that he fell ill. He had to be carried about in a chair, for he could hardly move his arms and legs. He was condemned to life imprisonment, and was put in the dungeon of a castle built on the summit of a high hill. No one knows how much he suffered during the five months he was there. He died in November 1579 and was given the burial of a criminal, in an unmarked grave.

After Francis David's death, a poem was found written on the wall of his cell. Part of it reads:

Twice ten years I have loyally served my country
And to the Prince my fidelity hath been proven.
Ask you the crime that the Fatherland hates so?
This alone is it: 'One God not three' I have worshipped.

The last lines of the poem are:

Nor lightening, nor cross, nor sword of the Pope,
    nor death's visible face,
No power whatever can stay the progress of Truth.
What I have felt I have written, with faithful heart
    I have spoken.
After my death the dogmas of untruth shall fall. [13]

o   o   o   o   o

Although David died, his movement continued; and indeed, for many years, the Transylvanian Unitarians were referred to as those who were 'of Francis David's religion'. Today his arguments are accepted as 'plain, straightforward and scriptural. The verdict of all reasonable men is given in favour of David.' [14]

Blandrata, who had played such a great part in David's death, became very popular with the Catholics and the king. He became so rich that his heir was not prepared to wait for his natural death to occur – and murdered him. Although the persecution of the Unitarians continued, it did not, as is usual, produce the result which the persecutors desired to achieve. David was soon sanctified as a martyr and his example provided the Unitarians with an inspiration which survived generations of organized persecution.

The number of Unitarians in Transylvania did nevertheless diminish considerably, but began to increase again in the south of Hungary which was under Turkish rule, for the Muslim rulers were enjoined by the Qur'an to allow the followers of other faiths to live in peace, provided that they did not interfere with the practices of Islam. Thus, under Turkish rule, all Christians – both Trinitarian as well as Unitarian – enjoyed a freedom which did not exist in any of the Christian countries. They were even allowed to practice their personal laws.

In taking advantage of this freedom, for example, one Calvinist bishop had a Unitarian hanged for heresy. Another Unitarian minister brought this action to the notice of the Turkish governor in Buda. He ordered the Calvinist bishop to appear before him, and after a trial, the bishop and his two assistants were sentenced to death as murderers. The Unitarian minister then interceded on behalf of the condemned bishop, saying that he had not sought revenge, but only wished that such incidents should be prevented from happening again. So the culprits were not hanged, but a heavy fine imposed on them instead.

The Unitarians enjoyed peace under Turkish rule for nearly a century and at one point they had about sixty churches in the country. With the decline of Turkish power, however, the freedom of belief which the Unitarians had enjoyed also declined, and people were again forced to become Roman Catholics. Those who refused were violently persecuted. By the end of the nineteenth century, however, it no longer became possible to persecute people openly, and the number of Unitarians again began to increase. The Unitarian movement still survives in Eastern Europe today, and David's influence is still to be found in the hearts of some people.

There is some speculation as to how much contact Francis David had with the Muslims. Certainly, his beliefs come very close to Islam, and at least in one place in his writings he openly refers to the Qur'an in support of these beliefs:

> It is not without reason said in Qur'an that Jesus can give no assistance to those who worship him because they would have him pass for God contrary to the doctrine taught by him ... so they are worthy of blame who teach that we ought to worship and invoke Jesus, he himself having taught that the Father is to be invoked ... God is not threefold but One. [15]

Of all the abuses which were hurled at David, however, he was never openly called a Muslim, perhaps because both the Calvinists and the Catholics feared that to say this would have brought the then powerful Turkish rulers to the aid of the Unitarians. The apparent ignorance of the Turkish rulers as regards the Unitarian movement, whose beliefs were so close to their own, can perhaps be ascribed to the degeneration of their own Islam.

One of the main criticisms of David was that if his views were accepted, then the distinction between Judaism and Christianity would tend to disappear, and the latter would relapse into the former. Even Blandrata openly taunted David by saying that he was returning to Judaism. He never refuted any of David's arguments, but attempted to discredit him by playing on the popular sentiment against the Jews – who were always held responsible by the misinformed European Christians for 'the murder of Christ' – and appeared to be oblivious of the fact that each new Prophet came to reaffirm and extend the teaching of the Prophet before him.

Part of Francis David's importance lies in the fact that by his affirmation of the Divine Unity he reaffirmed Jesus's position in the Prophetic tradition without denying in any way the Prophets who came before and after him, peace be all of them. In addition, he reminded people that true faith and trust in God, together with a life lived in accordance with the example and teaching of Jesus, peace be on him, are sufficient for this life and for the one after it. [16]

o   o   o   o   o

Lelio Francesco Maria Sozini (1525–1562)

Lelio Sozini was born in Bologna in 1525. He became a jurist whose legal studies led him to research into Hebrew and the Bible. When he was a young man, he left Bologna and moved to the area around Venice where a degree of religious freedom existed which was unknown in other parts of Italy. The writings of Servetus had found their way there and influenced many. Among those who embraced his belief, writes Wallace in his *Anti-trinitarian Biographies*, there were 'many persons of distinguished rank and eminent attainments in the city of Venice.' [17] Since these opinions were not openly tolerated by the Senate, those who held them began to meet in secret. Their intention was to study the truth of Christianity and to re-establish the teaching of Jesus in its purity. Lubinietski in his *History of the Reformation in Poland*, writes:

> They came to the conclusion that there is but one God. Jesus was truly a man. He was conceived by the operation of the Holy Ghost in the chaste womb of a virgin. The doctrine of Trinity and the divinity of Jesus were the opinions introduced by pagan philosophers.' [18]

Lelio met this group of Unitarians and, writes Wallace, 'soon became enamoured of these views and embraced them with all the ardour and ingenuousness of a youthful mind bent upon the pursuit and acquisition of religious truth.' [19] A gnostic called Camillo influenced him especially. A new vista opened up before him. Up until then, his mind had been inhibited by the rigid dogmas of the established Trinitarian Church. He now felt a new freedom which he had not experienced before. His life had taken on a new meaning, and he wished to devote himself to the search for truth.

It is known that the number of members in the Secret Society of Vinecenza, as it is known today, was over forty. When the existence of this society was ultimately discovered, some of its members were arrested and put to death, while others were fortunate enough to make their escape and find asylum in other countries. Other known members of this society besides Lelio Sozini, were Ochinus, Darius Sozini (Lelio's cousin), Alciati and Bucalis. There is a strong tradition that the last two of these men ultimately embraced Islam. Dr. White, in his Brompton lectures, called the disciples of Sozini 'followers of the Arabian prophet.' [20]

While the existence of this society was still a secret, Lelio Sozini's attention was drawn to two men outside it. One was Servetus and the other was Calvin. Servetus had the courage openly to declare his belief in the Divine Unity, whilst Calvin had made himself known as a force to be reckoned with in the Reformist circles of Europe. Lelio Sozini wanted to meet both of them and decided to see Calvin first. When Sozini met him, he was utterly disappointed to find that Calvin was as hide-bound as any Roman Catholic priest. This feeling soon changed to one of disgust when he discovered that Calvin himself had helped to have Servetus arrested. From then on, Sozini relied on the example of Servetus and the inspiration of Camillo in his extensive studies of the accepted doctrines of the established Church. In 1559 Lelio Sozini went to Zurich and spent the last three years of his life deep in reflection and study. He died in 1562 when he was thirty-seven years old.

Fausto Paolo Sozini (1539–1604)

Fausto Paolo Sozini, Lelio Sozini's nephew, was born in 1539. His uncle handed down to him all that he had acquired during his short but useful life. At the age of twenty-three, young Fausto Sozini, or Socianus as he became popularly known, became an heir not only to Lelio's inheritance, but also to the light of Camillo and the learning of Servetus. His most precious legacy, however, was the great number of manuscripts and exegetical notes left by his uncle.

Socianus received his early education in Sienna, where he had been born. On coming of age, he visited Lyons and Geneva. He returned to Italy in 1565. He went to Florence and entered the service of Isabella de Medeci. He received both position and honour from her. After her death, he left Italy and settled in Basle. Here, the young scholar soon attracted the attention of all those who were interested in the study of theology. He published a book, for private circulation anonymously, as it was very dangerous to openly differ from the official teaching of the Trinitarian Church.

His book reached the hands of Blandrata who, as we have already seen, was the court physician in Poland. At this stage, Blandrata had the courage, vision, ability, and ambition to free the minds of the common people from the dogmatic stranglehold which the established Trinitarian Church had imposed on them. The religious toleration of the rulers of Poland had made the country an attractive place for all those who wanted to freely discuss and act on their religious beliefs, and who did not wish to blindly follow the obtuse dogmatism of the established Church. Blandrata invited Socianus to Poland, and his offer was gladly accepted. In the free and congenial atmosphere that Socianus found there, he was at liberty to write in his own name without fear of persecution by the Trinitarian Church. Although his own person was safe, his property in Italy was confiscated. Socianus married a Polish woman and severed all connections with his native land.

The rulers of Poland at this time did not believe in the doctrine of Trinity, but they were still groping in the dark. They did not know what steps to take to produce a positive dogma. The presence of Socianus fulfilled this need and clearly gave satisfaction to both the rulers and the people alike. The knowledge which his uncle had passed on to him, together with the fruits of his own study, fused together in Socianus' intellect, and his writings had a powerful impact on the established Trinitarian Church.

In its anger, the Roman Catholic Church had him arrested and he was condemned to be burnt alive. However, popular support for Socianus was so great that the court decided to subject him to ordeal by water, in order to give their judgement greater weight. This test, along with that of ordeal by fire, had been adopted by the Trinitarian Church, and given the name of *judicum dei*, the judgement of God, although it had never been part of Jesus's, or even Paul's, teaching. The outcome of the ordeal was said to be the immediate judgement of God. In the ordeal by water the accused was thrown into deep water. If he drowned, he was guilty. Knowing full well that Socianus could not swim, the officiating clergy threw him into the sea. He was saved from drowning, however, and lived until he died in 1604.

In 1605, the writings of Socianus were collected together in a book. Since it was published in Rokow, it became popularly known as the *Racovian Catechism*. Originally published in the Polish language, it came to be translated into almost all the languages of Europe. In time, his teaching spread everywhere, and his school of theology became known as Socianism. Harnack, in his *Outlines of the History of Dogma*, ranks Socianism along with Roman Catholicism and Protestantism as the last of the final stages of Christian dogma. It is largely due to Socianus that the Unitarians became recognised as a separate entity within modern Christianity. Harnack concluded that Socianism had these characteristics:

- It had the courage to simplify questions concerning the reality and content of religion and to discard the burden of the ecclesiastical past.

- It broke the contracted bond between religion and philosophy, between Christianity and Platonism.

- It helped spread the idea that the religious statement of truth must be clear and intelligible if it is to have strength.

- It tried to free the study of the Holy Scriptures from the bondage of old dogmas which themselves were not in the Scriptures. It was said by someone that, 'The ignorance of the laity is the revenue of the clergy.' The teachings of Socianus did much to diminish both.

The Socian religion crossed Europe and spread to England. Bishop Hall of Norwich is recorded as bewailing the fact that 'the minds of Christian men were seduced ... through the infernal Socian heresy by Anti-trinitarians and New Arians so that the final destruction of Christianity was to be feared.' [21]

In 1638, a brutal and organised persecution of the Socians in Poland began. Their College at Rokow was closed down, and the followers of Socianus were deprived of all civil rights. Many people who affirmed the Unity of God were burnt alive. Thus in 1639, for example, Catherine Vogal, the wife of a jeweller in Poland was burnt alive at the age of eighty. Her crime was that she believed that God was One; that He was the Creator of the Seen and the Unseen worlds; and that God could not be conceived of by the human intellect. This is, of course, the pure metaphysics of Islam. Fuller writes that, 'such burning of heretics startled the common people, because of the hideousness of the punishment ... and so they were ready to entertain good thoughts even of the opinions of the heretics who sealed them so manfully with their blood.' [22] 'Therefore, adds Wallace, 'James I indulged his propensity for incendiarism by the more harmless practice of burning their books.' [23]

In 1658, the people of Poland were given the option of either accepting Roman Catholicism or else going into exile. The Unitarians dispersed throughout Europe. They spread with their teaching, and continued to remain a separate entity for a long time.

In the writings contained in the *Racovian Catechism*, Socianus struck at the very root of what had become orthodox Christianity by denying the doctrine of Atonement. Although he was ignorant of the fact that Jesus was neither crucified nor resurrected, and that therefore the doctrine is entirely without any foundation anyway, Socianus was able to establish the absurdity of the doctrine on other grounds.

Briefly speaking, the doctrine of Atonement preaches that man is born in a state of sin because of the first wrong action of Adam, and that Jesus, by his (supposed) crucifixion, atones for this state of sin and for all the personal wrong actions of all those who take baptism and follow him. According to orthodox Christianity, the Church is a religious fellowship, a society of divine origin which was founded by Christ through his atoning work for men. Only within its communion, it says, and by its office, can sinful men and women find their way to God. The Church – that is, the priesthood of the Church – is therefore considered to have more importance than and to take priority over the individual believer.

Socianus denied all this. He was sure that a person could have direct access to God without the need for any intermediaries. In order to attain salvation, he wrote, not baptism, but 'right reason' was needed, and it was not necessary to blindly follow the Church. By denying this doctrine, Socianus brought the whole authority of the Church and its *raison d'etre* into question. It was largely because of this that both the Catholics and Protestants joined forces with such fervour to fight Socianism. Socianus refuted the doctrine of atonement, *inter alia*, on the following grounds:

- Christ was not in a position to offer an infinite sacrifice for sin since Christ, according to the Gospel narration, suffered only for a short time.

- Even the most intense suffering for a limited period on earth is nothing compared with the eternal suffering in Hell to which man is liable.

- If it is argued that Christ's suffering was greater because he is an infinite being, then it must also be accepted that his ability to endure such suffering was correspondingly infinite. Thus even the suffering of an infinite being cannot atone for eternal suffering.

- If, for the sake of argument, it is conceded that Christ did somehow offer infinite atonement, then this makes it impossible to speak of the forgiveness of God, or of man's gratitude to Him for granting His forgiveness – since any person baptised in the name of Christ would automatically acquire atonement for his or her sins, even before God could grant forgiveness and remit the penalty for them.

- To accept the doctrine of Atonement means that God's Law is no longer binding on His servants since whatever they do, the penalty for all their sins has already been paid in full.

- Therefore, a person who believes in Christ is at full liberty to do whatever he or she likes – for since the offering of Christ was absolute and infinite, it therefore included everything and, therefore, universal salvation must necessarily follow.

- In other words, the logic inherent in the doctrine of Atonement demands that God has no right to add any further conditions to what He requires of man. The whole price has been paid – past, present and future – and, therefore, all debtors are now free, even before they have fallen into debt.

- For, suppose a number of men had owed a great debt to an earthly creditor and someone had paid it all off; then what right would the creditor have to make further demands or conditions on these men who were no longer indebted to him?

The doctrine of atonement was also implicitly criticised by Socianus simply by his affirming that Jesus was not God, but a man – for it is self-evident that there is no way that one man could possibly atone for all the wrong actions of all the people who believed in him, no matter how great both he and any suffering that he might have endured happened to be. This fact in itself is enough to expose the erroneous reasoning on which the established Church relies, and so dispel this mythical doctrine.

Socianus asserted that Jesus was truly a mortal man, even though he was born of a virgin. He was elevated above other men in degree due to the holiness of his life. He was not God, but he received inspiration from God. Thus he had divine vision and divine power, but he was not himself the source of that vision and power. He had been sent by God with His supreme God-given authority on a mission to mankind.

Socianus supported these beliefs with comprehensive citation and confident exegesis of the relevant passages from the Scriptures. His subtle and able argument gave a rational meaning to the words of Christ: Jesus was not the Word made flesh. He was a man who achieved victory over wrong action in his life in the flesh. He did not exist before the world came into existence. It was permissible to invoke the help of Jesus in prayer as long as he was not regarded or worshipped as God.

Socianus affirmed that God is the supreme Lord of all: Omnipotence is not only His attribute, he argued, but rules over every other attribute. There can be no question raised against God. The finite cannot be a measure of the infinite. Therefore, all human conceptions of the nature of God must be incomplete and accordingly considered as inadequate grounds on which to base a critical judgement about Him. God's will is free and not bound by any law that the human mind can envisage or formulate. His purpose and His will are hidden from the human mind. God's dominion comprises His absolute right and supreme authority to determine whatever He may choose, in respect of us all and all other things. He can read our thoughts even though they may be hidden in the innermost recesses of our hearts. He can, as He pleases, ordain laws and determine both reward and punishment for the purity and the lapses in a person's intentions and actions. Thus human beings have been given the freedom of choice, but are in fact powerless.

Since there cannot be more than one being who possesses supreme dominion over all things, asserted Socianus, to speak of three persons who are all supreme is to speak irrationally. The Essence of God is One, not only in attribute but also in number. It cannot in any way contain a plurality of persons. For example, an individual person possesses an individual intelligent essence, and wherever three numerical persons exist, then there must necessarily be reckoned three individual essences. If it is affirmed that there is one numerical essence, therefore, it must be held that accordingly there is one numerical person.

The doctrine of Trinity was also refuted by Socianus, as by others before him, on the grounds that it was not possible for Jesus to have two natures simultaneously. He said that two substances having opposite characteristics cannot combine into one person, and that in the case of Jesus and God, such characteristics are mortality – and immortality: having a beginning – and being without any beginning; being subject to change – and being immutable; having an end – and being without any ending.

Again, continued Socianus, two natures each of which is apt to constitute a separate person, cannot be huddled into one person. For, instead of one, there, of necessity, arise two persons and consequently, in the case of Jesus, they become two Christs, one divine and one human. The Church says that Christ is constituted of a divine and a human nature, just as a man is, having a body and a soul. Socianus replied that, in that case, this is widely different from the belief that the two natures in Christ are so united that Christ is thus constituted of a divine and a human body. In a man, body and soul are so conjoined that a man is neither only soul nor only body. For neither the soul nor the body separately constitute a person. Whereas, in the case of Jesus, the divine nature in itself constitutes a person – and therefore, of necessity, so must the human nature in itself also constitute a separate person.

Furthermore, argued Socianus, it is also repugnant to the Scriptures themselves that Christ should have a divine nature: Firstly, God created Jesus. Secondly, the Scriptures say that Jesus was a man. Thirdly, whatever excellence Jesus had is testified by the Scriptures to be the gift of God. Fourthly, the Scriptures most clearly indicate that Jesus perpetually ascribes all the miracles not to himself nor to any divine nature of his own, but to the Father. Jesus himself confirmed the Divine Will.

The following excerpt from the *Racovian Catechism* is to be found in Reland's *Historical and Critical Reflections upon Mahometanism and Socianism*:

> The opinion of those who attribute divinity to Jesus Christ is not only repugnant to right reason but likewise to the Holy Scriptures, and they are in gross error who believe that not only the Father but also the Son and the Holy Ghost are three persons in one deity ...

The essence of God is most simple and absolutely one, and therefore it is a downright contradiction for one to generate another if they are three independent persons. And the poor little reasons of our adversaries to the contrary to prove that the Father had begot a son of His own substance are ridiculous and impertinent ...

Always till the times of the Nicene Council and some time later as appears by the writings of those who lived then, the Father alone was acknowledged for the true God, and those who were of the contrary mind, such as the Sabellians and the like were accounted heretics ...

The spirit of the Anti-Christ hath not introduced more dangerous error into the Church of Christ than this doctrine which teaches that there are three distinct persons in the most simple essence of God each of which is itself God, and that the Father is not the only true God but that the Son and the Holy Ghost must be joined with Him. There is nothing more absurd or more impossible and more repugnant to right reason ...

Also Christians believe that Jesus Christ died to merit salvation for us and to satisfy the debts which we contracted by our sins, yet this opinion is false, erroneous and most pernicious. [24]

Socianus stated that one of the causes of the acceptance of the doctrine of Trinity was the influence of pagan philosophy, as this passage from Toland's *The Nazarenes* indicates:

The Socians and the other Unitarians no less confidently assert that the Gentiles did likewise introduce into Christianity their former polytheism and deifying of dead men: thus retaining the name of Christianity but quite altering the thing and suiting it as their interest or the necessity of their affairs required to all the opinions and customs anywhere in vogue from that time to this. [25]

It is clear why the writings of Socianus achieved such widespread acceptance. They not only took people back to a more accurate picture of who Jesus was and what he came for, but helped also to destroy much of the power which the Church had over people.

The greatness of Socianus lies in the fact that he produced a theology which was at once logical and yet based on the *Bible*. It was therefore very difficult for his opponents to dismiss his writings. For instance, when, in 1680, the Reverend George Ashwell found that the books of Socianus were becoming very popular among his students, he decided to write a book refuting the Socian religion. His assessment of Socianus is interesting, since it comes from the pen of an enemy:

> So great was the author and patron of this sect in whom all the qualities, which excite the admiration and attract the regard of men, were united; so that he charmed, as it were, by a kind of fascination all with whom he conversed, and left on the mind of all a strong impression of admiration and love. He so excelled in the loftiness of his genius and the suavity of his disposition, such was the strength of his reasoning and the force of his eloquence, so signal were the virtues which he displayed in the sight of all, which he possessed in an extraordinary degree; so great were his natural endowments and so exemplary was his life that he appeared to captivate the affection of mankind.

Then, after saying all this, Ashwell concludes that Socianus was the 'devil's great noose or snare'! [26]

Today many Christians do not share the same contradictory feelings about Socianus as the Reverend Ashwell. There is a dominant feeling of sympathy for Socianism and a sense of disquiet about the brutal way in which it was suppressed – and along with this there is a definite reaction against Trinitarianism. Many thinking Christians now agree with Socianus and are unable to accept the alleged divinity of Jesus and all that this mistaken belief implies.

John Biddle (1615-1662)

John Biddle, the Father of Unitarianism in England, was born in 1615. He was a brilliant student and was described as a man who 'outran his instructors and became tutor to himself.' [27] He went to Oxford University in 1634, and was awarded a B.A. in 1638 and an M.A. in 1641. After leaving Oxford he was appointed as a teacher in the Free School of St. Mary de Crypt in Gloucester. Here Biddle began to re-examine his religious views, and started to doubt the validity of the doctrine of the Trinity. He was influenced by the thought of the European Unitarians – for the teaching of Socianus had by now made its way to England.

A Latin version of the *Racovian Catechism* had been sent to England with a dedication to King James I. It was burnt by the hangman in public in 1614. Although the book may have been burnt, its contents caught the interest of the public, and steps were taken to discredit it. John Owen, who was commissioned by the Council of State under Oliver Cromwell to refute the teaching of Socianus, is recorded as saying: 'Do not look upon these things as things far off wherein you are little concerned, the evil is at the door; there is not a city, a town, scarce a village in England wherein some of the poison is not poured forth.' [28]

These attempts to uphold the official dogmas of the established Church did meet with some opposition. William Chillingworth, (1602-1644), for example, condemned, 'the mischief of creeds which lead to the persecution, burning, cursing and damning of men for not subscribing to the words of men, as the word of God.' [29] Jeremy Taylor and John Milton both affirmed that, 'the faithful pursuit of reason did not make a heretic. The mischief lay in the influences that perverted the will.' [30]

The debate spread, and more steps were taken by those in authority to 'protect' belief in the doctrine of Trinity. In June 1640, the Conventions of Canterbury and York decided to prohibit the import, printing and circulation of Socian books. Priests were ordered not to preach Socian doctrines, and everyone was warned that anyone who believed in these doctrines would be excommunicated. A number of authors and thinkers denounced this decision, but to no effect.

It was in this climate of reappraisal and fresh examination that Biddle's own views underwent a change, especially in connection with the doctrine of Trinity. He spoke freely about them and as a result was asked by the Magistrates, in 1644, to give them a written confession of faith. This he did in simple language: 'I believe there is one Almighty Essence called God. So there is only One person in Essence.' [31]

Biddle also published a pamphlet at this time entitled *Twelve Arguments Refuting the Deity of the Holy Spirit*. It was addressed 'To the Christian Reader'.

In 1645, the manuscript of the *Twelve Arguments* was seized and Biddle was imprisoned. He was called to appear before Parliament but still refused to accept the Deity of the Holy Spirit. He reprinted the pamphlet in 1647. On the 6th of September of the same year, Parliament ordered that the pamphlet be burnt by the hangman, and this was done. On the 2nd of May, 1648, a 'Severe Ordinance' was passed. It stated that anyone who denied the Trinity, or the divinity of Jesus or of the Holy Spirit, would suffer death without the benefit of clergy. A summary of the *Twelve Arguments*, the cause of such extreme measures, follows:

1. Whoever is distinguished from God is not God.
    The Holy Spirit is distinguished from God.
    Therefore the Holy Spirit is not God.

2. He Who gave the Holy Spirit to the Israelites is
    Jehova Alone.
    Therefore the Holy Spirit is not Jehova, or God.

3. Whoever does not speak of his own accord
    is not God.
    The Holy Spirit does not speak of his own accord.
    Therefore the Holy Spirit is not God.

4. Whoever is taught is not God.
    Whoever is told what to say by another
    is taught.
    Christ speaks what he is told.
    Therefore Christ is not God.

    (Here Biddle quotes *John 8: 26* where Jesus says:
    'Whatsoever I have heard from Him, these things I
    speak.')

5. In *John 16: 14* Jesus says:
    'God is He that giveth all things to all.'
    He that receives from another is not God.

6. He that is sent by another is not God.
    The Holy Spirit is sent by God.
    Therefore the Holy Spirit is not God.

7. Whoever is not the giver of all things is not God.
   Whoever is a gift of God is not the giver
       of all things.
   Whoever is a gift of God is himself given.
   The gift is within the power of the giver.
   God can never be within the power of another.

   (Here Biddle quotes *Acts 17: 25*: 'God giveth to all,
   life, breath and all things.')

8. Whoever changes place is not God.
   The Holy Spirit changes place.
   Therefore the Holy Spirit is not God.

   (Biddle further explained this syllogism by saying that
   if God were to change place then He would cease to
   be where He was before and begin to be where he
   was not before – which would be a contradiction of
   His attribute of being Omnipresent, and therefore of
   His Deity. Therefore it could not have been God who
   came to Jesus, but an Angel who appeared as a person in the Name of God.)

9. Whoever prays to Christ to come to judgement
       is not God.
   The Holy Spirit does this.
   Therefore the Holy Spirit is not God.

10. In *Romans 10: 14* it reads, 'How shall they believe in
    him of whom they have not heard. He in whom men
    have not believed, yet were disciples.'

    He who is not believed in is not God.
    Men have not believed in the Holy Spirit,
        yet were disciples.
    Therefore the Holy Spirit is not God.

11. Whoever is told by God through an intermediary
        what he is to say – i.e. Jesus –
    has an understanding distinct from God.
    Therefore Jesus is not God.

And whoever hears from God what he
   – i.e. Jesus – is to say is taught by God.
The Holy Spirit does so.
Therefore the Holy Spirit is not God.

12. Whoever has a will which is distinct
   from the will of God is not God.
The Holy Spirit has a will which is distinct
   from the will of God.
Therefore the Holy Spirit is not God.

(Here Biddle quotes *Romans 8.26-27* which reads: 'Likewise the Spirit also helpeth ... for we know not how to pray as we ought, but the Spirit maketh intercession for us with groans unutterable ... he maketh intercession for the saints according to the will of God.')

Biddle also discussed the one verse in the *New Testament* which the priesthood of the established Trinitarian Church used to quote in support of their view of the doctrine Trinity, 1 *John 5: 7*, which reads: 'For there are three that bear record in heaven – the Father, the Word, and the Holy Ghost; and these three are One.'

Biddle stated that the verse was contrary to common sense. It contradicted other verses in the Scriptures, and it only signified union of consent and agreement, but never of essence. Furthermore, he pointed out, the verse did not even appear in the oldest Greek copies of the gospel, nor in the Syriac translations, nor in the very old Latin editions. It seemed therefore that the verse had been interpolated, and was rejected as such by interpreters both ancient and modern. [32]

Despite the Act of 1648, Biddle published two further tracts, for which he was put in prison and would probably have been hanged had he not been helped by a number of independent members of Parliament. One of them was called *A Confession of Faith Touching the Holy Trinity According to the Scripture*. It was composed of six articles, each illustrated with passages from the *Bible* and supported with his arguments. In the Preface, he boldly talks of the evils resulting from belief in the doctrine of Trinity and says that the arguments used by the Trinitarians are 'fitter for conjurers than Christians.' [33] Here is an excerpt from Biddle's *Confession of Faith*:

I believe that there is one most High God, Creator of heaven and earth and the first Cause of all things and consequently the ultimate object of our faith and worship.

I believe in Jesus, to the extent that he might be our brother, and have a fellow feeling of our infirmities and so become more ready to help us. He has only human nature. He is subordinate to God. And he is not another God. There are not two Gods.

The Holy Spirit is an angel who due to his eminence and intimacy with God is singled out to carry His message. [34]

The other work Biddle published at this time was called *The Testimonies of Iranaeus, Justin Martyr, Etc., Concerning One God and the Persons of the Holy Trinity.*

After a long wait in prison, a magistrate stood bail for Biddle, and he was released. The name of the magistrate was kept secret since he feared for his safety. Biddle had not enjoyed his liberty for very long before he was again thrown into prison. The magistrate died soon after, and although he left a small legacy to Biddle, this was soon eaten up by the high costs of the prison, and for a while Biddle's food was reduced to a small quantity of milk taken in the morning and in the evening. His situation was eased when a London publisher employed him while still in prison as a proof reader for a new edition of the *Septuagint*, the first Greek translation of the *Old Testament* which was originally done, it is said, by seventy-two learned Jews in seventy days on the Greek island of Pharos in the 3rd century AD.

Then on the 16th of February 1652, the Act of Oblivion was passed and Biddle was set free. An English version of the *Racovian Catechism* was printed in Amsterdam during the same year, and immediately became popular in England. Biddle printed a book on Unitarianism in 1654, again in Amsterdam, and it was widely read in England. During this period of relative freedom, Biddle began to meet with other Unitarians every Sunday to worship God in their own way. Those who attended did not believe either in the concept of Original Sin or in the doctrine of Atonement. On the 13th of December 1654, Biddle, who had recently published two catechisms, was again arrested and sent to prison. He was forbidden the use of pen, ink and paper and was not allowed to have any visitors. All copies of his books were ordered to be burnt.

Biddle appealed, and was released on the 28th of May 1655. However, once again, it was not long before Biddle again clashed with the authorities: A public debate was taking place. The speaker commenced the dispute by asking if there was anyone present who denied that Christ was God most High. Biddle promptly and firmly declared, 'I deny it.' When he supported this statement with arguments which his adversaries could not refute, it was decided to halt the proceedings and to continue on another day. Biddle was then reported to the authorities, and before the day fixed for the debate had arrived he was again arrested and put in prison.

To begin with, Biddle was denied the services of a lawyer, perhaps because it was doubtful whether there was a law in force at the time under which he could be convicted. His friends who were well aware of this decided to approach Cromwell directly. They drew up a petition and sent it to him. Before it could reach him, however, the petition had been so altered and disfigured that its original authors had to openly disown it as a forgery. [35]

Cromwell, who was at his wits end, found a way out of this difficult situation by banishing Biddle to the Scilly Islands on the 5th of October 1655. He was to remain in custody in the Castle of St. Mary's for the rest of his life and would be paid an allowance of one hundred crowns *per annum*. During his captivity there, Biddle wrote an indignant poem, a few lines of which follow:

> The conclave met, the judge was set,
> Man mounted on God's throne;
> And they did judge a matter there,
> That rests with Him alone;
> A brother's faith they made a crime,
> And crushed thought's native right sublime. [36]

The more Biddle suffered, the more convinced he became of the errors that were inherent in the prevailing religion which was being supported by the established Trinitarian Church. Thomas Firmin, who had helped Biddle in the past, continued to help him by providing him with enough money to make his life in prison as comfortable as it could be.

Meanwhile sympathy for Biddle increased far and wide. The more he suffered the more popular his beliefs became, until the government had to asked Dr. John Owen to counteract the effects which Biddle's teaching was having.

After holding a survey in which he discovered that a large number of Englishmen were Unitarians, Owen published a reply to Biddle in 1655. In a way Cromwell's actions helped Biddle: Supported by his allowance, Biddle was out of reach of his enemies and could spend his time in contemplation and prayer. He remained a prisoner in the Castle of St. Mary's until 1658, when, due to the increased pressure for his release, he regained his freedom.

As soon as he had come out of prison, Biddle began to hold public meetings during which he examined the Scriptures in order to demonstrate the Unity of God and to show the falsehood of the doctrine of Trinity. These meetings developed into regular Unitarian worship according to their faith. This had never happened in England before.

On the 1st of June 1662 Biddle was again arrested together with some of his friends in the middle of one of their meetings. They were all put in prison and bail was refused. There was no statute under which they could be punished so they were prosecuted under Common Law. Biddle was fined one hundred pounds and condemned to lie in prison until the sum was paid. His fellow worshippers were fined twenty pounds each. Biddle was ill-treated in prison and kept in solitary confinement. This, together with the foul air of the prison brought on a disease which resulted in his death in less than five weeks. He died on the 22nd September 1662.

Biddle's death, together with the effects of the Act of Uniformity, passed in the same year, meant that public worship which followed the pattern established by Biddle could not take place. Under the Act 2,257 priests were ejected from their 'living.' Their fate is unknown. But it is known that about 8,000 people died in prison for refusing to accept the doctrine of Trinity during this particular era in England. The author of a biography about Biddle, written about twenty years after his death, preferred to remain anonymous for safety's sake. However, Unitarianism continued as a school of thought and its adherents grew. Using force to bring back people into the established Church only helped to win many people over to the beliefs of Socianus and Biddle, and it is significant that many of the leading intellects of the age, including John Milton, Sir Isaac Newton and John Locke, secretly affirmed the Divine Unity.

The degree to which the authorities attempted to stamp out Unitarianism during this period can be measured by the laws which they passed: An act of 1664 condemned all persons convicted of refusing to go to an established church with banishment. Should such a person return, he or she would be hanged. There were also penalties for anyone who attended a religious meeting of five or more persons not authorised by the official Trinitarian Church. Should anyone commit this offence a second time, they would be banished to America, and in case of return or escape would suffer death without benefit of clergy.

The Test Act of 1673 provided that, apart from the punishment provided for in the Act of 1664, any person who did not receive the sacrament according to the usage of the Church of England would on conviction be no longer able to sue anyone or bring any action in the law courts. He could no longer be a guardian of any child, or an executor, or the recipient of any legacy or deed or gift. Should anyone convicted under this law attempt to do any of these things, they were liable to a five hundred pound fine.

In 1689 the Toleration Act was passed. However, toleration was denied to all those who did not accept the doctrine of Trinity. Naturally the Unitarians condemned the intolerance of the Toleration Act. Parliament replied by condemning Unitarianism as an 'obnoxious heresy'. The penalty for this 'crime' was the loss of all civil rights together with imprisonment for three years. However what Biddle had stood for could not be removed from men's hearts by statute alone, even though such laws prevented many from openly professing their faith.

Those who felt they were unable to defy the law and openly denounce the doctrine of Trinity resorted to various expedients in order to quieten the reproaches of their conscience. Some quietly omitted those parts of the Athanasian Creed of which they did not approve. Some had it read by the parish clerk. One priest is said to have shown his disrespect for the creed by having it sung to a popular hunting tune. Another priest, before he read out the Trinitarian creed as prescribed by law, used to say, 'Brethren, this is the creed of St. Athanasius, but God forbid that it should be the creed of any other man!' [37] However, on the whole, those who believed in the Divine Unity did not generally dare to openly declare their faith.

Biddle was a serious scholar, and his formulations were the result of profound study. He was convinced that he could best serve mankind by fearlessly bearing witness to the truth, even if this meant reproach and persecution. He was prepared to accept poverty, the dungeon and exile. He wanted men to leave the churches which he regarded as corrupt, and to renounce all outward conformity to any profession of error. He had the courage of a martyr – and he died as one.

John Milton (1608-1674)

Milton, who lived at the same time as Biddle and shared many of his views, was not as outspoken as Biddle, preferring to lead his life outside prison. Thus in Volume Two of his *Treatise on True Religion* for example, his criticisms are veiled. He says:

> 'The Arians and Socians are charged to dispute against Trinity. They affirm to believe the Father, Son and Holy Ghost according to Scripture and the Apostolic Creed. As for terms of trinity, tri-unity, co-essentiality, tri-personality, they reject them as scholastic notions not to be found in Scripture which by general Protestant maxim is plain and perspicuous abundantly to express its own meaning in the properest words belonging to so high a matter and so necessary to be known, a mystery indeed in their sophistic subtleties but in scripture a plain doctrine.' [38]

In another of his books Milton was more direct. He said that the power exercised by Popes, Councils, Bishops and Presbyters was to be classified as among the rankest and most odious of tyrannies. He continued, 'All imposition of ordinances, ceremonies and doctrines are an unwarranted invasion of liberty.' [39]

The poet did not openly defy the civil authority of the country, but he kept to himself as a protest against the bigotry and intolerance of the established Church. Like a number of leading intellectuals, he stopped going to any church. Dr. Johnson said of Milton:

> 'He has not associated with any denomination of Protestants. We know rather what he was not than what he was. He was not of the Church of Rome. He was not of the Church of England. Milton grew old without any visible worship. In his distribution of his hours there was no hour of prayer – his work and his meditation were an habitual prayer.' [40]

It is clear that Dr. Johnson was not aware of a book written by Milton and discovered nearly a hundred and fifty years after his death in 1823. The manuscript was found in the old State Paper Office in

Whitehall and was entitled *A Treatise Relating to God.* Written while
he was a Latin secretary to Cromwell, it was obviously not intended
to be published during Milton's life. In Part One, Chapter Two,
Milton writes about the attributes of God and the Divine Unity:

> Though there be not a few who deny the existence of
> God, 'for the fool hath said in his heart there is no God',
> *Psalm 14: 1,* yet the Deity has imprinted upon the hu-
> man mind so many unquestionable tokens of Himself
> and so many traces of Him are apparent throughout the
> whole of nature that no one in his senses can remain
> ignorant of truth. There can be no doubt that everything
> in the world by the beauty of its order and the evidence
> of a determinate and beneficial purpose which pervades
> it, testifies that some supreme efficient Power must have
> pre-existed by which the whole was ordained for a spe-
> cific end.
>
> No one however can have right thoughts of God with
> nature, or reason alone as his guide, independent of the
> word or message of God ... God therefore has made as
> full a revelation of Himself as our minds can conceive
> or the weakness of our nature can bear ... Such knowl-
> edge of the Deity as was necessary for the salvation of
> man, He has Himself of His goodness been pleased to
> reveal abundantly ... The names and attributes of God
> either show His nature or His divine power and excel-
> lence.

Milton then lists some of the attributes of God: Truth, Spirit (I am
that I am), Immensity and Infinity, Eternity, Immutability (I change
not), Incorruptibility, Immortality, Omnipresence, Omnipotence,
and finally, Unity, which he says 'proceeds necessarily from all the
foregoing attributes.' Milton then lists the following proofs from
the Bible:

> Jehova, He is God, there is none besides Him.
> (*Deuteronomy 4: 35*).

> Jehova, He is God in the heavens above and upon the
> earth beneath: there is none else. (*Deuteronomy 4: 39*).

1, even 1, am He and there is no God with Me.
(*Deuteronomy 32: 39*).

... that all the people of the earth may know that Jehova is God and that there is none else. (*I Kings 8: 60*).

... Thou art the God, even Thou alone, of all the king-doms of the earth.   (*2 Kings 19: 15*).

Is there a god besides Me? Yea, there is no god.
(*Isaiah 44: 8*).

I am Jehova and there is no god besides Me.
(*Isaiah 45: 5*).

There is no god else besides Me ...
there is none besides Me.   (*Isaiah 45: 21*).

I am God and there is none else. (*Isaiah 45: 22*).

(Commenting on the above verse, Milton says, 'that is, no spirit, no person, no being beside Him is God for 'none' is a universal negative.')

I am God and there is none else. I am God
and there is none like Me.   (*Isaiah 46: 9*).

Milton continues:

What can be plainer, what more distinct, what more suitable to general comprehension and the ordinary forms of speech, for the purpose of impressing on the people of God that there was numerically One God and One Spirit in the common acceptation of numerical unity? It was in truth fitting and highly agreeable to rea-son that the first and consequentially the greatest com-mandment to which even the lowest of the people were required to pay scrupulous obedience should be deliv-ered in so plain a manner that no ambiguous or obscure expressions might lead His worshippers into error or keep them in suspense or doubt. Accordingly, the Isra-

elites under the Law and their Prophets always understood it to mean that God was numerically One God
besides Whom there was none other, much less any
equal. For the schoolmen had not as yet appeared who
through their confidence in their own sagacity, or more
properly speaking on arguments purely contradictory,
impugned the doctrine itself of the Unity of God, which
they pretended to assert. But as with regard to the Omnipotence of the Deity, it is universally allowed, as has
been stated before, that He can do nothing which involves a contradiction: so it must always be remembered
in this place that nothing can be said of the One God
which is inconsistent with His Unity, and which assigns
to Him at the same time the attributes of unity and plurality. *Mark 12: 29-32*: 'Hear O Israel, the Lord our God
is One Lord.' To which answer the scribe asserted, 'Well,
Master, thou hast said the truth: for there is One God;
and there is none other than He.'

Milton then goes on to discuss the nature of the Holy Spirit. The
Scripture, he says, is silent on its nature, in what manner it exists,
and from whence it arose. He continues:

It is exceedingly unreasonable not to say dangerous that
in a matter of so much difficulty believers should be
required to receive a doctrine represented by its advocates as of primary importance and of undoubted certainty on anything less than the clearest testimony of
Scriptures, and that a point that is confessedly contrary
to reason should nevertheless be considered as susceptible of proof from human reason only or rather from
doubtful and obscure disputations.

Milton points out that the Holy Ghost must be inferior to both God
and Jesus, since his duties were to carry messages from the One to
the other. On his own he could do nothing. He was therefore subservient and obedient to God in all things. He was sent by God
and said nothing other than what he had been told to say.

Milton then comes to the following conclusions based on his
knowledge of the Bible: The Holy Spirit is not omniscient. The Holy
Spirit is not omnipresent. It cannot be said that because the Holy

Spirit carries out the work of God, therefore he is part of God. If this was so, then why is the Holy Spirit called the Comforter, who will come after Jesus, who speaks not of himself nor in his own name, and whose power therefore is acquired? (*John 16: 7-14*). It therefore becomes clear that instead of accepting the term 'Comforter' in its obvious sense as a Prophet who will come after Jesus, to call him Holy Spirit and yet call him God creates a confusion which cannot be ended. [41]

Milton agrees with Arius that Jesus was not eternal. He points out that it was in God's power to create or not to create Jesus. He concludes that Jesus was born 'within the limits of time'. He is at a loss to find any passage of Scripture which would support the 'eternal generation of Jesus'. He asserts that the hypothesis that Jesus, though personally and numerically another, is yet essentially one with God is both strange and repugnant to reason. This dogma, he adds, does violence not only to reason but also to Scriptural evidence. Milton agrees with the 'Israelitish people' that God is the One and only God. It is so evident that it requires no explanation – that God alone is the self-existing God, and that a being that is not self-existing cannot be God. He concludes:

> It is wonderful with what futile subtleties or rather with what juggling artifices certain individuals have endeavoured to elude or obscure the plain meaning of the passages of the Scriptures. [42]

Milton felt that he could not express these views openly, for to have done so would have been to endanger his own personal safety, and to expose himself to the same treatment that Biddle and many others like him had suffered.

In 1611, for example – that is within Milton's lifetime – two men called Mr. Legatt and Mr. Wightman were burnt alive with the king's permission because they believed that there was no Trinity of persons, Father, Son and Holy Spirit, in the Unity of Godhead; that Jesus Christ was neither the natural true son of God, nor of the same substance, eternity and majesty with the Father in respect to his godhead; and that Jesus Christ was a man only and a mere creature, and not God and man together in one person.

Milton's silence on these matters while he was alive was therefore an understandable one.

John Locke (1632-1704)

John Locke, who is best known for his treatises on the social contract, was also a man who held Unitarian views but was afraid to openly declare them. At one point, he was forced to leave England on account of his political views. On his return, after the revolution of 1688, he made sure that he did not directly offend the powers of the official Church, since he feared further persecution. Even his monograph supporting reason was not liked by the Church, and another tract written by him had to be published anonymously.

It is known, however, that Locke did study the teachings of the early disciples of Christ and could find no justification for the belief in Trinity. He was a close friend of Newton and obviously discussed this matter, which was so much in dispute in that age, with him. Le Clere, a friend of Locke and Newton, observes that no controversy was ever conducted with so much skill on the one hand or, on the other, with so much misrepresentation, confusion and ignorance. It is said that the terms of the Toleration Act of 1689 were negotiated by Locke.

Sir Isaac Newton (1642-1727)

Newton's illustrious life has been summed up by Pope, the famous English poet, in these words:

> Nature and nature's laws lay hid in night
> God said, 'Let Newton be!' – and all was light. [43]

And yet Newton was another man who felt it unwise to profess his beliefs openly:

In 1690, for example, Newton sent John Locke a small packet containing his written observations on the corruption of the text of the *New Testament* as regards *1 John 5: 7* and *1 Timothy 3: 16* – both of which verses, he concluded, had been introduced into the *New Testament* at a much later stage, since they do not appear in the earliest Greek manuscripts, and were never quoted during any of the arguments and debates that arose between the Unitarian Christians and the Paulinian Christians in the early days of the Church – simply because they did not exist at that time and had not yet been invented.

Newton hoped that Locke could help him have the manuscript translated into French and published in France, since he felt it would be too dangerous to print it in England. It was called *An Historical Account of Two Notable Corruptions of Scripture*. In 1692, an attempt was made to publish a Latin translation of it anonymously. When he heard of this, Newton entreated Locke to take steps to prevent this publication, since he felt that the time was not yet ripe for it. In his *Historical Account*, Newton says, referring to *1 John 5: 7*:

> In all the vehement universal and lasting controversy about the Trinity in Jerome's time and both before and long enough after it, this text of the 'three in heaven' was never once thought of. It is now in everybody's mouth and accounted the main text for the business and would assuredly have been so too with them, had it been in their books.

He continues:

> Let them make good sense of it who are able. For my part I can make none. If it be said that we are not to determine what is Scripture and what not by our private judgements, I confess it in places not controverted, but in disputed places I love to take up with what I can best understand. It is the temper of the hot and superstitious part of mankind in matters of religion ever to be fond of mysteries, and for that reason to like best what they understand least. Such men may use the Apostle John as they please, but I have that honour for him as to believe that he wrote good sense and therefore take that to be his which is the best. [44]

According to Newton, *1 John 5: 7* appeared for the first time in the third edition of Erasmus's *New Testament*. He believed that before the publication of this edition, the 'spurious text' was not to be found in the *New Testament*: 'When they got the Trinity into his edition they threw by their manuscript, if they had one, as an almanac out of date. And can such shuffling dealings satisfy considering men?' He continues, 'It is rather a danger in religion than an advantage to make it now lean on a broken reed.'

In referring to *1 Timothy 3: 16*, Newton says: 'In all the times of the hot and lasting Arian controversy it never came into play ... they that now read, "God manifested in the flesh," think it one of the most obvious and pertinent texts for the business.' [45]

Newton was opposed to the allegorical or double interpretation of the *Old Testament*. He did not regard all the books of the Scriptures as having the same authority. According to Whiston, Newton also wrote a dissertation upon two other texts which Athanasius had attempted to corrupt, but there is no trace of it today. Finally, Newton also had this to say:

> The word 'Deity' imports exercise of dominion over subordinate beings and the word 'God' most frequently signifies Lord. Every lord is not God. The exercise of dominion in a spiritual being constitutes a God. If that dominion be real that being is the real God; if it be fictitious, a false God; if it be supreme, a supreme God. [46]

Thomas Emlyn (1663-1741)

Thomas Emlyn was born on the 27th of May 1663. He went to Cambridge in 1678 and, having concluded his studies there, returned to Dublin, where he soon became a very popular preacher. This Presbyterian Minister preached his first sermon in 1682, and for the next ten years his reputation as a good preacher grew.

In about 1702, a member of his congregation observed that Emlyn avoided certain well-known pulpit expressions and the arguments usually employed in support of the dogma of Trinity. This lead to his being questioned as to what he thought about the concept of the Trinity. Since he was asked so pointedly, Emlyn found himself bound to express his views openly and without reserve:

He admitted that he believed in One God. He declared that God was Alone the Supreme Being and that Jesus derived all authority and power from Him alone. He added that if the congregation found his views obnoxious, he was quite willing to resign to enable them to choose a minister who supported their own opinions. The majority of the congregation did not want this, but the situation was such that he resigned, much to their sorrow. He was advised to go to England for a short while to let things calm down. This he did.

After he had been in England for ten weeks, Emlyn returned to Dublin in order to collect and bring his family back to England. Before he could do so, he was arrested, in 1703, and charged with being a heretic. It had been discovered that he was responsible for publishing a book on Unitarianism entitled *An Humble Inquiry into the Scripture Account of Jesus Christ*, and this provided the prosecution with all the evidence that they needed. The entire book is based fundamentally on the text in *John 14: 28* in which Jesus is reported as saying, 'The Father is Greater than I.' Emlyn sought to establish that Jesus was a mediator between man and God. Thus, in a subtle way, he indicated that Jesus was indeed separate from God – and, in so doing, he demolished the concept of the Trinity.

On account of the difficulty felt by his opponents in wording the indictment against him, Emlyn's trial was deferred for a few months, which he spent in prison. When the trial finally commenced, a 'gentlemen of the long robe' informed him that he would not be permitted to defend himself, but that it was designed 'to run him down like a wolf without law or game.' [47] It is accordingly not surprising that Emlyn was convicted and found guilty of 'writing and publishing an infamous and scandalous bible declaring that Jesus Christ is not the Supreme God.' [48] Emlyn was given the choice of being imprisoned for one year, or of paying a fine of one thousand pounds. He was to remain in prison until the fine was paid.

In the appeals against conviction and sentence which followed, Emlyn was dragged from court to court and paraded as a heretic before the public. This disgraceful treatment was described by his captors as a display of mercy – for if he had been in Spain or France, it was pointed out, he would have been burned alive by the Inquisition. After a great deal of pressure had been exerted on the government, the fine was reduced to seventy pounds. It was paid and Emlyn left prison and Ireland. An eminent priest, when commenting on the treatment meted out to heretics, declared that, 'the enlightening faculty of a dungeon and fine is very convincing.' [49]

Emlyn thus joined the distinguished saints who dared deny the doctrine of Trinity and affirm the faith in One and only One God. In the Divine revelation of the *Qur'an*, the whole matter is made clear. God is supreme and there is no one like Him. No one else is mentioned as God. Unfortunately, it is not so in the *Bible*. Emlyn therefore tried to clear up this confusion in his writings.

God, according to Emlyn, 'sometimes signifies the most High, Perfect, and Infinite Being, Who is of Himself Alone, and owes neither His Being nor His Authority, nor anything else to another; and this is what is most commonly intended when we speak of God in ordinary Discourse, and Prayer, and Praise; we mean it of God in the most eminent sense.'

Emlyn then goes on to demonstrate that in the *Bible*, although the word 'God' is often employed, it is sometimes used to signify persons who are invested with subordinate authority and power in comparison with the Supreme Being:

> Angels are styled as God ... 'Thou hast made him a little lower than the Gods.' (*Psalm 8: 5*); Magistrates are Gods. (*Exodus 22: 28, Psalm 82: 1, John 10: 34-35*); sometimes a person is styled as God, as Moses is twice called a God to Aaron, and afterwards a God to Pharaoh; and the Devil is also called the God of this World, i.e. the Prince and mighty ruler of it, who by unjust usurpation and God's permission occupies this position. Now as He Who alone is God in the former sense is infinitely above all these, so we find Him distinguished from all others who are called Gods.

To further clarify this distinction, Emlyn quoted Philo who describes the Supreme Being as 'not only God of men, but God of Gods.' This is the highest and most glorious epithet given to God in the *Old Testament*, when it is designed to make a most magnificent mention of His Greatness and Glory.

Having established that the *Bible* uses the term 'God' to describe God and to describe beings inferior to God, Emlyn then proceeded to try and resolve the question: 'In which of the two senses is Christ said to be 'God' in the Holy Scriptures?'

Emlyn concluded that Christ was an inferior being compared to the God of Gods, (see *I Corinthians 8: 5*). He reached this conclusion by asking himself this crucial question: 'Has Jesus Christ any God over him, who has greater Authority, and greater ability than himself, or not?' The reply to this question would decide the status of Jesus one way or the other. If God was above him, then clearly he could not also be the Absolutely Supreme God. Emlyn's reply to the question he had posed was 'Yes', and he provided three arguments to support his answer:

- Jesus expressly speaks of a God other than himself.

- He accepts his God to be above or over himself.

- He asks for perfection since he lacks those super-eminent and infinite perfections which belong only to God, the Supreme Being.

Emlyn felt that these three points had to be elaborated on in a way which would be understood by the general public. He decried the practice of those who wrote about the Scriptures in a manner unintelligible to the people and yet who expected them to believe in the dogma their writings described. Emlyn expanded these three points thus:

Firstly, Jesus speaks of another God distinct from himself. Several times we find him saying, 'My God' of another: 'My God, my God, why hast Thou forsaken me?' (*Matthew 27: 46*); 'I am returning to my Father and your Father, to my God and your God.' (*John 20: 17*). Surely, he intended not saying, 'My Self, My Self, why hast thou forsaken me?' This God was distinct from himself, as he declares in other places, in *John 8: 42*, where it is to be noted that he does not distinguish himself from Him as the Father, but as God, and therefore, in all just construction, he cannot be supposed to be the selfsame God, from whom he distinguished himself ...

Secondly, Jesus owns, not only another than himself to be God, but also that he is above or over himself, which is plainly intimated also by his Apostles. He himself loudly proclaims his subjection to the Father in many instances. In general, he declares his Father to be greater than himself. He says he came not to do anything on his own, but only in his Father's name and authority. He sought not his own, but God's Glory; nor made his own will, but God's his rule. In such a posture of subjection he came down from heaven into this earth. Again he owns his dependence upon God, even for those things, which it is pretended belong to him, as God, *viz.,* the power of working miracles, of raising the dead, of executing universal judgement: all of which he says, 'of my own self I can do nothing.' (*John 5: 30*).

Thirdly, Jesus disclaims those infinite perfections (underived power, absolute goodness, unlimited knowledge), which belong only to the Supreme God of Gods. And it is most certain that, if he lacks one or any of these perfections that are essential to the Deity he is not God in the same sense. If we find him disclaiming the one, he cannot challenge the other, for to deny himself to have all Divine Perfections, or to deny himself to be the Infinite God is the same thing.

Emlyn then goes on to give some examples in order to illustrate this last point:

One great and peculiar Perfection of the Deity, is absolute and underived Omnipotence. He who cannot work all miracles, and do whatever he wills by himself can never be the Supreme Being if he cannot do it without the help of another. He appears to be an imperfect defective being, comparatively, since he needs help, and asks for additional strength from another than himself.

Now it is most evident, that Jesus, (whatever power he had), confesses again and again, that he had not infinite power by himself: 'Of myself I can do nothing.' (*John 5: 30*). He had been speaking of great miracles, *viz.*: raising the dead, of executing universal judgement; he makes it quite clear, that men should know that his sufficiency for these things was of God. In the beginning he says, 'The son can do nothing but what he sees the Father do.' So in the middle he says the same thing. As if he could never too much inculcate this great truth, he adds towards the conclusion, 'I can do nothing of myself ...' Surely this is not the Voice of God, but of man! The Most High can receive from none. He cannot be made more mighty or wise, because to absolute Perfection, there can be no addition. Since power in God is an essential Perfection, it follows that if it be derived, then so would be the essence or Being itself, which is blasphemy against the most High. To number Him among dependent derivative beings will be tantamount to 'un-God' Him. The supreme God indeed is only He who is the first Cause and absolute original of all.

Emlyn also considered the statement which is attributed to Jesus in *Mark* 13: 32. Speaking of the Day of Judgement, Jesus is reported to have said, 'Of that day knows no man, no, not the angels of heaven, not the son, but the Father only.' Emlyn observed that for anyone who believed in the divinity of Jesus this statement would imply that God had two natures, or two different states of awareness simultaneously. It would put Him in the ridiculous position of knowing and not knowing something at the same time. If Jesus was Divine and God had this knowledge then Jesus would not have made this statement, since by having this nature he too would have possessed that knowledge.

Thomas Emlyn, who died in July 1741, was well aware that he would be misunderstood by a large number of Christians. In defending his belief he made it clear in his *Confession of Christianity* that he regarded Jesus as his teacher, whom he admired and loved beyond father, mother or friends. He continued, 'I know that Jesus loves nothing but Truth, and will never be offended with anyone who stands by his words, *viz.*, that, "the Father is greater than I," (*John* 14: 28).' In view of this statement, argued Emlyn, it would be dangerous to say, 'God is not greater than Jesus.' [50]

Thomas Emlyn was a learned man of God who was distinguished by his learning and integrity, and for the firmness with which he endured persecution rather than compromise his beliefs. He belongs to the galaxy of saints who defied those who opposed and persecuted them. They suffered imprisonment, torture and even death, but did not falter before the might of the established Trinitarian Church and State which so often combined forces to eliminate them. On the whole, each instance of persecution only added to the popularity of their message which was, simply:

There are not Three but only One God.

Emlyn was one of the first of the Protestant dissenters who had the courage to publicly pronounce their disbelief in the doctrine of the Trinity. The number of Presbyterian ministers who joined him, and who embraced Arian and other Unitarian beliefs at the beginning of the eighteenth century was considerable. Ten years after Emlyn's trial, for example, the muffled unrest which had been felt in the Church of England as a result of the questioning of Jesus's supposed divinity exploded with the publication in 1712 of Samuel

Clarke's *Scripture Doctrine of the Trinity*. In this book, he cited 1,251 passages from the Scriptures to prove that God the Father was Supreme, and that Christ and the Holy Spirit were subordinate to Him. Clarke later published an edited version of the Book of Common Prayer omitting the Athanasian Creed and other Trinitarian features.

Theophilus Lindsey (1723-1808)

Theophilus Lindsey was born in 1723. He was the organiser of the first Unitarian congregation in England. Using a reformed order of service based on Samuel Clarke's revision of sixty years earlier, and robed without the traditional white surplice, Lindsey conducted the first service in an auction room on Essex Street in London. It was the 17th of April, 1774. The service was attended by a large congregation including Benjamin Franklin and Joseph Priestly. Here is Lindsey's account of the occasion, which is contained in a letter which he wrote to a friend the next day:

> You will be pleased to hear that everything passed off very well yesterday; a large and much more respectable audience than I could have expected, who behaved with great decency and in general appeared, and many of them expressed themselves, to be much satisfied with the whole of the service. Some disturbance was apprehended, and foreboded to me by the great names, but not the least movement of the kind. The only fault found with it, was that it was too small. From the impressions that seemed to be made, and the general seriousness and satisfaction, I am persuaded that this attempt will, through the divine blessing, be of singular usefulness. The contrast between ours and the church-service strikes everyone. Forgive me for saying, that I should have blushed to have appeared in a white garment. No one seemed in the least to want it. I am happy not to be hampered with anything – but entirely satisfied with the whole of the service; a satisfaction never before known – I must again say it, and bless God for it, that we were enabled to being well. And we only desire to go on as through His blessing we have begun ... [51]

The formation of the Essex Street congregation soon inspired other Unitarian 'chapels' to be built in Birmingham, Manchester, and other English cities. Ecclesiastical independence fostered doctrinal freedom, so that in 1790, in an address to the students of Oxford and Cambridge, Lindsey asserted the following 'facts, clear and plain to every understanding ... which all men, who believe the scriptures, sooner or later must bow down to and acknowledge':

- There is One God, one single person, Who is God, the sole Creator and sovereign Lord of all things;

- The holy Jesus was a man of the Jewish nation, the servant of this God, highly honoured and distinguished by Him;

- The Spirit, or Holy Spirit, was not a person, or an intelligent being; but only the extraordinary power or gift of God, imparted to Jesus Christ himself, in his life-time; and afterwards, to the apostles and many of the first Christians, to empower them to preach and propagate the Gospel with success (*Acts 1: 2*); and

- This was the doctrine concerning God, and Christ, and the Holy Spirit, which was taught by the apostles and preached to the Jews and heathens. [52]

With these almost modern convictions, English Unitarianism entered its greatest age. In his writings, Lindsey made the following points in order to demonstrate the fact that Jesus Christ is not God:

- Jesus never styles himself as God; nor does he give even the least intimation that he was the person by whom all things were made.

- The Scriptures of the *Old Testament* throughout speak of but one Person, one Jehova, as God by Himself, Alone and Creator of all things. With reference to *1 John 5: 7*, it is therefore not credible that John, a pious Hebrew, should all at once introduce another creator, a new God, without any notice. It is not known whence he drew this strange doctrine, or by what authority he delivered it; especially when we consider that by the law of Moses, whose divine authority he acknowledged, it was the crime of idolatry and blasphemy to have, or to worship, any other God but Jehova. His lord and master, Jesus, made mention of no other God but Jehova, and never took upon himself to speak anything of himself; but as the Father, whose messenger he was, gave him commandment what he should say and what he should speak. (*John 12: 49*).

(*Note*: It would appear from what Lindsey says here, that at this stage the discovery by Sir Isaac Newton that *I John 5: 7* is a forgery had not yet come to light.)

- The writers of the Gospel history speak of one divine person, the Father, as the only true God. (*John 17: 3*).

- Mark, Matthew and Luke appear to have written their Gospels without consulting each other. They never even give a hint of Jesus being God. It cannot be believed or imagined that these men, if they had known him to be God and Creator of the World, would have kept silent on such an important matter.

- John, who begins his Gospel by saying that the Word was God and that Jesus was the Word made flesh, does not ascribe this name to him once in the rest of his Gospel.

- An examination of Luke's gospel shows that he believed that Jesus had no existence before he was born of his mother, Mary, since:

    - In *Luke 3: 23-38*, a lineal descent of Jesus is given.

    - In *Luke 4: 24* and *13: 33*, Jesus is acknowledged to be a Prophet of God.

    - In *Luke 7: 16* and *24: 19*, Jesus is called a Prophet.

    - In *Luke 9: 20* and *26* and in *Luke 22: 27* and *29*, Peter and some of the other apostles call Jesus the servant of God.

- In *Luke 5: 24* and in *Luke 17: 24* and *30*, Luke describes Jesus as the 'son of man', appointed to an important office under God that made the world.

Lindsey asked those who worshipped Jesus as if he were God what their replies would be if Jesus – who is often described in the Gospels as praying to God, but never to himself – appeared to them and asked the following questions:

- Why did you address your devotions to me? Did I ever direct you to do it, or propose myself as an object of religious worship?

- Did I not uniformly and to the last set you an example myself of praying to the Father, to my Father and your Father, to my God and your God? (*John 20: 17*).

- When my disciples requested me to teach them to pray (*Luke 11: 1-4*), did I teach them to pray to myself or to any other person but the Father?

- Did I ever call myself God, or tell you that I was the maker of the world, and to be worshipped?

- Did not Solomon, after building the Temple, say, 'Will God indeed dwell on the earth? Behold the heaven and heaven of heavens cannot contain Thee; how much less this house which I have built.'? (*1 Kings 8: 27*). [53]

Lindsey's belief in the Divine Unity is evident from these words of his:

The Infinite Creator should be worshipped in all places for He is everywhere … no place is more sacred than another, but every place is sacred for the prayer. The worshipper makes the place. Whenever there is a devout humble mind that looks to God, God is there. A mind free from sin is the true temple of God. [54]

Joseph Priestly (1733-1804)

Joseph Priestly was born in the little hamlet of Fieldhead six miles south-west of Leeds in 1733. He was the eldest child of a domestic cloth-maker. His mother died when he was six years old. At home he was given a strict Calvinist upbringing, but at school his teachers were dissenting ministers, that is to say, priests who did not agree with all the doctrines of the Trinitarian Church of England. With a view to becoming a minister, Priestly became well-grounded in Latin, Greek and Hebrew. The Elders of the Quakers refused to admit him, however, as he did not demonstrate sufficient repentance for Adam's sins. Similarly, the universities refused to accept anyone who did not subscribe to all the doctrines of the orthodox Church.

Instead, Priestly was sent to a well-known academy where the teachers and students were divided between the 'orthodoxy' of the established Church and the 'heresy' of belief in One God. Here Priestly began to doubt the truth of the fundamental dogmas of the official Christian church in earnest, especially that of the doctrine of Trinity. The more he studied the *Bible*, the more convinced of his own views Priestly became. The writings of Arius, Servetus, and Socianus left a profound impression on him and like them, he also came to the conclusion that the Scriptures provided meagre support for the doctrines of Trinity, Original Sin, and the Atonement and Redemption of Sins. The result was that on completion of his studies he left the Academy as a confirmed Arian.

Priestly was subsequently appointed as an assistant to a minister at a salary of thirty pounds *per annum*. When it was discovered that he was an Arian, he was dismissed. In 1758 he succeeded in securing another appointment as a minister in Nantwich, in Cheshire. He served there for three years. His income was small but he supplemented it by giving private tuition. He soon acquired the reputation of being a good teacher.

The Arians had established an Academy at Warrington in 1757, and on leaving Nantwich, Priestly became a teacher there. He used to visit London during the vacations, and it was on one of these visits that he met Benjamin Franklin for the first time.

In 1767 Priestly came to preach nearer his old home, becoming the minister in Mill Hill in Leeds. He stayed there for six years. It was in Leeds that Priestly printed a number of tracts and he soon became well-known as an outstanding and authoritative spokesman for Unitarianism.

In his spare time, Priestly began to study chemistry with considerable success. He won recognition from the Royal Society, and in 1774 made his crowning discovery of oxygen, which made him famous. In the research which followed, Priestly discovered more new gases than all his predecessors had done before him. However, he was more interested in religion than in physical science and regarded these discoveries as a theologian's pastime. In his personal memoirs, he passes over these achievements in the space of about a page. He once wrote, 'I have made discoveries in some branches of Chemistry. I never gave much attention to the common routine of it, and know but little of the common processes.'[55]

Priestly next joined the Earl of Shellburne as his librarian and literary companion. He was given a generous salary and a life annuity with the freedom to do what he pleased. He remained at this post for seven years, spending the summers in the Earl's country mansion and the winters in London. He also accompanied the Earl on his journeys to Paris, Holland, Belgium and Germany. The Earl found Priestly's friendship with Benjamin Franklin an embarrassment, since the latter was all in favour of the Revolution taking place in France at this time. Priestly formally terminated his friendship with Franklin and shortly afterwards went to stay in Birmingham. His stay in this city lasted for eleven years, and although it ended in a crushing tragedy, it was perhaps the happiest period of his life. His duties as a priest were confined to Sundays and so during the rest of the week he was free to work in his laboratory and to write whatever he wished.

It was in Birmingham that Priestly produced his most important and influential work, *A History of the Corruptions of Christianity*, which greatly angered the established Church. He not only denied the validity of the doctrine of Trinity, but also affirmed the humanity of Jesus. He pointed out that the biblical narratives of the birth of Jesus were inconsistent with one another. He believed that Jesus was a man, constituted in all respects like other men, and subject to the same infirmities, the same ignorance, the same prejudices and the same frailties. He was chosen by God, however, to introduce a moral dispensation into the world. He was instructed in the nature of his mission, and invested with miraculous powers. Jesus was sent to reveal the great knowledge of the next life in which men would be rewarded according to their acts in this life and not merely by virtue of their having been baptised. These views were not liked either by the government or by the official Church.

Priestly not only affirmed the humanity of Jesus, but also denied the immaculate conception. He thus laid the foundation of the new thinking which resulted in Unitarianism becoming like a voyage in a boat without a rudder riding on a turbulent sea. A sense of direction is totally missing in the movement known as Unitarian Universalism.

This denial of the immaculate conception – which is confirmed by the *Qur'an* – led to a totally unnecessary and bitter controversy that did more harm than good to those who affirmed the Divine Unity. A similar movement had contributed towards the French Revolution and its Reign of Terror. These events on the other side of the Channel had unnerved many people in England. The orthodox Church made it appear that the teachings of Priestly would result in the same kind of tragedy in England. Countless insulting and threatening letters began to arrive at his doorstep, and his effigy was burned in different parts of the country.

On July the 14th 1791, a group of people were celebrating the anniversary of the fall of the Bastille in a Birmingham hotel. A mob, whose leaders were the justices of the town, gathered outside and, thinking Priestly was taking part in the celebrations, smashed the hotel windows. Dr. Priestly was not there. The mob then went to his house which, Priestly writes in his memoirs, was 'plundered and burnt without mercy.' [56] His library, his laboratory and all his papers and manuscripts were destroyed in the fire. Priestly, who had been forewarned by a friend, barely escaped with his life.

The next day, the houses of all the important Unitarians in Birmingham were burnt, and in the two days which followed the mob began to burn the houses of those people who were not even professed Unitarians, but who had given shelter and protection to the Unitarians who had been made homeless. During this time the people of Birmingham were in a panic. All the shops were closed, and people cried out and wrote on their houses 'Church and King' to escape the fury of the mob. It was not until the army was called in that the rioters melted away.

It was now too dangerous for Priestly to remain in Birmingham, and he left for London in disguise. Writing about his experiences in Birmingham, he said, 'Instead of flying from lawless violence, I had been flying from public justice. I could not have been pursued with more rancour.' [57] In London he was unable to openly walk on the streets lest he be recognised and the house of his host attacked and destroyed. After a while he rented a house. The landlord was afraid that not only this house, but also his own might be destroyed.

In 1794, Priestly sailed for America with Benjamin Franklin. There they opened some of the first Unitarian churches in and around Philadelphia. In the years that followed, the situation in England became more relaxed. In 1802, Priestly's old congregation opened a chapel, and Bilsham, a leading Unitarian, was invited to preach the opening sermon. Priestly, however, was content to remain in America, where he died in 1804.

Joseph Priestly's main contribution to the Unitarians in England were his comprehensive arguments, both historical and philosophical, in support of the Unity of God. They were drawn from the Scriptures and the writings of the old Christian fathers, interpreted by reason, and rigorously applied to the religious and political problems of his day. 'Absurdity supported by power,' he wrote, 'will never be able to stand its ground against the efforts of reason.' [58]

Of all Priestly's religious works, the most influential was his *History of the Corruptions of Christianity*, written in two volumes, in which he sought to show that true Christianity, as embodied in the beliefs of the early Church, was Unitarian – and that all departures from that faith were corruptions. The book infuriated the orthodox and delighted the liberals in both England and America. It was publicly burned in Holland. Here follows Priestly's own summary of his work:

> To consider the system of Christianity, one would think it very liable to corruption, or abuse. The great outline of it is that the Universal Parent of mankind commissioned Jesus Christ to invite men to practice virtue, by the assurance of His mercy to the penitent, and of His purpose to raise to immortal life and happiness all the virtuous and good. Here is nothing that any person could imagine would lead to much subtle speculation, at least such as could excite animosity. The doctrine itself is so plain, that one would think the learned and the unlearned were upon a level with respect to it. And a person unacquainted with the state of things, at the time of its promulgation would look in vain for any probable source of the monstrous corruptions and abuses which crept into the system afterwards. Jesus,

however, and his apostles, foretold that there would be a great departure from the truth, and that something would arise in the Church altogether unlike the doctrine which they taught, and even subversive of it.

In reality, however, the causes of the succeeding corruptions did then exist, and accordingly, without anything more than their natural operation, all the abuses rose to their full height; and what is more wonderful still, by the operation of natural causes also, we see the abuses gradually corrected, and Christianity recovering its primitive beauty and glory.

The causes of the corruptions were almost wholly contained in the established opinions of the heathen world, and especially the philosophical part of it, so that when those heathens embraced Christianity, they mixed their former tenets and prejudices with it. Also, both Jews and heathens were so much scandalised at the idea of being disciples of a man who had been crucified as a common malefactor, that Christians in general were sufficiently disposed to adopt any opinion that would most effectually wipe away this reproach.

The opinion that the mental faculties of man belonging to a substance distinct from his body or brain, and of this invisible spiritual part, or soul, being capable of subsisting before and after its union with the body, which had taken the deepest root in all schools of philosophy, was wonderfully calculated to answer this purpose. For by this means Christians were enabled to give to the soul of Christ what rank they pleased in the heavenly region before he was born. On this principle went the Gnostics, deriving their doctrine from the received oriental philosophy. Afterwards, the philosophising Christians went upon another principle, personifying the wisdom, or Logos, of God the Father, equal to God the Father Himself ...

The abuses of the positive institutions of Christianity, monstrous as they were, naturally arose from the opinion of the purifying and sanctifying virtues of rites and ceremonies, which was the very basis of all the worships of the heathens! And they were also similar to the abuses of the Jewish religion. We likewise see the rudiments of all the monkish austerities in the opinions and practices of the heathens, who thought to purify and exalt the soul by macerating and mortifying the body.

As to the abuses of the government of the Church, they are as easily accounted for as abuses in civil government; worldly-minded men being always ready to lay hold of every opportunity of increasing their power; and in the dark ages too many circumstances concurred to give the Christian clergy peculiar advantages over the laity in this respect.

Upon the whole, I flatter myself that, to an attentive reader of this work, it will appear, that the Corruption of Christianity, in every article of faith or practice, was the natural consequence of the circumstances in which it was promulgated; and also that its recovery from these corruptions is the natural consequence of different circumstances.

To bring the whole (false Christian position) into a short compass:

1. The General Council gave the Son the same nature with the Father.

2. Admitted the Holy Spirit into the Trinity.

3. Consigned to Christ a human soul in conjunction with the Logos.

4. Settled the hypothetical union of the divine and human nature of Christ, and

5. Affirmed, that in consequence of this union, the two natures constituted only one person.

It requires a pretty good memory to retain these distinctions, it being a business of words only, and ideas are not concerned in it. [59]

Priestly also wrote another book called *The History of Jesus Christ*, some of which is reprinted here:

When we inquire into the doctrine of any book, or set of books, concerning any subject, and particular passages are alleged in favour of different opinions, we should chiefly consider what is the general tenor of the whole work with respect to it, or what impression the first careful perusal of it would make upon an impartial reader...

If we consult Moses' account of the creation, we shall find that he makes no mention of more than one God, Who made the heavens and the earth, Who supplied the earth with plants and animals, and Who also formed man. The plural number, indeed, is made use of when God is represented as saying, (*Genesis 1: 26*), 'Let Us make man'; but that this is mere phraseology is evident from its being said immediately after, in the singular number, (*Genesis 1: 27*), 'God created man in His own image', so that the Creator was still One Being. Also, in the account of the building of the Tower of Babel, we read, (*Genesis 11: 7*), that God said, 'Come, let Us go down and there confound their language'; but we find, in the very next verse, that it was One Being only Who actually effected this.

In all the intercourse of God with Adam, Noah, and the other patriarchs, no mention is made of more than One Being who addressed them under that character. The name by which he is distinguished is sometimes 'Jehova', and at other times, 'the God of Abraham', *etc.*, but no doubt can be entertained that this was the same Being who is first mentioned under the general title of God, and to Whom the making of the heavens and the earth is ascribed.

Frequent mention is made in the Scriptures of 'angels', who sometimes speak in the Name of God, but then they are always represented as the creatures and the servants of God ... On no account, however, can these angels be considered as 'Gods', rivals of the Supreme Being, or of the same rank with Him.

The most express declarations concerning the Unity of God, and of the importance of the belief of it, are frequent in the *Old Testament*. The first commandment is, (*Exodus 20: 3*), 'Thou shalt have no other gods before Me.' This is repeated in the most emphatical manner,

(*Deuteronomy* 6: 4), 'Hear, O Israel, the Lord thy God is one Lord.' I have no occasion to repeat what occurs on this subject in the later prophets. It appears, indeed, to have been the great object of the religion of the Jews, and of their being distinguished from other nations by the superior presence and superintendence of God, to preserve among them the knowledge of the Divine Unity, while the rest of the world were falling into idolatry. And by means of this nation, and the discipline which it underwent, that great doctrine was effectually preserved among men, and continues to be so to this day.

Had there been any distinction of persons in the Divine Nature, such as the doctrine of the Trinity supposes, it is at least so like an infringement of the fundamental doctrine of the Jewish religion, that it certainly required to be explained, and the obvious inference from it to be guarded against. Had the eternal Father had a Son, and also a Spirit, each of them equal in power and glory to Himself, though there should have been a sense in which each of them was truly God, and yet there was, properly speaking, only One God; at least the more obvious inference would have been, that if each of the three persons was properly God, they would all together make three Gods. Since, therefore, nothing of this kind is said in the *Old Testament*, as the objection is never made, nor answered, it is evident that the idea had not then occurred. No expression, or appearance, had at that time even suggested the difficulty.

If we guide ourselves by the sense in which the Jews understood their own sacred books, we cannot but conclude that they contained no such doctrine as that of the Christian Trinity. For it does not appear that any Jew, of ancient or modern times, ever deduced such a doctrine from them. The Jews always interpreted their Scriptures as teaching that God is simply One, without distinction of persons, and that the same Being Who made the world, did also speak to the patriarchs and the Prophets without the intervention of any other beings besides angels.

Christians have imagined that the Messiah was to be the second person in the divine trinity; but the Jews themselves, great as were their expectations from the Messiah, never supposed any such thing. And if we consider the prophecies concerning this great personage, we shall be satisfied that they could not possibly have led them to expect any other than a man in that character. The Messiah is supposed to be announced to our first parents under the title of 'the seed of the woman', (*Genesis 3: 15*) ...

God promised to Abraham, (*Genesis 12: 3*), that 'in his seed all the families of the earth should be blessed.' This, if it relate to the Messiah at all, can give us no other idea than that one of his seed or posterity, should be the means of conferring great blessings on mankind. What else, also, could be suggested by the description which Moses is supposed to give of the Messiah, when he said, (*Deuteronomy 18: 18*), 'I will raise them up a Prophet, from among their brethren, like unto thee, and will put my words in his mouth, and he shall speak unto them all that I shall command him.'? Here is nothing like a second person in the trinity, a person equal to the Father, but a mere Prophet, delivering in the Name of God, whatever he is ordered to do ...

In the *New Testament* we find the same doctrine concerning God that we do in the Old. To the scribe who inquired which was the first and the greatest commandment, our Saviour answered, (*Mark 12: 29*), 'The first of all the commandments is, "Hear O Israel, the Lord our God is One Lord,"' *etc.*, and the scribe answered to him, 'Well, master, thou hast said the truth; for there is One God, and there is none other but He,' *etc.*

Christ himself always prayed to this One God, as his God and Father. He always spoke of himself as receiving his doctrine and his power from Him, and again and again disclaimed having any power of his own. (*John 5: 19*): 'Then answered Jesus and said unto them, "Verily, verily, I say unto you, the Son can do nothing of himself."' (*John 14: 10*): 'The words which I speak unto you, I speak not of myself, but the Father that dwelleth in me, he doth the works.' (*John 20: 17*): 'Go to my brethren, and say unto them, "I ascend unto my Father, and your Father, and unto my God and your God."' It cannot, surely, be God who uses such language as this.

The apostles to the latest period of their writings, speak the same language; representing the Father as the only true God, and Christ as a man, the servant of God, who raised him from the dead, and gave him all the power of which he is possessed, as a reward of his obedience. (*Acts* 2: 22): Peter says, 'Ye men of Israel, hear these words, Jesus of Nazareth, a man approved of God among you, by miracles, and wonders, and signs, which God did by him, *etc.*, whom God has raised up.' Paul also says, (*l Timothy* 2: 5), 'There is One God, and one mediator between God and men, the man Christ Jesus.'

Priestly continues:

It will be seen in the course of this history that the common people, for whose use the books of the *New Testament* were written, saw nothing in them of the doctrines of the pre-existence or divinity of Christ, which many persons of this day are so confident that they see in them ... Why was not the doctrine of the trinity taught as explicitly, and in as definite a manner in the *New Testament* at least, as the doctrine of the Divine Unity is taught in both the *Old* and *New Testament*, if it be a truth? And why is the doctrine of the Unity always delivered in so unguarded a manner, and without any exception made in favour of a trinity, to prevent any mistake with respect to it, as is always now done in our orthodox catechisms, creeds, and discourses on the subject? ... Divines are content to build the strange and inexplicable doctrine of the trinity upon mere inferences from casual expressions, and cannot pretend to one clear, express, and unequivocal textual source.

There are many, very many, passages of Scripture, which inculcate the doctrine of the Divine Unity in the clearest and strongest manner. Let one such passage be produced in favour of the trinity. And why should we believe things so mysterious without the clearest and most express evidence?

There is also another consideration which should be recommended to those who maintain that Christ is either God, or the maker of the world under God. It is this: The manner in which our lord speaks of himself, and of the power by which he worked miracles, is inconsistent, according to the common construction of language, with the idea of his being possessed of any proper power of his own, more than other men have.

If Christ was the maker of the world he could not have said that of himself he could do nothing, that the words which he spoke were not his own, and that the Father within him did the works. For if any ordinary man, doing what other men usually do, should apply this language to himself, and say that it was not he that spoke or acted, but God Who spoke and acted by him, and that otherwise he was not capable of so speaking or acting at all, we should not hesitate to say that his language was either false or blasphemous …

It would also be an abuse of language if Christ could be supposed to say that his Father was greater than he, and yet secretly mean his human nature only, while his divine nature was at the same time fully equal to that of the Father. There is nothing that can be called an account of the divine, or even the super-angelic nature of Christ in the Gospels of Matthew, Mark, or Luke; and allowing that there may be some colour for it in the introduction to the gospel of John, it is remarkable that there are many passages in his Gospel which are decisively in favour of his simple humanity.

Now these evangelists could not imagine that either the Jews or the Gentiles, for whose use their Gospels were written, would not stand in need of information on a subject of so much importance, which was so very remote from the apprehensions of them both, and which would at the same time have so effectually covered the reproach of the cross, which was continually abject to the Christians of that age. If the doctrines of the divinity, or pre-existence, of Christ are true, they are no doubt in the highest degree important and interesting. Since, therefore, these evangelists give no certain and distinct account of them, and say nothing at all of their importance, it may be safely inferred that they were unknown to them.

It must also be asked how the apostles could continue to call Christ a man, as they always do, both in the book of Acts, and in their epistles, after they had discovered him to be either God, or a super-angelic being, the maker of the world under God. After this, it must have been highly degrading, unnatural, and improper, notwithstanding his appearance in human form ...

Let us put ourselves in the place of the apostles and first disciples of Christ. They certainly saw and conversed with him at first on the supposition that he was a man like themselves. Of this there can be no doubt. Their surprise, therefore, upon being informed that he was not a man, but really God, or even the maker of the world under God, would be of the same nature as ours on discovering that a man of our acquaintance was supposed to be in reality God, or the maker of the world. Let us consider then, how we should feel, how we should behave towards such a person, and how we should speak of him afterwards. No one, I am confident, would ever call any person a man, after he was convinced he was either God, or an angel. He would always speak of him in a manner suitable to his proper rank.

Suppose that any two men of our acquaintance, should appear, on examination to be the angels Michael and Gabriel, would we call them men after that? Certainly not. We would naturally say to our friends, 'Those two persons whom we took to be men, are not men, but angels in disguise.' This language would be natural. Had Christ, therefore, been anything more than man before he came into the world, and especially had he been either God, or the maker of the world, he never could have been considered as being a man, while he was in it; for he could not divest himself of his superior and proper nature. However disguised, he would always in fact have been whatever he had been before, and would have been so styled by all who truly knew him ...

It must strike every person who gives the least attention to the phraseology of the *New Testament*, that the terms 'Christ' and 'God', are perpetually used in contradistinction to each other, as much as 'God' and 'man';

and if we consider the natural use of words, we become satisfied that this would not have been the case, if the former could have been predicated of the latter, that is, if Christ had been God.

We say 'the prince and the king', because the prince is not a king. If he had been, we should have had recourse to some other distinction, as that of 'greater and less', 'senior and junior', 'father and son', *etc.* When therefore, the apostle Paul said that the Church at Corinth was Christ's, and that Christ was God's, and that manner of distinguishing them is recurrent in the *New Testament*, it is evident that he could have no idea of Christ being God, in any meaningful sense of the word.

In like manner, Clemens Romanus, calling Christ the 'sceptre of the Majesty of God', sufficiently proves that in his idea the sceptre was one thing, and the God whose sceptre it was, another. This, I say, must have been the case when this language was first adopted.

Having shown that the general tenor of the Scriptures, and several considerations that obviously may be deduced from them are highly unfavourable to the doctrine of the trinity, or to those of the divinity or pre-existence of Christ, there arises another consideration, which has been little attended to, but which seems very strongly to go against either of these doctrines having been known in the time of the apostles, and therefore against their being the doctrine of the Scriptures. That Jesus was even the Messiah, was divulged with the greatest caution, both to the apostles and to the body of the Jews. For a long time our Lord said nothing explicit on this subject, but left his disciples, as well as the Jews at large, to judge him from what they saw. In this manner only he replied to the messengers that John the Baptist sent to him.

If the high-priest expressed his horror, by rending his clothes, on Jesus avowing himself to be the Messiah, what would he have done if he had heard or suspected, that he had made any higher pretensions? And if he had made them, they must have transpired. When the people in general saw his miraculous works, they only wondered that God should have given such power to a man,

(*Matthew* 9: 8): 'When the multitude saw it, they marvelled, and glorified God, who had given such power
unto men.'

At the time that Herod heard of him, it was conjec-
tured by some that he was Elias, by others, a Prophet,
and by some that he was John risen from the dead; but
none of them imagined that he was either the most high
God Himself, or the maker of the world under God. It
was not so much as suggested by any person that Jesus
performed his mighty works by any power of his own.

If the doctrine of the divinity of Christ had been actually preached by the apostles, and the Jewish converts
in general had adopted it, it could not but have been
well known to the unbelieving Jews. And would they,
who were at that time, and have been ever since, so exceedingly zealous with respect to the doctrine of the
Divine Unity, not have taken the alarm, and have urged
this objection to Christianity, as teaching the belief of
more Gods than one in the apostolic age?

And yet no trace of anything of this nature can be
perceived in the whole history of the book of Acts, or
anywhere else in the *New Testament*. To answer the
charge of holding two or three Gods, is a very considerable article in the writings of several of the ancient Christian Fathers. Why then do we find nothing of this kind
in the age of the apostles? The only answer is, that then
there was no occasion for it, the doctrine of the divinity
of Christ not then having been put forward.

What was the accusation against Stephen, (*Acts* 6: 13),
but his speaking blasphemous things against the temple and the law? If we accompany the apostle Paul in
all his travels, and attend to his discourses with the Jews
in their synagogues, and their perpetual and inveterate
persecution of him, we shall find no trace of their so
much as suspecting that he preached a new divinity, as
the godhead of Christ must have appeared, and always
has appeared to them.

Is it possible to give due attention to these considerations, and not be aware that the apostles had never been
instructed in any such doctrines as those of the divinity
or pre-existence of Christ? If they had, as the doctrines

were quite new, and must have appeared extraordinary, we should certainly have been able to trace the time when they were communicated to them. They would naturally have expressed some surprise, if they had intimated no doubt about the truth of the information. If they received them with unshaken faith themselves, they would have taught them to others, who would not have received them so readily. They would have had the doubts of some to encounter, and the objections of others to answer. And yet, in all their history, and copious writings, we perceive no trace of their own surprise, or doubts or of the surprise, doubts, or objections of others.

It must be acknowledged that the proper object of prayer is God the Father, Who is called the first person in the trinity. Indeed, we cannot find in the Scriptures either any precept that will authorise us to address ourselves to any other person, or any proper example of it. The sort of thing that can be alleged to this purpose, like Stephen's short address to Christ after he had seen him in vision, is very inconsiderable. Jesus himself always prayed to his Father, and with as much humility and resignation as the most dependent being in the universe could possibly do; always addressing him as his Father, or the Author of his being; and he directs his disciples to pray to the same Being, the One, he says, we ought to serve.

Accordingly, the practice of praying to the Father only was long universal in the Christian church. The short addresses to Christ, as those in the Litany, 'Lord have mercy upon us, Christ have mercy upon us,' being comparatively of late date. In the Clementine liturgy, the oldest that is extant, contained in the Apostolical Constitutions, which were probably composed about the fourth century, there is no trace of any such thing. Origen, in a large treatise on the subject of prayer, urges very forcibly the propriety of praying to the Father only, and not to Christ; and as he gives no hint that the public forms of prayer had anything reprehensible in them in that respect, we are naturally led to conclude that, in his time, such petitions to Christ were unknown in the public assemblies of Christians.

Let us now attend to some particulars in the history of the apostles. When Herod had put to death James, the brother of John, and imprisoned Peter, we read, (*Acts 12: 5*), that, 'prayer was made without ceasing of the church unto God,' not to Christ, 'for him.' When Paul and Silas were in prison at Philippi, we read, (*Acts 16: 25*), that they 'sung praises to God,' not to Christ. And when Paul was warned of what would befall him if he went to Jerusalem, (*Acts 21: 14*), he said, 'The will of the Lord be done.' This, it must be supposed, was meant of God the Father, because Christ himself used the same language in this sense: when praying to the Father, (*Luke 22: 42*), he said, 'Not my will, but Thine be done ...'

It has been shown that there is no such doctrine as that of the trinity in the scriptures. The doctrine itself, as has been clearly demonstrated, has proved impossible for reasonable men to accept or even hold in their minds, as it implies contradictions which render it meaningless.

The Athanasian doctrine of the trinity asserts in effect that nothing is wanting in either the Father, the Son, or the Spirit, to let any one of them truly and properly be God, each of them being equal in eternity, and all divine perfections; and yet these three are not three Gods, but only one God. They are therefore both one and many in the same respect – in each being perfect God.

This is certainly as much a contradiction, as to say that Peter, James, and John, having each of them everything that is requisite to constitute a complete man, are yet all together not three men, but only one man. For the ideas annexed to the words 'God', or 'man', cannot make any difference in the nature of the two propositions. After the Council of Nicea, there are instances of the doctrine of the trinity being explained in this very manner. The Fathers of that age being particularly intent on preserving the full equality of the three persons, entirely lost sight of their proper unity. Thus no matter how this doctrine is explained, one of these always has to be sacrificed to the other. As people are apt to confuse themselves with the use of the words 'person' and 'being', these should be defined.

The term 'being' may be predicated of every thing, and therefore of each of the three persons in the trinity. For to say that Christ, for instance, is God, but that there is no being, no substance to which His attributes may be referred, would be manifestly absurd; and therefore when it is said that each of these persons is by himself God, the meaning must be that the Father, separately considered, has a being; that the Son, separately considered, has a being, and likewise that the Holy Spirit, separately considered, has a being. Here then are no less than three beings, as well as three persons, and what can these three beings be but three Gods, without supposing that there are 'three co-ordinate persons, or three Fathers, three Sons, or three Holy Ghosts?'

If this mysterious power of generation be peculiar to the Father, why does it not still operate? Is He not an unchangeable being, the same now that He was from the beginning, His perfections the same, and His power of contemplating them the same? Why then are not more sons produced? Has He become incapable of this generation, as the orthodox Fathers used to ask, or does it depend upon His will and pleasure whether He will exert this power of generation? If so, is not the Son as much a creature, depending on the will of the Creator, as anything else produced by Him, though in another manner; and this whether he be of the same substance with Him, or not?

It must also be asked in what manner the third person of the trinity was produced. Was it by the joint exertion of the first two, in the contemplation of their respective perfections? If so, why does not the same operation in them produce a fourth and so on?

Admitting, however, this strange account of the generation of the trinity, that the personal existence of the Son necessarily flows from the intellect of the Father exerted on itself; it certainly implies a virtual priority, or superiority in the Father with respect to the Son; and no being can be properly God, who has any superior. In short, this scheme effectually overturns the doctrine of the proper equality, as well as the unity of the three persons in the trinity.

The great objection to the doctrine of the trinity is that it is an infringement of the doctrine of the Unity of God, as the sole object of worship, which it was the primary design of Divine Revelation to establish. Any modification of this doctrine, therefore, or any other system whatever, ought to be regarded with suspicion, in proportion as it makes a multiplicity of objects of worship, for that is to introduce idolatry. [60]

○   ○   ○   ○   ○

The Unitarian movement in England had a profound effect in America, where it began as an off-shoot of Calvinism – but by the seventeenth century, the different foundations gradually changed into different religious denominations, with not so much emphasis being placed on dogma. As a result, the way ahead was opened up for gradual theological change:

Charles Chauncy (1705-1757), of Boston, gave a definite impetus and direction to the establishment of belief in the Divine Unity. Under James Freeman (1759-1835), the congregation of King's Chapel in Boston purged their Anglican Liturgy of all references to the doctrine of Trinity. This took place in 1785. Thus, the first Unitarian Church came into existence in the New World. Here, the doctrines of Priestly were openly printed and freely distributed, and they were accepted by the majority of the people in Boston. The result was that Unitarianism was accepted by all the ministers in Boston except one.

In other words, the religious intolerance which had characterised the attitude of the various established Trinitarian Churches – whether Roman Catholic or Protestant – in Europe was not exported to the New World in its entirety. Although the Roman Catholic armies succeeded in massacring vast numbers of the indigenous inhabitants of the West Indies and South America – in the name of Jesus Christ, and although the Protestants succeeded in massacring vast numbers of the indigenous inhabitants of North America – in the name of Jesus Christ, there was nevertheless a sufficient amount of open space and a sufficient degree of human tolerance in the New World to permit Unitarianism to grow.

○   ○   ○   ○   ○

William Ellery Channing (1780-1842)

William Channing was born in 1780. At the age of twenty-three he came to Boston and began his ministry which was to have a great influence on Unitarian thought. Channing had never accepted the doctrine of Trinity, but it was then not considered safe to openly denounce it. Along with other Unitarian ministers, he was accused of secretly spreading his views against the doctrine of Trinity. Channing replied that their views on Trinity were not concealed, but that they preached as if this doctrine had never been known. Channing said that they had adopted this approach so as not to divide the Christians against each other. Thus, at this stage, the Unitarian movement had not yet come out fully into the open.

In 1819, Channing gave a discourse at the ordination of the Reverend Jared Sparks. In his inimitable way, he outlined the salient features of Unitarian belief. He asserted that the *New Testament* was based on the *Old Testament*, and that the teaching which had been dispensed to the Christians was a continuation of the Jewish one. It was the completion of a vast scheme of Providence which required a vast perspective to be understood.

(Clearly Channing had not been granted access to a reliable translation of the *Qur'an* – which not only confirms the link between and continuity of the teachings of Moses and Jesus, but also confirms that the teachings of Muhammad are in turn a continuation of their teachings, may the blessings and peace of God be on him and them, and in fact the completion of the Prophetic tradition within God's 'vast scheme of Providence', which does indeed require a vast perspective to be understood.)

Keeping this in mind, said Channing, he affirmed the belief that God never contradicts in one part of the Scripture what He teaches in the other, and that He 'never contradicts in revelation, what He teaches in His works and providence. And we therefore distrust every interpretation, which, after deliberate attention, seems repugnant to any established truth.' Channing was insistent that man should make use of his reason:

> God has given us a rational nature, and will call us to account for it. We may let it sleep, but we do so at our peril. Revelation is addressed to us as rational beings.

We may wish, in our sloth, that God had given us a system demanding no labour of comparing, limiting, and inferring. But such a system would be at variance with the whole character of our present existence; and it is the part of wisdom to take revelation as it is given to us, and to interpret it by the help of the faculties, which it everywhere supposes, and on which it is founded.

Channing went on to say that:

If God be infinitely wise, He cannot sport with the understanding of His creatures. A wise teacher discovers his wisdom in adapting himself to the capacities of his pupils, not in perplexing them with what is unintelligible, not in distressing with apparent contradictions ... It is not the mark of wisdom to use an unintelligible phraseology to communicate what is above our capacity, to confuse and unsettle the intellect by appearance of contradictions ... A revelation is a gift of light. It cannot thicken our darkness and multiply our perplexities.

Following these principles, Channing continued:

In the first place, we believe in the doctrine of God's Unity, or that there is One God and One only. To this truth we give infinite importance and we feel ourselves bound to take heed lest any man spoil us of it by vain philosophy. The proposition that there is One God seems to us exceedingly plain. We understand by it that there is One Being. One Mind, One Person, One Intelligent Agent and One only to Whom underived and infinite perfection and dominion belongs. We conceive that these words could have conveyed no other meaning to the simple and uncultivated people who were set apart to be the depositaries of this great truth and who were utterly incapable of understanding those hair-breadth distinctions between being and person which the sagacity of later ages has discovered. We find no intimation that God's Unity was a quite different thing from the oneness of other intelligent beings.

We object to the doctrine of the Trinity, that whilst acknowledging in words, it subverts in effect, the Unity of God. According to this doctrine, there are three infinite and equal persons, possessing supreme divinity, called the Father, Son and Holy Ghost. Each of these persons, as described by theologians, has his own particular consciousness, will and perceptions. They love each other, converse with each other, and delight in each other's society. They perform different parts in man's redemption, each having his appropriate office, and neither doing the work of the other. The Son is mediator and not the Father. The Father sends the Son, and is not himself sent; nor is he conscious, like the Son, of taking flesh. Here, then, we have three intelligent agents, possessed of different consciousness, different wills, and different perceptions, performing different acts, and sustaining different relations; and if these things do not imply and constitute three minds or beings, we are utterly at a loss to know how three minds or beings are to be formed.

It is a difference of properties, and acts, and consciousness, which leads us to the belief of different intelligent beings, and if this mark fails us, our whole knowledge falls; we have no proof, that all the agents and persons in the universe are not one and the same mind. When we attempt to conceive of three Gods, we can do nothing more than represent to ourselves three agents, distinguished from each other by similar marks and peculiarities to those which separate the persons of the Trinity; and when common Christians hear these persons spoken of as conversing with each other, loving each other, and performing different acts, how can they not help regarding them as different beings, different minds?

We do, then with all earnestness, though without reproaching our brethren, protest against the irrational and unscriptural doctrine of the Trinity. 'To us,' as to the Apostle and the primitive Christians, 'there is One God, even the Father.' With Jesus, we worship the Father, as the only living and true God. We are astonished, that any man can read the *New Testament*, and avoid the conviction, that the Father alone is God.

We hear our Saviour continually distinguished from Jesus by this title: 'God sent His Son,' ... 'God anointed Jesus.' Now, how singular and inexplicable is this phraseology, which fills the *New Testament*, if this title belong equally to Jesus, and if a principal object of this book is to reveal him as God, as partaking equally with the Father in supreme divinity! We challenge our opponents to adduce one passage in the *New Testament*, where the word God means three persons, where it is not limited to one person, and where, unless turned from its usual sense by the connection, it does not mean the Father. Can stronger proof be given, that the doctrine of three persons in the Godhead is not a fundamental doctrine of Christianity?

This doctrine, were it true, must, from its difficulty, singularity, and importance, have been laid down with great clearness, guarded with great care, and stated with all possible precision. But where does this statement appear? From the many passages which treat of God, we ask for one, one only, in which we are told, that He is a three-fold being, or, that He is three persons, or that He is Father, Son, and Holy Ghost. On the contrary, in the *New Testament*, where, at least, we might expect many express assertions of this nature, God is declared to be One, without the least attempt to prevent the acceptation of the words in their common sense; and He is always spoken of and addressed in the singular number, that is, in language which was universally understood to intend a single person, and to which no other idea could have been attached, without an express admonition. So entirely do the Scriptures abstain from stating the Trinity, that when our opponents would insert it into their creeds and doxologies, they are compelled to leave the *Bible*, and to invent forms of words altogether unsanctioned by Scriptural phraseology. That a doctrine so strange, so liable to misapprehension, so fundamental as this is said to be, and requiring such careful exposition, should be left so undefined and unprotected, to be made out by inference, and to be hunted through distant and detached parts of Scripture, this is a difficulty, which, we think, no ingenuity can explain.

We have another difficulty. Christianity, it must be remembered, was planted and grew up amidst sharp-sighted enemies, who overlooked no objectionable part of the system, and who must have fastened with great earnestness on a doctrine involving such apparent contradictions as the Trinity. We cannot conceive an opinion, against which the Jews, who prided themselves on an adherence to God's Unity, would have raised an equal clamour. Now, how happens it, that in the apostolic writings, which relate so much to objections against Christianity, and to the controversies which grew out of this religion, not one word is said, implying that objections were brought against the Gospel from the doctrine of the Trinity, not one word is uttered in its defence and explanation, not a word to rescue it from reproach and mistake? This argument has almost the force of demonstration. We are persuaded, that had three divine persons been announced by the first preachers of Christianity, all equal, and all infinite, one of whom was the very Jesus who had lately died on a cross, this peculiarity of Christianity would have almost absorbed every other, and the great labour of the Apostles would have been to repel the continual assaults, which it would have awakened. But the fact is, that not a whisper of objection to Christianity, on that account, reaches our ears from the apostolic age. In the Epistles we see not a trace of controversy called forth by the Trinity.

We have further objections to this doctrine, drawn from its practical influence. We regard it as unfavourable to devotion, by dividing and distracting the mind in its communion with God. It is a great excellence of the doctrine of God's Unity, that it offers to us One object of supreme homage, adoration, and love, One Infinite Father, One Being of beings, One Original and Fountain, to Whom we may refer all good, in Whom all our powers and affections may be concentrated, and Whose lovely and venerable nature may pervade all our thoughts. True piety, when directed to an undivided Deity, has a chasteness, a singleness, most favourable to religious awe and love.

Now the Trinity sets before us three distinct objects of supreme adoration; three infinite persons, having equal claims on our hearts; three divine agents, performing different offices, and to be acknowledged and worshipped in different relations. And is it possible, we ask, that the weak and limited mind of man can attach itself to these with the same power and joy, as to One Infinite Father, the only First Cause, in Whom all the blessings of nature and redemption meet as their centre and source? Must not devotion be distracted by the equal and rival claims of three equal persons, and must not the worship of the conscientious, consistent Christian be disturbed by an apprehension, lest he withhold from one or another of these, his due proportion of homage?

We also think, that the doctrine of the Trinity injures devotion, not only by joining to the Father other objects of worship, but by taking from the Father the supreme affection, which is His due, and transferring it to the Son. This is a most important view. That Jesus Christ, if exalted into the infinite Divinity, should be more interesting than the Father, is precisely what might be expected from history, and from the principles of human nature. Men want an object of worship like themselves, and the great secret of idolatry lies in this propensity. A God, clothed in our form, and feeling our wants and sorrows, speaks to our weak nature more strongly than a Father in heaven, a pure spirit, invisible and unapproachable, save by the reflecting and purified mind.

We think too, that the peculiar offices ascribed to Jesus by the popular theology, make him the most attractive person in the Godhead. The Father is the depository of the justice, the vindicator of the rights, the avenger of the laws of the Divinity. On the other hand, the Son, the brightness of the divine mercy, stands between the incensed Deity and guilty humanity, exposes his meek head to the storms, and his compassionate breast to the sword of the divine justice, bears our whole load of punishment, and purchases with his blood every blessing which descends from heaven. Need we state the effect of these representations, especially on common minds, for whom Christianity was chiefly designed, and whom it seeks to bring to the Father as the loveliest being?

Having thus given our views of the Unity of God, I proceed in the second place to observe, that we believe in the unity of Jesus Christ. We believe that Jesus is one mind, one soul, one being, as truly as we are, and equally distinct from the One God. We complain of the doctrine of the Trinity, that not satisfied with making God three beings, it makes Jesus Christ two beings, and thus introduces infinite confusion into our conceptions of his character. This corruption of Christianity, alike repugnant to common sense and to the general strain of Scripture, is a remarkable proof of the power of a false philosophy in disfiguring the simple truth of Jesus.

According to this doctrine, Jesus Christ, instead of being one mind, one conscious intelligent principle, whom we can understand, consists of two souls, two minds; the one divine, the other human. Now we maintain, that this is to make Christ two beings. To denominate him one person, one being, and yet to suppose him made up of two minds, infinitely different from each other, is to abuse and confound language, and to throw darkness over all our conceptions of intelligent natures. According to the common doctrine, each of these two minds in Christ has its own consciousness, its own will, its own perceptions. They have in fact no common properties. The divine mind feels none of the wants and sorrows of the human, and the human is infinitely removed from the perfection and happiness of the divine. Can you conceive of two beings in the universe more distinct? We have always thought that one person was constituted and distinguished by one consciousness. The doctrine, that one and the same person, should have two consciousnesses, two wills, two souls, infinitely different from each other, this we think an enormous tax on human credulity.

We say, that if a doctrine so strange, so difficult, so remote from all the previous conceptions of men, be indeed a part and an essential part of revelation, it must be taught with great distinctions, and we ask our brethren to point to some plain, direct passage, where Christ is said to be composed of two minds infinitely different, yet constituting one person. We find none. Other Christians, indeed, tell us, that this doctrine is necessary to the harmony of the Scriptures, that some texts ascribe to Jesus Christ human, and others, divine properties, and that to reconcile these, we must suppose two minds, to which these properties may be referred. In other words, for the purpose of reconciling certain difficult passages ... we must invent an hypothesis vastly more difficult, and involving gross absurdity. We are to find our way out of a labyrinth, by a clue which conducts us into mazes more inextricable.

Surely, if Jesus Christ felt that he consisted of two minds, and that this was a leading feature of his religion, his phraseology respecting himself would have been coloured by this peculiarity. The universal language of men is framed upon the idea, that one person is one person, is one mind, and one soul, and when the multitude heard this language from the lips of Jesus, they must have taken it in its usual sense, and must have referred to a single soul all of which he spoke, unless expressly instructed to interpret it differently. But where do we find this instruction? Where do you meet, in the *New Testament*, the phraseology which abounds in Trinitarian books, and which necessarily grows from the doctrine of two natures in Jesus? Where does this divine teacher say, 'This I speak as God, and this as man; this is true only of my human mind, this only of my divine'? Where do we find in the Epistles a trace of this strange phraseology? Nowhere. It was not needed in that day. It was demanded by the errors of a later age.

We believe then, that Christ is one mind, one being, and, I add, a being distinct from the one God ... We wish, that those from whom we differ, would weigh one striking fact: Jesus, in his preaching, continually spoke of God. The word was always in his mouth. We ask, does he, by this word, ever mean himself? We say, never. On the contrary, he most plainly distinguishes between God and himself, and so do his disciples. How this is to be reconciled with the idea, that the manifestation of Christ, as God, was a primary object of Christianity, our adversaries must determine.

If we examine the passages in which Jesus is distinguished from God, we shall see, that they not only speak of him as another being, but seem to labour to express his inferiority. He is continually spoken of as the Son of God, sent of God, receiving all his powers from God, working miracles because God was with him, judging justly because God taught him, having claims on our belief, because he was anointed and sealed by God, and was able of himself to do nothing. The *New Testament* is filled with this language. Now, we ask, what impression this language was fitted and intended to make? Could any, who heard it, have imagined that Jesus was the very God to whom he was so industriously declared to be inferior; the very Being by Whom he was sent, and from Whom he professed to have received his message and power?

Trinitarians profess to derive some important advantages from their mode of viewing Christ. It furnishes them, they tell us, with an infinite atonement, for it shows them an infinite being suffering for their sins. The confidence with which this fallacy is repeated astonishes us. When pressed with the question, whether they really believe, that the infinite and unchangeable God suffered and died on the cross, they acknowledge that this is not true, but that Christ's human mind alone sustained the pains of death. How have we, then, an infinite sufferer? This language seems to us an imposition on common minds, and very derogatory to God's justice, as if this attribute could be satisfied by a sophism and a fiction ... [61]

Thus, even though Channing mistakenly believed that Jesus was crucified and was resurrected, he was still able to illustrate the absurdity of the doctrine of the Atonement and Redemption of Sins, despite his ignorance of the fact that the alleged events on which this doctrine is based never took place. Channing further refuted the doctrine on the following grounds:

- There is no passage in the *Bible* in which we are told that the son of man is infinite and needs infinite atonement. This doctrine teaches that man, although created by God a frail, erring and imperfect being, is regarded by the Creator as an infinite offender. Surely God can forgive sin without this rigid expedient.

- This doctrine which talks of God becoming a victim and a sacrifice for His own rebellious subjects is as irrational as it is unscriptural. Atonement should be made to and not by God. If infinite atonement was necessary, which only God could require, then God would have to become a sufferer and take upon Himself our pain and woe – a thought of which the mind cannot conceive. To escape this difficulty, we are told that Christ suffered as man and not as God. But if he only suffered for a short and limited period, then how was the necessity for infinite atonement satisfied?

- If we have God in heaven with infinite goodness and power, we need no other infinite person to save us. This doctrine dishonours God when it says that without the help of a second and a third deity, He could not save man.

- If infinite atonement in order to satisfy the demands of justice was indispensable for man's salvation, then this should have been expressed clearly and definitely in at least one passage of the *Bible*. This doctrine may be compared to a judge who punishes himself for the crimes committed by a transgressor appearing in his court – whereas the *Bible* says, 'For we must all appear before the judgement seat of Christ, that each one may receive what is due to him for the things done while in the body, whether good or bad.' (*2 Corinthians 5: 10*). And again, 'Each of us will give an account of himself to God.' (*Romans 14: 12*).

- If by the crucifixion of Jesus, God's justice is satisfied for sins past, present and to come, then God has lost all power to enjoin godliness and a virtuous life, and also all prerogative in either forgiving or punishing disobedience. If God punishes a Christian sinner on the Day of Judgement, then it will mean that either God will have committed a breach of faith – or else that the doctrine of atonement is not true.

⊙   ⊙   ⊙   ⊙   ⊙

Up until 1819, the congregations of the Unitarians in Boston were held either in private houses or in the hall of the Medical College in Barclay Street. In 1820, the construction of a building for Unitarian worship was started. It was completed in 1821. In spite of this indication that they were becoming more established, the Unitarians were still called 'a crew of heretics, infidels, or atheists.' [62]

There was, however, a change in their policy of cautious preaching, and Channing, who had so far received the narrow and bitter attacks from the pulpits of the orthodox Trinitarian Church without retaliating, felt that the time had come for him to strike back with all the force at his command and to speak out boldly in support of his faith, and against the prejudices of orthodoxy. In his book, *A History of Unitarianism*, E. M. Wilber writes of Channing that:

> His theme was that the Scriptures, when reasonably interpreted, teach the doctrine held by the Unitarians. It took up the main doctrines on which the Unitarians depart from the orthodox and held them up one by one for searching examination … it made an eloquent and lofty appeal against a scheme so full of unreason, inhumanity and gloom as Calvinism … and impeached the orthodoxy of the day before the bar of popular reason and conscience. [63]

The cause of Unitarianism in America was further helped by a convention held at Massachusetts in 1823, when the orthodox Church made an unsuccessful attempt to have a doctrinal test imposed on ministers who wished to preach to Unitarian congregations. This failure in fact succeeded in bringing the Unitarian movement out into the open, and served to unite its members in the defence of a common cause.

In 1827, a second Unitarian church was opened with a famous sermon by Channing. To him, wrote E. M. Wilber, should go the credit for the fact that, 'even if not explicitly acknowledged, the doctrine of Trinity, even if still formally confessed, had ceased to be the centre of orthodox faith, and was no longer given its old emphasis; and that the outstanding doctrines of Calvinism had received new interpretations which the fathers would have rejected with horror.' [64]

These developments did not occur unopposed. In 1833, the Unitarians were condemned as 'cold-blooded infidels' and abuses were hurled that were 'unparalleled even in the days of theological intolerance and bigotry.' [65] It is recorded that even as late as 1924, thirty or forty Unitarians met in Boston to form an anonymous association, which might indicate that although there was no likelihood of their sharing the same fate as earlier Unitarians, there was still an element of danger for a Christian who affirmed the Divine Unity.

Channing remained a firm Unitarian to the end of his days. To him, Jesus was not only human, but also an inspired Prophet of God. In contrast to the doctrines attributed to Calvin which focus on 'human depravity', the 'wrath of God', and the 'atoning sacrifice of Christ', Channing proclaimed 'one sublime idea' which he defined as 'the greatness of the soul, its union with God by spiritual likeness, its receptivity of His spirit, its self-forming power, its destination to the ineffable and its immortality.' [66]

This was a refreshing change to the cold logic and emphasis placed on the phenomenal world by Priestly. Channing breathed life into the Unitarian movement, not only in America, but also in England. Priestly was after all a physical scientist. His reasoning was sound, but his outlook was materialistic. In asserting that 'man's rational nature was from God,' [67] Channing elevated Unitarian thought to new spiritual heights, and his words made a deep impression on both sides of the Atlantic.

Channing protested against every form of sectarian narrowness. Denominational aggression was foreign to his nature, and this spirit was infused in the leaders of the movement which culminated in the founding of the Divinity School of Harvard University in 1861. Part of its constitution reads:

> It being understood that every encouragement be given to the serious, impartial and unbiased investigation of Christian truth and that no assent to the peculiarities of any denomination be required of either the students or professors or instructors. [68]

In 1825, the American Association was formed, the same year as was done in England. Ralph Waldo Emerson (1803-1882) resigned the pulpit in Boston and the breach between the old and the new thinking was complete. The religion of Jesus was proclaimed to be the love of God and service of man, and an 'absolute religion'.

O   O   O   O   O

Unitarianism within Christianity has continued up to the present day. Many of the Christian sects, although they have little access to the existential reality of Jesus – of how he behaved towards people and conducted his transactions with them, of how he did every-thing and lived his life – do believe in One God and seek to live according to the *Bible's* precepts, despite the contradictions within it. However, the confusion caused by the doctrines of Original Sin, of the Atonement and Redemption of Sins, and of the Trinity, com-bined with the absence of any real transmitted guidance as to how to live the way Jesus lived, peace be on him, have caused the now almost complete rejection of the various forms of Christianity which existed a hundred years ago.

Today many churches lie empty, and the relatively new and more cheerful, at times even ecstatic, congregations which now tend to be more popular in some quarters are characterised more by their refusal to be bound by the outmoded European Christian dogmas of the past than anything else.

It is significant, however, that the old doctrines continue to manifest in new forms. Although less emphasis is placed on the doctrine of Original Sin, for example, the majority of 'modern' Christians still believe that the only way to get to heaven is by believing in Jesus Christ – who, they will still enthusiastically main-tain, died on the cross in order to atone for all the sins of whoever believes in him.

Thus the doctrine of the Atonement and Redemption of Sins still plays an important part in 'modern Christianity', and it is be-cause of this that Jesus is still regarded as being 'God-like', if not God Himself. He is sometimes treated as God in certain contexts and situations, even if many Christians really believe that he is not actually God. In other words, although some – although by no means all – of today's Trinitarian Christians no longer indulge in the semantics and the sophistry and the casuistry of their Euro-pean predecessors, there is nevertheless an underlying orthodoxy to the modern forms of Christianity which is rooted in the past, which is supported by the ecumenical movement as far as it goes, which is Trinitarian, and which is now propagated and imposed by more subtle means than those once utilised by the notorious Inquisition – notably by the various forms of electronic mass-communication. The absence of any ongoing debate between the Unitarians and the Trinitarians testifies to the 'success' of these new techniques.

Although many Christians today will cheerfully agree that there is only One God, and assert that they *are* Unitarians, the underlying structure of their belief-system remains Trinitarian – for its origins are Trinitarian. Although most 'born again' Christians will agree that God cannot die, even temporarily, most of them will be only too happy to say in one breath that Jesus is their Lord – God – and in the next breath that Jesus died in order to redeem the sins of whoever believes in him, and in the next breath that whoever truly believes in him is filled with the Holy Spirit and so 'born again' in this world and saved in the next world – saved by God. Although the word 'Trinity' may not actually be used in the course of this explanation, it is clear that within this circular belief-structure there are three distinct elements or persons – God, Jesus (who in fact is God), and the Holy Spirit (of God) – who are nevertheless united as a whole, making One. And so the doctrine of the Trinity continues to survive, even though it just does not make sense!

As long as awkward questions – such as, 'If Jesus is God, then how can God die?' or, 'If Jesus is God, and if God was dead for three days, then who sustained the Universe and every living thing in it during that period?' or, 'If Jesus was God, then to whom was he always praying?' – as long as awkward questions such as these are ignored or avoided, then for many it is still possible to sustain the Trinitarian belief-structure, even in this modern age, and often with the help of the sense of euphoria which can be experienced by whoever believes that they have indeed been 'saved'.

It is this emotional response towards Jesus – 'Jesus loves you!' – in which his original ties with the Tribe of Israel and his original commitment to uphold and live by the Law of Moses are either not known, or else ignored, or even vetoed thanks to the doctrine of the 'New Covenant' (of Paul, it must be emphasised, not Jesus or God) – that has enabled the ecumenical movement to make some 'progress' during the last fifty years.

Common sense dictates that everyone who claims to be following Jesus should be united, but what the commonly shared principles on which such unity should be founded has, as we have seen, always been a matter of intense argument and debate, and even bloodshed.

It has been possible in the more recent past, however, to avoid disunity to a certain extent simply by avoiding rational argument and only selectively quoting the passages from the *Bible* which appear to support the Paulinian hypothesis without contradicting each other. An uncritical acceptance of the 'absolute redemption' which is apparently offered by God in exchange for an unconditional belief in Jesus, exercised in conjunction with complete reliance on Paul's words that, 'The entire Law is summed up in a single command, "Love your neighbour as yourself,"' (*Galations 5: 14*), have resulted in a blurring of the main issues and a clouding over of the intellectual dilemmas and discrepancies which have always characterised the debates and conflicts both with and within the Trinitarian Church in the past.

Nevertheless, any modern Unitarian Church which still insists that there is only One God – and that Jesus was no more or less than a Prophet of God, and that each person is answerable for his or her own actions in this life and will have to answer for them on the Day of Resurrection – will not find itself particularly welcomed by the ecumenical movement which is essentially Trinitarian in religious nature and general outlook, but rather it will be ignored and isolated and alienated by it in a society which is now so fragmented that everyone is free to disagree with everyone else without any threat of retribution, simply because any such dissent is no longer a threat to those who now maintain the present *status quo* and who, in any case, are no longer Trinitarian Christians.

In other words, although the modern forms of Trinitarian Christianity still continue to support the structure of the modern state, in which the new cathedrals are the international banks, they no longer control it – and in this situation the most that the believing Christians can hope to achieve is to combine together in order to protect their common interests and their religion.

In spite of modern Christianity's beleaguered situation, however, the views of the Unitarians and the Trinitarians continue to remain diametrically opposed to each other – as in the past, so also today – and this will never change.

And if the Unitarian view is unacceptable to the Trinitarians, then the Muslim view – which not only confirms the Unitarian view but also asserts, on the basis of the Divine revelation of the *Qur'an*, that Jesus was definitely not even crucified – is even more unacceptable to the Trinitarians, for this means that there is neither any foundation whatsoever nor any truth in either the doctrine of the Atonement and Redemption of Sins, or in the doctrine of Trinity, whatever form these doctrines may take, ancient or modern.

o   o   o   o   o

Chapter Nine

Christianity Today

In order to ascertain the nature of Christianity today, it is necessary to bear in mind the distinction between knowledge which is arrived at by observation and deduction, and knowledge which is revealed to man through no power of his own. Deductive knowledge is always changing in the light of fresh observations and new experience. It therefore lacks certainty. Revealed knowledge is from God. In every revealed message, there is a metaphysical aspect and a physical. The metaphysical teaches the nature of the Divine Unity. The physical provides a code of behaviour. Revealed knowledge has always been brought by a messenger who embodied it. The way he lives is the message. To behave as the messenger did is to have knowledge of the message, and in this knowledge is certainty.

Christianity today is said to be based on revealed knowledge, but none of the *Bible* contains the message of Jesus intact, and exactly as it was revealed to him, peace be on him. There is hardly any record of his code of behaviour. The books in the *New Testament* do not even contain eye-witness accounts of his sayings and actions. They were written by people who derived their knowledge second-hand. These records are not comprehensive and have never been satisfactorily authenticated. Everything which Jesus said and did which has not been recorded has been lost forever.

Those who seek to verify what is in the *New Testament* claim that even if by no means comprehensive, it is at least accurate. However, it is significant that all the oldest surviving manuscripts of the *New Testament*, from which all the present translations of the *Bible* derive, were written after the Council of Nicea. The *Codex Sinaiticus* and the *Codex Vaticanus* date from the late 4th or 5th century, and the *Codex Alexandrius* from the 5th century AD. As a result of the Council of Nicea, nearly three hundred other accounts of the life of Jesus, many of them eye-witness accounts, were systematically destroyed. As we have seen, the events leading up to the Council of Nicea indicate that the Pauline Church had every reason to change the contents of the four Gospels which survived.

Clearly, the manuscripts of the *New Testament* which were written after the Council of Nicea are different from the manuscripts which existed before the Council. It is significant that publication of some of the *Dead Sea Scrolls*, when they do not verify the post-Nicene manuscripts, have been withheld.

The unreliability of the officially accepted Gospels appears to be admitted by the Church itself: The metaphysics of Christianity today are not even based on what is in the Gospels. The established Church is founded on the doctrines of Original Sin, of the Atonement and Redemption of Sins, of the divinity of Jesus, of the divinity of the Holy Ghost, of Trinity, and of the New Covenant. None of these doctrines are to be found within the Gospels. They were neither explained nor taught by Jesus. They were the fruits of Paul's innovations, combined with the influence of Greek culture and philosophy, and compounded by the speculation of latter-day European Christians who did not know what they were talking about. Paul never personally experienced either the company or the direct transmission of knowledge from Jesus. Before his 'conversion', he vigorously persecuted the followers of Jesus, and after it he was largely responsible for abandoning the code of behaviour of Jesus when he took 'Christianity' to the non-Jews of Greece and beyond. The figure of 'Christ' whom he claimed taught him his new doctrine is an imagination. His rejection of the Law of Moses – to which he nevertheless continued to refer whenever it suited him – is without divine sanction, and his teaching is based on an event which never took place, the supposed death and resurrection of Jesus.

Despite their extremely doubtful origins, the doctrines of the established Trinitarian Church form an integral part of the social conditioning of anyone who is given a 'Christian education'. Although many have rejected some or all of these doctrines, the magic they exercise is such that those who give them credibility are lead by their logic to believe in the notorious principle: 'Outside the Church, no salvation.' The Church's metaphysical construct is this: The doctrine of the Atonement and Redemption of Sins says that Christ who was of God took on human form and became Jesus, who then died for all believers to atone for all their sins. The Church accordingly guarantees forgiveness of sins and salvation on the Day of Judgement, for any one who believes in 'Christ' and who follows the guidance of the Church. Further, it is believed that this contract is available to all people until the end of the world. The natural consequences of this belief are these:

Firstly, it implies that believing Christians are not responsible for their actions in this world and that they will not be held to account for them after their deaths – for whatever they do in this world, they believe that they will nevertheless be redeemed by 'Christ's sacrifice' – while all those who are not believing Christians will be automatically doomed to eternal damnation in Hell, no matter how good the lives they have led. However, this does not mean a life of joy on earth for all believing Christians. Their belief in the doctrine of Original Sin, which states that because of the fall of Adam, all men are born sinful, means that while they are alive it follows that their condition is one of unworthiness and incompleteness. This tragic view of life is reflected in the following statement of J. G. Vos, a Christian, in which he compares Islam and Christianity:

There is nothing in Islam to lead a man to say, 'Oh wretched man that I am, who shall deliver me from the body of this death?' or, 'I know that in me; that is, in my flesh, dwelleth no good thing.' A religion with reasonable attainable objectives ... does not give the sinner the anguish of a guilty conscience nor the frustration of trying without success to attain in practical living the requirements of an absolute moral standard. In brief, Islam makes a man feel good, while Christianity necessarily first, and often thereafter, makes a man feel bad. The religion of the broken heart is Christianity, not Islam. [1]

Secondly, belief in the doctrine of the Atonement and Redemption of Sins only leads to confusion when believing Christians attempt to reconcile the other teachings God has revealed to man with their own belief. The doctrine clearly implies that 'Christ's sacrifice' and 'message' are unique and final, and that therefore believing Christians cannot accept the teachings of other Prophets. At the same time, they cannot deny the truth which they inevitably find within them. Thus, for example, believing Christians are obliged to reject Judaism, and yet accept the *Old Testament*, which as we have seen is at least partially derived from the teachings which Moses brought to the Jews. Thus believing Christians find themselves in the impossible position of having to accept two contradictory beliefs – simultaneously – as this passage shows:

There are elements of relative good in the non-Christian faiths. While the call for separation from false religions is certainly Biblical, and the demonic character of pagan religions is taught in Scripture ... still it is also true that elements of limited relative good exist in these religions. While it is true that they are demonic in character, it is also true (and Scriptural) that they are products of man's distorted interpretation of God's revelation in nature. Even though they may be works of the devil, still they are not simply works of the devil, but partly products of God's common grace and partly products of sinful man's abuse of God's revelation in nature.[2]

It is significant that Vos does not mention all the 'distorted interpretation' which the *New Testament* is known to have undergone.

Attempts to avoid the dilemma of simultaneous acceptance and rejection of non-Christian faiths has been made by arguing that some Christians 'discern in them the influence of the 'cosmic Christ' who, as the eternal Logos or revealer of the Godhead, is the 'light that enlightens every man.' This view was summed up by William Temple when he wrote:

By the word of God – that is to say, Jesus Christ – Isaiah and Plato, Zoroaster, Buddha, and Confucius uttered and wrote such truths as they declared. There is only one Divine Light, and every man in his own measure is enlightened by it.[3]

The reasoning in this passage relies on the assumption that the 'one Divine Light' and 'Christ' are one and the same. Since 'Christ' is an imagination, the doctrine fails, and the dilemma remains. It can only be avoided by resorting to what George Orwell called 'doublethink'. He defined it thus:

Doublethink means the power of holding two contradictory beliefs simultaneously, and accepting both of them. The party intellectual knows that he is playing tricks with reality, but by the exercise of doublethink he also satisfies himself that reality is not violated.[4]

Doublethink lies at the root of believing Christians' fundamental assumption that 'Christ' is God. It is around this assumption that the controversy of the two natures of Jesus has continued to rage for centuries. One moment he is human. The next moment he is divine. First he is Jesus, then he is Christ. It is only by the exercise of doublethink that a person can hold these two contradictory beliefs simultaneously. It is only by the exercise of doublethink that belief in the illusory doctrine of Trinity can be maintained.

Article VII of the *Thirty-Nine Articles of the Church of England* begins: 'The *Old Testament* is not contrary to the *New* ...' As Milton has so clearly shown, the *Old Testament* is full of passages affirming the One-ness of God. There is not one passage which describes the Divine Reality in any of the terms used by believing Christians to describe the doctrine of Trinity. The act of affirming what is in the *Old Testament* – and in fact the Gospels for that matter – and at the same time affirming belief in the doctrine of Trinity, is probably the greatest illustration of the exercise of doublethink within Christianity today.

The logic of the established Church's metaphysic, based on doctrines which were not taught by Jesus, obscures not only the nature of Jesus, but also the Divine Unity. Thus the metaphysic of Christianity today is totally opposed to the metaphysic which was originally taught by Jesus.

The physical aspect of what Jesus brought, his code of behaviour, is today irrecoverably lost. To live as Jesus lived is to understand his message, yet there is virtually no existing record of how Jesus behaved. And what little knowledge exists is often ignored. The most fundamental daily act of Jesus was that of worship of the Creator – the whole purpose for which man was created. Yet it is evident that no Christian today makes the same acts of worship which Jesus made. Jesus was educated in the synagogue in Jerusalem from the age of twelve. He preached in the synagogue. He used to keep the synagogue clean. No Christian today can be found performing any of these actions. How many Christians have even been circumcised in the manner that Jesus was? Jesus usually prayed in the synagogue. He prayed at appointed times each day, in the morning, at mid-day, and in the evening. He used to wash with water before he prayed. The exact form of his prayer is no longer practised, but it is known that it was based on the prayer which Moses was given, and that it probably included the positions of standing, bowing, prostrating and sitting.

Jesus said that he had come to uphold the Law of Moses and not to destroy it one jot or one tittle.

The services now held in today's churches were developed long after Jesus had disappeared. Many of them come directly from the pagan Graeco-Roman mythological rites. The prayers they use are not the prayers which Jesus made. The hymns they sing are not the praises which Jesus sung. Believing Christians today worship God as they think best, not as He originally commanded Jesus and his true followers.

Due to the innovations of Paul and his followers, there is no revealed teaching left as to what to eat and what not to eat. Anyone given a 'Christian education' today eats what he or she feels like. Yet Jesus and his true followers only ate *kosher* meat and were forbidden to eat pig's flesh. Most believing Christians today are unaware of the fact that the food which God has forbidden them to eat, such as pork and blood, is forbidden because it is not good for them. Instead they believe that these 'dietary requirements' belong to another age before fridges were invented, and that 'Christian' scientists in white coats know best.

The last meal Jesus is known to have eaten before his disappearance was the Passover meal. No Christian today celebrates this long-standing Jewish tradition to which Jesus so meticulously held. It is no longer known in what manner Jesus ate and drank, who he would eat with and who he would not eat with, where he would eat and where he would not eat, when he would eat and when he would not eat. Jesus fasted, but again it is not known how, where and when he fasted. His science of fasting has been lost. There is no record of the food he liked especially, and the food of which he was not particularly fond.

Jesus did not marry while he was on earth, but he did not forbid marriage. There is no passage in the Gospels which states that a follower of Jesus must take a vow of celibacy. Nor is there any authority for the establishment of single-sex communities such as monasteries or convents, although these could owe their origin to communities such as the Essenes. The early followers of Jesus who were married followed the code of behaviour within marriage which Moses brought. Their example is no longer emulated by believing Christians today, and the current breakdown and collapse of the family structure in the Christian West today demonstrates the lack of effective guidance as regards behaviour within a

Christian marriage – of how a man should behave towards a woman, and a woman towards a man.

This has been exacerbated by many of the official Churches' current permissive attitudes towards extra-marital sex, homosexuality and lesbianism – all of which are forbidden by the teachings of all the Prophets, including Moses, Jesus and Muhammad, may the blessings and peace of God be on them and on whoever follows their example.

Extracting moral principles from the Gospels and trying to live in accordance with them is not the same as acting in a certain manner because it is known that Jesus acted that way in that situation. One course of action is the fruit of deductive knowledge, the other course of action is based on revealed knowledge. Only the former can be changed and manipulated; the latter cannot – it can only be ignored.

There is neither any written record, nor any living existentially transmitted human record, of how Jesus walked, of how he sat, of how he stood, of how he kept himself clean, of how he went to the toilet, of how he went to sleep, of how he woke up, of how he greeted people, of how he was with old people, of how he was with young people, of how he was with old women, of how he was with young women, of how he was with strangers, of how he was with guests, of how he was with his enemies, of how he conducted his transactions in the market place, of how he travelled, of what he was allowed to do and of what he was not allowed to do.

The records of Jesus' message as revealed to him by God are incomplete and inaccurate. The doctrines on which Christianity today is based are not to be found within these records. The record of how Jesus acted is almost non--existent, and what little is known is virtually ignored. Yet the institution of the Church, in whatever form, has always claimed to be the interpreter and guardian of Jesus' message. The Church was not instituted by Jesus. He did not establish a hierarchy of priests to act as mediators between God and man. Yet the established Pauline church, from very early on, always taught Christians to believe that their salvation was assured if they acted and believed as the Church told them. From where did the Church derive its authority?

This claim for authority, in its most extreme form, is to be found in the Roman Catholic Church's doctrine of papal infallibility. Cardinal Heenan has summed it up in these words:

This secret of this wonderful unity of our Church is Christ's promise that the Church will never fail to teach the truth. Once we know what the Church teaches we accept it. For we know it must be true ... All Catholic priests teach the same doctrine because they all obey the Vicar of Christ. The word 'vicar' means 'one who takes the place of another.' The Pope is the Vicar of Christ because he takes the place of Christ as Head of the Church on earth. The Church remains one because all her members believe the same Faith. They believe it because the Church cannot teach what is false. This is what we mean when we say that the Church is infallible. Christ promised to guide his Church. One of the ways Christ chose to guide the Church was by leaving his Vicar on earth to speak for him. That is why we say the Pope is infallible. He is the Head of the infallible Church. God could not allow him to lead it into error. [5]

It is significant that Cardinal Heenan talks only of 'Christ', and not of Jesus. He does not refer to the Gospels to support his claims – because there is in fact nothing in the Gospels to support them!

The dogma of papal infallibility has often proved awkward, and especially in retrospect. For, as we have already seen, if all the Popes were infallible, then why was Pope Honorius anathematised? Does the relatively recent papal encyclical which states that the Jews were not responsible for the supposed crucifixion of Jesus mean that all the preceding Popes who were of the opinion that the Jews were responsible were not infallible after all? And since Jesus was in fact not crucified at all, does this not mean that all the Popes who have believed that he was crucified were not infallible at all?

Many Roman Catholics today have rejected the validity of 'Christ's promise that the Church will never fail to teach the truth,' which is not to be found in any of the Gospels: The great gap between Church teaching and practice, to give some examples of contemporary attitudes, troubled Cincinnati's Archbishop Joseph L. Bernadin, who said in an interview in U.S. Catholic:

So many consider themselves good Catholics, even though their beliefs and practices seem to conflict with the official teaching in the Church. This is almost a new concept of what it means to be a Catholic today ... Once it became legitimate (in 1966) to eat meat on Friday one could doubt the authority of the Pope, practice birth control, leave the priesthood and get married or indeed do anything else one wanted to.

(*Note*: The practice of abstaining from meat on Friday, meant to emulate Jesus's fasting and to commemorate the day on which he was supposed to have been crucified, eventually became a Church commandment and for centuries served as a kind of Roman Catholic badge.)

And:

'Vatican II, (the Second Vatican Council of 1962), amazed me,' wrote author, Doris Grumbach, in the Critic, 'because it raised the possibility of more answers than one, of gray areas, of a private world of conscience and behaviour. But like all places in human experience of rigour and rule, once the window was opened, everything came under question. No constants remained, no absolutes, and the Church became for me a debatable question. I still cling to the Gospels, to Christ and some of his followers as central to my life, but the institution no longer seems important to me. I no longer live in it.' [6]

The investment and exercise of considerable authority in the established Trinitarian Church, if not its complete infallibility, nevertheless still remains. It is evident, all these centuries later, even within the Churches which have long rejected the authority of the Pope over them. However, the validity of any form of religious authority is today being doubted and rejected on a scale that has never been known before. In the words of George Harrison:

When you're young you get taken to church by your parents and you get pushed into religion at school. They're trying to put something into your mind. Obviously because nobody goes to church and nobody believes in God. Why? Because they haven't interpreted the *Bible* as it was intended. I didn't really believe in God as I'd been taught it. It was just like something out of a science fiction novel. You're taught just to have faith, you don't have to worry about it, just believe what we're telling you. [7]

Between the two poles of complete acceptance and complete rejection of the established Church's reliability as the guardians of the message of Jesus, there lies every shade of opinions as to what it is to be a believing Christian. Wilfred Cantwell Smith writes:

> There is so much diversity and clash, so much chaos, in the Christian Church today that the old ideal of a unified or systematic Christian truth has gone. For this, the ecumenical movement is too late. What has happened is that the Christian world has moved into that situation of open variety, of optional alternatives. It would seem no longer possible for anyone to be told or even to imagine that he can be told, what it means or should mean, formally and generically, to be a Christian. He must decide for himself – and only for himself. [8]

This conclusion implies that there are as many versions of Christianity today as there are Christians, and that the role of the Church, as an institution which is the guardian of Jesus's message, has largely ceased to exist: A graduate student at U.C.L.A. asked: 'What is the point of a Church if it's always up to my own conscience?' [9] However, the Church remains an integral part of Western culture today, and the relationship between the two is an interesting one.

o   o   o   o   o

Vast amounts of literature have been written in the West during the last few centuries, in the attempt to understand the nature of existence. They provide a catalogue of all the possible avenues of thought a person's mind will pursue when he or she does not have the certainty of revealed knowledge to live and understand his or her life by. Some writers such as Pascal have realised that the mind is a limited tool, and that the heart is the centre of their being, and the container of real knowledge:

> The heart has its reasons which are unknown to reason … It is the heart which is aware of God and not reason. This is what faith is: God perceived intuitively by the heart, not by reason. [10]

In the attempt to gain access to the heart many have rejected Christianity and experimented with other means:

Mystical experience is said to lead to real knowledge of 'the truth' about the universe. This truth is inexpressible in words, but it can be felt. The medium can be music, drugs, meditation … [11]

These alternative approaches to understanding Reality have been adapted by people in the West on a vast scale, often only as a means of self-gratification, rather than as part of a serious attempt to find out what life is all about.

The Trinitarian Church has greatly accommodated itself to these new trends in the culture of the West. In their attempts to keep the churches full, some priests have introduced pop-groups and discotheques into their routine to attract young people. Concerts, exhibitions and jumble-sales cater for more conservative tastes. Charitable concerns help establish a sense of purpose for those who indulge in them. These attempts to 'modernise' the established Church and keep it 'up to date' are in keeping with the Pauline Church's long-standing tradition of compromise by all means. If it cannot pass on the message of Jesus, it must at least provide a 'useful social function'.

This process of compromise, especially during the present century, has resulted both in the continued absorption of the Church into the culture, and of the re-absorption of the culture into this changing structure of the Church. It is a two-way process which has endlessly been alternating since Paul and his followers set it in motion. Many people have 'returned to Christianity' as a result of their experience with music, drugs and meditation. They tend either to completely reject these experiences, and adopt a puritanical form of Christianity, or else they incorporate their new way of life into their own updated version of Christianity. Both these trends cover up the prophethood of Jesus. He is either exalted as God or regarded as no more than a charismatic cult figure, a 'Jesus Christ Superstar' who meant well, but was misunderstood.

The continuing identification of the established Trinitarian Church with the culture of the West and the two-way assimilation process between the two is clearly apparent simply by observing how people live today: With the exception of those who have withdrawn into monasteries and convents to remember God, the life-style of those who call themselves Christians often closely resembles the life-styles of those who claim to be agnostics, humanists or atheists. Their beliefs may be different, but their general behaviour is the same.

The laws which exist in the 'Christian' countries of the West today – the laws governing birth and death, the formation and dissolution of marriage, the rights over property within and outside marriage, or in the event of divorce or death, adoption and guardianship, commerce and industry and all the rest – are not to be found in the Gospels. The laws which define what constitutes criminal behaviour and the various penalties for such behaviour, are no longer derived from the *Bible*. Murderers are no longer executed, for example, and adulterers are no longer stoned to death. Some laws, such as those which legalise usury in all its forms, flatly contradict what has in fact always been forbidden by God.

Most of these laws are not laws which have been revealed to man by God. They are the fruits of deductive knowledge. They are either inherited from the Roman system of law, or are based on the common practice of people over a long period of time, or are statutes formulated and amended whenever it is considered necessary in accordance with the democratic method, which is alleged to be the bequest of the ancient Greeks. No one in today's courts of law can refer to the Gospels as a binding authority in his or her dealings with another person, and have their submissions or representations based on them judicially accepted. A person may swear to tell the truth on the *Bible* – but it must remain tightly shut!

The Christianity of today is inseparable from the culture of the West, which has now been successfully exported virtually throughout the world. The established Christian Church and the State are at one with each other and support each other. And the individuals who work within their respective institutions do not live as Jesus lived, however much some of them may wish that they were.

The spiritual impoverishment of Christianity today is due to the inescapable fact that the believing Christians of today lack a science of social behaviour, based on that which was originally embodied by Jesus and his true followers – and that lack has left them at a loss in this life and unprepared for what happens after death. As Wilfred Cantwell Smith writes:

> To say that Christianity is true is to say nothing significant; the only question that concerns either God or me, or my neighbour is whether my Christianity is true, and whether yours is. And to that question, a truly cosmic one, in my case the only valid answer is a sorrowful 'not very ...' [12]

It is scarcely surprising, in the light of all this, that as the churches of the world are emptying, the mosques of Islam are filling up, for in this age, as for the last fourteen centuries, the knowledge about Jesus to which only the Muslims have access, is far more accurate and far more reliable than any of the perversions of the original teachings of and accounts about Jesus which still exist today – and which are all that today's believing Christians, whether Unitarian or Trinitarian, have – and in this age, as for the last fourteen centuries, the only way to truly follow Jesus, Prophet of Islam, peace be on him, is by following the way of Islam, the way of the Prophet Muhammad, may the blessings and peace of God be on him and on all the Prophets of God, and on all their true followers, until …

the Last Day

Chapter Ten

Jesus in Hadith and Muslim Traditions

The *Hadith* are another source of knowledge about Jesus, peace be on him, about which many students of Christianity have been kept in the dark. The *Hadith* consist principally of records of eyewitness accounts of what the Prophet Muhammad, may the peace and blessings of God be on him, said and did during his life-time. The *Hadith* have always been carefully distinguished from the *Qur'an* which is the revelation which was revealed to the Prophet Muhammad by God through the angel Gabriel. Thus the *Hadith* literature complements the *Qur'an* and even contains commentaries on passages from the *Qur'an* – but the two are never confused with each other. The *Qur'an* is the Word of God. The *Hadith* contain the words of people.

Faced with the impossibility of verifying their own texts, a highly sophisticated pseudo-scholarship was set up by the Roman Catholic Church and Protestant Christian missionaries in the last century to discredit the Muslim *Hadith* literature – which had already undergone the most scrupulous checking and verification in the history of recorded scholarship, for, unlike the officially accepted Gospels of the *New Testament* – and indeed the *Gospel of Barnabas* for that matter – which purport to record some of the actions and words of Jesus, peace be on him, during his life-time – but which in the absence of any early records are incapable of being thoroughly authenticated – a *hadith* which records the words or actions of the Prophet Muhammad, may God bless him and grant him peace, is not accepted as being reliable unless it can be traced back through a chain of human transmission made up of reliable people, from person to person, back to someone who was a companion of the Prophet Muhammad and who actually witnessed the event or heard the words which the *hadith* describes or relates.

The most reliable sources of the *Hadith* were those people who loved and feared God and His Messenger the most. After a relatively short time, most of the *Hadith* which had been transmitted orally were recorded in written form, including the details of who all the people in the human chain of transmission were. The more reliable the people in any particular chain of transmission were, and the more different chains of transmission there are for the same *hadith*, the more reliable any particular *hadith* is considered. At a later stage, usually during the 1st or 2nd centuries after the death of Muhammad, in 632 AD, large collections of the *Hadith* were gathered together, in order to ensure that they were not lost.

Among the most important collections of the *Hadith* are those made by *Imam* al-Bukhari and *Imam* Muslim, which were compiled about two hundred years after the Prophet Muhammad's death, may the peace and blessings of God be on him, and which describe and record every aspect of his life and knowledge. Thus the *Hadith* form an essential part of the record of the teaching and the history and the biography of the Prophet Muhammad, being as they are reliable contemporary eyewitness accounts. Thus, as Iftekhar Bano Hussain points out in her book, *Prophets in the Qur'an, Volume Two: The Later Prophets*:

> Accordingly any quotations concerning *sayyedina* 'Isa from any of the Gospels, or from any other ancient source, cannot be given the same weight or accepted with the same confidence as a reliable, fully authenticated *hadith*, no matter how compelling its words may be – although of course sometimes the truth of what is said is so self-evident that it cannot be ignored. This is probably particularly true of those traditions which were transmitted by the very early Unitarian followers of Jesus whose descendants eventually embraced Islam during the 7th and 8th centuries CE.
>
> For as well as those *hadith* of the Prophet Muhammad which refer specifically to *sayyedina* 'Isa, may the blessings and peace of Allah be on them, there are also many other Muslim traditions which give accounts of the sayings and deeds of *sayyedina* 'Isa. These traditions were originally gathered together by the early followers of *sayyedina* 'Isa, especially those early Unitarian followers who spread to Arabia and North Africa. When

the Prophet Muhammad, may Allah bless him and grant him peace, came, many of the followers of these followers embraced Islam. They had retained these traditions about *sayyedina* 'Isa, peace be on him, and had passed them down from generation to generation. [1]

These traditions were then passed down from generation to generation by the Muslims and many of them were finally gathered together in Ath-Tha'labi's *Stories of the Prophets* and in Al-Ghazzali's *Revival of the Life-Transaction Sciences*. It is significant to see how these traditions give a clear and unified picture of the ascetic Prophet who prepared the way for the final Messenger:

> Ka'b al-Akbar said, 'Jesus, son of Mary, was a ruddy man, inclined to white; he did not have long hair, and he never anointed his head. Jesus used to walk barefoot, and he took no house, or adornment, or goods, or clothes, or provision, except his day's food. Wherever the sun set, he arranged his feet in prayer till the morning came. He was curing the blind from birth, and the leper, and raising the dead by God's permission, and was telling his people what they were eating in their houses and what they were storing up for the morrow, and he was walking on the surface of the water in the sea. His head was dishevelled and his face was small; he was an ascetic in the world, longing for the next world and eager for the worship of God. He was a pilgrim in the earth till the Jews sought him and desired to kill him. Then God raised him up to heaven; and God knows best.'

> Malik, son of Dinar, said, 'Jesus, peace be upon him, and the disciples with him passed by the carcass of a dog. A disciple said, "What a stench this dog makes!" Then he, (blessings and peace by upon him), said, "How white are its teeth!"'

> It is related on the authority of Ma'ruf al-Karkhi that Jesus, peace be upon him, said, 'Remember cotton when it is put over your eyes.'

It is said that Jesus, son of Mary, peace be upon him, met a man and said to him, 'What are you doing?' He replied, 'I am devoting myself to God.' He said, 'Who is giving you what you need?' He said, 'My brother.' Jesus said, 'He is more devoted to God than you.'

Jesus, son of Mary, peace be upon him, said, 'The world consists of three days: yesterday which has passed, from which you have nothing in your hand; tomorrow of which you do not know whether you will reach it or not; and today in which you are, so avail yourself of it.'

The disciples said to Jesus, peace be upon him, 'How is it that you can walk on water and we cannot?' Then he said to them, 'What do you think of the *dinar* and the *dirham*?' (pieces of money). They replied, 'They are good.' He said, 'But they and mud are alike to me.'

When Jesus was asked, 'How are you this morning?', he would answer, 'Unable to forestall what I hope, or to put off what I fear, bound by my works, with all my good in another's hand. There is no poor man poorer than I.'

And he said also, 'The world is both seeking and sought. He who seeks the next world, this world seeks him until his provision in it is complete; and he who seeks the present world, the next world seeks him until death comes and seizes him by the neck.'

If you wish, you may follow him who was the Spirit and the Word, Jesus, son of Mary, peace be upon him, for he used to say, 'My seasoning is hunger, my under-garment is fear of God, my outer-garment is wool, my fire in winter is the rays of the sun, my lamp is the moon, my riding beast is my feet, and my food and fruit are what the earth brings forth (i.e. without cultivation). At night I have nothing and in the morning I have nothing, yet there is no one on earth richer than I.'

Jesus, peace be upon him, said, 'He who seeks after the world is like one who drinks sea water; the more he drinks, the more his thirst increases, until it kills him.'

It is related that the Messiah, peace be upon him, passed in his wandering a man asleep, wrapped up in his cloak; then he wakened him and said, 'O sleeper, arise and glorify God! Exalted is He!' Then the man said, 'What do you want from me? Truly I have abandoned the world to its people.' So he said to him, 'Sleep then, my friend.'

Obaid, son of 'Umar, said, 'The Messiah, son of Mary, peace be upon him, used to wear hair clothing, and eat wild fruits, and he had no son to die, and no house to be demolished, and he stored up nothing for the morrow. He slept wherever the evening overtook him.'

Jesus, the Messiah, peace be upon him, used to take nothing with him but a comb and a jug. Then he saw a man combing his beard with his fingers, so he threw away the comb; and he saw another drinking from a river with the palms of his hands, so he threw away the jug.

Jesus, peace be upon him, said to the disciples, 'Take the places of worship as houses, and the houses as alighting places; and eat wild vegetables, and drink pure water, and escape safe from the world.'

Jesus, son of Mary, peace be upon him, said, 'In the last days there will be learned men who teach abstinence in the world but will not be abstinent themselves, who will teach men to take delight in the next world but will not take delight in it themselves, and who will warn men against coming before rulers but will not refrain themselves. They will draw near to the rich and keep far from the poor; they will be pleasant to great men but will shrink from humble men. Those are the brethren of the devils and the enemies of the Merciful.'

The following is related from Jabir, from Laith:

A man accompanied Jesus, son of Mary, peace be upon him, and said, 'I will be with you and will accompany you.' So they set off and came to the bank of a river and sat down to breakfast; and they had three loaves. They ate two loaves, and a third loaf was left over. Then Jesus, peace be upon him, rose up and went to the river and drank, after which he returned, but did not find the loaf; so he said to the man, 'Who took the loaf?' He replied, 'I do not know.'

Then he set off with his companion and saw a gazelle with two of her young. The narrator said: he called one of them and it came to him; then he cut its throat and roasted part of it, and he and that man ate. Then he said to the young gazelle, 'Rise, by the permission of God.' When it arose and went away, he said to the man, 'I ask you by Him Who has shown you this sign, who took the loaf?' He replied, 'I do not know.'

Afterwards they came to a wadi with water in it and Jesus took the man's hand and they walked on the water. Then, when they had crossed, he said to him, 'I ask you by Him Who has shown you this sign, who took the loaf?' He replied, 'I do not know.'

Then they came to a desert and sat down, and Jesus, peace be upon him, began to collect earth and a heap of sand, after which he said, 'Become gold, by the permission of God, Exalted be He!' It became gold, and he divided it into three parts and said, 'A third is for me, a third for you, and a third for him who took the loaf.' Then he said, 'I am the one who took the loaf.' He said, 'It is all yours.'

Jesus, peace be upon him, then left him, and two men came to him in the desert while he had the wealth with him and wished to take it from him and kill him. He said, 'It is among us in thirds; so send one of you to the village to buy food for us to eat.'

The narrator said: they sent one of them, and he who was sent said to himself, 'Why should I divide this wealth with these men? I shall put poison in this food and kill them and take the wealth myself.' So he did so. And these two men said, 'Why should we give this man a third of the wealth? When he returns we shall kill him, and divide the wealth between us.'

The narrator said: so when he returned they killed him and ate the food and died; and that wealth remained in the desert with those three men lying dead beside it. Then Jesus, peace be upon him, passed them in that condition and said to his companions, 'This is the world, so beware of it.'

It is related that Jesus, peace be upon him, passed three people whose bodies were wasted and who were pale and said, 'What has brought on you that which I see?' They replied, 'Fear of the Fire.' He said, 'It is God's duty to render secure him who fears.' Afterwards he passed from them and came to another three, and lo, they were in greater emaciation and paleness, so he said, 'What has brought on you that which I see?' They replied, 'Desire for the Garden.' He said, 'It is God's duty to give you what you hope for.' After that he passed from them and came to another three, and lo, they were in still greater emaciation and paleness as though mirrors of light were over their faces, so he said, 'What has brought on you that which I see?' They replied, 'We love God, Great and Glorious is He.' He said, 'You are those who are nearest to God; you are those who are nearest to God; you are those who are nearest to God.'

It is related on the authority of Muhammad, son of Abu Musa, concerning Jesus, son of Mary, peace be on him, that he passed an afflicted man and treated him kindly and said, 'Oh God, I beseech You to heal him.' Then God, Exalted is He, revealed to him, 'How can I heal him from that with which I am healing him?'

It is related that Jesus, peace be upon him, one day passed a hill in which he saw a cave. He drew near it and found in it a devotee whose back was bent, whose body was wasted, and in whom austerity had reached its utmost limits. Jesus greeted him and wondered at the evidences (of devotion) which he saw. So Jesus said to him, 'How long have you been in this place?' He replied, 'For seventy years I have been asking Him for one thing which He has not granted me yet. Perhaps you, O Spirit of God, may intercede for me concerning it; then possibly it may be granted.' Jesus said, 'What is your requirement?' He replied, 'I asked Him to let me taste the amount of an atom of His pure love.' Jesus said to him, 'I shall pray to God for you about that.'

So he prayed for him that night, and God, Exalted is He, revealed to him, 'I have accepted your intercession and granted your request.' Jesus, peace be upon him, returned to him to the place after some days to see what the condition of the devotee was, and saw the cave had fallen in and a great fissure had appeared in the ground below it. Jesus, peace be upon him, went down into that fissure and went some leagues in it and saw the devotee in a cave under that hill standing with his eyes staring and his mouth open. Then Jesus, peace be upon him, greeted him, but he did not give him an answer.

While Jesus was wondering at his condition a voice said to him, 'O Jesus, he asked Us for something like an atom of Our pure love, and We knew that he was not able for that, so We gave him a seventieth part of an atom, and he is bewildered in it thus; so what would it have been like if We had given him more than that?'

Whoever is familiar with the main events in the Prophet Muhammad's life, may God bless him and grant him peace, will already know that not long after he had begun calling people to worship God – and only God – he was taken on a miraculous night journey (*al-'isra' wa'l-mi'raj*) on a winged mount called the *Buraq* with the angel Gabriel to Jerusalem – and from there through the seven heavens, past the limit of forms, to the very Presence of God – not in the sense of physical proximity of course, for God is already closer to everyone than their jugular vein, but in the sense of spiritual nearness and intimacy. In each of the seven heavens, he met one of the earlier Prophets, peace be on all of them, who had preceded him – and one of these Prophets was Jesus. Thus we know from this that for the time being at least, Jesus is in one of the seven heavens, in the Unseen, and as yet has not experienced death.'

The Prophet Muhammad, may the blessings and peace of God be on him, also confirmed on more than one occasion that towards the end of time Jesus would return to this world in order to destroy the AntiChrist (the *Dajjal*) and his followers, and that after this had occurred, the way of Islam would be established throughout the world. Among the many *hadith* which record what the Prophet Muhammad said about Jesus, may the blessings and peace of God be on both of them, are these:

> It has been related by Ibn Mas'ud, may God be pleased with him, that the Prophet Muhammad, may God bless him and grant him peace, said, 'On the night of the *'isra'* (the night journey), I met my father Abraham, Moses and Jesus, and they discussed the Hour. The matter was referred first to Abraham, then to Moses, and both said, "I have no knowledge of it."
>
> 'Then it was referred to Jesus, who said, "No-one knows about its timing except God; what my Lord told me was that the *Dajjal* will appear, and when he sees me he will begin to melt like lead. God will destroy him when he sees me. The Muslims will fight against the disbelievers, and even the trees and rocks will say, 'O Muslim, there is a disbeliever hiding behind me – come and kill him!' God will destroy the disbelievers, and the people will return to their own lands. Then Gog and Magog will appear from all directions, eating and drinking everything they find. The people will complain to me, so I will pray to God and He will destroy them, so that the earth will be filled with their stench. God will send rain which will wash their bodies into the sea. My Lord has told me that when that happens, the Hour will be very close, like a pregnant woman whose time is due, but her family do not know exactly when she will deliver."' (*Ahmad ibn Hanbal: Musnad, 1.375*).

These events are described in greater detail in the following *hadith*:

> An-Nuwas ibn Sam'an said, 'One morning the Prophet, may God bless him and grant him peace, spoke about the *Dajjal*. Sometimes he described him as insignificant,

and sometimes he described him as so dangerous that we thought he was in the clump of date-palms nearby. When we went to him later on, he noticed that fear in our faces, and asked, "What is the matter with you?" We said, "O Messenger of God, this morning you spoke of the *Dajjal*; sometimes you described him as insignificant, and sometimes you described him as being so dangerous that we thought he was in the clump of date-palms nearby."

'The Prophet, may God bless him and grant him peace, said, "I fear for you in other matters besides the *Dajjal*. If he appears whilst I am among you, I will contend with him on your behalf. But if he appears while I am not among you, then each man must contend with him on his own behalf, and God will take care of every Muslim on my behalf. The *Dajjal* will be a young man, with short, curly hair, and one eye floating. I would liken him to Abdal-'Uzza ibn Qatan. Whoever amongst you lives to see him should recite the opening verses of Surat al-Kahf. He will appear on the way between Syria and Iraq, and will create disaster left and right. O servants of God, adhere to the Path of Truth."

'We said, "O Messenger of God, how long will he stay on the earth?" He said, "For forty days, one day like a year, and one day like a month, and one day like a week, and the rest of the days will be like your days.'

'We said, "O Messenger of God, for the day which is like a year, will one day's prayers be sufficient?" He said, "No, you must make an estimate of the time, and then observe the prayers."

'We asked, "O Messenger of God, how quickly will he walk upon the earth?" He said, "Like a cloud driven by the wind. He will come to the people and call them (to a false religion), and they will believe in him and respond to him. He will issue a command to the sky, and it will rain; and to the earth, and it will produce crops. After grazing on these crops, their animals will return with their udders full of milk and their flanks stretched. Then he will come to another people and will call them (to a false religion), but they will reject his call. He will depart from them; they will suffer famine and will possess nothing in the form of wealth. Then he will pass through the wasteland and will say, 'Bring forth your treasures', and the treasures will come forth, like swarms of bees. Then he will call a man brimming with youth; he will strike him with a sword and cut him in two, then place the two pieces at the distance between an archer and his target. Then he will call him, and the young man will come running and laughing.

'"At that point, God will send the Messiah, son of Mary, and he will descend to the white minaret in the east of Damascus, wearing two garments dyed with saffron, placing his hands on the wings of two angels. When he lowers his head, beads of perspiration will fall from it, and when he raises his head, beads like pearls will scatter from it. Every disbeliever who smells his fragrance will die, and his breath will reach as far as he can see. He will search for the *Dajjal* until he finds him at the gate of Ludd (the biblical Lydda, now known as Lod), where he will kill him.

'"Then a people whom God has protected will come to Jesus son of Mary, and he will wipe their faces (i.e. wipe the traces of hardship from their faces) and tell them of their status in Paradise. At that time God will reveal to Jesus: 'I have brought forth some of My servants whom no-one will be able to fight. Take My servants safely to at-Tur.'

'"Then God will send Gog and Magog, and they will swarm down from every slope. The first of them will pass by the Lake of Tiberias, and will drink some of its water; the last of them will pass by it and say, 'There used to be water here.' Jesus, the Prophet of God, and his Companions will be besieged until a bull's head will be dearer to them than one hundred *dinars* are to you nowadays.

'"Then Jesus and his Companions will pray to God, and He will send insects who will bite the people of Gog and Magog on their necks, so that in the morning they will all perish as one. Then Jesus and his Companions will come down and will not find any nook or cranny on earth which is free from their putrid stench. Jesus and his Companions will again pray to God, Who will send birds like the necks of camels; they will seize the bodies of Gog and Magog and throw them wherever God wills. Then God will send rain which no house or tent will be able to keep out, and the earth will be cleansed, until it will look like a mirror. Then the earth will be told to bring forth its fruit and restore its blessing.

On that day, a group of people will be able to eat from a single pomegranate and seek shelter under its skin (i.e. the fruit will be so large). A milch-camel will give so much milk that a whole party will be able to drink from it; a cow will give so much milk that a whole tribe will be able to drink from it; and a milch-sheep will give so much milk that a whole family will be able to drink from it.

At that time, God will send a pleasant wind which will soothe them even under their armpits, and will take the soul of every Muslim. Only the most wicked people will be left, and they will fornicate like asses; then the Last Hour will come upon them.'"(*Sahih Muslim, Kitab al-Fitan wa Ashrat as-Sa'ah, 8.196-199*).

The Prophet Muhammad also confirmed that after the *Dajjal* and his followers had been killed, Jesus would then follow the way of Muhammad, breaking all the crosses, because he is not the 'son' of God and he was not crucified, and marrying and having children and governing as a just ruler in accordance with the *Qur'an* and the *Sunnah*, and finally, after his death, being buried next to the Prophet Muhammad in Madina, where they will remain until they are brought back to life on the Day of Rising and Judgement, may the blessings and peace of God be on both of them:

It has been related by Abu Hurayra, may God be pleased with him, that the Prophet Muhammad, may God bless him and grant him peace, said, 'By the One in Whose hand my soul is, the son of Mary will soon descend among you as a just judge, and he will break the crosses, and kill pigs, and abolish the *jizya*, and wealth will pour forth to such an extent that no one will accept it, and one prostration (in prayer) will be better than the world and what it contains.' Then Abu Hurayra added, 'If you wish, you can recite, '**And there is not one of the People of the Book but will certainly believe in him before his death – and on the Day of Standing he will be a witness against them.**' (*Qur'an 4: 159*). (*Al-Bukhari*).

And:

It has been related by Abu Hurayra, may God be pleased with him, that the Prophet Muhammad, may God bless him and grant him peace, said, 'The Prophets are like brothers: they have different mothers but their way of life is one. I am the closest of all the people to Jesus son of Mary, because there is no other Prophet between him and myself. He will come again, and when you see him, you will recognise him. He is of medium height and his colouring is reddish-white. He will be wearing two garments, and his hair will look wet. He will break the cross, kill the pigs, abolish the *jizya* and call the people to Islam. During his time, God will end every religion and sect other than Islam, and will destroy the *Dajjal*. Then peace and security will prevail on earth, so that lions will graze with camels, tigers with cattle, and wolves with sheep; children will be able to play with snakes without coming to any harm. Jesus will remain for forty years, then die, and the Muslims will pray for him.' (*Ahmad ibn Hanbal: Musnad, 2: 406*).

And:

It has been related by Abu Hurayra, may God be pleased with him, that the Prophet Muhammad, may God bless him and grant him peace, said, 'What will you do when the son of Mary descends amongst you and leads you as one of you?' Ibn Abi Dhi'b, on the authority of Abu Hurayra narrated 'your leader amongst you'. Ibn Abi Dhi'b said, 'Do you know what the words "and leads you as one of you" mean?' I said, 'Explain these to me.' He said, 'He will lead you in accordance with the Book of your Lord, may He be glorified and exalted, (the *Qur'an*), and the *Sunnah* of your Messenger, may God bless him and grant him peace.' (*Muslim*).

And:

> 'Abd'Allah bin Amr reported Muhammad, may the
> peace and blessings of God be on him, as saying, 'Jesus,
> son of Mary, will descend to the earth, will marry, have
> children, and remain forty-five years, after which he will
> die and be buried along with me in my grave. Then Jesus,
> son of Mary, and I shall arise from one grave between
> Abu Bakr and 'Umar.' (*Ibn al-Jauzi in Kitab al-Wafa'*).

And:

> It has been transmitted by 'Abdullah ibn 'Umar that the
> Prophet Muhammad, may God bless him and grant him
> peace, said, 'I dreamt at night that I was at the *Ka'ba*,
> and I saw a dark man like the most handsome of dark
> men you have ever seen. He had hair reaching to be-
> tween his ears and his shoulders like the most excellent
> of such hair that you have seen. He had combed his hair,
> and water was dripping from it. He was leaning on two
> men or on the shoulders of two men doing *tawaf* around
> *Ka'ba*. I asked, "Who is this?" It was said, "The Messiah,
> son of Mary." Then we were with a man with wiry hair
> and blind in his right eye, as if it was a floating grape. I
> asked, "Who is this?" It was said to me, "This is the
> AntiChrist."' (*Al-Muwatta' of Imam Malik: 49: 2.2*).

Many of those who profess to be followers of Jesus today are often
totally unaware of the deep spiritual connection which exists between Jesus and Muhammad, may the blessings and peace of God
be on them both, and indeed are more accustomed to regarding
those who profess to be followers of Muhammad as 'them' and not
'us', and even as 'the enemy'. It is clear from all the above *hadith*,
however, that Jesus is indeed a Prophet of Islam – and that the
only way to follow Jesus today is by following the way of Muhammad, may God bless them both and grant them peace, for, as we
have seen, this is what Jesus himself will do when he returns to
this world.

   O   O   O   O   O

And if he were to walk up to you right now, then Jesus, peace be on him, would say, 'If you wish to follow me – then follow Muhammad!'

> It has been transmitted by Abu Hurayra, may God be pleased with him, that the Prophet Muhammad, may God bless him and grant him peace, said, 'By Him in Whose hand is the life of Muhammad, whoever of the Jews or Christians hears about me, but does not affirm belief in what I have been sent with (the *Qur'an*), and dies in this state, will be one of the inhabitants of the Fire of Hell.' (*Muslim*).

> It has been transmitted by Abu Musa al-Ash'ari, may God be pleased with him, that the Prophet Muhammad, may God bless him and grant him peace, said, 'If anyone believes in Jesus son of Mary and then believes in me, then he will have a double reward.' (*Al-Bukhari*).

> It has been transmitted by 'Ubada, may God be pleased with him, that the Prophet Muhammad, may God bless him and grant him peace, said, 'Whoever bears witness that there is no god except God, alone without any partner; and that Muhammad is His slave and His Messenger; and that Jesus is the slave of God and His Messenger and His Word which he bestowed on Mary and a Spirit from Him; and that the Garden is true and the Fire is true, then God will make him enter the Garden, however few his good actions may have been. (*Al-Bukhari*).

> Abu Hurayra reported God's Messenger, may the peace and blessings of God be upon him, as saying, 'I am the nearest of kin to Jesus, son of Mary, in this world and in the next. The prophets are brothers, sons of one father by co-wives. Their mothers are different, but their way of life is one. There has been no prophet between us.' (*From Bukhari and Muslim*)

In this famous statement, the last of the Prophets and Messengers, our master Muhammad, may the peace and blessings of God be upon him, summed up the whole matter:

The prophets are brothers: they are all the same; there is no distinction between them.

Sons of one father: they all declare one doctrine – *La ilaha il'Allah. There is no god but Allah, the One.* Nothing can be associated with Him in His Divinity.

Their mothers are different: each Prophet has been sent to a particular people at a particular time. The Prophet of the time has had revealed to him a *Sunnah*, or life-form, a practice, a social pattern by which his community should live. Whenever a new Prophet came to a people, he brought a new form of this *Sunnah* to accord with the new age. This is the *Shari'ah* or Road of the Prophets. Thus, with the coming of our master Muhammad, may the peace and blessings of God be upon him, the Divine Transaction is complete. Messengership is sealed in the last revealed Book, the *Glorious Qur'an.*

Prophethood is sealed with the *Shari'ah* and the *Sunnah* of the compassionate Prophet, Muhammad, may the peace and blessings of God be upon him.

The science of worship, itself the means of approach to God, is sealed in the Book (the *Qur'an*) and the *Sunnah* of the first of the sons of Adam, peace be upon him. The Way of Jesus, Prophet of Islam, is over. The Way of Muhammad, Prophet of Islam, has begun.

This verse of the *Qur'an*, the last to be revealed, disclosed the tremendous matter to be complete:

This day I have perfected your way of life for you, and I have completed My blessing upon you, and I have chosen AL-ISLAM for you as your way of life.

(Qur'an 5: 3).

○   ○   ○   ○   ○

Chapter Eleven

Jesus in Qur'an

The *Qur'an*, the last of the Divine Books, revealed by the Creator to the last of the Messengers – Muhammad, may God bless him and grant him peace – is a source of knowledge about Jesus, peace be upon him, which is not generally known to most students of Christianity. The *Qur'an* not only leads us towards a better understanding of who Jesus was, but also, through that understanding, it increases our respect and love for him. The last Revelation, coming as it did some six hundred years after the birth of Jesus, tells what is important for us to know about his life and teachings, and places his role as Prophet in the vast perspective that the Unitarians realised lay behind prophecy itself. The *Qur'an* alone gives us that perspective – which no other source today can provide.

The *Qur'an* does not cover the life of Jesus in any great detail as regards specific events. The miracles and powers which he was given are mentioned including some which are not even described in the *Bible* – but mostly in general terms. Similarly, the Book which Jesus was given by God, the *Ingil*, is mentioned several times, but its exact contents are not indicated. However, the *Qur'an* is very specific as to his purpose, how he appeared on earth, who he was, and, equally important, who he was not, and how his mission ended.

Before looking at the verses which describe the life of Jesus himself, it would be helpful to examine the verses which delineate what his function on earth was, and how he fits into the broader pattern of what came before him and what was to come after him:

It is stated again and again that Jesus was one of the long line of Prophets who had been sent to the peoples of this earth; that he was a Messenger whose guidance and teachings were a reaffirmation and an extension of the guidance which the Prophets before him had brought – and a preparation for the guidance which the Prophet coming after him would bring, may God bless him and grant him peace.

The *Qur'an* makes it clear that Jesus was the son of Mary, the daughter of 'Imran, who was descended from the Prophet Solomon, the son of the Prophet David who was descended from Judah, one of the twelve sons of the Prophet Jacob – who was otherwise known as Israel – who was descended from the Prophet Isaac, the son of the Prophet Abraham, may the blessings and peace of God be on all of them.

The *Qur'an* also makes it clear that there is absolutely no doubt about the fact that Jesus was the promised Messiah – descended from the family of David, from the family of Jacob, from the family of the Prophet Abraham through his son Isaac – whose coming had been foretold in the original *Torah* of Moses, may the blessings and peace of God be on all of them:

> And We indeed gave Moses the Book, and We made a succession of Messengers follow after him, and We gave Jesus son of Mary clear proofs and We helped him with the pure spirit (the angel Gabriel). (*Qur'an 2: 87*).

The following passage reminds us of the line of Prophets of which Jesus was a part. After referring to Abraham, it continues:

> And We gave him (Abraham) Isaac and Jacob, and We guided each of them – and before that We guided Noah and, from among his descendants, David and Solomon and Job and Joseph and Moses and Aaron – and that is how We reward those who are good; and Zachariah and John and Jesus and Elijah – each of them was from among the righteous; and Ishmael and Elisha and Jonah and Lot – and We favoured each of them in all the worlds, as well as some of their forefathers and their descendants and their brothers; and We chose them and guided them to a straight path. (*Qur'an 6: 84-87*).

And this list of Prophets is by no means complete, as the following passage addressed to the Prophet Muhammad, makes clear:

> Surely We have inspired you (Muhammad) just as We inspired Noah and the Prophets after him, as We inspired Abraham and Ishmael and Isaac and Jacob and the tribes (of Israel) and Jesus and Job and Jonah and Aaron and Solomon, and David to whom We gave the

Zabur, and Messengers whom we have told you about and Messengers whom we have not told you about, and Moses to whom God spoke directly – Messengers who brought good news and a warning so that mankind would not have any argument against God after the Messengers; and God has always been Mighty, Wise. (*Qur'an 4: 163-165*).

In fact the Prophet Muhammad said that Jesus was one of one hundred and twenty-four thousand Prophets, may the blessings and peace of God be on all of them, between whom there is no cause for conflict or argument. Thus God commands the Muslims as follows:

Say: 'We believe in God, and in what has been revealed to us, and in what was revealed to Abraham and to Ishmael and to Isaac and to Jacob and to the Tribes (of Israel), and in what was given to Moses and Jesus and the Prophets from their Lord – we make no distinction between any of them, and to Him we have submitted.' And as for whoever desires a life transaction other than Islam, it will not be accepted from him, and in the next life he will be among the losers. (*Qur'an 3: 84-85*).

Furthermore, it is clear from the *Qur'an* that all of the Prophets were well aware that they had been sent by God for the same purpose and with basically the same message:

And (remember) when We made a covenant with the Prophets – with you (Muhammad), and with Noah, and Abraham, and Moses, and Jesus son of Mary – and We made them make a solemn covenant, so that the truthful might be asked about their truthfulness – and He has prepared a painful punishment for the disbelievers. (*Qur'an 33: 7-8*).

And:

O Messengers, eat what is good and do good – surely I am aware of what you do – and surely this community of yours is one community, and I am your Lord, so fear Me. (*Qur'an 23: 51-52*).

And:

> He has commanded you to follow the same life-trans-
> action that He decreed for Noah, and which We have
> revealed to you (O Muhammad), and which We decreed
> for Abraham, and for Moses, and for Jesus, saying, 'Es-
> tablish the life-transaction and do not become divided
> in it.' (*Qur'an 42: 13*).

Part of the covenant which all the Prophets made with God was to
tell their followers about the coming of Muhammad, may God bless
him and grant him peace, and to follow him should he come during their lifetime:

> And when God made His covenant with the Prophets,
> (He said), 'This is what I have given you as a Book and
> wisdom, and then a Messenger (Muhammad) will come
> to you confirming what you have – and you will be-
> lieve in him and you will help him.' He said, 'Will you
> be bound by this and will you accept this obligation?'
> They replied, 'We will be bound by it.' He said, 'Then
> bear witness to it – and I will bear witness with you –
> and as for whoever turns away after this, then they will
> be the ones who disobey.' (*Qur'an 3: 81-82*).

Thus the picture of Jesus which unfolds in the *Qur'an* is not that of
some remarkable man who appeared on earth as an isolated event
in an otherwise somewhat chaotic world, but of a Messenger who,
like all the other Messengers, was sent for his time and his age, a
part of the ordered unfolding of the universe:

> And We sent Jesus son of Mary in their footsteps,
> confirming what was (revealed) before him in the *To-
> rah*; and We gave him the *Ingil* – in which there was
> guidance and light – confirming what was (revealed)
> before it in the *Torah*, and a guidance and a warning for
> those who fear God. And let the people of the *Ingil* judge
> by what God has revealed in it. And whoever does not
> judge by what God has revealed, then they are evil liv-
> ers. (*Qur'an 5: 46-47*).

And furthermore, a time which, as Jesus was well aware, had limits – a time which was bounded by the time before his time, and by the time after it:

> And (remember) when Moses said to his people, 'O my people, why do you persecute me when you well know that I am the Messenger of God to you?' So when they went astray God sent their hearts astray. And God does not guide the people who are evil.
>
> And (remember) when Jesus son of Mary said, 'O Tribe of Israel, surely I am the Messenger of God to you, confirming what was (revealed) before me in the *Torah*, and bringing good news of a Messenger who will come after me, whose name is the Praised One (*Ahmad*).'
>
> ('*Ahmad*' is one of the names of the Prophet Muhammad, may God bless him and grant him peace, meaning 'the Most Praiseworthy', 'the One who Distinguishes between Truth and Falsehood', and 'the Comforter'. Its equivalent in Greek is '*Parakletos*' or '*Parakleitos*', meaning 'the Comforter' or 'the Praised One'.)
>
> Yet when he came to them with clear proofs, they said, 'This is clearly magic.'
>
> And who does greater wrong than the one who makes up a lie against God when he is called to Islam? And God does not guide people who do wrong. They desire to put out the Light of God with their words, but God will perfect His Light however much those who disbelieve detest it. He it is Who has sent His Messenger with the guidance and the true life-transaction, so that He may make it overcome all other religions, however much the idol worshippers detest it.
>
> O you who trust, shall I lead you to a bargain that will save you from a painful punishment? You should believe in God and His Messenger, and fight in the way of God with your wealth and your selves. That is better

for you, if only you knew. He will forgive you your wrong actions and bring you into Gardens underneath which rivers flow and pleasant dwellings in Gardens of Eden. That is the supreme success. And He will give you something else that you love: Help from God and victory that is near – and give good news to the believers!

O you who believe, be God's helpers, just as when Jesus son of Mary said to the disciples, 'Who will be my helpers for God?' and the disciples replied, 'We are God's helpers.' And a party of the Tribe of Israel believed, and a party disbelieved, and We strengthened those who believed against their enemy, and so they became the ones who prevailed. (*Qur'an* 61: 5-14).

Jesus's conception and birth are recorded by the *Qur'an* in great detail. It would be illuminating to begin with his mother's birth and upbringing, for it helps us to see how Mary was chosen and prepared by God to be the mother of Jesus:

Surely God chose Adam and Noah and the family of Abraham and the family of 'Imran above all the worlds – they were descended from each other – and God is Hearing, Knowing. (And remember) when the wife of 'Imran said, 'My Lord, surely I have vowed that what is in my womb will be dedicated to You – so accept it from me. Surely it is You Who are the Hearer, the Knower.' And when she had given birth to her, she said, 'My Lord, surely I have given birth to a girl,' and God knew best to whom she had given birth – a boy is not like a girl, 'and surely I have named her Mary, and surely I seek protection in You for her and her offspring from the outcast *shaytan*.'

And her Lord accepted her with complete acceptance, and made her grow in complete health, and made Zachariah her guardian. And whenever Zachariah entered the sanctuary where she was, he found that she had food. He said, 'O Mary, from where has this come?' She replied, 'It is from God – surely God provides for whomever He wishes without reckoning.' Then Zachariah prayed to his Lord, saying, 'My Lord, grant me good offspring from Your presence – surely You hear prayer.' And the angels called to him as he stood in prayer in the sanctuary, 'Surely God gives you good news of John, who will confirm a Word (Jesus) from God, and who will be honourable and chaste and one of the righteous Prophets.' He said, 'My Lord, how can I have a son, when I have become old and my wife is barren?' He replied, 'Just like that – God does what He wants.' He said, 'My Lord, give me a sign.' He replied, 'Your sign shall be that you will not speak to anyone for three days except by sign-language, and remember your Lord much and glorify Him at nightfall and in the early morning.'

And (remember) when the angels said, 'O Mary, surely God has chosen you, and He has made you pure, and He has preferred you above all women in all the worlds. O Mary, be obedient to your Lord, and prostrate and bow down in worship (before Him) with those who bow down in worship.'

This is from tidings of the Unseen which We reveal to you – and you were not there with them when they cast their reeds (to decide) which of them should be Mary's guardian, and you were not there with them when they argued about it. (*Qur'an 3: 33-44*).

John was the Prophet who directly preceded Jesus. It is said that his mother, Elisabeth, and Mary's mother, Hannah, were either sisters or cousins, which means that Jesus and John were cousins. The miraculous birth of John is also mentioned in the following passages:

And (remember) when Zachariah called to his Lord, 'My Lord, do not leave me without a child – and You are the best of those who grant inheritance.' And We heard his prayer, and We gave him John, and We made his wife fertile – surely they were swift to do good, and they prayed to Us with longing and fear, and they were in awe of Us. And (remember) the one who remained chaste (Mary), and so We breathed in her of Our Spirit, and made her and her son (Jesus) a sign for all the worlds. (*Qur'an 21: 89-91*).

And:

> (This is) a reminder of the mercy of your Lord to His
> slave, Zachariah, when he called to his Lord in secret
> prayer, saying, 'My Lord, surely my bones have become
> fragile, and my head shines with grey hair, and my
> prayers to You, my Lord, have never been in vain, and
> surely I am concerned about who will succeed me, as
> my wife is barren – so grant me a successor from Your
> presence who will inherit from me, and who will in-
> herit from the family of Jacob, and make him, my Lord,
> pleasing (to You).'

> (It was said to him), 'O Zachariah, surely We give you
> good news of a son whose name is John – and We have
> never given that name to anyone before him.' He said,
> 'My Lord, how can I have a son when my wife is barren
> and I have become old and weak?' He replied, 'Just like
> that – your Lord says, "It is easy for Me, just as I created
> you in the past, when you were not anything."' He said,
> 'My Lord, give me a sign.' He replied, 'Your sign shall
> be that you will not speak to anyone for three nights
> even though you are well.' Then he came out to his peo-
> ple from the sanctuary and gestured to them to glorify
> (God) in the early morning and at nightfall.

> (And it was said to his son), 'O John, hold fast to the
> Book!' And We gave him wisdom when he was a boy,
> and compassion from Our presence, and purity – and
> he was devout, and he was kind to his parents, and he
> was never tyrannical or rebellious. So peace be on him
> the day he was born, and the day he died, and the day
> he will be brought back to life! (*Qur'an 19: 2-15*).

The story of the miraculous conception and birth of Jesus is related
in two different places in the *Qur'an*:

> (And remember) when the angels said, 'O Mary, surely
> God gives you good news of a Word from Him, whose
> name is the Messiah, Jesus son of Mary, who will be hon-
> oured in this world and in the next world, and who will

be one of those who are near (to God) – and he will speak to people from his cradle and when he is a man, and he will be one of those who are righteous.' She replied, 'My Lord, how can I have a child, when no man has touched me?' He replied, 'Just like that – God creates whatever He wants. When He decrees something, then all He says to it is, "Be!" and it is. And He will teach him the Book, and wisdom, and the *Torah*, and the *Ingil*, and he will be a Messenger to the Tribe of Israel, (saying), "Surely I have come to you with a sign from your Lord – surely I will make the shape of a bird from clay for you, and then breathe into it, and it will become a bird by the permission of God; and I will heal him who was born blind and the leper, and I will bring the dead to life by the permission of God; and I will tell you what you have had to eat and what you have stored away in your houses – surely in that there is certainly a sign for you, if you are believers. And (I have come) to confirm what was before me from the *Torah*, and to make some of what used to be forbidden for you lawful for you – and I have come to you with a sign from your Lord, so fear God and obey me. Surely God is my Lord and your Lord, so worship Him – that is the straight path."'

And when Jesus perceived their disbelief, he said, 'Who will be my helpers for God?' The disciples replied, 'We are God's helpers – we believe in God, so bear witness that we are Muslims! O our Lord, we believe in what You have revealed and we follow the Messenger, so record us among those who bear witness.' (*Qur'an 3: 45-53*).

The story is also told in Surah Maryam:

And mention Mary in the Book – when she withdrew from her people to a place in the east and chose seclusion from them, then We sent Our spirit (the angel Gabriel) to her, and he appeared to her as a perfect man. She said, 'Surely I seek refuge in the Merciful One from you, if you fear God.' He said, 'Surely I am only a Messenger from your Lord, to give you news of a pure son.' She replied, 'How can I have a son when no man has

touched me, and when I have never been immoral?' He
said, 'Just like that – your Lord says, "It is easy for Me –
and We shall make him a sign for mankind, and a mercy
from Us – and it is something which has already been
decreed."'

And so she conceived him, and she withdrew with him
to a place which was far away, and the pains of child-
birth drove her to the trunk of a palm tree – she said, 'O
would that I had died before this and become nothing,
forgotten!' And then it was said to her from below her,
'Do not be sad – your Lord has placed a small stream
beneath you, and shake the trunk of the palm tree towards you - you will make fresh ripe dates fall around
you. So eat and drink and be comforted. And if you meet
any man, then say, "Surely I have made a vow to the
Merciful One to fast, and I may not speak to anyone
today."'

Then she brought him to her people, carrying him. They
said, 'O Mary, you have indeed come with something
deceitful! O sister of Aaron, your father was not a wicked
man, and your mother was never immoral!' Then she
pointed to him. They said, 'How can we talk to a baby
in his cradle?' He said, 'Surely I am the slave of God –
He has given me the Book, and He has made me a
Prophet, and He has made me blessed wherever I may
be, and He has made the prayer and *zakat* obligatory for
me as long as I live, and He has made me obedient towards the one who bore me, and He has not made me
tyrannical or ungrateful – and peace be on me the day I
was born, and the day I die, and the day I shall be
brought back to life!'

Such was Jesus son of Mary – (this is) a statement of the
truth about which they are in doubt. It is not how it is
for God to choose any son – glory be to Him! When He
decrees something, then all He says to it is 'Be!' and it is.

'And surely God is my Lord and your Lord, so worship
Him. This is the straight path.' (*Qur'an 19: 16-36*).

The place where Jesus was born is also mentioned in one other passage in the *Qur'an*:

> And We made a sign of the son of Mary and his mother, and We gave them a place of refuge in a high place, where there was safety and running water. (*Qur'an 23: 50*).

It is also said that this passage refers to the place where Mary and Jesus took refuge after his birth, and after they had been forced to leave Jerusalem and flee to Egypt, where they stayed during the early part of Jesus's childhood. God knows best.

Jesus's childhood, his return to Jerusalem from Egypt with his mother, and his early manhood, are not mentioned in the *Qur'an*, but there are several references to what happened once he began to call the Tribe of Israel to only worship God and to follow the teachings of Moses which were in the *Torah*. The following passage, for example, refers to the response of the men who became Jesus's disciples:

> O you who believe, be God' helpers, just as when Jesus son of Mary said to the disciples, 'Who will be my helpers for God?' and the disciples replied, 'We are God's helpers.' And a party of the Tribe of Israel believed, and a party disbelieved, and We strengthened those who believed against their enemy, and so they became the ones who prevailed. (*Qur'an 61: 14*).

The conflict between those who accepted Jesus and those who rejected him, peace be on him, often focused around his extraordinary miracles, which he always attributed to God and not to himself. It is not surprising, in view of these miracles, that some of those who accepted Jesus did so rather too enthusiastically, and in so doing mistakenly considered him to be the 'son' of God, thereby idolising him and making him an object of worship. God refers to this misconception in the following passage from Surat al-Ma'ida, which refers to God's questioning all His Messengers on the Last Day:

> On the Day when God will gather all the Messengers together and will say, 'What was the response to you?' they will say, 'We do not know – surely it is only You Who knows what is hidden.'

And God will say, 'O Jesus son of Mary, remember My blessing on you and on your mother – how I strengthened you with the pure spirit (the angel Gabriel), so that you spoke to people from the cradle and as a man; and how I taught you the Book, and wisdom and the *Torah* and the *Injil*; and how you made the shape of a bird from clay by My permission, and then breathed into it, so that it became a bird by My permission; and how you healed him who was born blind and the leper by My permission; and how you raised the dead by My permission; and how I restrained the Tribe of Israel from harming you when you came to them with clear proofs, and those of them who disbelieved said, "Surely this is nothing but magic!" And (remember) when I inspired the disciples to, "Believe in Me and in My Messenger," and they said, "We believe, so bear witness that we are Muslims!"'

And (remember) when the disciples said, 'O Jesus son of Mary, is your Lord able to send down a table from heaven for us?' He replied, 'Fear God if you are believers!' They said, 'We want to eat from it, and put our hearts at ease, and know that you have told us the truth, and be among those who witness it.' Jesus son of Mary said, 'O God, our Lord, send down a table from heaven for us with a feast for us, for the first of us and the last of us, and as a sign from You, and provide for us – and You are the Best of those who provide.' God said, 'Surely I will send it down for you – and if any of you disbelieves afterwards, then I will surely punish him with a punishment with which I have never punished anyone else in all the worlds before!'

(It is said that this feast replenished itself as long as no one stored up any of it for the next day, and that as soon as someone did this, it disappeared. God knows best.)

And when God says, 'O Jesus son of Mary, did you say to people, "Take me and my mother as two gods instead of God,"?' he will reply, 'Glory be to You – it was not for me to say what I had no right to say! If I ever said that, then You would certainly know it. You know what is in me, and I do not know what is in You – surely it is only You Who knows what is hidden. I only told them what You commanded me – to, "Worship God, my Lord and your Lord," and while I dwelt among them I was a watcher over them, and when You took me up, then You were a Watcher over them – and You watch over everything. If You punish them, then surely they are Your slaves, and if You forgive them, then surely You are the Mighty, the Wise.'

God will say, 'This is a Day when the truthful will benefit from their truthfulness, for gardens underneath which rivers flow will be theirs, dwelling there for ever – God is pleased with them and they are pleased with Him – that is the great success.' The dominion of the heavens and the earth and whatever is in them belongs to God – and He has power over everything. (*Qur'an 5: 109-120*).

Elsewhere in the *Qur'an*, God makes it perfectly clear that both Jesus and Mary were only human beings:

The Messiah son of Mary was only a Messenger like the Messengers who went before him and his mother was a truthful woman and they both used to eat food. See how We clarify the signs for them – and then see how they make up lies! Say: 'Do you worship what does not have any power to either harm or benefit you, instead of God?' And it is God Who is the One Who Hears, the One Who Knows. (*Qur'an 5: 75-76*).

It follows that Jesus could not possibly be the 'son' of God:

And they say, 'God has chosen a son.' Glory be to Him! Indeed whatever is in the heavens and the earth is His. Everything is subservient to Him, the Bringer into Being of the heavens and the earth – and when He decrees a matter, then all He says to it is 'Be!' and it is. (*Qur'an 2: 116-117*).

And:

> God has not chosen any son, and there is not any other
> god as well as Him – otherwise each god would cer-
> tainly have taken over what it had created, and some
> would have exalted themselves over others. Glory be to
> God above what they assert – the Knower of the Un-
> seen and the Seen, may He be exalted far above the part-
> ners they associate with Him! (*Qur'an 23: 91-92*).

And:

> Surely the life-transaction is only for God. And those
> who choose guardians other than Him (say), 'We only
> worship them so that they will bring us nearer to God.'
> – Surely God will judge between them concerning what
> they used to disagree about. Surely God does not guide
> whoever denies in disbelief. If God had wanted to have
> a son, He could certainly have chosen whatever He
> wanted from His creation – Glory be to Him! He is God,
> the One, the Compeller! (*Qur'an 39: 3-4*).

And:

> Say: 'If the Merciful did have a son, then I would be the
> foremost of the worshippers.' Glory be to the Lord of
> the heavens and the earth, the Lord of the Throne, above
> what they assert. (*Qur'an 43: 81-82*).

And:

> And certainly if you ask them, 'Who created the heav-
> ens and the earth?' they will certainly say, 'God.' Say:
> 'Do you not see, regarding whatever you pray to instead
> of God, that if God wished to harm me, how could they
> protect me from His harm – or if He wished to show
> mercy to me, how could they withhold His mercy?' Say:
> 'God is enough for me – in Him do those who trust put
> their trust.' (*Qur'an 39: 38*).

And:

Say: 'Are you telling me to worship other than God? –
You fools!' (*Qur'an 39: 64*).

And:

Blessed is the One Who has revealed the Discrimination (between right and wrong) to His slave (Muhammad), so that he might be a warner to all the worlds –
the One to Whom the dominion of the heavens and the
earth belongs – and He has not chosen a son, and He
does not have any partner to share the dominion, and
He has created everything and determined its destiny.
– And yet they have chosen gods instead of Him who
cannot create anything but are themselves created, and
who do not have any power either to harm or to benefit
themselves, and who do not have any power over either death, or life, or raising the dead! (*Qur'an 25: 1-3*).

And:

And they say, 'The Merciful has chosen a son.' You have
indeed come up with something terrible – so that the
heavens are almost torn apart, and the earth split open,
and the mountains scattered in pieces – that you should
claim that the Merciful has a son! And it is not in the
nature of things for the Merciful to choose a son – when
every one in the heavens and the earth only comes to the
Merciful as a slave. He certainly knows them all – and
He knows their number exactly – and each of them will
come to Him on the Day of Standing, alone. (*Qur'an 19:
88-95*).

And:

And We did not send any Messenger in the past without inspiring in him, 'Surely there is no god except Me
– so worship Me.' And they say, 'The Merciful has chosen a son.' Glory be to Him! – They are only slaves who
have been honoured:

They do not speak before He has spoken, and what they do is by His command. He knows what is ahead of them and what is behind them, and they cannot intercede except on behalf of whomever is pleasing to Him, and they tremble in fear of Him. And if one of them were to say, 'Surely I am God and not Him,' then we would repay anyone like that with Hell – that is how We reward wrong doers. (*Qur'an 21: 25-29*).

And:

They say: 'God has chosen a son.' – Glory be to Him! – He is the Self-Sufficient! Whatever is in the heavens and whatever is in the earth belongs to Him. You do not have any authority for (saying) this. Why do you say things about God of which you have no knowledge? Say: 'Surely those who make up a lie about God will not be successful.' They will pass their time in this world, and then to Us they will return, and then We will make them taste intense punishment because they used to disbelieve. (*Qur'an 10: 68-70*).

Thus in the opening *ayat* of Surat al-Kahf, God states that one of the reasons why the *Qur'an* has been revealed is to warn those who claim that God has a son:

In the Name of God the Merciful the Compassionate

Praise belongs to God Who has revealed the Book to His slave (Muhammad). And He has not put any distortion in it, only clarity, in order to warn of a severe punishment from Him, and to give good news to the believers who do good that theirs will be a good reward, where they will dwell for ever, and to warn those who say, 'God has chosen a son,' which is something they know nothing about, and neither did their fathers. The words which they utter are dreadful – surely what they say is nothing but a lie. (*Qur'an 18: 1-5*).

For:

It is not how it is for God to choose any son. – Glory be
to Him! – When He decrees a matter, then all He says to
it is 'Be!' and it is. (*Qur'an* 19: 35).

And:

> O mankind, a simile is coined for you – so pay attention
> to it: Surely those to whom you pray instead of God
> could never create a fly, even if they all tried together –
> and if the fly took something from them, they could not
> retrieve it from it: How weak are both the seeker and
> the sought! (*Qur'an* 22: 73).

Thus it also follows that anyone who thinks – by virtue of Mary's
degree of perfection, and by virtue of the miraculous nature of the
immaculate conception – that Jesus can somehow be associated
with being God in any way is mistaken:

> Those who say, 'Surely God is the Messiah, son of Mary,'
> have indeed disbelieved. Say: 'And who would have
> any power at all over God if He wished to destroy the
> Messiah son of Mary, and his mother, and whoever is
> on earth, all together? And dominion over the heavens
> and the earth and what is between them belongs to God
> – He creates what He wants – and God has power over
> everything. (*Qur'an* 5: 17).

It also follows that any concept of a Trinity is false:

> O People of the Book, do not go to extremes in your
> religion, and do not say anything about God except the
> truth. Surely the Messiah Jesus son of Mary was a Mes-
> senger of God, and His Word which He sent down into
> Mary, and a Spirit from Him – so believe in God and
> His Messengers, and do not say, 'Three.' Stop it! (That
> would be) better for you. Surely God is only One God!
> Glory be to Him – far beyond His having a son – when
> whatever is in the heavens and whatever is in the earth
> is His. And God is enough to look after it.

The Messiah would never be too proud to be a slave of God, and neither would the angels who are near (to God). And as for whoever is too proud to be His slave, and is arrogant, He will gather them altogether to Him. And as for those who believed and did good, He will give them their reward in full, and increase it for them out of His generosity – and as for those who were proud and arrogant, He will punish them with a painful punishment, and they will not find anyone to be their friend or helper instead of God. (*Qur'an 4: 171-173*).

And:

Those who say, 'Surely God is the Messiah, son of Mary,' are certainly disbelievers. And the Messiah said: 'O Tribe of Israel, worship God, my Lord and your Lord. As for whoever associates partners with God, surely God has certainly forbidden him the Garden and his abode will be the Fire – and for the wrong doers there will be no helpers.' Those who say, 'Surely God is one of three in a trinity,' are certainly disbelievers – for there is no god except the One God. And if they do not desist from what they are saying, a painful punishment will certainly befall those of them who disbelieve. Will they not rather turn to God in repentance and seek His forgiveness? And God is Forgiving, Compassionate. (*Qur'an 5: 72-74*).

Jesus is also referred to in this passage from Surat al-Baqara, in which God indicates that although some of His Messengers were more blessed than others, this does not mean that they were not human beings:

And of these Messengers We have made some to excel others: among them are those to whom God spoke, and among them are those whom He exalted in degree above others; and We gave Jesus son of Mary clear signs and strengthened him with the pure spirit (the angel Gabriel). And if God had wanted, those who came after them would not have fought with each other, after the clear signs that had come to them – but they differed, and from among them were those who believed, and from among them were those who disbelieved; and if God had wanted, they would not have fought with each other, but God does what He wants. (*Qur'an 2: 253*)

Thus in spite of his extraordinary purity, and the piercing clarity of his words and signs, there were inevitably people who rejected Jesus, both while he was on earth and after he had been taken away from it:

And when the son of Mary is given as an example your people turn away from it and say, 'Are our gods better, or him?' And they only mention him for the sake of argument – indeed, they are an argumentative people! Surely he was only a slave whom We blessed, and whom We gave as an example to the Tribe of Israel. And if We had wanted, We could certainly have put angels among you to be leaders in the earth; and surely there is certainly knowledge about the Hour, so do not be in any doubt about it, and follow Me – that is the straight path; and do not let *shaytan* lead you astray – surely he is clearly your enemy.

And when Jesus came with clear proofs, he said, 'I have indeed come to you with wisdom and in order to clarify what you used to disagree about for you – so fear God and obey me. Surely it is God Who is my Lord and your Lord, so worship Him – that is the straight path.'

But the groups among them disagreed – so woe to those who do wrong, from the punishment of a painful Day. (*Qur'an 43: 57-65*).

And:

And We certainly sent Noah and Abraham, and placed the prophethood and the Book among their descendants: among them is he who is rightly guided, and many of them are evil-livers. Then We made Our Messengers follow in their footsteps, and We made Jesus son of Mary follow on, and We gave him the *Ingil*, and We placed compassion and mercy in the hearts of those who fol-

lowed him; and it was they who invented monasticism
– We did not ordain it for them – only seeking the pleasure of God; but they did not observe it with true observ-
ance, so We give those of them who believe their reward
but many of them are evil livers. (*Qur'an* 57: 26-27).

Although both the Romans and the Pharisees wanted Jesus dead,
albeit for different reasons, God makes it clear that they did not
kill Jesus, even though it was their intention to do so:

And they plotted, and God plotted – and God is the best
of plotters. (And remember) when God said, 'O Jesus,
surely I am going to take you up, and raise you up to
Me, and free you from those who disbelieve – and I will
put those who follow you above those who disbelieve
until the Day of Standing – and then you will all return
to Me, and I will judge between you concerning what
you used to disagree about. And as for those who disbelieve, I shall punish them with an intense punishment
in this world and in the next world – and they will not
have any helpers.' And as for those who believe and do
good, He will give them their reward in full – and God
does not love wrong doers. 'And what We are telling
you is from among the signs, and a wise reminder.'

Surely the similarity of Jesus with God is like the similarity of Adam. He created him from dust, and then said
to him, 'Be!' – and he is. This is the truth from your Lord,
so do not be one of those who doubt.

And as for whoever argues with you about him (Jesus),
after the knowledge which has come to you, then say:
'Come, let us summon our sons and your sons, and our
women and your women, and ourselves and yourselves,
and then let us humbly pray, and invoke the curse of
God upon those who lie.'

Surely this explanation is certainly true, and there is not
any god except God – and surely God is certainly the
Mighty, the Wise. And if they turn away, then surely
God is aware of those who are corrupt. (*Qur'an* 3: 54-63).

God also refers to the fact that Jesus was neither killed nor crucified in the following passage from Surat an-Nisa, in which He describes the consequences of the actions of those from among the Tribe of Israel who disbelieved and broke their covenant with God:

> And because of their breaking their covenant, and their rejecting the signs of God, and their killing the Prophets without any justification, and their saying, 'Our hearts are covered over,'– indeed God has set a seal on them because of their disbelief so that they will not believe except for a few – and because of their disbelief and their spreading a great slander against Mary, and their saying, 'Surely we killed the Messiah, Jesus son of Mary', a Messenger of God – and they did not kill him and they did not crucify him, but it appeared so to them. And surely those who disagree about it are certainly in doubt about it; they have no knowledge about it but only follow speculation. And they did not kill him for certain, but God took him up to Himself. And God was ever Mighty, Wise. And there is not one of the People of the Book but will certainly believe in him before his death, and on the Day of Standing he will be a witness against them – and because of the wrong doing of the Jews, We forbade them the good things which were permitted for them (before), and because of their turning away from the way of God so much, and their taking usury – and they were indeed forbidden it – and their devouring people's wealth through deception, We have prepared a painful punishment for those of them who disbelieve. But those of them who are firm in knowledge, and the believers, believe in what has been revealed to you (Muhammad), and in what has been revealed before you – and those who establish the prayer, and those who pay the *zakat*, and those who believe in God and the Last Day – to these we shall give a great reward. (*Qur'an* 4: 155-162).

The *Qur'an* makes it clear that the last Messenger to be sent by God, not only to the Tribe of Israel, but to all mankind, and to the *jinn*, was the Prophet Muhammad, may God bless him and grant him peace, who confirmed the teachings of both Moses and Jesus, while at the same time simplifying and abrogating their Law:

> And God indeed made a covenant with the Tribe of Israel, and We raised up twelve leaders from among them, and God said: 'Surely I am with you. If you establish the prayer and pay the *zakat*, and accept My Messengers and honour them, and lend to God a good loan, surely I will remit your sins, and surely I will bring you into Gardens underneath which rivers flow. So whoever of you disbelieves after this will certainly go astray from the right way.'
>
> And because of their breaking their covenant, We have cursed them and made their hearts grow hard. They separate words from their meanings and forget about part of what they have been reminded; and you will not cease finding treachery from all except a few of them – but forgive them and pardon them. Surely God loves those who do good.
>
> And We made a covenant with those who say, 'Surely we are Christians,' but they forgot a part of what they had been reminded – so We have stirred up enmity and hatred among them until the Day of Standing, when God will show them what they were doing.
>
> O People of the Book, now has Our Messenger (Muhammad) indeed come to you, making clear to you much of what you used to hide in the Book, and forgiving much. Now there has indeed come to you from God a Light and a clear Book, whereby God guides whoever seeks His pleasure to paths of peace – and He brings them out of darkness into light by His decree, and guides them to a straight path. (*Qur'an* 5: 12-16).

As the above passage indicates, it was inevitable that when the Prophet Muhammad, may God bless him and grant him peace, began to call people to only worship God, many of them would be those who claimed to be following either Moses or Jesus, and it is for this reason that there are so many passages in the *Qur'an* which are addressed to such people, who are often referred to as the 'People of the Book' a title indicating – more then than now – both their common genealogical link with the Tribe of Israel as well as the fact that their way of life was, and is, at least to some extent still based on one of the earlier divine revelations.

Although many of these passages may appear to have been directed primarily towards the followers of Middle Eastern and North African Judaism and Christianity who were alive when the *Qur'an* was first revealed during the early 7th century AD, it is clear that they often apply equally, if not more so, to the followers of the various European versions of Judaism and Christianity which, as we have already seen, developed at a later stage. It is equally clear that they still often apply towards today's Jews and Christians, whatever the version of Judaism or Christianity that they may now claim to be following. In the *Qur'an* God promises those from among the People of the Book who are sincere in their actions that they will have nothing to fear:

> Surely those who believe and those who are Jews and the Sabaeans and the Christians – whoever believes in God and the Last Day and does good – they shall not be afraid and they shall not be sad. (*Qur'an* 5: 69).

And that they will receive what is due to them:

> Surely those who believe and those who are Jews and the Christians and the Sabaeans – whoever believes in God and the Last Day and does good – surely their reward is with their Lord and they shall not be afraid and they shall not be sad. (*Qur'an* 2: 62).

And that God will judge between them on the Last Day:

> Surely those who believe and those who are Jews and the Sabaeans and the Christians and the Magians and those who worship idols – surely God will judge between them on the Day of Standing; surely God is Witness of every thing. (*Qur'an* 22: 17).

Again, when addressing the Muslims, God says:

> You are the best community that has been raised up for
> mankind, commanding what is good and forbidding
> what is bad and believing in God. And if only the Peo-
> ple of the Book had believed, it would certainly have
> been better for them. Some of them are believers, but
> most of them are evil livers. They will not harm you
> except for a little annoyance, and if they fight against
> you they will turn their backs on you and flee – and
> then they will not be helped. They will be stamped with
> humiliation wherever they are found, except when they
> have a covenant with God and a covenant with people
> – for they have incurred the anger of God and so pov-
> erty will be stamped on them – that is because they re-
> jected the signs of God and killed the Prophets without
> any justification. That is because they rebelled and were
> wicked.
>
> They are not all alike. There is an upright community of
> the People of the Book who recite the revelations of God
> in the night time and who prostrate themselves (before
> Him). They believe in God and the Last Day, and they
> command what is right and forbid what is wrong, and
> they are swift to do good – and these are among the
> righteous, and as for whatever good they do, none of it
> will be rejected. And God knows those who are devout.
> (*Qur'an 3: 110-115*).

And:

> And surely among the People of the Book there are some
> who believe in God and in what has been revealed to
> you and in what has been revealed to them – humble
> before God, they do not exchange the signs of God for
> something of little value. As for them, their reward is
> with their Lord – surely God is swift at the reckoning.
> (*Qur'an 3: 199*).

And:

As for those to whom We gave the Book before it (the *Qur'an*), they believe in it, and when it is recited to them they say, 'We believe in it – surely it is the truth from our Lord – surely even before it we were Muslims.' These will be given their reward twice over – because they are patient, and they repel evil with good, and they spend from what We have provided for them, and when they hear idle talk they turn away from it and say, 'To us our actions, and to you your actions, peace on you, we do not want to be among those who are ignorant.' (*Qur'an 28: 52-55*).

And:

O you who believe, fear God and believe in His Messenger (Muhammad), and He will give you a double taste of His mercy, and He will give you a light in which to walk, and He will forgive you – and God is Forgiving, Compassionate – so that the People of the Book may know that they do not have any control over any of the generosity of God, and that generosity is in God's hand to give to whomever He wishes – and God's generosity is vast. (*Qur'an 57: 28-29*).

And:

And do not argue with the People of the Book – except for those of them who do wrong – unless it is with what is best, and say, 'We believe in what has been revealed to us and in what has been revealed to you – and our God and your God is One, and it is to Him that we submit.' (*Qur'an 29: 46*).

It is clear from the following passages, however, that not all of the Jews and the Christians have the same attitude or degree of understanding:

And they say, 'No one will enter the Garden except for whoever is a Jew or a Christian.' This is what they want. Say: 'Show your proof, if you are speaking the truth.'

Indeed, and as for whoever submits his will to God while doing good, then his reward is with his Lord – and they shall not be afraid and they shall not be sad. And the Jews say, 'The Christians do not have anything,' and the Christians say, 'The Jews do not have anything,' – and they both recite the Book! That is how those who do not know speak – and God will judge between them, concerning what they used to disagree about, on the Day of Standing. (*Qur'an* 2: 111-113).

And:

And the Jews and the Christians say, 'We are sons of God and His loved ones.' Say: 'Then why does He punish you for your wrong actions?' – Certainly you are human beings whom He has created. He forgives whomever He wishes, and He punishes whomever He wishes, and dominion over the heavens and the earth and what is between them belongs to God – and the journeying is to Him. (*Qur'an* 5: 18).

And certainly God makes it clear that He can forgive anything except *shirk*, which is worshipping other than Him instead of Him:

Surely God does not forgive partners being associated with Him, but He forgives whomever He wishes anything other than that – and whoever associates partners with God has certainly gone far astray. (*Qur'an* 4: 116).

And certainly God makes it clear that it is He Who decides who is for the Fire and who is for the Garden, and not anyone else:

And as for those who believe and do good, We shall bring them into Gardens underneath which rivers flow, in which they will dwell for ever. It is a promise from God which is true, and who can be more truthful than God in what is said? It will not be as you wish, and it will not be as the People of the Book wish: Whoever does evil will receive its reward – and will not find any friend or any helper other than God. And whoever does good – whether male or female – and is a believer, then they will enter the Garden, and they will not be wronged (even as much as) the speck on a date-stone.

And who is better in their life-transaction than whoever submits their will to God while doing good and follows the way of Abraham, the naturally pure? – And God chose Abraham as an intimate friend. And whatever is in the heavens and whatever is in the earth belongs to God, and God is always encompassing everything. (*Qur'an 4: 122-126*).

Thus it is the pure and simple life-transaction embodied by Abraham to which all believers today are called :

And they say, 'Be Jews or Christians,' and you will be rightly guided. Say: 'No, rather the way of Ibrahim, the naturally pure – and he was not one of the idol worshippers.'

Say: 'We believe in God and in what has been revealed to us and in what was revealed to Abraham and to Ishmael and to Isaac and to Jacob and to the tribes (of Israel), and in what Moses and Jesus were given and in what the Prophets received from their Lord; we make no distinction between any of them, and to Him we have surrendered.' And if they believe in the like of what you believe in, then they are rightly guided; and if they turn away, then they have separated; and God is enough for you; and He is the Hearer, the Knower. '(We take our) colour from God – and who is better than God at giving colour? – and we are His worshippers.'

Say: 'Are you going to argue with us about God, when He is our Lord and your Lord? We have our actions, and you have your actions, and we are being sincere to Him – or do you say that Abraham and Ishmael and Isaac and Jacob and the tribes (of Israel) were Jews or Christians?' Say: 'Do you know best, or does God? (*Qur'an 2: 135-140*).

Thus the *Qur'an* makes it clear that the Muslims are those who believe not only in the Prophet Muhammad, may God bless him and grant him peace, but also in all the Prophets who came before him, may the blessings and peace of God be on all of them – and in the One Who sent them, and in the prophetic life-transaction which they all shared and embodied:

Say: 'O People of the Book, let us come to an agreement between us and you: that we shall worship none but God, and that we shall not associate any partner with Him, and that none of us shall take others for lords instead of God.'

And if they turn away, then say: 'Bear witness that we are Muslims.'

O People of the Book, why do you argue about Abraham, when the *Torah* and the *Ingil* were not revealed until after him? Have you no intellect? You certainly argue about what you have some knowledge about, but why argue about what you have no knowledge about? – And God knows, and you do not know. Abraham was not a Jew, and he was not a Christian, but he was naturally pure – a Muslim – and he was not one of those who worship idols. Surely the people who are closest to Abraham are those who followed him, and this Prophet (Muhammad), and those who believe – and God is the Friend of the believers.

A party of the People of the Book would love to lead you astray – but they do not lead anyone astray except themselves, although they do not perceive this. O People of the Book, why do you reject the signs of God, when you witness them? O People of the Book, why do you cover up the truth with falsehood and knowingly conceal the truth? And a party of the People of the Book say, 'Believe in what has been revealed to those who believe at the start of the day, and then at its end reject it, so that perhaps they may return (to disbelief) – and do not believe anyone except whoever follows your own religion.'

Say: 'Surely God's guidance is the guidance – whether (or not) anyone is given the like of what you were given, and whether (or not) they argue with you in the presence of your Lord.'

Say: 'Surely generosity is in God's hand – He gives it to whomever He wants – and God is Immense, Knowing. He chooses whomever He wishes for His mercy – and God's generosity is vast.'

And from among the People of the Book there is the one who, if you entrust him with a *qintar*, will return it to you – and from among them is the one who, if you entrust him with a *dinar*, will not return it to you unless you keep on asking him for it. That is because they say, 'We have no obligation towards the *goyim*,' – and this, which they say is from God, is a lie, and they know it. Indeed – and as for whoever keeps his promise and fears God, then surely God loves those who are fearful.

As for those who exchange their covenant with God and the promises they have made for a small gain – surely they will have no share of good in the next world, and God will not speak to them and He will not look at them on the Day of Standing, and He will not purify them – and theirs will be a painful punishment. And surely there is certainly a group of them who distort what is in the Book with what they say, so as to make you think that it is from the Book when it is not from the Book – and they say, 'This is from God,' when it is not from God – and this, which they say is from God, is a lie, and they know it.

It is not possible for any man to whom God has given the Book and wisdom and prophethood to then say to people, 'Worship me instead of God,' but only, 'Worship your Lord – by your spreading knowledge of the Book, and by your studying it.' And he did not command you to take the angels and the Prophets as your lords – would he command you to disbelief after you had become Muslims?

And when God made His covenant with the Prophets, (He said), 'This is what I have given you as a Book and wisdom, and then a Messenger (Muhammad) will come to you confirming what you have – and you will believe in him and you will help him.' He said, 'Will you be bound by this and will you accept this obligation?' They replied, 'We will be bound by it.' He said, 'Then bear witness to it – and I will bear witness with you – and as for whoever turns away after this, then they will be the ones who disobey.' Do they desire other than the life-transaction of God, when whatever is in the heavens or the earth submits to Him, willingly or unwillingly, and to Him they will return?

Say: 'We believe in God, and in what has been revealed to us, and in what was revealed to Abraham and to Ishmael and to Isaac and to Jacob and to the tribes (of Israel), and in what was given to Moses and Jesus and the Prophets from their Lord – we make no distinction between any of them, and to Him we have submitted.'

And as for whoever desires a life-transaction other than Islam, it will not be accepted from him, and in the next life he will be among the losers. (*Qur'an 3: 64-85*).

The *Qur'an* also confirms that even though some of the People of the Book *know* that their teachings have been altered and that the teachings of the Prophet Muhammad are pure, they still nevertheless prefer the falsehood to the truth:

And (remember) when God made a covenant with those who were given the Book to, 'Make it clear to people, and do not conceal it,' but they hid it behind their backs and exchanged it for something of little value – and what they have in exchange is awful. Do not think that those who exult in what they have given and who love to be praised for what they have not done – do not think that they are safe from punishment – and theirs will be a painful punishment. And the dominion of the heavens and the earth belongs to God – and God has power over everything. (*Qur'an 3: 187-189*).

And:

> Do you not see that those who have been given part of
> the Book have exchanged it for going astray, and that
> they want you also to go astray from the way? And God
> knows best who your enemies are – and God is enough
> as a Guardian, and God is enough as a Helper. (*Qur'an*
> 4: 44-45).

And:

> Those who have been given the Book recognise this
> (*Qur'an*) just as they recognise their own sons – but they
> deceive themselves and so they will not believe. (*Qur'an*
> 6: 20).

And:

> Say: 'O People of the Book, why do you reject the signs
> of God when (you know that) God is witnessing what
> you are doing?'

> Say: 'O you who believe, if you were to obey a group of
> those who were given the Book, they would make you
> become disbelievers again after your belief.' And how
> can you disbelieve, when the signs of God are recited to
> you and His Messenger is among you? And whoever
> holds on firmly to God will indeed be guided on a
> straight path. O you who believe, fear God with the fear
> which is due to Him, and do not die except as Muslims.
> (*Qur'an* 3: 98-102).

God tells the followers of the Prophet Muhammad what to say to
those of the People of the Book who oppose the Muslims:

> Say: 'O People of the Book, do you reject us just because
> we believe in God, and in what has been revealed to us,
> and in what was revealed in the past, and because most
> of you are evil livers?' Say: 'Shall I tell you what is worse
> than that as far as retribution from God is concerned? It
> is for whomever God has cursed and is angry with –

and whomever of these He has turned into apes and pigs – and whoever worships false gods. These are in a worse situation and are further astray from the right way.' And when they come to you, they say, 'We believe,' – when in fact they came in not believing and they certainly left the same way – and God knows best what they were concealing. And you see many of them competing with each other in wickedness and enmity and devouring what is forbidden – what they are doing is certainly awful. Why do the rabbis and the priests not forbid their evil words and their devouring what is forbidden? What they are doing is certainly awful. (*Qur'an 5: 59-63*).

And:

And the Jews say, 'Ezra is the son of God,' and the Christians say, 'The Messiah is the son of God.' These are the words that they utter, which are like the words of those who disbelieved in the past – God curse them – what liars they are! They have taken their rabbis and their monks as their lords instead of God – and the Messiah son of Mary – and they were commanded only to worship One God. There is no god except Him. Glory be to Him, above what they associate with Him. They want to put out the Light of God with their mouths, but God seeks only to perfect His Light, however much those who reject may detest it. He is the One who has sent His Messenger with guidance and the true life-transaction so that it may overcome all other religions, however much those who worship idols may detest it. Oh you who believe, surely many of the rabbis and the monks certainly devour the wealth of people through deception and lead them away from the way of God. And as for those who hoard up gold and silver and do not spend it in the way of God, tell them of a painful punishment – on a Day when it will be heated up in the Fire of Hell, and then their foreheads and their sides and their backs will be branded with it, (and they will be told), 'This is what you used to hoard up for yourselves – so have a taste of what you used to hoard!' (*Qur'an 9: 30-35*).

Fortunately not all of the People of the Book oppose the Muslims with the same degree of intensity:

> You will certainly find that the most implacable of people in their enmity towards those who believe are the Jews and those who worship idols, and you will certainly find that the nearest in their affection towards those who believe are those who say, 'Surely we are Christians.' That is because there are priests and monks among them, and because they are not proud.
>
> And when they listen to what has been revealed to the Messenger, you see their eyes fill with tears as they recognise the truth. They say, 'Our Lord, we believe – so record us as being among those who bear witness. And how can we not believe in God and in what has come to us of the truth – and (how can we not) hope that our Lord will lead us in (to the Garden) with the people who are righteous?' And God has rewarded them for what they say, with Gardens underneath which rivers flow, in which they shall dwell for ever – and that is the reward for those who do good. And as for those who disbelieve and deny Our signs – these are the people of Hell. (*Qur'an* 5: 82-86).

It is clear from the *Qur'an*, however, that wherever their sympathies may lie, those Christians who refuse to accept Islam are more closely allied with the Jews than with the Muslims, and God warns the Muslims not to take them as their friends:

> And the Jews will not be pleased with you, and neither will the Christians, until you follow their system. Say: 'Surely the guidance of God is the only guidance.' And if you were to follow their desires, after the knowledge which has come to you, you would not have in God any friend or helper. Those to whom We have given the Book and who read it as it should be read, these believe in it – and as for whoever rejects it, then these are the losers. (*Qur'an* 2: 120-121).

And:

> O you who believe, do not take the Jews and the Chris-
> tians as friends – they are friends to one another – and
> whoever of you makes friends with them is surely one
> of them. Surely God does not guide people who are
> wrong doers. And you see those in whose hearts there
> is a sickness going hastily over to them, saying, 'We are
> afraid that we are going to suffer a change of fortune.'
> And it may be that God will grant (you) victory, or a
> decree directly from Him, so that they may feel remorse
> about what they secretly kept to themselves. And then
> those who believe will say, 'Are these the ones who
> swore by God their most binding oaths that they were
> surely with you?' – Their actions have proved fruitless,
> and they have become losers. (*Qur'an 5: 51-53*).

And:

> O you who believe, do not make friends with those from
> among those who were given the Book before you, and
> from among the disbelievers, who treat your way of life
> as a joke and a game. And fear God, if you are indeed
> believers. And when you call (them) to the prayer, they
> treat it as a joke and a game – that is because they are a
> people who have no intellect. (*Qur'an 5: 57-58*).

And:

> O you who believe, do not make close friends with those
> who are not like you – who will not stop trying to cor-
> rupt you and who would love to destroy you. Their
> hatred is indeed apparent from what they say, but what
> their hearts conceal is worse – We have indeed made
> the signs clear to you, if you have any intellect. Although
> you are the ones who love them, they do not love you –
> and you believe in all of the Book. And when they meet
> you, they say, 'We believe,' – but when they are alone,
> they bite their finger-tips in their rage at you.
>
> Say: 'May you die with rage!'

Surely God knows what is hidden in your hearts. If good comes to you it grieves them, and if bad strikes you it makes them glad, but if you are patient and fear God, then their cunning will not harm you at all – surely God encompasses whatever they are doing. (*Qur'an 3: 118-120*).

God tells the followers of the Prophet Muhammad how to treat those from among the People of the Book who are openly opposed to the Muslims:

Fight those from among those who have been given the Book who do not believe in God or in the Last Day, and who do not forbid what God and His Messenger have forbidden, and who do not follow the true life-transaction – until they pay the *jizya* of their own accord, after they have been subdued. (*Qur'an 9: 29*).

In spite of sustained opposition throughout the last fourteen centuries to God, and to the Prophet Muhammad, may God bless him and grant him peace, and to the *Qur'an*, the invitation to the People of the Book in every age to obey God and His Messenger has always remained the same:

O People of the Book, now has Our Messenger indeed come to you, making clear to you much of what you used to hide in the Book, and forgiving much. Now there has indeed come to you from God a Light and a clear Book, whereby God guides whoever seeks His pleasure to paths of peace – and He brings them out of darkness into light by His decree, and guides them to a straight path. (*Qur'an 5: 15-16*).

And:

O People of the Book, now has Our Messenger indeed come to you to make things clear to you after an interval between Messengers, lest you should say, 'Neither a bringer of good news nor a warner ever came to us.' And now a bringer of good news and a warner has indeed come to you – and God has power over everything. (*Qur'an 5: 19*).

God also says in the *Qur'an*:

> In the Name of God the Merciful the Compassionate
>
> Those who disbelieve from among the People of the
> Book and those who worship idols could not have
> ceased (doing so) until clear proof came to them: A
> Messenger from God, reciting from a Book free from im-
> purity containing true revelations.
>
> And the People who were given the Book did not be-
> come divided until after clear proof came to them, and
> they were not commanded (to do) anything other than
> to worship God, sincere to Him in their life-transaction
> – naturally pure – and to establish the prayer and to
> pay the *zakat* – and that is the true life-transaction. Surely
> those who disbelieve from among the People of the Book
> and those who worship idols will abide in the Fire of
> Hell for ever. They are the worst of created beings. Surely
> those who trust and do good are the best of created be-
> ings. Their reward is with their Lord – Gardens of Eden
> underneath which rivers flow, in which they will dwell
> for ever. God is pleased with them and they are pleased
> with Him. – This is for whoever fears his Lord. (*Qur'an
> 98: 1-8*).

And:

> Whoever purifies his self, and remembers the Name of
> his Lord, and does the prayer, is indeed successful – but
> you prefer the life of this world, even though the next
> life is better and more lasting! Surely this is certainly in
> the earlier Books, the Books of Abraham and Moses.
> (*Qur'an 87: 14-19*).

Again, in Surat al-Mai'dah, God reminds the People of the Book of
the reward that awaits those who follow the Prophet Muhammad
– the same reward which awaits whoever has truly followed not
only Moses and Jesus, but indeed all of the Prophets and Messengers who came before and after them, may the blessings and peace
of God be on all of them:

And if only the People of the Book would trust and fear God, We would certainly remit their sins for them, and We would certainly bring them into Gardens of Delight. And if they had only followed the *Torah* and the *Ingil* and what was revealed to them from their Lord, they would certainly have been nourished from above them and from beneath their feet. Among them there is a community who are on the right path – but what many of them do is evil. (*Qur'an 5: 65-66*).

And:

Say: 'O People of the Book, you will not have anything until you follow the *Torah* and the *Injil* and what has been revealed to you from your Lord.' And what has been revealed to you from your Lord is certain to increase the disobedience and disbelief of many of them – but do not feel sorry for people who are disbelievers. (*Qur'an 5: 68*).

And:

Say: 'O People of the Book, do not emphasise anything other than the truth in your religion, and do not follow the desires of people who certainly went astray in the past, and who led many astray, and who went astray from the right way.' (*Qur'an 5: 77*).

When describing those who believe in the signs of God – including the Prophet Muhammad, may God bless him and grant him peace – God refers to:

Those who follow the Messenger, the Prophet who can neither read nor write, whom they will find described in the *Torah* and the *Ingil* which are with them – he will enjoin what is right on them and forbid them what is wrong, and he will make the good things lawful for them and prohibit them the foul things, and he will relieve them of their burden and the chains they used to wear. So those who believe in him, and honour him, and help him, and follow the light which is sent down with him – they are the successful ones.

Say (O Muhammad): 'O mankind, surely I am the
Messenger of God – the One to Whom the dominion of
the heavens and the earth belongs – to all of you. There
is no god except Him – He gives life and He gives death
– so believe in God and His Messenger, the Prophet who
can neither read nor write, who believes in God and His
words – and follow him so that you may be rightly
guided.' (*Qur'an 7: 157-158*).

And:

Certainly there is a good example in the Messenger of
God for you – for whoever regards God and the Last
Day with hope and remembers God a great deal. (*Qur'an
33: 21*).

And:

Muhammad is not the father of any man among you,
but he is the Messenger of God, and the Seal of the
Prophets – and God is always aware of everything.

O you who believe, remember God with a great deal of
remembrance, and glorify Him in the early morning and
in the evening. He is the One who blesses you – and His
angels – so that He may bring you out of darkness into
light; and He is always Compassionate with the believers. Their greeting on the Day that they meet Him will
be, 'Peace'; and He has prepared a generous reward for
them. (*Qur'an 33: 40-44*).

And:

O you who believe, bow down, and prostrate, and worship your Lord, and do good, so that you may be successful – and strive for God with the striving which is
due to Him. He has chosen you and He has not imposed
anything difficult on you in the life-transaction – the
way of your forefather Abraham. He has described you
as Muslims, both in the past and in this (*Qur'an*), so that
the Messenger (Muhammad) may be a witness for you,
and so that you may be witnesses for mankind; so es-

tablish the prayer and pay the *zakat* and hold firmly to God – He is your Protector, a blessed Protector and a blessed Helper. (*Qur'an* 22: 77-78).

And:

And as for whoever obeys God and the Messenger, they are with those whom God has blessed – the Prophets, and those who speak the truth, and the martyrs, and the righteous – and they are the best company! (*Qur'an* 4: 69).

And:

He has commanded you to follow the same life-trans-action that He decreed for Noah, and which We have revealed to you (O Muhammad), and which We decreed for Abraham, and for Moses, and for Jesus, saying, 'Establish the life-transaction and do not become divided in it.' What you are calling the idol worshippers to follow is dreadful for them, but God chooses whomever He wishes for Himself, and He guides whoever turns to Him to Himself. And they did not become divided until after knowledge had come to them, out of rivalry amongst themselves, and if it had not been for a decree for an appointed term which had already come from your Lord, judgement concerning them would certainly have been passed – and surely those who have inherited the Book after them are hopelessly in doubt about it. (*Qur'an* 42: 13-14).

And:

Surely the life-transaction with God is Islam.

And those who were given the Book (in the past) did not disagree until after knowledge had come to them, out of rivalry amongst themselves – and as for whoever rejects the signs of God, then surely God is swift at the reckoning. And if they argue with you, then say, 'I have submitted my will to God – together with whoever follows me.'

And say to those who were given the Book (in the past) and to those who are illiterate, 'Have you accepted Islam?' And if they have accepted Islam then they are indeed rightly guided, and if they turn away then it is only up to you to deliver the message – and God is All-Seeing over (His) slaves.

As for those who reject the signs of God, and who kill the Prophets without any justification, and who kill those people who demand justice – tell them of a painful punishment. These are the ones whose actions have failed both in this world and in the next world – and they will not have any helpers. Have you not seen how those who have been given part of the Book invoke the Book of God to reach a judgement between them – and then a group of them turn away in disagreement? That is because they say, 'The Fire will not touch us except for a certain number of days,' – and so what they used to make up in their religion has deceived them.

How will it be when We have gathered them all together on a Day about which there is no doubt, when every self will be paid in full for what it has earned – and they will not be wronged? (*Qur'an 3: 19-25*).

And:

And the different groups among them disagree with each other – so woe to those who disbelieve in the meeting on a mighty Day: listen to them, and look, on the Day they meet Us! – and today the wrong doers are clearly astray, so warn them about the Day of regret when the matter will be judged, for now they are careless and they do not believe. Surely it is We Who will inherit the earth and whatever is in it – and it is to Us they will return. (*Qur'an 19: 37-40*).

And:

And what will tell you what the Day of Judgement is? Again, what will tell you what the Day of Judgement is?

A Day on which no one has any power over any one else at all – on that Day the affair will belong entirely to God. (*Qur'an 82: 17-19*).

And:

Say: 'O God, the King Who has the dominion, You give power to whomever You wish and You take away power from whomever You wish; and You exalt whomever You wish and You humiliate whomever You wish – good is in Your hand – surely You have power over everything. 'You make the night turn into the day and You make the day turn into the night; and You bring out the living from the dead and You bring out the dead from the living – and You provide for whomever You wish without calculating. (*Qur'an 3: 26-27*).

And:

In the Name of God the Merciful the Compassionate

Say: 'He is God the One – God the Everlasting – no one is born from Him and He is not born from anything – and there is nothing like Him.' (*Qur'an 112: 1-4*).

And:

In the Name of God the Merciful the Compassionate

Praise belongs to God, Lord of the Worlds,
the Merciful the Compassionate,
King of the Day of the Life-Transaction.
Only You we worship and only You we ask for help.
Lead us on the Straight Path,
The path of those whom You have blessed,
Not of those with whom You are angry,
and not of those who are astray.

(*Qur'an 1: 1-7*)

Amin

And when Allah says, 'O Jesus son of Mary, did you say to people, "Take me and my mother as two gods instead of Allah,"?' he will reply, 'Glory be to You – it was not for me to say what I had no right to say! If I ever said that, then You would certainly know it. You know what is in me, and I do not know what is in You – surely it is only You Who knows what is hidden. I only told them what You commanded me – to, "Worship Allah, my Lord and your Lord," and while I dwelt among them I was a watcher over them, and when You took me up, then You were a Watcher over them – and You watch over everything.

(Qur'an: Surat al-Ma'ida – 5: 116-117)

Chapter Notes

Chapter One: The Unitarian View and Christianity

1. *The Apostolic Fathers*, E.J. Goodspeed.
2. *Articles of the Apostolic Creed*, Theodore Zahn, pp. 33-37.
3. *Tetradymus*, John Toland.
4. *Outlines of the History of Dogma*, Adolf Harnack.
5. *What Is Christianity?*, Adolf Harnack, p. 20.
6. *The Jesus Report*, J. Lehman (quoting from *Krewz Verlag*, Stuttgart, 2nd ed., 1960, p. 112).
7. *Articles of the Apostolic Creed*, Theodore Zahn.
8. *Erasmi Epistolai*, 1834 ed., P.S. Allen, V, pp. 173-92.

Chapter Two: An Historical Account of Jesus

1. *The Bible, the Qur'an and Science*, M. Bucaille, p. 105.
2. *The Bible, the Qur'an and Science*, M. Bucaille, p. 90.
3. *The Jesus Report*, J. Lehman, pp. 14-15.
4. *The Bible, the Qur'an and Science*, M. Bucaille, p. 96.
5. *The Wilderness Revolt*, Bishop Pike, p. 101.
6. *The Dead Sea Scrolls*, Edmund Wilson.
7. *The Bible, the Qur'an and Science*, M. Bucaille, p. 29.
8. *The Bible, the Qur'an and Science*, M. Bucaille, p. 33.
9. *The Bible, the Qur'an and Science*, M. Bucaille, pp.33-34.
10. *The Bible, the Qur'an and Science*, M. Bucaille, p. 34.
11. *Prophets in the Qur'an, Volume Two: The Later Prophets*, Iftekhar Bano Hussain, pp. 112-113.
12. *The Death of Jesus*, Joel Carmichael, p. 141.
13. *The Dead Sea Scrolls*, Edmund Wilson, p. 94.
14. *The Bible, the Qur'an and Science*, M. Bucaille, p. 115.
15. *The Death of Jesus*, Joel Carmichael, p. 139.
16. *The Jesus Scroll*, D. Joyce, p. 126.
17. *The Nazarenes*, John Toland, p. 18.
18. *The Life of Jesus*, Carveri.
19. *The Bible, the Qur'an and Science*, M. Bucaille, p. 64.

Chapter Three: Barnabas and the Early Christians

1. *The Kingdom of God and Primitive Christian Belief*, Albert Schweitzer, p. 149.
2. *Lebuch II*, Heinrich Holzmann, pp. 256, 376.
3. *The Jesus Report*, Johannes Lehman, p. 123.
4. *The Beginning of the Christian Church*, Hanz Lietzman, p. 104.
5. *Paul and His Interpreters*, Albert Schweitzer, p. 198.
6. *The Nazarenes*, John Toland, Preface, p. 6.
7. *A History of Christianity in the Apostolic Age*, A.C. MacGiffert, pp. 216, 231, 424-5.
8. Quoted in *The Jesus Report*, Johannes Lehman, p. 126.
9. Quoted in *The Jesus Report*, Johannes Lehman, p. 127.
10. Quoted in *The Jesus Report*, Johannes Lehman, p. 128.
11. *The Nazarenes*, John Toland, pp. 73-76.

Chapter Four: Early Unitarians in Christianity

1. *Constantine the Great*, J.B. Firth, pp. 190-191.
2. *A History of the Eastern Church*, A.R. Stanley, p. 94.
3. *A History of Christianity in the Apostolic Age*, A.C. MacGiffert, p. 172.
4. *The Donatist Church*, W.H.C. Frend, p. 153.
5. *The Donatist Church*, W.H.C. Frend, p. 164.
6. *The Donatist Church*, W.H.C. Frend.
7. *The Donatist Church*, W.H.C. Frend.
8. *The Donatist Church*, W.H.C. Frend.
9. *Constantine the Great*, J.B. Firth.
10. *Constantine the Great*, J.B. Firth.
11. *The Donatist Church*, W.H.C. Frend, p. 164.
12. *The Donatist Church*, W.H.C. Frend, p. 326.
13. *John 14.28*, The Bible.
14. *Constantine the Great*, J.B. Firth.
15. *Constantine the Great*, J.B. Firth.
16. *Constantine the Great*, J.B. Firth.
17. *Constantine the Great*, J.B. Firth.
18. *Constantine the Great*, J.B. Firth.
19. *The Council of Nicea*, J. Kaye, pp. 23-25.
20. *Constantine the Great*, J.B. Firth, p. 60.

21. *Arius*, Prof. Gwatkin.
22. *Arius*, Prof. Gwatkin.
23. *Arius*, Prof. Gwatkin.
24. *Tetradymus*, J. Toland.
25. *Tetradymus*, J. Toland.
26. *Tetradymus*, J. Toland.
27. *Tetradymus*, J. Toland.
28. *Tetradymus*, J. Toland.
29. *A History of Christianity in the Apostolic Age,* A.C. MacGiffert.
30. *The Bible, the Qur'an and Science*, M. Bucaille, p. 64.
31. *The Bible, the Qur'an and Science*, M. Bucaille, p. 67.

Chapter Five: The Gospel of Barnabas

1. *The Bible, the Qur'an and Science*, M. Bucaille, pp. 68-70.
2. *The Nazarenes*, John Toland, pp. 6-8.
3. *Spicilegium i* (ex Cod. Barocc. 39), Grabe.
4. *Islamic Horizons, February 1985*, S A Johnson.
5. *The Nazarenes*, John Toland, pp. 15-16.
6. *The Gospel of Barnabas*, David Sox, p. 106.
7. *The Bible, the Qur'an and Science*, M. Bucaille, pp. 86-87.
8. *The Apostolic Fathers*, E. J. Goodspeed, p. 266.
9. *The Bible, the Qur'an and Science*, M. Bucaille, pp. 91-92.
10. *The Bible, the Qur'an and Science*, M. Bucaille, pp. 92-93.
11. *The Gospel of Barnabas*, David Sox, p. 92.

Chapter Six: The Shepherd of Hermas

1. *The Apostolic Fathers*, Edgar J. Goodspeed.

Chapter Seven: Trinitarian Christianity in Europe

1. *The Condemnation of Pope Honorius*, John Chapman.
2. *The Condemnation of Pope Honorius*, John Chapman.
3. *The Condemnation of Pope Honorius*, John Chapman.

Chapter Eight: Later Unitarians in Christianity

1. *The Hunted Heretic*, R.H. Bainton.
2. *A History of Unitarianism*, E.M. Wilbur.
3. *Challenge of a Liberal Faith*, G.N. Marshall.
4. *Anti-trinitarian Biographies*, A. Wallace.
5. *Rise of the Dutch Republic*, Motley.
6. *The Epic of Unitarianism*, D.B. Parke, pp. 5-6.
7. *Treatises Concerning the Mohametons*, A. Reland, pp. 215-223.
8. *Francis David*, W.C. Gannett.
9. *Francis David*, W.C. Gannett.
10. *A History of Unitarianism*, E.M. Wilbur.
11. *Francis David*, W.C. Gannett.
12. *Francis David*, W.C. Gannett.
13. *Francis David*, W.C. Gannett.
14. *A History of Unitarianism*, E.M. Wilbur, p. 78.
15. *Treatises Concerning the Mohametons*, A. Reland, p. 190.
16. *Francis David*, W.C. Gannett.
17. *Anti-trinitanan Biographies*, A. Wallace.
18. *A History of the Reformation in Poland*, Lubinietski.
19. *Anti-trinitarian Biographies*, A. Wallace.
20. *Anti-trinitarian Biographies*, A. Wallace.
21. *Anti-trinitarian Biographies*, A. Wallace, Introduction, p. 79.
22. *Anti-trinitarian Biographies*, A. Wallace, p. 44.
23. *Anti-trinitarian Biographies*, A. Wallace, p. 45.
24. *Historical and Critical Reflections Upon Mohametonism and Socianism*, A. Reland.
25. *The Nazarenes*, John Toland.
26. *Anti-trinitarian Biographies, III*, A. Wallace.
27. *Anti-trinitarian Biographies, III*, A. Wallace.
28. *Anti-trinitarian Biographies, III*, A. Wallace.
29. *The Religion of the Protestants*, W. Chillingworth.
30. *The Religion of the Protestants*, W. Chillingworth.
31. *Anti-trinitarian Biographies, III*, A. Wallace.
32. *True Opinion Concerning the Holy Trinity*, J. Biddle.
33. *Anti-trinitarian Biographies, III*, A. Wallace.
34. *The Epic of Unitarianism*, D.B. Parke, pp. 31-32.
35. *Anti-trinitarian Biographies, III*, A. Wallace.

36. *Anti-trinitarian Biographies, III*, A. Wallace.
37. *Anti-trinitarian Biographies, III*, A. Wallace.
38. *The Christian Doctrine*, J. Milton.
39. *The Christian Doctrine*, J. Milton.
40. *Anti-trinitarian Biographies, III*, A. Wallace.
41. *The Christian Doctrine*, J. Milton.
42. *The Christian Doctrine*, J. Milton.
43. *Anti-trinitarian Biographies, III*, A. Wallace, p. 428.
44. *Anti-trinitarian Biographies, III*, A. Wallace, p. 438.
45. *Anti-trinitarian Biographies, III*, A. Wallace.
46. *Anti-trinitanan Biographies, III*, A. Wallace.
47. *Anti-trinitarian Biographies, III*, A. Wallace, p. 517.
48. *Anti-trinitarian Biographies, III*, A. Wallace.
49. *Anti-trinitarian Biographies, III*, A. Wallace.
50. *Anti-trinitarian Biographies, III*, A. Wallace.
51. *The Epic of Unitarianism*, D.B. Parke, p. 46.
52. *The Epic of Unitarianism*, D.B. Parke, p. 47.
53. *A List of False Reading of the Scripture*, T. Lindsey.
54. *Two Dissertations*, T. Lindsey.
55. *Memoirs of Dr. Priestly*, J. Priestly.
56. *Memoirs of Dr. Priestly*, J. Priestly, p. 76.
57. *Memoirs of Dr. Priestly*, J. Priestly, p. 89.
58. *The Epic of Unitarianism*, D.B. Parke, p. 48.
59. *A History of the Corruptions of Christianity*, J. Priestly.
60. *The History of Jesus Christ*, J. Priestly.
61. *Anti-trinitarian Biographies*, A. Wallace.
62. *Anti-trinitarian Biographies*, A. Wallace.
63. *A History of Unitarianism*, E.M. Wilbur, p. 424.
64. *A History of Unitarianism*, E.M. Wilbur.
65. *Anti-trinitarian Biographies*, A. Wallace.
66. *The Epic of Unitarianism*, D.B. Parke.
67. *Challenge of a Liberal Faith*, G.N. Marshall.
68. *A History of Unitarianism*, E.M. Wilbur.

Chapter Nine: Christianity Today

1. *A Christian Introduction to Religions of the World*,
   J.G. Vos, pp. 66-67.
2. *A Christian Introduction to Religions of the World*,
   J.G. Vos, p. 27.

3. *The World's Religions*, N. Anderson, p. 232.
4. *'1984'*, G. Orwell, p. 220.
5. *Christianity on Trial*, I, Colin Chapman, pp. 32-33.
6. *Time Magazine*, May 24th, 1976, pp. 42-43.
7. *Christianity on Trial*, I, Colin Chapman, p. 37.
8. *Christianity on Trial*, I, Colin Chapman, pp. 51-52.
9. *Time Magazine*, May 24th, 1976, p. 46.
10. *Christianity on Trial*, I, Colin Chapman, p. 63.
11. *Christianity on Trial*, I, Colin Chapman, p. 74.
12. *Christianity on Trial*, 1, Colin Chapman, p. 61.

Chapter Ten: Jesus in Hadith and Muslim Traditions

1. *Prophets in the Qur'an, Volume Two: The Later Prophets*, Iftekhar Bano Hussain, p. 120.

○   ○   ○   ○   ○

Bibliography

The *Qur'an*
The Meaning of the Glorious Qur'an (A translation by
  Muhammad Pickthall), 1930.
The *Hadith* Collections of *Imam* al-Bukhari
  and *Imam* Muslim.
Al-Muwatta' of Imam Malik, (translated by 'A'isha
  'Abdarahman at-Tarjumana and Ya'qub Johnson), 1982.
The *Bible* (King James and New International Versions).

'Abdal-Qadir as-Sufi, *The Way of Muhammad*,
  Diwan Press, 1975.
Allegro, *The Dead Sea Scrolls*.
Allen, P.S., *Erasmi Epistolai*, 1834 Edn.
Alton, *Religious Opinions of Milton, Locke, and Newton*,
  1833.
Anderson, Norman, *The World's Religions*, 1975.
Apuleius, Lucius, *Metamorphosis - The Golden Ass*, (trans-
  lated by T. Taylor), 1822.

Backwell, R.H., *The Christianity of Jesus*, 1972.
Bainton, R.H., *The Hunted Heretic*, 1953.
Beattie, *The New Theology and the Old*, 1910.
Becker, *The Dead Sea Scrolls*.
Begin, Menachem, *The Revolt. The Story of the Irgun*.
  (translated by Samuel Karr).
Belloc, J.H.D., *An Open Letter on the Decay of Faith*, 1906.
Biddle, John, *True Opinion Concerning the Holy Trinity
  (Twelve Arguments)*, 1653.
Bigg, *The Origin of Christianity*, 1909.
Blackney, E.H., *The Problems of Higher Criticism*, 1905.
Brown, David, *The Structure of the Apocalypse*, 1891.
Brown, W.E., *The Revision of the Prayer Book – A Criticism*,
  1909.
Bruce, Frederick, *Jesus and Christian Origins Outside the
  New Testament*, 1974.
Bruce, F.F., *The New Testament Documents*, 1943.
Bruce, F.F., *The Books and the Parchments*, 1950.

Bucaille, Dr. M., *The Bible, the Qur'an and Science*, 4th Edn.

Burnet, Gilbert, *An Abridgement of the History of the Reformation*.

Bury, Arthur, *The Naked Gospel*, 1699.

Carmichael, Joel, *The Death of Jesus*, 1962.

Carnegie, W.H., *Why and What I Believe in Christianity*, 1910.

Carveri, *The Life of Jesus*.

Cary, *Parsons and Pagans – An Indictment of Christianity*, 1906.

Celsus, *Arguments of Celsus* (translated by Lardner), 1830.

Chadwick, H., *Alexandrian Christianity*, 1954.

Chadwick, H., *The Early Church*, 1967.

Channing, W.E., *The Character and Writing of Milton*, 1826.

Channing, W.E., *The Superior Tendency of Unitarianism*, 1831.

Channing, W.E., *The Works of Channing*, 1840-1844.

Chapman, Colin, *Christianity on Trial*, 1974.

Chapman, John, *The Condemnation of Pope Honorius*, 1907.

Charles, R.H., *The Book of Jublilees*, 1917.

Charles, R.H., *The Apocrypha and Pseudo-Epiapapha of the Old Testament*.

Chesterton, G.K., *Orthodoxy*, 1909.

Chillingworth, W., *The Religion of the Protestants*.

Clarke, Samuel, *The Bible*, 1867.

Clodd, Edward, *Gibbon and Christianity*, 1916

Cooke, Rev., *Reply to Montgomery*, 1883.

Cooke, Rev., *True to Himself*, 1883.

Corelli, Marie, *Barnabas - A Novel*, 1893.

Corelli, Marie, *Council of Nicea and St. Athanasius*, 1898.

Cox, Edwin, *The Elusive Jesus*.

Craver, Marcello, *The Life of Jesus*, 1967.

Cross, Frank Moore, *The Ancient Library of Qumran and Modern Biblical Studies*.

Culligan, *The Arian Movement*, 1913.

Cummins, G.D., *The Childhood of Jesus*, 1972.

Cunningham, Francis, *A Dissertation on the Books of Origen Against Celsus*, 1812.

Curll, Edward, *Historical Account of the Life of John Toland*, 1728.

Davies, W.D., *Paul and Rabbinic Judaism.*
Dinwiddie, *The Times Before the Reformation*, 1883.
Disciple, *Gospel of the Holy Twelve.*
DuPont-Sommer, *The Jewish Sect of Qumran and the
Essenes*, (translated by RD. Barnett).

Emlyn, T., *An Humble Enquiry into Scripture*, 1756.
Eusebius, *Church History – Life of Constantine the Great*,
(translated by MacGiffert), 1890.
Eusebius, *The Ecclesiastic History*, 1847.
Eusebius, *A Select Library of Nicene and post-Nicene Fathers
of the Christian Church*, (translated by A.C. MacGiffert,
Ph.D.), 1890.
Everett, C.C., *Theism and the Christian Faith.*

Firth, J.B., *Constantine the Great*, 1890.
Frazer, W., *The Golden Bough.*
Frend, W.H.C., *The Early Church.*
Frend, W.H.C., *Persecution in the Early Church.*
Frend, W.H.C., *An Address to the Inhabitants of Cambridge*,
1788.
Frend, W.H.C., *The Rise of the Monophysite Movement.*
Frend, W.H.C., *Coulthurst's Blunders Exposed*, 1788-89.
Frend, W.H.C., *The Donatist Church.*
Froude, *The Life and Letters of Erasmus*, 1916.

Gannett, D., *Francis David, Founder of Unitananism*, 1914.
Gibbon, Edward, *Christianity*, 1930.
Gibbon, Edward, *Decline and Fall of the Roman Empire*,
1909-1914.
Gibson, J.M., *Inspiration and Authority of the Holy Scrip-
tures.*
Glover, T.R., *Jesus of History*, 1919.
Goodspeed, E.J., *The Letter of Barnabas*, 1950.
Goodspeed, E.J., *The Apostolic Fathers*, 1950.
Gordon, Alexander, *Heresy.*
Grant & Fridman, *The Secret Sayings of Jesus*, 1960.
Green, *Sir Isaac Newton's Views*, 1871.
Guthrie, D., *A Shorter Life of Christ*, 1970.
Gwatkin, *Arius.*

Haines, *Religious Persecution*.
Hall, L, *The Continuity of Revelation*, 1908.
Harnack, Adolf, *Christianity and History*, (translated by Saunders), 1900.
Harnack, Adolf, *Outlines of the History of Dogma*, 1900.
Harnack, Adolf, *What is Christianity?*, 1901.
Harris, J.R., *Celsus and Aristedes*, 1921.
Harwood, P., *Priestly and Unitarianism*, 1842.
Hastings, *Dictionary of Christ and the Gospel*.
Hay, J.S., *Heliogabalus*, 1911.
Haygood, A.G., *The Monk and the Prince*, 1895.
Hayne, S., *The General View of the Holy Scripture*, 1607.
Heinimann, *John Toland*, 1944.
Hermes, *Hermes – A Disciple of Jesus*, 1888.
Holzmann, Heinrich, *Lebuch II*.
Hone, W., *The Apocryphal New Testament*, 1820.
Hort, F.J.A., *Six Lectures on the Ante-Nicene Fathers*, 1895.
Huddleston, *Toland's History of the Druids*, 1814.
Hunt, *Jesus Christ*, 1904.
Hussain, Iftekhar Bano, *Prophets in the Qur'an, Volume Two: The Later Prophets*, 1995.
Hynes, S., *The Manifesto*, 1697.

Ibn Kathir, *The Signs before the Day of Judgement*, (translated by Huda Khattab), 1991.

Jan, *John Hus - His Life*, 1915.
Josephus, *The Works of Flavius Josephus*, (translated by William Whitson), 1840.
Joyce, D., *The Jesus Scroll*, 1973.

Kamen, H.A.R., *The Spanish Inquisition*, 1965.
Kaye, J., *The Council of Nicea*, 1853.
Kaye, J., *The Ecclesiastic History of the 2nd & 3rd Centuries*, 1893.
Kaye, J., *The Sermons*, 1850.
Kaspary, J., *The Life of the Real Jesus*, 1904.
Kaspary, J., *The Origin, Growth, and Decline of Christianity*, 1904-10.
Kelly, J.N.D., *Early Christian Creeds*, 1949.
Kirkgaldy, *The New Theology and the Old*, 1910.

Knight, *The Life of Faustus Socianus*, (translated by Biddle), 1653.
Knox, W.L., *The Sources of the Synoptic Gospels*, 1953.
Konstantinides, *Saint Barnabas*, 1971.

Lardner, N., *A History of Heretics*, 1780.
Lardner, N., *Two Schemes of Trinity*, 1829.
Latourette, K.C., *A History of the Expansion of Christianity*, 1953.
Leany, A.R.C., *The Dead Sea Scrolls*.
Leany, A.R.C., *The Rule of Qumran*.
Lehman, Johannes, *The Jesus Report*, 1972.
Lietzman, Hanz, *The Beginning of the Christian Church*, 1949.
Lietzman, Hanz, *A History of the Early Church*, 1961.
Lindsey, T., *Two Dissertations*, 1779.
Lindsey, T., *An Historical View of the State of Unitarian Doctrine*, 1783.
Lindsey, T., *A List of False Readings of the Scripture*, 1790.
Lubinietski, *A History of the Reformation in Poland*.

MacGiffert, A.C., *The Apostles' Creed*, 1902.
MacGiffert, A.C., *The God of the Early Christians*, 1924.
MacGiffert, A.C., *A History of Christianity in the Apostolic Age*, 1897.
MacLachlan, *The Religious Opinions of Milton, Locke, and Newton*, 1941.
Madden, *Life and Martyrdom of Savonarola*, 1854.
Major, John, *'Sentences'*.
Marshall, G.N., *Challenge of a Liberal Faith*, 1966.
Marshall, G.N., *Understanding of Albert Schweitzer*, 1966.
Masters, John, *Baptismal Vows, or the Feast of St. Barnabas*, 1866.
Mellone, S.H., *Unitarianism and the New Theology*, 1908.
Miller, F., *The History of the Jewish People in the Age of Jesus Christ*.
Milton, J., *Treatise of Civil Power*.
Milton, J., *The Christian Doctrine*, 1825.
Motley, *Rise of the Dutch Republic*.
Mowry, Lucetta, *The Dead Sea Scrolls and the Early Church*.
Murray, G.G.A., *Five Stages of Greek Religion*.

Newman, A., *Jesus* (with a Preface by Dr. Schmeidal), 1907.
Newman, J.H., *Arianism of the Fourth Century*, 1833.
Newton, *Sir Isaac Newton Daniel*, 1922.

Orwell, G., *'1984'*.
Oxyrhynchus, *New Sayings of Jesus and Fragments of a Lost Gospel*, (translated by B.P. Grenfell & A.S. Hunt), 1897.

Parke, D.B., *The Epic of Unitarianism*, 1957.
Patrick, John, *The Apology of Origen in Reply to Celsus*, 1892.
Pike, E.R., *Spiritual Basis of Nonconformity*, 1897.
Pike, J.A., *If This Be Heresy*, 1967.
Pike, J.A., *Time for Christian Candour*, 1965.
Pike, J.A., *The Wilderness Revolt*, 1972.
Priestly, Joseph, *A General History of the Christian Church*, 1802.
Priestly, Joseph, *A History of the Corruption of Christianity*, 1871.
Priestly, Joseph, *History of Jesus Christ*, 1786.
Priestly, Joseph, *Memoirs of Dr. Priestly*, 1904.
Priestly, Joseph, *Socrates and Jesus*, 1803.
Priestly, Joseph, *Three Tracts*, 1791.
Priestly, Joseph, *Dr. Priestly 's Catechism*, 1796.
Priestly, Joseph, *A New Song*, 1876.
Puccinelli, P., *Vita de S. Barnaba Apostolo*.

Quick, Murid, *The Story of Barnabas*.

Ragg, Lonsdale and Laura, *The Gospel of Barnabas*, (edited and translated from the Italian Ms. in the Imperial Library at Vienna), 1921.
Reed, Douglas, *The Controversy of Zion*, 1985.
Reland, Adrian, *Historical and Critical Reflections upon Mohametanism and Socianism*, 1712.
Reland, Adrian, *Treatises concerning the Mohametons*.
Rice, D.T., *Byzantine Art*, 1954.
Rice, Michael, *False Inheritance*, 1994.
Robinson, J.A., *Barnabas, Hermas and the Didache*, 1920.
Robinson, J.A.T., *Honest to God*, 1964.

Robinson, J.M., *The New Quest of the Historical Jesus*, 1959.
Robinson, J.M., *Problem of History in Mark*, 1957.
Robertson, J .M., *The Historical Jesus*, 1916.
Robson, Rev. James, *Christ in Islam*, 1929.
Ruinus, *Commentary on the Apostles' Creed*, 1955.
Rylcy, G.B., *Barnabas, or the Great Renunciation*, 1893.

Sanday, *Outlines of the Life of Christ*.
Sandmel, S., *We Jews and Jesus*, 1973.
Santucci, L., *Wrestling with Jesus*, 1972.
Savonarola, *Verity of Christian Faith*, 1651.
Schmiedel, P.W., *Jesus in Modern Criticism*, 1907.
Schokel, L.A., *Understanding Bibical Research*, 1968.
Schweitzer, Albert, *Christianity and the Religions of the World*, 1923.
Schweitzer, Albert, *The Mysticism of Paul the Apostle*, 1953.
Schweitzer, Albert, *Paul and his Interpreters*.
Schweitzer, Albert, *The Kingdom of God and Primitive Christianity*, 1968.
Schweitzer, Albert, *The Philosophy of Civilization*, 1946.
Schweitzer, Albert, *A Psychiatric Study of Jesus*, 1958.
Schweitzer, Albert, *The Story of Albert Schweitzer*.
Sox, David, *The Gospel of Barnabas*, 1984.
Spark, *Unitarian Miscellany*.
Spark, *Christian Reformer*.
Stanley, A.P., *The Eastern Church*, 1869.
Stanley, A.P., *The Athanasian Creed*, 1871.
Stanley, A.P., *Lectures on the History of the Eastern Church*, 1883.
Stevenson, J., *Creeds, Councils, and Controversies*.
Stevenson, J., *Studies in Eusebius*, 1929.
Stevenson, J., *The New Eusebius*.

Taylor, John, *The Scriptural Doctrine of Original Sin*.
Taylor, John, *A History of the Octagon Church*.
Thomas-a-Kempis, *Imitation of Christ*, (translated by John Wesley), 1903.
Thompson, F.A., *Goths in Spain*, 1969.
Toland, John, *Hypathia*, 1753.
Toland, John, *The Nazarenes*, 1718.

Toland, John, *Theological and Philosophical Works*, 1732.
Toland, John, *Tetradymus*.
Towgood, *Serious and Free Thoughts on the Present State of the Church*.

Vermas, G., *Jesus, the Jew*, 1973.
Vos, J.G., *A Christian Introduction to Religions of the World*, 1965.

Wallace, *Anti-trinitarian Biographies*, 1850.
Warchaurr, J., *Jesus or Christ?*, 1909.
Warfield, B.B., *Jesus or Christ?*, 1909.
Whittaker, T., *The Origins of Christianity*, 1933.
Wilbur, E.M., *A History of Unitarianism in Transylvania, England, and America*.
Williamson, G.A., *The History of the Church*, 1965.
Williamson, G.A., *The Jewish War*, 1959.
Wilson, E.M., *The Dead Sea Scrolls*, 1969.
Wisaart, H.S., *Socialism and Christ, the Great Enemy of the Human Race*, 1905.
Workman, H.B., *Persecution in the Early Church*, 1960.

Zahn, T., *The Articles of the Apostles' Creed*, 1899.
Zahn, T., *Introduction to the New Testament*, 1909.
Zahn, T., *Peter, Saint and Apostle*, 1889.

Periodicals

Christian Examiner, Jan. 1924-Dec. 1925.
Edinburgh Review, Vol. XII, 1825.
Hibbert Journal Supplement, *Jesus or Christ*, Vol. VII, 1909.
Harvard Theological Review, *Theism and the Christian Faith*, 1909.
Islamic Horizons, Feb. 1985, *Today's Gospel of Barnabas – Is it Authentic?*
Neale, Samuel, *A select series of biographical narratives, etc.*, Vol. VIII, 1845.
Review Biblique, 1950.
Time Magazine, May 24, 1976.

o   o   o   o   o

About the Authors

Muhammad Ata'ur-Rahim lived much of his life in Hyderabad, India, before moving to Pakistan at the time of the Partition in 1947. He was awarded the degrees of BT, LLB and MA at the Muslim University of Aligarh, before completing his further studies in education at the Universities of Edinburgh and London, where he was awarded his MRST. He was the Government of India Scholar in the Archaeology, Art and Religion of Ancient India. After being promoted to the rank of Colonel during the Second World War, in which he served with distinction, Muhammad Ata'ur-Rahim became the Principal of the Urdu College in Karachi, Pakistan. His other books include *Unitarianism in Christianity* and *The Meeting Ground of Islam and Christianity*. He died in 1978, *'alehi rahma.*

Ahmad Thomson was born in Chipata, Zambia, on the 23rd of April, 1950, towards the end of the British colonial period in Africa. Educated in both Zimbabwe and England, and widely travelled, he was fortunate enough to escape having too rigid a cultural moulding or social conditioning, and accordingly, although brought up as a Christian, recognised and embraced Islam for what it is when he encountered it, clearly and existentially embodied by real Muslims.

Soon after embracing Islam, the author met Colonel Muhammad Ata'ur-Rahim, who had come to England in order to pursue his studies of Jesus, peace be upon him, and Christianity in greater depth, and at the suggestion of Shaykh 'Abd al-Qadir al-Murabit they began to work together. As a result of their joint research three books were written, *Jesus, Prophet of Islam, Jesus in Qur'an,* and *Blood on the Cross* which was completed after the author had been on pilgrimage to Makka and after Colonel Rahim had died, *'alehi rahma.*

Other books written by Ahmad Thomson include *Dajjal - The King who has no clothes*, which is a contemporary study of the Anti-Christ written from a Qur'anic perspective and based on some of the recorded sayings of the Prophet Muhammad, may the blessings and peace of Allah be on him and his family and his Companions and all who follow him and them in what they are able with sincerity until the Last Day. Amin.